BUILDING THE EMPIRE STATE

AMERICAN BUSINESS, POLITICS, AND SOCIETY

Series editors:
Andrew Wender Cohen, Pamela Walker Laird,
Mark H. Rose, and Elizabeth Tandy Shermer

Books in the series American Business, Politics, and Society explore
the relationships over time between governmental institutions and
the creation and performance of markets, firms, and industries large
and small. The central theme of this series is that politics, law, and
public policy—understood broadly to embrace not only lawmaking
but also the structuring presence of governmental institutions—have
been fundamental to the evolution of American business from the
colonial era to the present. The series aims to explore, in particular,
developments that have enduring consequences.

BUILDING THE
EMPIRE STATE

Political Economy in the Early Republic

Brian Phillips Murphy

PENN

UNIVERSITY OF PENNSYLVANIA PRESS

PHILADELPHIA

Published by
University of Pennsylvania Press
Philadelphia, Pennsylvania 19104-4112
www.upenn.edu/pennpress

Printed in the United States of America
on acid-free paper

1 3 5 7 9 10 8 6 4 2

Library of Congress Cataloging-in-Publication Data
Murphy, Brian Phillips.
   Building the empire state : political economy in the early
republic / Brian Phillips Murphy.
       pages cm — (American business, politics, and society)
   Includes bibliographical references and index.
   ISBN 978-0-8122-4716-9
   1. New York (State)—History—1775–1865. 2. New York (State)—
Politics and government—1775–1865. 3. New York (State)—
Economic conditions—History—18th century. 4. New York
(State)—Economic conditions—History—19th century. 5. Finance,
Public—United States—New York (State)—1789–1801. 6. Finance,
Public—United States—New York (State)—1801–1861. I. Title.
II. Series: American business, politics, and society.
F123.M93 2015
974.7'03—dc23
                                                    2014040796

For my father, James J. Murphy III
(1943–2013)

CONTENTS

NOTE ON BANKING TERMS

At its core, a bank is an organization that lends money and extends credit to people on the basis of its assets and their ability to repay obligations. Those assets could be money—piles of gold and silver coins, say—or anything with a recognizable value as collateral. For example, *land banks*, sometimes called *country banks*, accepted mortgaged real estate as a form of capital, enabling landlords to turn their normally illiquid holdings into paper banknotes. *Money* or *commercial banks*, by contrast, preferred coined money that was called *specie*. Not surprisingly, cash-rich and land-poor merchants favored money banks to the land banks desired by landlords.

Organizationally, banks could be wholly private enterprises. A simple contract drawn between two partners who loaned money at interest could be considered a private bank. Incorporated and joint-stock banks were composed of shareholders who each held fractional ownership in the institution, which they could buy and sell. The owners did not need to know each other because the institution itself was governed by a stable set of rules and regulations and administered by an elected board of directors and hired staff.

A joint-stock company that received an incorporation grant gained rights and legal privileges that distinguished it from other companies lacking such a useful instrumentality. A corporation possessed a fictitious legal "personhood" that allowed its directors and shareholders to sue and be sued in court as a single entity and to hold common property as shares changed hands and membership on the board of directors rotated. An incorporated bank might also operate on a larger scale than an unincorporated joint-stock sibling because it enjoyed a privilege of limited liability, protecting shareholders from being responsible for debts incurred by the bank above the amount of their investments. An unincorporated partnership that went bankrupt could haunt generations of heirs and descendants, but the failure of an incorporated bank wiped out only its shareholders' equity investments in the enterprise; their other assets were shielded from legal claims. Incorporated banks, then, possessed advantages that other commercial enterprises and unincorporated institutions did not. With those privileges, however, came an enormous amount of discretion; bankers chose who they would do business with, making those banks desirable for investors and well-connected borrowers but resented by those left on the sidelines. This aspect of banking became far more intense if a bank's charter was exclusive, giving it a monopoly within a city or state by barring the creation of competing institutions.

A bank's principal function in this period was to provide a sound medium of exchange: called *banknotes*, these were pieces of bank-printed money that could be redeemed on demand for gold or silver, making it a very safe and desirable form of currency.

In contrast to banks that developed in the mid-nineteenth century and are familiar to twenty-first-century readers, banks in the early republic served the interests of commercial firms rather than individual consumers by providing financiers, businesspeople, and merchants with access to credit and capital. Without satellite branches, banks typically conducted business locally, "discounting" notes—IOUs—in exchange for an equal amount of the bank's own printed currency, minus interest. It was called a "discount" because the bank collected its interest payment up front. At a 6 percent annual interest rate, a bank would lend someone $100 for a three-month term by giving them $98.50 in the bank's own banknotes; $100 would be due at the end of the loan. Banks discounted both commercial paper—short-term IOUs used in lieu of cash—and longer-term, renewable accommodation notes. Both types of loans had to be endorsed by guarantors known to the bank's directors, making borrowers and endorsers jointly responsible for debts. Thus, banking privileges were personalized and reputation-dependent.

Boards of directors, cashiers, and clerks were all responsible for making sure that the paper money banknotes and checks paid by the bank were authentic, not counterfeit. But this task was mere housekeeping compared to the directors' obligation to ensure that the bank's customers—the recipients of its credit—were worthy of the risks entailed in allowing them to become debtors. A bank that was incorporated or formed by a joint-stock company typically loaned twice as much as its capitalization (the sum it had raised initially by offering its shares for sale). For example, a bank that sold one thousand shares priced at $500 each was capitalized at $500,000 and might loan as much as $1 million. Because the bank was extending itself in this way, each time it decided to offer credit to a client it was taking a risk. This necessarily meant that personal relationships became important factors in determining who received credit. Similarly, any person accepting a check had to make a judgment about the person passing the check, the name of the person who had signed it, and the bank's ability to pay the check. The person who redeemed a check might be the second, third, or even fourth person to hold it. A bank, then, created networks of credit by taking risks and acting as a financial intermediary, providing tangible and reliable paper banknotes and checks that facilitated the buying and selling of goods and services in a local and regional economy.

Strength in Structure

One late spring day in Manhattan in 1784, Robert Robert Livingston Jr. did something he and his peers did nearly every day of their adult lives: he sat down, pulled out a sheaf of paper, and began scribbling.[1]

For the past seven years, the 37-year-old aristocrat had been New York State's chancellor, one of its top judicial officials. The position had been created under a new state constitution New York adopted in 1777 after the separation from Great Britain. Livingston coauthored that document and all but inherited the newly created post; his late father, Robert R. "Judge" Livingston Sr. had also been a prominent jurist and politician in colonial New York.

Politics was one of the Livingston family's businesses, and Robert Junior had long been busy at the center of the politics of Revolution. In 1775 he became a delegate to the Continental Congress in Philadelphia, and in 1776 he was one-fifth of the Committee of Five tasked with drawing up a Declaration of Independence. He returned to New York to frame that state's 1777 constitution, was named the state's chancellor by a provisional governing body, and left again in 1781 to serve as his country's first secretary of foreign affairs, its senior-most diplomatic official.[2]

But now all of that was in the past.

As the national capital ambled from Philadelphia to Princeton to Annapolis, the center of its politics drifted further and further from Livingston's reach and from New York itself, where the Livingston name—one that had dominated colonial politics for a century—seemed to be at a nadir. In the New York legislature, some of the Revolution's leaders, whom the chancellor had labeled "warm & hotheaded Whigs," seemed determined to permanently keep men like him from wielding anything like his former power.[3] Having come under fire for being an absentee state officeholder, Livingston resigned his foreign affairs post in 1783 and returned home to mend ties in New York.

He spent months battling the allegation by the Whigs that he had in fact vacated the office of chancellor once he began serving in Congress. Even after that controversy quieted, a smaller contingent of legislators pestered the chancellor by proposing to cut his £400 salary in half while debating a bill that gave raises to the governor and every other judge in the state.[4]

Livingston quietly began plotting his recovery by falling back on a playbook his family had (successfully) used for generations: rebuilding his political capital by rebuilding his financial capital. As a political entrepreneur descended from several generations of political entrepreneurs—people who sought to translate their influence and connections into sources of income and opportunity—Livingston was used to living in a state where the official apparatus of government was his collaborative and encouraging partner, aiding his enterprises and giving a boost to his personal ambitions and those he had for the civic well-being of New York City. The animating energy of colonial government had long come from collaborations between official entities and local private interests. In Livingston's mind, the propriety of that relationship had in no way been discredited by the Revolution. Restoring those pre-Revolutionary practices would favor Livingston's family and others with capital to invest and influence to exercise, and for the next thirty years Robert Livingston planned and profited from political-economy practices he helped set.[5]

During the fall of 1783, Livingston began spending money and political capital to reestablish both the city of New York and his footing within it. He began enticing friends and associates to join him in buying houses and estates vacated during the war or abandoned by Tory Loyalists who had fled the country. Livingston had already invested £2,800 in such properties and was seeking a credit line of £8,000 to plunge even deeper into the venture. At the same time, he was assembling a portfolio of associates to cofound a so-called land bank where such real estate holdings could be mortgaged for paper money.

What frustrated Robert Livingston enough to decry the city's "notorious" greed in early 1784 was that the official apparatus of New York's government—both its state legislature and the city corporation governing New York City through an appointed mayor and an elected board of aldermen—was not reciprocating. As he read newspaper articles about other states' willingness to use incorporation grants to harness civic energy and mobilize private capital, Livingston saw New York failing to support the ambitions he and other New Yorkers harbored for their city and state. His bid for a bank charter was stalled in the state legislature, and New York's municipal government seemed to be immobilized and subject to the whims of petty entrenched interests looking to preserve their own narrow privileges at the expense of others.

Pouring his angst onto four long, narrow ledger-sized sheets of laid cotton paper—the kind lawyers used for formal court filings and Livingston used for everything—the chancellor fumed that "since the peace, a rage has prevailed in the neighboring states for corporations" that "annex ideas of utility to them." But in New York "we have not been so fortunate." Although "the fire" of 1776 "left open a door for improvement" and history had provided London's 1666 singe as a model for what an active and ambitious city government could do under such circumstances, New Yorkers refused to "[do] things themselves or [avail] themselves of the spirit of enterprise that the war has left with us."

According to the chancellor, New York City's government had become incapable of following through on even basic tasks. New Yorkers had gotten good at "[projecting] useful schemes for posterity to carry into effect," the chancellor wrote. Streets that should have been repaired for "the health & embellishment of the town" had instead become "the abode of verb & excuses." The city corporation had planned to plant trees that would re-create the "cool & shady walks" New Yorkers had enjoyed before the war. With the planting season nearly over, however, the chancellor marveled, "[N]o step has yet been taken." "Even this shadowy improvement," he predicted, "is liable to cheat our hopes." A "scheme," Livingston reflected, "is extinguished with the same rapidity that it was embraced." "Half a dozen old women" could arrest work on a project by merely "scold[ing] . . . the profanity" entailed in "[exposing] dark recesses of stone street . . . to publick view."

Livingston thought city leaders had been cowed into inaction by incumbent interests and entrenched monopolists who were "too powerful for the rest of the citizens" to defeat. The influence of these forces, Livingston believed, distorted the city's political economy and marketplace to the detriment of consumer-citizens. Spoiled bread flour that should have been "held up to public view" by a regime of city-appointed inspectors was instead being sold to unsuspecting buyers, all to keep "the customs of our ancestors, encourage luxury, and discourage . . . the sale of unmarketable flour." An abundance of fresh water that could have provided "comfortable refreshments" to residents while "guard[ing] us against the alarming ravages of fire" was instead unavailable—all because the proprietors of a spring-fed well called the

"Tea-Water Pump" stood in the way. "It is a notorious fact," he wrote, "that the greed of this city is worse than that of any other place upon the continent." "[A]las we have little hope to expect," Livingston sighed, that such an improvement "will be crowned with [success] while there are tea-water men, and tea-water women & tea-water children" insisting they alone had gained in 1757 the permanent and exclusive right to supply the city with water for all time. As long as their government refused to challenge the status quo, New Yorkers would be left with no choice than to be "tormented from seeing the cup glide by them after it was brought to their chins," destined "neither to eat or drink like other folk." "It is our common reproach to want bread and water" even though "the means of obtaining both are in our power." The only public project New Yorkers could truly be proud of, Livingston bitterly concluded, was the city's decades-old gallows. They were "distinguished," he noted, by their strength, and were "in the word[s] of Hamlet's grave digger, built stronger than the carpenter or mason."[6]

In his lifetime, Robert Livingston sent thousands of letters and published nearly a dozen widely read essays. This, however, was not one of them.

There is no indication that Livingston returned to this essay or revised it or that it was ever sent—to anyone. One of Livingston's biographers linked it to another letter sent to New York City mayor James Duane—the husband of one of the chancellor's cousins. But that missive is mocking and mischievous in tone, clearly intended to irk the mayor. This letter was a bridge-burner that flayed both the city's political leadership and the public alike and was originally written for publication in a newspaper.[7] It was an essay written at a moment when, in a bitter letter to his friend John Jay, the chancellor said he had "concluded my political career."[8]

Livingston might have simply wanted to spare his family embarrassment or shield himself from this momentary departure from rhetorical elegance. However, his statement to Jay about having "concluded" his political life cries out for further scrutiny. By what measure could Livingston credibly claim to be exiting politics? It certainly would have surprised New York State's legal and political community to learn that their sitting chancellor considered himself retired, particularly when his daily actions and ongoing engagements plainly contradicted this statement. As a man raised in the innermost circles of New York politics during British dominion, Livingston was clearly irritated and even disturbed by his state's postwar politics during these first years of American independence now called the Critical Period.[9]

The Revolution fundamentally challenged the colonial status quo, empowering people who wanted to deny former colonial aristocrats the chance to return to their positions at the top of the new nation's political and socio-economic ladders. Some ideological imperatives, therefore, demanded that Robert Livingston feel frustrated in 1784, and a cadre of state legislators stood ready to make his political life as difficult as possible.[10] Livingston's reaction was evidence of just how unfamiliar, at least to him, this new environment had become. He remained determined, however, to turn his lands, money, connections, and family name into sources of profit and influence—not as an aristocrat but as a political entrepreneur.

Yet the chancellor was all too aware that not every New Yorker with capital was committed to the same agenda. When the chancellor railed against the "notorious fact" of the "greed of [New York City]," he was drawing a contrast between himself and others who sought privileges in the political marketplace. Livingston saw himself as a positive force in his country's politics. Profit was just one of several reasons he was interested in banking and real estate investing, activities that he viewed as constructive contributions toward the commercial success and political stability of his state. The marketplace regulations and interventions he desired—flour inspections, freshwater supplies, street paving, tree planting—had long been permissible and even definitional duties of municipal governments that had been constituted under a royal charter, operated within common law, and rechartered following independence.[11]

Although localities, states, and the developing national confederation had adopted formal articles and constitutions, the nation's actual day-to-day governing habits—its *applied* political economy—were still up for grabs at this moment in American history.[12] In New York, as in the nation, the proper extent of the state's mixed economy of public-private enterprises had hardly been debated, let alone defined. The ideological imperatives of the Revolution were competing with familiar practices of pre-Revolutionary governance, and although some lawmakers wanted to further exploit their opportunity to effect social and economic change, others sought to settle the Revolution as soon as possible. The state government, Livingston told Robert Morris, was "weak, unsettled."[13] The monopoly-holders of the Tea-Water Pump and deceitful flour merchants were fine with that and with exploiting a lack of competition in the political marketplace to wring profits from an already anemic economy. To Livingston, their greed was parasitic, and the city government's inaction amounted to a betrayal of the Revolution's "spirit of enterprise" that was to be "encourage[d] . . . in others." Livingston's essay, therefore, did not merely address a personal agenda; the larger question hovering over his words and the country as a whole in 1784 was: What happens now?

Political economy is a well-defined term in American history: the way that states and governments ordered the economy and operated within the marketplace.[14] As much as is known about it in theory, however, less is understood about the interactions among legal and extralegal voluntary associations, chartered and informal institutions, and political officials with backgrounds and futures in commercial and transportation development.[15] But these ground-level machinations, complex and often messy, are what political economy *is* once it is operationalized.[16]

Building the Empire State surveys and samples the changing institutional ecology of New York State during the first five decades following independence, a period my fellow historians call the early republic, by following a community of entrepreneurs like Robert R. Livingston, and their enterprises. New York was a onetime mercantile colony that, as a state, became home to the first bank incorporated after the Revolution (the Bank of New-York), utilities, canals, railroads, and other internal improvement companies, as well as the country's most powerful steamboat monopoly and the largest public works project of the early republic: the Erie Canal.[17] Within this geographical context, this book investigates political economy in practice: I ask how ideas and ideologies gave way to actions and policies, and I explore the political, economic, and legal consequences of chartering particular institutions and organizing the marketplace in certain ways. In this period, New York's state government was busy opening avenues for profit and influence to its citizens, prompting them to organize and mobilize as economic interests in order to take advantage of these opportunities. By asserting authority in creating and regulating institutions that facilitated and intermediated private commercial transactions throughout the northeastern United States and toward the expanding westward frontier, New York's political officials set the formal rules of the game and defined the informal norms of behavior in one of the nation's busiest commercial centers and largest economies, demonstrating that "the state" was one of the primary agents of change in the early republic's economy.[18]

But although early American states were important in this era, they were hardly omnipotent. Operating within a layered federal regime of divided and shared sovereignties; early state governments lacked the jurisdictional authority, fiscal imagination, and public consent to directly undertake comprehensive revenue-intensive programs of nation-building.[19] To compensate, lawmakers tapped the rule-making powers that were implicit in American statehood and constitution-making in order to reward private coalitions' capital-formation abilities with formal institutional structures and legal privileges. Legal tools that had been the legacy of British imperial rule—charters for business corporations and banks, and monopoly grants for technology and transportation, for example—were repurposed by American lawmakers to serve the republic's domestic needs.[20] By restructuring and selectively bestowing these useful instrumentalities on favored groups, New York State political leaders created an economy of political opportunity that linked private ambition to the public weal.

Flinging the doors of statehouse chambers open to petitioners eager to gain legal privileges and realize exclusive profits resurrected the familiar pre-Revolutionary practice of engaging private entities to finance, construct, and manage civic institutions and ostensibly public assets. The landscape of political opportunity in the early republic was dominated by an economy of influence in which financial capital readily purchased political and regulatory power; this incentivized coalition-building and rewarded legislative skill. It also empowered public officials to steer private capital toward building a financial and transportation infrastructure capable of encouraging further commercial ambition and hastening economic development. Government therefore got things done by deliberately bestowing public authority on individuals and institutions in order to tap private capital and channel self-interest toward public goods and civic ends.[21] As a consequence, legislators willingly—and in some cases inadvertently—sustained the influence of a cadre of unelected political actors whose stature flowed from their personal access to private capital: political entrepreneurs.[22]

Once they were organized into legally sanctioned and formalized partnerships and corporations, these out-of-doors unelected operatives and political entrepreneurs began curating their interests; they recruited supporters from the ranks of elected officials to deepen and widen their ties to voters. Though far from uniform or unanimous, support for politically oriented entrepreneurs among a growing interlocking directorate of citizen-shareholders and corporate directors frustrated the practical day-to-day efforts of constitution-writers and lawmakers to collar unelected individuals' and associations' capabilities to bend the vast power of the state's rule-making regulatory apparatus in their favor. Successful political entrepreneurs actively interested people in their enterprises by building networks of credit that offered access to debt and capital, by transforming the transactional relationship between modest citizen-shareholder investors and high-born corporate officers into durable long-term political alliances, and by constructing a partisan infrastructure to bring institutional discipline to the state's official sources of political authority. In the new nation's political economy, therefore, the energies of government, subordinate political institutions, and political parties were all fueled in large measure by extra-legislative, out-of-doors mobilizations undertaken for economic and material reasons.[23]

For elected officials and appointees, catering to constituents' material interests was no distraction; it was the daily grind of the business of governing. Perusing the journals of legislative houses and statute books makes clear that such work consumed a great deal of attention from New York's political class in the early republic. Across a spectrum of letters of affection and agitation, it is clear that there was a consensus position shared among a broad swath of political entrepreneurs in the early republic—George and DeWitt Clinton, Robert R. Livingston, Robert Fulton, Aaron Burr, and Alexander Hamilton, accompanied by a large and wide cohort of less-studied figures—that a chief purpose of politics and government was to advance citizens' material interests and promote a commercial agenda. Creating a dynamic marketplace required the interposition of state power, and in the view of this cohort, government was supposed to be actively aiding the ambitions of the ambitious; for them, the controversy most often concerned whose enterprising plans merited support.

Although it is not surprising that capital and corporations exercised political power in the early republic (as they still do) or that political actors responded to them (ditto), it was not a given that the institutional ecology of New York State would evolve to revolve around the community of political entrepreneurs at the center of these enterprises. These experiments in privilege and monopoly were tests of the public's patience for private enterprises entrusted with exclusive rights to execute a public mission. And the political intensity of American corporations' early origins—particularly banks and transportation enterprises—helps explain why contemporaries and historians alike frequently cast a skeptical eye toward their emergence in the early republic.

This story is, after all, a paradox: corporations morphed from being objects of suspicion and symbols of monarchy in the late eighteenth century to being the dominant tool for capital formation and business organization by the middle of the nineteenth century.[24]

From the seemingly anti-bank, anticorporate, and antimonopoly political-economy rhetoric of the 1780s, an interwoven set of incorporated banks emerged in the United States that financed a set of semi-exclusive transportation initiatives. It is easy to explain this development as an enlargement of privileges among an already privileged cadre of self-dealing political leaders who succumbed to corruption and materialist temptations. Certainly the metaphysical efforts of political-economy theorists to sort out distinctions between public and private spheres of action was undermined by the state's adoption of corporations and monopoly grants to run mixed-economy enterprises.[25] Most efforts to use politics to restrain the influence of capital in early America were struggles that seem destined to fail.

Yet the subtle, often unspoken assumption underlying many histories of the politics and political economy of the early republic is that angst concerning corporations and concentrations of capital was widespread across thirteen states' legislatures and the public.[26] Through the ideological prisms of republicanism and liberalism, our unfortunate present-day predicament can seem avoidable and even accidental.[27] The shorthand narrative goes something like this: starting with the creation of incorporated banks after the Revolution, capital was unleashed with the emergence of rapacious railroads, a "Market Revolution," and a more laissez-faire marketplace that came to be dominated by trusts and monopolies in the Gilded Age.[28] Economic histories of the period often rely on the same narrative to reach a strikingly different conclusion: one celebrating laissez-faire as the demise of the anticapitalist radicalism of the American Revolution and the blossoming of a more nearly perfect and correct set of institutional arrangements between the public and private sectors.[29]

Historians have identified a spectrum of "good founders" who presciently recognized that corporations, monopolies, and other institutions for capital formation and the aggregation of influence had the potential to endanger the institutions of government and civil society; some believed they had no place in the nation's political economy, while others thought they could be unleashed only after first being mastered.[30] A cadre of state legislators in Pennsylvania held firm in opposing all incorporated banks and trying to repeal an existing bank's charter, while in Massachusetts lawmakers sought to house-train corporations by tinkering with the details and complexities of corporate charter language.[31] These histories of politics and political economy look to the founding generation for the answers they formulated to questions concerning how interests were to be managed in the young republic, poring over warning signs our forebears missed in this "lost moment" when history could have unfolded in a different way.

But this is precisely why context is key.

Early American lawmakers considering petitions for legal privileges needed to look no further than the 1773 Tea Act for an example of how a corporation's shareholders could sway parliamentarians' votes, distorting an empire's political economy and propelling its colonies into open rebellion. The East India Company, however, was a unique institution without a North American equivalent.[32]

By contrast, American historians writing in the twentieth and twenty-first centuries approach this subject with their own particular constellation of references. Whenever most people are asked what the word *corporation* means to them—whether they are detached scholars and journalists, interested policy makers and politicos, or students considering the question for the first time—they conjure answers that reference the signposts of our era. They do not think of the British East India Company or its favored position in the eighteenth-century tea market but settle their brains on the twenty-first-century companies they interact with on a regular basis. To live in the United States today is to live in a nation where well-organized private interests dominate the defense, health-care, banking and finance, and media and publishing industries, as well as science, all manner of transportation, and much of the everyday commerce of nearly 300 million citizens.

Despite the sticky web of complication woven by this system as it was practiced, the vocabulary we use in our present political discourse continues to insist that somewhere, deep under layers of institutions, money, motives, and grey shades of legality, an identifiable line once existed that demarcated the boundary between What Is Public and What Is Private.[33]

This assumption lies at the heart of decades of state legislative and congressional lawmaking and United States Supreme Court litigation aiming to limit the influence of corporations and wealthy individuals on elections and policy making. But even after drawing and redrawing limitations on who can participate in a campaign, when and how much they can contribute, and in what places and spaces candidates and lawmakers can solicit support, little seems to have been redeemed. Despite the creation of a Federal Election Commission (FEC) in 1974; the Court's 1976 decision in *Buckley v. Valeo*; the adoption of the Bipartisan Campaign Reform Act (McCain-Feingold) in 2002; internal efforts by congressional ethics committees; audits by the executive branch; state governments' oversight and policing of agencies, officials, and legislators; and citizens' activities in monitoring disclosure reports, filing Freedom of Information Act (FOIA) requests, and signing Public Interest Research Group (PIRG) petitions, the applied political economy of the United States remains inherently muddled.

The federal regime's regulatory apparatus often appears to be deliberately designed to be captured by the industries being monitored.[34] Many sectors of the U.S. economy are dominated by just a handful of corporations, often operating as duopolies or monopolies. And although these firms are said to be part of the free and private marketplace, their positions are protected and their power is undeniably felt throughout the public sector. In the formal exercise of policy making, rule-making, lawmaking, and the crafting and enforcement of administrative regulations, and in the informal but highly lucrative economy of influence sustained by lobbying, deal-making, political fundraising, and seasonal electioneering, any lines that might separate public and private spheres and markets in our era seem blurred beyond recognition. The most fundamental, basic tasks of the modern American state—"to insure domestic Tranquility, provide for the common defense, promote the general Welfare"—are today executed within the mixed economy of socialized risks, private rewards, public funds, public oversight, and private profit.

Judges, policy makers, and even government activists do not seem able to carve out distinct public and private spheres in thinking about how America's political economy should work, largely because reforms fail to take full notice of how that political economy works in practice.

What if there was no lost moment? What if, instead of swinging into action as an afterthought to restrain a politics driven by ideology (or honor or culture) in the early republic—think of James Madison's *Federalist* No. 51—material interests were instead at the very heart of post-Revolutionary and post-Constitutional Convention politics, used to both excite and temper competing imperatives? If true, we could then view the "emergence" of corporations and economic institutions as a continuation of past practices adjusted to fit new political arrangements.[35]

Much rhetoric of the American Revolution redefined civic space by drawing boundaries around influence and power. Pamphleteers, Continental congressmen, and minutemen all evinced hostility to accumulations of wealth, concentrations of political authority in a single individual or among a court of collaborators, and the conflation of personal wealth with a right-to-rule that was common in pre-Revolutionary times. The idea that a man's political power emanated from his person, was legitimated by his property, and automatically elevated him to a stature sufficient to merit an office might not have been explicitly annihilated by the Revolution, but it was certainly disrupted by challenges to authority, aristocracy, and deference. Although wealth itself was not abolished, it was nevertheless divested of any implied grant of authority. Inheritances and marriages were no longer investiture ceremonies. The Revolution formally decoupled fitness for office from accidents of birth, marriage, and fortune once the legitimate source of government authority was relocated from the King, his ministers, and his imperial dependents to the sovereign people and their duly elected deputies in legislatures, councils, and congresses.

Yet this legacy was fundamentally jeopardized by the building of an institutional matrix of state-chartered enterprises responsible for igniting both financial and transportation "revolutions" in this era. To fund and run these corporations, monopolies, and other projects, lawmakers politically empowered a particular class of individuals: people with capital. Political entrepreneurs were people without boundaries, not at all self-conscious or deeply conflicted about using political leverage to gain economic advantages and deploying capital to win political disputes. They embodied in their person powers that were, in theory, reserved only for public bodies and to be dispensed only by popular consent in the new democratic republic. This form of authority nevertheless radiated throughout the institutions of New York's economic life.[36] Participating in the marketplace as a corporate director or shareholder; as a licensee of a state monopoly or partner in a state-sanctioned venture; as a holder and defender of a federal patent; as a bank depositor or borrower; as a bond holder in federal, state, or corporate securities; or even as a single signer among hundreds on a petition on behalf of a canal, railroad, or other project sent to the state capital were all avenues to participate in the state's political and civic life, demolishing any pretense of there being boundaries between the two.[37]

Ordinarily we think of this process as one of exploitation or regulatory capture that occurs when private firms gain sway over their public regulators. But what we learn in *Building the Empire State* is that no such coup d'état happened; it was never necessary. American capitalism instead grew out of collaborations between political and economic interests—a dynamic in which business strategies and institutions were shaped by political strategies and institutions, and vice versa.[38] In the case of Robert Livingston, self-interested and civic motives could be harmonious; he had no qualms about positioning himself and his investments for a favorable outcome if his larger

civic plans became a reality or in gaining personal political power by circum-
venting the electoral process to become the principal of a commercially and
financially influential extra-legislative institution. For him, no meaningful
distinction existed between public authority and private capital. Politics existed, in part, to ensure that the two were intertwined; Livingston and his
peers built their coalitions of investors with an eye toward translating money
into political leverage.

Although business, banking, and corporate histories are often indexed by
the formal names of firms and institutions, the process of actually creating a
political economy is personal and contingent.[39] This is not a study that rests
comfortably in the gallery of a legislature to rehash debates over a banking
bill, nor does it dwell in casebooks or libraries. Thanks to almost two decades
of brilliant interdisciplinary studies into political culture and a push to move
"beyond the Founders," we know that politics is not confined to recorded
debates at the federal level. If we want to know what happened and how
things really worked, we need to recover what happened out of sight in conference rooms and out of doors in the streets of the states and localities that
composed the federal union.[40] At each layer of the regime, officials were regularly besieged with proposals and petitions from people promising access to
financial capital. But awarding privileges to these applicants was not a blind
process favoring just anyone with money; legislators did not turn to strangers
to build the republic. Instead, successful petitioners were more likely to be
coalitions and partnerships that deliberately blended financial capital, political capital, and human capital in the form of technological, engineering, or
other forms of specialized expertise. At the friction point where private initiative met public authority, well-crafted coalitions were represented by lobbyists, current and former legislators, officials, and opinion leaders who, in
turn, seduced other lawmakers with personal assurances that a coalition had
the know-how and capital to plan, execute, and complete a project, delivering
a public good in return for a publicly given privilege and an opportunity for
private profit. Therefore, the very process of creating a financial and transportation infrastructure in the early republic had structural incentives that
favored a particular species of business coalition—one assembled with political savvy—because the winnowing process used by legislators to cull through
stacks of petitions demanded no less.

As Robert Livingston observed in 1784, officials charged with policy making in the new republic—city aldermen, state legislators, judges, governors
and their small circles of advisers—all were more responsive to organized

interests than airy notions of the public good or specific demands backed by a disorganized—if unified—"popular" will. For lawmakers and government officials "the public good" was not a self-evident vision; even at rare moments of apparent consensus, opposing economic interests could use their institutional advantages to thwart policies intended to serve that public, civic good. Therefore the legal privileges conferred on particular groups long ago and under a now-deposed regime had given them an institutional permanence that was undeniably difficult to overcome. Being so well established in the political marketplace allowed these groups to amplify their wishes—however narrow and selfish—giving them an outsized voice in policy making. Moreover, the state's inaction reinforced this institutional asymmetry by discouraging the formation of countervailing rival institutions and coalitions.

In the emerging American political system, therefore, the pre-Revolutionary habit of attending to organized, mobilized, and institutionalized interests had remained in place. Government responded to pressure from established interests; it was irrelevant whether those interests were discredited so long as they faced no meaningful opposition. In pondering the failures of the early 1780s, Robert Livingston had come to appreciate the important role that the institutionalization of political interests played in creating engaged and competent public and mixed-economy enterprises. For Livingston, the novelty of this situation was that it was an institutional problem he could not change by leaning on his aristocratic name or his immense inherited land holdings. The sellers of spoiled bread flour and "Tea-Water men" had enfeebled the city government's capacity to address matters of public health and commercial regulation, not because those ideas lacked merit or because the city lacked the legal authority to assert its police powers in those areas but because no countervailing interests existed to agitate for those measures. The chancellor and others, therefore, could pine all they wanted for more energetic public authorities and more civically oriented projects, but these plans would always be at risk of being defeated so long as advocates were unorganized and unstructured. Being interested was not the same as being an interest, let alone an institution. A hungrier and thirstier population might be unhappy, but unless they were mobilized and organized, they were unlikely to see the government change its course. Electing a slate of more favorable candidates to the state legislature or the city's board of aldermen would not provide a cure because the underlying problem was a lopsided institutional ecosystem.

With this realization Livingston had discovered a loophole in the radicalism of the American Revolution: a small number of people could multiply their impact by organizing themselves into associations and institutions with permanence and influence. For this reason, Robert Livingston, who hailed from one of the nation's most wealthy and aristocratic families, had been at the apex of Revolutionary politics, and claimed to have "concluded my political career," decided in early 1784 to write, circulate, and submit a petition asking the state legislature to create a corporation. Livingston saw commerce, and banking in particular, as a useful tool for revolutionary settlement—the process of bringing the Revolution to a close now that the war was over. He believed commerce could mend the frayed relationship between the city and state's revolutionary Patriots—Whigs both mild and "hot-headed"—and those former Tory Loyalists who decided to remain in America and cast their lot with the new republic. If Livingston could channel influence and money toward the common goal of repairing and rebuilding the city's physical plant, he could help New York City reemerge from the conflict as a commercial center with a vigorous mixed economy and population of Tories and Patriots who were each stakeholders in the city's success. Meanwhile, he could personally profit from his investments while gaining leverage over and influence within the city and state's political economy by installing himself and select like-minded associates at the head of what would become the state's most influential financial institution. In the months following a Revolution against imperial abuses, unaccountable power, and monarchical tyranny, New York's chancellor had decided how he would maximize his influence in the new nation's political system: he would become a banker.

In creating a market, therefore, the state had defined what was at stake in political competition. By simply responding to interests, the state encouraged the formation of interests that would marshal financial, human, and technical capital on behalf of proposed projects. In addition, lawmakers prodded aspiring citizen-shareholders to organize plans; identify, recruit, and mobilize supporters: consolidate investor capital: and circulate petitions later unfurled in lobbies and cloakrooms in Manhattan, Albany, and Washington. Once legislators had decided to engage outside interests in the act of state formation, the boundary between politics and capital became as thin as the paper petitions for those charters and grants.

Embracing the complexities and context of these narratives is crucial; the instinct to search for clean hands and pure intentions is little different from the temptation to impose ahistorical "public" and "private" categories on mixed-economy institutions. The early republic's applied political economy was consciously manipulated by its participants in a way that militates against such neatness. Once the first shovel of canal dirt or turnpike mud was turned over by a worker paid in paper banknotes that had been carried upriver aboard a privately owned state-licensed steamboat and unloaded on a private pier at a public port, any bright categorical lines we imagine had long been trampled underfoot. Similarly, divisions between partisanship and supposedly apolitical business relationships crumbled once people began identifying themselves as Federalists, Republicans, or Whigs, for personal financial reasons, and switched affiliations if such a move would deliver advantages in business, credit, legal privileges, or political appointments. Even during the Critical Period and "Revolution of 1800," when ideological commitments reached high-water marks, political leaders were busy constructing legislative and electoral majorities with promises of public patronage, private favoritism, and competitive advantages in commerce and business. Taken together, these statutes, petitions, and journals; the debates they ignited; and the institutions they spawned are the clearest articulation of what Americans expected from their government and envisioned for their political economy in this era.

The key to understanding the political economy of the early American republic is to appreciate that there was strength in numbers, so too was there strength in structure. Government was now under the control of a more popular politics; the key to gaining leverage in the city and state's political economy lay in mobilizing the people who were the constituent members of the sovereign state of New York's body politic. Like it or not, the most durable and useful legal tool to accomplish that turned out to be the corporation, the legacy of which we continue to wrestle with today.[41]

Case Studies in Empire Building

The chapters in this book are chronologically organized as case studies, examining how the business strategies of political entrepreneurs were directly related to the political structures of the state and responsive to the wishes of lawmakers.

Chapter 1 details the introduction of finance capital and commercial banking into the un-banked mercantile community of New York City. Propelled by newly won state sovereignty and seeking competitive advantages in politics, policy making, and commerce, several separate cohorts of elite New

Yorkers tried to found incorporated banks in 1784. When only one of those proposed banks, the Bank of New-York, opened its doors and did so without the state's blessing, it nevertheless gained legitimacy by rooting itself in the state's institutional ecosystem as a lender to the state and municipal government and a bulwark against the incursions of a federal bank.

Chapter 2 examines the founding of the Northern and Western Inland Lock Navigation Companies, two Albany-area canal companies chartered in the early 1790s to connect the Hudson River to Lake Erie and Lake Champlain. Both companies failed and were seen as cautionary precursors to the Erie Canal.

Chapter 3 looks at how a clever cabal of elites manipulated the corporate chartering process to launch a bank from within a water utility, called the Manhattan Company, in 1799. For nearly a decade, the Bank of New-York used its financial leverage to sway political favor and block new entrants from opening rival banks until Aaron Burr and other New York Democratic-Republicans seized an opportunity to open their own bank. Amid the controversy, partisans and bankers confronted the political implications of partisan corporations and the propriety of using credit as a tool in electoral competition.

Chapter 4 examines the complicated political economy of monopoly rights in the early republic during the beginning of the nineteenth century. Even more so than the corporation, the embrace of monopoly privileges by early American states was a continuation of an imperial practice that was unquestionably monarchical: giving one person or association a long-term exclusive right to a route, waterway, structure, type of business, or stream of revenue. A paradox emerged in the republic's use of the privilege: a successful monopoly inspired legal and political challenges, forcing its proprietors to be open to partnerships with would-be rivals. In the case of the steamboat, state legal protections were ultimately more useful in maintaining a monopoly's viability than any federal patent protection for technology.

Chapter 5 considers the implications of New York lawmakers' 1817 decision to directly manage and publicly finance the Erie Canal, which fundamentally changed the relationship between the state government and its maturing institutional ecosystem. The diminishing appeal of exclusive privileges led to a fundamental reorientation in state policy with the public mobilization on behalf of the Erie Canal and legislative wrangling over how it would be financed. Although it is thought of as a "public" project and one of the first of its kind, beneath that veneer it was a hybrid—a desirable investment among wide slices of the electorate who included proprietors of incorporated financial institutions and land speculators who stood to benefit from its operation, and a civic project that legislators and merchants realized would bring the western United States into the close orbit of New York, creating the conditions for the city and state to become the commercial epicenter of the eastern seaboard.

CHAPTER 1

"The Most Dangerous and Effectual Engine of Power"

New York officially became an American city at one o'clock in the afternoon on 25 November 1783. To the sound of pealing bells, Major General Henry Knox and a retinue of horse-mounted dignitaries left Bowling Green, at the foot of Broadway in Manhattan, setting off to the Bull's Head Tavern on the Bowery, accompanied by a crowd that had assembled at the city's "Tea-Water Pump" and followed on foot. There they met George Washington, New York governor George Clinton, Chancellor Robert R. Livingston, and other members of a provisional government, which was about to take possession of the southern parts of New York that had been under British occupation for the last seven years.

The thousands of spectators reviewing columns of troops that day were firsthand witnesses to spectacles of regime change reflected even in the naming of New York's taverns. Evening festivities were hosted at Cape's Tavern, a site formerly known as the "Province Arms" and then the "City Arms" when it was a favored haunt for the officers of His Majesty's occupying forces. After being purchased by John Cape, the new proprietor's first public act was to replace a thirty-year-old sign that had hung above the door with a new one bearing the armorial insignia of the now-independent state of New York.[1]

However meaningful, the symbolic acts of replacing signs and changing flags were inherently complicated by some unpleasant facts concerning New York City's population and prospects. With the evacuation of more than twenty-nine thousand British Loyalists complete, there remained just twelve thousand people living inside the belt of Manhattan's terraqueous border.[2] Although people could strip away physical vestiges of British dominion and occupation, the uncomfortable truth was that many of those who remained in the city could be classified as British Loyalists: Tories who had cooperated in the British occupation but who were not so loyal that they felt compelled to leave the United States after the war's end.

To people like Chancellor Robert Livingston and his circle of correspondents, which included George Washington, foreign affairs minister John Jay, and former New York congressmen Gouverneur Morris and Alexander Hamilton, the presence of those Tories was essential if the city were to rebound as a commercially viable destination for goods and capital. Americans had rejected British imperial governance during the Revolution, but the mercantilist practices and habits of the British Atlantic remained intact and Hamilton in particular was convinced that the new nation needed Tories to help negotiate that world. The willingness of the Tories to participate in American commerce would entangle the city, state, and nation in a web of trade that, both Livingston and Hamilton hoped, would foster geopolitical stability for the United States as a whole. Furthermore, the treatment of those Tories would speak volumes about the intentions and nature of the new American regime and its ability to reconcile with its former kin. And finally, in the view of Livingston's cohort, New York desperately needed the Tories' money. The city was hemorrhaging coined metal—gold and silver—that was essential to participate in international trade. There was a real risk that Tories' capital and connections could be lost for good.

But not everyone was enthusiastic about continuing to host these former Loyalists. During the Revolution, New York legislators punished British collaborators by confiscating their estates and chopping them up to be sold to (ostensibly) patriotic rent-paying tenants.[3] Although the war was now over, such punitive acts showed no signs of abating. For months, vitriolic attacks circulated in New York under the "Whig Party" moniker, while self-identifying Whigs in the legislature stoked their countrymen's passions by calling for the expulsion of Tories and pressing for invasive new laws to forever bar them from owning property, holding office, or voting, effectively rendering them civically and financially dead. An August 1783 broadside addressed from "Brutus" to the "Tories of New York"—likely penned by Albany county state senator Abraham Yates—delighted in the "remorse, despair and shame cloud[ed] upon [Tories'] imaginations" by fear of American reprisals. "A review of the treason, murder and robberies, which you [Tories] have committed, with a long catalogue of your aggravated offenses against an oppressed but zealous band of patriots," would follow the war, he predicted. His advice to Tories was to "flee then while it is in your power, for the day is at hand, when, to your confusion and dismay" they would face "just vengeance" from "collected citizens."[4] The day was coming, these Whigs promised, when Loyalists would not be able to hide from the things they had done.

As Yates and his colleagues attempted to foment and channel popular anger against Tories, Robert Livingston chalked their motivations up to greed and self-interest. "We have many people who wish to govern this city," Livingston told his friend Robert Morris, "and who have acquired influence in turbulent times which they are unwilling to loose in more tranquil seasons." These legislators had won votes from vengeful and frightened voters, and they wanted to keep those voters vengeful and frightened, even if it meant proposing anti-Tory laws they knew they would never actually adopt into law. The chancellor also believed that Whig legislators were using this veneer of patriotism to enrich themselves. Behind their "violent spirit of persecution," Livingston told Alexander Hamilton, was a "most sordid interest" in "wish[ing] to possess the house of some wretched Tory" or trying to "engross the trade & manufactures of [New York]" for themselves by driving out a Tory "rival" in "trade or commerce." Some Whigs wanted to avoid repaying lawful debts owed to Tories, and others wanted to lower real estate values and the "price of Living" by "depopulating the town" of Manhattan. "It is a sad misfortune," Livingston concluded, "that the more we know of our fellow creatures, the less reason we have to esteem them."[5]

But however base these motives might have been, Livingston saw real dangers lurking in New York's political currents. Calling anti-Tory hostilities a "gathering storm," he worried that the "smallest spark" might cause the city to "take fire" and overwhelm "all [the] barriers which our weak unsettled government oppose" by transforming rhetoric into riot.[6] The city's "violent papers" were encouraging a "spirit of [Tory] emigration," observed Hamilton. "Many merchants of second class, characters of no political consequence," were "carry[ing] away eight or ten thousand guineas" from the "popular frenzy" in New York—a loss of capital he predicted "our state will feel for twenty years at least.[7] Writing from Paris to raise alarm with both Livingston and Hamilton, John Jay hoped the "indiscriminate Expulsion and Ruin" of Tories would not come to pass; he reported that "the Tories are almost as much pitied in these Countries, as they are execrated in ours." "Violences and associations against the Tories pay an ill compliment to Government and impeach our good Faith," he wrote. Events in New York were being read as a sign of "unnecessary Rigour and unmanly Revenge without a parallel except in the annals of religious Rage in Times of Bigotry and Blindness." Whigs were "carry[ing] the Matter too far." Their actions were "impolitic as well as unjustifiable."[8]

In the weeks that followed the British evacuation, Robert Livingston, Alexander Hamilton, and a cohort of like-minded, self-styled moderates tried to assuage Whig-Tory tensions in the city of New York by appealing to social ties, crafting legal arguments in favor of revolutionary settlement, and attempting to influence the direction of the city and state's politics. When those tactics failed, they separately decided that their best chance for success was to found a bank.

In the first three months of 1784, three distinct coalitions began publicly organizing themselves to launch what they hoped would become the first incorporated bank in the state of New York. Each group made it far enough to file petitions with the New York state legislature seeking charters of incorporation. Two of the groups publicly solicited stock subscriptions from investors in advance of those filings. And even after the legislature declined to grant any of their requests for a charter in 1784, one faction went ahead and opened a bank anyway: the Bank of New-York. The directors of that institution persistently filed incorporation petitions throughout the remainder of the decade.

This chapter focuses on illuminating the appeal of incorporated banks at this moment of history in the early American republic. After all, given the avenues open to elite New Yorkers in 1784—from launching a new social club or society to replicating one of the Revolution's many semi-official committees of notables—why create a bank? And why not simply form a private bank rather than seek state permission for an incorporated one?

On its face, the corporate form is a useful legal instrument that enables a rotating group of people to hold common property over long periods of time and to be a fictitious "person" who could sue and be sued in court as a single entity. But in practice the corporation is a vehicle for the accumulation of capital and influence. The extent of that influence is determined by the underlying purpose and function of the corporation at hand, and a bank's essential institutional function is to amass capital and offer credit. As institutions that unite human, financial, and political capital under one roof, banks are different from ordinary firms that buy and sell goods. As a route to participation in the Atlantic economy that would reestablish New Yorkers' access to British and Continental credit, an incorporated bank would present a familiar and reassuring façade to foreign creditors, which would inspire confidence and initiate mutually beneficial transatlantic mercantile alliances.

At the heart of those alliances were transactions; banks could enable them by connecting borrowers with lenders. Yet because a bank's resources were finite, its directors and managers had no choice but to exercise discretion in deciding who was eligible to gain access to that credit and the institution's other services. Each time the bank extended itself it was taking a risk; personal relationships therefore were important factors in determining who received credit. Outside the bank's offices, any person accepting a check drawn on a bank as a substitute for gold coins or paper money had to make a similar set of judgments: about the person passing the check, the name of the person on the check itself, and the bank's ability to pay that check. Banks, then, were not primarily vaults or even offices. By printing reliable paper money and checks that facilitated the buying and selling of goods and services, they provided a crucial medium of exchange in the local and regional economy. And by lending to borrowers and accepting capital from creditors, banks created institutional networks of obligation and dependence.

For the economically and politically ambitious, no institution in the early American republic offered a more tempting array of advantages than a bank. Bank proprietors and clients were dealmakers and brokers in opportunity, making fortunes for those fortunate enough to be members of its network. The act of granting and tapering access to credit while excluding others from having it is what gives bankers their power; that access was preferential and

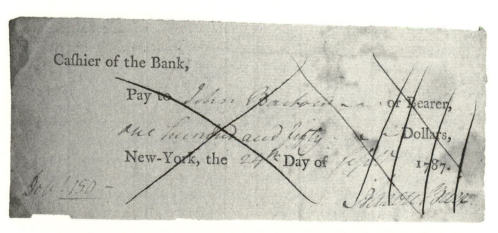

Figure 1. Partly printed check endorsed by Aaron Burr, 24 April 1788. This is an example of an early American bank check issued by the Bank of New-York. Note that because there was only one bank in New York City, the check refers to the Bank of New-York simply as "the Bank." Source: Private collection.

revocable, enabling bank directors to shower preferred treatment on favored clients, projects, or politics. Banks therefore shape their clients' interests, and if a bank is a lender to local or state government, its directors calibrate the capabilities and interests of those public entities as well. The existing banks familiar to former British colonists in the late eighteenth century—namely, the Bank of England in London and the Bank of North America in Philadelphia— were quasi-independent arms of the state; no other type of institution was more likely to be regarded with skepticism, suspicion, and outright fear by the public and elected officials alike.[9]

Understanding the utility of banks and the opposition they provoked is crucial to understanding the development of this era's political economy, but despite the multiple efforts launched to win bank incorporation charters in New York in 1784, the ferocious competition for that prize has all but vanished from modern accounts of this period.[10] Histories of early American banking instead tend to settle their gaze on just one of these associations: the Bank of New-York. The reasons are understandable: it was the only one of the proposed banks to open its doors in 1784, it remained the city's only bank until a branch of the Bank of the United States opened in 1791, and it operated under its own name until a 2007 merger. In addition, the bank has one particularly prominent name tied to its origin story: future Treasury secretary Alexander Hamilton. His role in the bank's founding and early operations invites observers to view it as an intellectual antecedent of his political and economic philosophy in establishing the first Bank of the United States and a securitized, tradable national debt. Before one can understand Hamilton, the thinking goes, one must study "his" bank.[11] Yet the Bank of New-York's early years—the seven years it operated before it was incorporated—are often ignored in studies of early American finance that rely on quantitative data. The bank did not begin keeping a single set of archived account books or minutes of the meetings of its board of directors until the bank was chartered; therefore, the precise details of its finances remain opaque and unknowable. Approaching the Bank of New-York through Hamilton can be more distorting than illuminating. Hamilton's position was initially tangential and his influence within the bank was diluted by other directors and shareholders. He owned, after all, just one symbolic share of its stock. Acting as an agent for two wealthy out-of-town merchants, Hamilton had initially planned to help them found their own bank. Once he learned that a coalition had already met to organize a commercially oriented bank, he joined that group and was welcomed by promoters who were as eager to gain access to two large investors as they were to Hamilton's thoughts on finance. Therefore, studies of New York banks that fixate on Hamilton's role at the Bank of New-York risk overstating his indispensability and overshadowing the institution's more authentic originators: New York City merchants and the competition for charters in New York City during the winter and spring of 1784.

The various bank cohorts in New York in 1784 were united by motivations to ameliorate ongoing tensions between New York's Whigs and Tories by creating a venue for what Robert Livingston called "social intercourse" that would "wear down mutual prejudices." The bank promoters agreed that anti-Tory politics were blinding both lawmakers and voters to the obvious contributions Tories could make to the city and nation's commercial and political life, and there seemed to be no easy way to rhetorically persuade political leaders that their long-term self-interest lay in changing course. Moreover, none of the state's existing institutions had the capacity to offer the favors, privileges, and opportunities that could reorganize the rivalries and contain the animosities threatening to destabilize the infant republic. As he watched the local economy of New York City deteriorate, Robert Livingston ridiculed the lack of money and credit in the city as "republican economics." Having driven Tories and their capital abroad, the chancellor feared that New York would eventually have to go abroad in search of funds to operate its state government.

Each pro-bank mobilization therefore sought to reach beyond rhetoric by launching an institution capable of offering financial incentives to Tories and Whigs who found common cause with one another, replacing mutual hostilities with transactional trust. Livingston thought a bank would aid New Yorkers in financing their own future and secure the confederation among the new states, "[helping] cement a union that separate [state] debts would weaken."[12] Alexander Hamilton and a group of Manhattan merchants shared similar views regarding the potential for commercial relationships to mend divisions between rival parties. Hamilton proposed that different interests not merely acknowledge mutual ambitions and symbiotic relationships but act on them, too. A bank could fulfill his wish to "make" durable alliances by encouraging Tories and Whigs to "participate" in the "privileges" of the new regime while resetting peacetime trade with Britain.[13] The pro-bank activists of 1784 therefore considered commercial and business relationships to be essential features in the civic ecology of a stable and thriving state as well as a union of states. In this way, economic materialism did not merely peacefully coexist alongside democratic political institutions; instead, the two seemed to be fundamentally linked. Business interests tamed the passions and rival-ries that deference, aristocracy, and politeness could not master. If the state created the market, the market in turn stabilized the state and gave it the ca-pacity to govern.

Beyond resuscitating the local economy and strengthening the nation's prestige and power abroad, an incorporated bank would strengthen bank pe-titioners' hands in New York State's political arena. In replacing animosities with alliances, bankers would constrain the ability of New York politicians to continue to exploit anti-Tory sentiment among voters. On a practical level, Tory bank clients would quickly find themselves ensnared in legal contracts and credit relationships, making future legislative assaults more difficult to justify and frustrating to enforce. A Tory-Whig bank would place Tory capi-tal beyond lawmakers' reach by comingling Tories' "Loyalist" assets and cap-ital with those of "patriots," thereby sheltering them from confiscation or seizure. Even as they were being asked for charters of incorporation, there-fore, lawmakers were being kept in the dark about one of the true motives behind the pro-bank mobilizations of 1784: an incorporated bank, clothed in the legitimate authority of the state, would become an institutional counter-weight to the state legislature. New York officials were being asked to create an institution that would be used to undermine their own governing agenda.

The competing coalitions of 1784 shared another reason for wanting to found a bank in New York: neither the state nor city already had one. Al-though competition between banks was feared as a potentially destabilizing rivalry, the absence of institutional banking in New York meant that mer-chants and mechanics alike lacked a stable supply of money and credit, creat-ing logistical challenges for individuals engaged in all kinds of transactions, from buying flour to paying taxes. As Alexander Hamilton argued in a 1783 letter to New York governor George Clinton, without an "incorporation of creditors in the nature of banks" people would be "deprive[d]" of "the benefit of an increased circulation" and would, "of course . . . [be] disable[d]" from "paying the taxes for want of a sufficient medium." The consequences were both local and national: a lack of sound money and available credit con-strained local commerce and injured the "national faith honor and reputa-tion" of the United States as a whole. "It will be a shocking and indeed an eternal reproach of this country," he wrote, "if we begin peaceable enjoyment of our independence by a violation of all the principles of honesty & true policy" because of an inability to conduct basic exchanges.[14]

Yet despite their commonalities, the coalitions who petitioned the New

York state legislature for a bank charter in 1784 had inherent differences. Each proposed to serve different interests by prioritizing different functions. The Bank of New-York opened as a *money bank*, meaning that its paper banknotes were backed by deposits of gold and silver coins called *specie*. Such a bank principally supported merchants engaged in importing goods to the city, investing in small manufacturing enterprises, and granting credit to each other and a limited circle of dependents. By contrast, the Livingston-backed Bank of the State of New York would be a *land bank*: its paper banknotes were to be backed with a portfolio of mortgaged lands as well as coins. Such a bank was designed to take advantage of a short-term depression in the city's real estate market and provide a vehicle for converting existing land holdings into circulating money. Livingston hoped it would become a deposit institution for governments, churches, and charities, enabling the bank to pay regular dividends on its stock and become a profitable investment for its shareholders. Yet it would also inevitably and primarily benefit landowners.

These distinctions are important. By proposing to tether paper banknotes to different forms of collateral, bank petitioners presented lawmakers with a choice about the future direction of the state's economy. Determining which type of capital—land or coins—was more suitable as a basis for a financial institution's operations would also determine what interests—landed or mercantile—would gain access to credit in the near future. This choice carried long-term implications for what kinds of economic activities would take root in New York and which professions—landlords or merchants, for example—would make decisions about how to allocate resources and dispense credit in and around the state's commercial hub of New York City. Therefore, bank coalitions were not simply asking lawmakers to award a bank charter to their favorite interest. Much more was at stake. They were asking the legislators to select a particular kind of bank and—by extension—a particular form of capitalism.

These were weighty options, but they were being laid before New York legislators at a moment when it seemed like lawmakers might welcome a momentous opportunity to shape the state's future direction by incorporating its first bank. Despite Robert Livingston's complaint that the state had been stingy in issuing corporate charters, New York City merchants were, in early 1784, already petitioning the state legislature to reintroduce the corporate form to the state's institutional landscape by reissuing a charter of incorporation to the Chamber of Commerce.[15] This move came on the heels of lawmakers intervening in a Whig–Tory dispute among the parishioners of Manhattan's Trinity Church in late 1783, when the state legislature overturned the election of a Tory rector by opening the church's 1696 charter of incorporation to vest governing authority in a new state-created board of nine trustees.[16] Corporate charters were exceedingly rare in New York in the 1780s, but no more so than in the rest of the nation.[17] And although the process of wrangling an act of incorporation from a legislature was no easy task, once state lawmakers had demonstrated their willingness to receive and consider petitions concerning corporate privileges, they created an incentive for new interests to mobilize and lobby for similar benefits. In nearby Philadelphia, some of the city's wealthiest merchants had recently begun organizing a second bank in their city that would, in the words of Gouverneur Morris, be a "coalition" of "violent Whigs and violent Tories." Although they had "turned their Backs upon every Body else about two years ago," these patriots and Loyalists "each performed a Semi Circle and met at the Opposite Point." New Yorkers need only read their newspapers to learn of these events.[18]

Therefore, despite the anti-bank and anticorporate suspicions and rhetoric permeating the new nation's political culture, it was reasonable for New York's bank promoters in 1784 to think that their state legislature not only could be nudged toward chartering an incorporated bank but also might have actually wanted to receive and approve such a proposal.[19] The push for incorporated banks was encouraged by legislators who collaborated with petitioners to define an economy of influence. This helps explain the paradox that emerged in New York City's (and New York State's) political economy during the first six months of peaceful American independence: in the immediate aftermath of a revolution waged against monarchy, monopoly, and privilege, New Yorkers saw a stampede in favor of corporations—an imperial vestige that linked all three. Elite merchants and landowners certainly envisioned their proposed corporate banks as mixed-economy public-private institutions that would enable them to gain (and regain) leverage over New York's official political institutions and policy-making apparatus while profiting from their newfound influence. Yet those proposals also reflected a perceived climate of political opportunity. Livingston, Hamilton, and other political entrepreneurs interwove their business and political strategies to appeal to elected public officials. The corporation was not an unwelcome alien in the early republic; among petitioners and some legislators, it was an invited guest.[20]

The Land Bank

Robert Livingston was a latecomer to the realization that a corporation—and a bank, specifically—could help him gain financial leverage over New York politics. Initially his plan was to wield power and make profits by speculating in Manhattan real estate. Looking around the city, the chancellor saw prices that he believed were too low and would quickly rebound once the city's population began to grow.[21]

Livingston whetted his appetite in late 1783 by buying £2,000 of "good substantial brick houses" that he predicted would bring in £350 of rental income per year. But the estates he truly coveted were far more lavish and ambitious investments. One had recently been the seat of the Loyalist DeLancey family; its current owner, the chancellor suspected, could not afford the home's upkeep or taxes, and he thought it could be bought for five or six thousand pounds sterling. For Livingston, however, there was a catch: although he was certainly a rich man, he was primarily rich in land. Unless he converted that wealth into credit and cash, he was destined to be little more than a spectator in the real estate boom he was so certain would arrive in the next year.

Livingston's first instinct was not to seek anything as formal as a corporate charter. He wanted partners with capital, and soon after the British evacuation it seemed Livingston might have found some. Circulating among the merchants trying to mend relations between New York's Whigs and Tories in late 1783 was Stephen Sayre, a former London sheriff and an ally of the radical journalist and parliamentarian John Wilkes, who supported the American cause during the war. Sayre once ran a private bank in London and had returned to Manhattan—his birthplace—in the fall of 1783 seeking to make a new fortune. There he began attending the Whig-Tory "dancing assemblies," where he met Major General Henry Knox, Chancellor Livingston, and Livingston's brother-in-law John Stevens, a merchant. Sayre also resumed a past friendship with Isaac Sears, a longtime member of the New York City Chamber of Commerce. Sayre and Livingston quickly began using these social events as they were intended to be used: as venues to generate business relationships that would sow political reconciliation and reinvigorate commerce. They recruited Stevens and Sears to be their partners in real estate speculation.[22]

According to Livingston, Sayre first proposed that the cadre broker a Dutch loan that would enable New York's state government to help repay its war debts. At the time, Sayre claimed to have good contacts in Holland but not in New York; therefore, he needed Livingston, Stevens, and Sears to exercise their influence with decision makers in the state and city to make a Dutch loan palatable at home. If the partners could collect fees and commissions for marketing and handling the transaction, Sayre suggested, they could use those proceeds to build the real estate portfolio Livingston had been eyeing.

Chancellor Livingston was never enthusiastic about this plan, and "discouraged" Sayre from pursuing it any further. Livingston did not want New York, or any state, to "contract a foreign debt independent" of the money "borrowed [abroad] by the United States." Congress's national debts, he explained, "help[ed] cement a union that separate [state] debts would weaken." Livingston was therefore unwilling to put profits ahead of principles if it meant jeopardizing the union that existed among the new states.[23]

In response, Sayre pitched a second idea: why not simply use a Dutch line of credit to make "loan[s] to individuals on real property"? This plan would appeal to Livingston, who was eager to see his vast land holdings become a source of ready, liquid money; it would provide him with cash and make him a patron who could offer credit to others.

Livingston liked the idea. However, he also seemed to believe that his aristocratic name alone could open doors and opportunities that were off limits to others. Before committing himself to support Sayre's initiative, the chancellor wanted to find out for himself whether Sayre's Dutch contacts would find it acceptable. He also wanted to see if he could go behind the backs of his partners to carve out a more lucrative side deal for himself. So he wrote to the Dutch minister to the United States, Peter J. Van Berckel, to find out whether he "approved or disapproved" of a credit-for-land idea. He explained to Van Berckel that "in every monied transaction" he preferred to "deal with the Lenders himself than (by a Broker) thru a third person."

Livingston plainly hoped that he could enlist Van Berckel to use his influence at home and abroad, swaying Dutch investors to support a land-investment plan and structure their loan in a way that would make Livingston the leading partner by displacing Stephen Sayre. To the Dutch minister, Livingston offered unequivocal support for the propriety and profitability of land investments. The departure of Tories who had "quited the state," he said, combined with the "little command that any persons among us have of money," had "opened a large field" for investments in real estate. He predicted that before "ten or twelve months or the restoration of commerce & the arrival of strangers" in New York City, these land purchases could "make immediately" an 8 or even 10 percent profit.

Livingston saw himself buying and selling these properties, he told Van Berckel, rather than working with partners and splitting commissions as he would have to under Sayre's proposal. He hoped the minister and his "friends" would "think the interest I offer sufficient to enduce you to lend your money . . . draw[ing] bills upon England or Holland" to "put into my hands;" it would then "be vested in real property." Offering that he was "not nor ever was engaged in trade" as a merchant and that his "property consists of . . . land and houses as I live within my income," Livingston even assured Van Berckel that he would offer a personal bond as security for a Dutch loan of £6,000. "It is impossible," he boasted, "for any person to offer better securities than I can." Moreover, if the minister personally became an investor, Livingston could advance him funds for a shared "joint account" that he would personally manage on Van Berckel's behalf.[24]

This was a bold and an underhanded offer on Livingston's part. And he knew that if his letter were shared, its contents would be toxic both to his reputation and to the opportunities at hand. Livingston not only would be betraying his partners but also would be putting their entire scheme at risk by tipping off other investors about gains to be made in New York. Moreover, if Van Berckel shared the letter's contents, the chancellor feared that people in Philadelphia might initiate "speculations that serve to empower enemies."

"Enemies" might seem a hyperbolic term to use in the context of real estate speculation, but Livingston was not referring to business rivalries or the scandal of being exposed as a double-dealing partner. Rather, he was worried that faraway Philadelphia investors could "empower" already mobilized factions of mutually suspicious Tories and Whigs in New York City. Thus there would be no better way to "empower enemies" in New York than by revealing that there were large profits to be made from the purchase and sale of Tory estates. Should they learn that out-of-state and foreign investors were pooling their capital to take advantage of the state's real estate market, New York lawmakers might be tempted to intensify anti-Tory hostilities and adopt even more aggressive laws to punish Tories and seize their property, violating the spirit and letter of the peace treaty between Britain and the United States and upending the revolutionary settlement that Livingston, Jay, and other moderate Whigs hoped to achieve.[25]

Making matters even more potentially explosive, Livingston was seeking British credit to finance his plans. The chancellor had asked John Jay to "establish . . . a credit for me upon some good house (either in England or Holland)" that could be used by him and his partners, who were likely spending their time casting about in London, Liverpool, and Amsterdam in search of credit as well. Therefore, as they conspired to profit from anti-Tory hostilities and expulsions by speculating in real estate that had been seized from or abandoned by Tories, they were looking to make those purchases with foreign—and even British—credit. No wonder Livingston feared that "hotheaded" Whigs would paint him and his associates as "suspected." If anyone found out about his partners' plans and his own personal duplicity, his credibility could be devastated.[26] As reckless as these actions might seem, Robert Livingston took them as a man of sound mind. He was a political entrepreneur and an aristocrat operating in New York during the immediate months that followed the end of the Revolution—a man who felt at liberty to conduct business as he saw fit, negotiating and negating agreements that privately contradicted his public statements. Perhaps because he did not feel that Stephen Sayre was one of his peers, Livingston considered their arrangements to be provisional. He saw himself as a man without boundaries.

Yet Livingston was about to learn that both his name and the pre-Revolutionary habits and impulses with which he had been raised would prove to be insufficient in helping him successfully navigate the political economy of post-Revolutionary New York. Only days after sending his letter to Peter Van Berckel, Livingston received a reply. In it, the Dutch minister declined his request for credit. He simply did not have "time enough to write to my friends" in Amsterdam right then. Then Van Berckel revealed that he could not partner with Livingston since he had already "thought it prudent to join with gentlemen" who were pursuing a similar scheme to invest in Tory-owned New York properties. They included Gouverneur Morris, New York land baron Philip Van Rensselaer, and Robert Morris. These men, the minister explained, had "experience and knowledge" and his "engagement" with them "put out of any power to do for another what I want to do for myself." Van Berckel closed his letter by suggesting that Livingston lift his request for silence; he wanted to know if the chancellor would be willing to join with them to everyone's "mutual advantage."[27] In reply, Livingston had no choice but to grudgingly "congratulate" Peter Van Berckel for making allies with men of "judgment & integrity." He hoped, however, that their "objects may not be the same" as his, and steered them away from "this Island" of Manhattan toward "improved and unimproved Land in other parts of the State."[28]

Thus it turned out that Livingston would need his partners after all. Without credit from Van Berckel or Jay, he also needed a new plan.

It was at this moment that Livingston decided to try to become a banker. A corporation offered the institutional advantage of installing himself and his partners at the center of their real estate speculations, and an incorporated bank—particularly a land bank—would enable him to raise outside investment capital and convert his personal land holdings into cash.

Although Livingston's shift of priority from real estate speculation to bank proprietorship had taken place in just under two weeks and smacked of pragmatic opportunism, it nevertheless forced him to recalibrate both his goals and his stated agenda. When dealing solely with private partners, the chancellor had mainly expressed interest in the private profits to be had in real estate speculation. But once he began pressing for a bank charter, Livingston began highlighting the civic benefits such an institution could deliver to the city and state.

Newspaper advertisements placed in the 12 February 1784 editions of the New York *Independent Gazette* and the New York *Packet* claimed that the land bank would be both a "place of safety for cash" and a tool that "renders aid to merchant and tradesman." Livingston and his partners pointed to Venice, Amsterdam, London, and even Philadelphia in its "infancy" as places where "great profits" had rewarded the "proprietors" of banks and "supported and created a system of credit extremely advantageous to . . . trade and revenues." They suggested the bank could reconcile Whigs and Tories by tying the two groups together through business relationships and pushing back against aggressive anti-Tory legislators. It was "universally acknowledged," they claimed, that there were "great benefits to commerce and society at large, to be derived from well regulated BANKS, especially in republican governments, where the hand of arbitrary power is restrained by law." In addition, banks created order in commerce and society by "compelling society to punctuality in contracts," enabling people to "make fresh ones." They made it possible to do "more business in less time and with greater facility."[29]

These public statements about banking were not about profits; they offered a prospectus of civic benefits, reflecting an awareness that the public good would have to be served by the state's first incorporated bank. Livingston, the consummate political operator and entrepreneur, simply did not feel that it was appropriate to seek a corporate charter to serve his private ambitions. There was something inherently transactional about applying to the state legislature for a bank charter. Even Robert Livingston felt that it was appropriate to place the public character of that institution at the center of his mobilization efforts. As an institutional extension of the state, a bank would be an agent of regulation, making commerce orderly, monitored, and efficient. And as an institution operating within the apparatus of the state, a bank could act as a safeguard against abusive legislators. In this vision, there was no conflict between incorporated banking and the flowering of a democratic republic; banking, in fact, promised to stabilize the regime. Incorporated banking was therefore being sold to the investing public as a commercial activity that had an inherently political character, and bank directors would be individuals who would wield both political and financial power within the early republic's economy of influence. For these reasons, the Livingston-backed proposal was to be called the "Bank of the State of New York," soliciting investments from an office at No. 6 Wall Street.

According to published details, the bank was to be managed by six directors who would be elected once the bank recruited its first 300 subscribers.[30] One thousand shares would be available for purchase; each was to cost $750, with one-third of that paid in cash and the remainder pledged in "landed security"—mortgaged properties in New York or New Jersey that would be credited for two-thirds of their assessed value. Shareholders would be allowed to borrow money from the bank, up to one-third of the assessed value of the lands they mortgaged. The bank would therefore enable land-owners to transform their properties into circulating, liquid money. All told, the bank's credit would be based on assets worth $1 million: $250,000 in gold and silver specie and $750,000 in mortgaged land titles. The bank promoters knew this investment would present risks to shareholders, but they promised that investors' other assets would be shielded in the event of the bank's failure; no subscriber was "liable for debts beyond his stock." Moreover, no salaries would be paid to the directors or clerks of the bank until shareholders were first paid a dividend.

To observers, it should have been obvious from the 12 February newspaper advertisements that the land-bank proprietors intended to forge a formal relationship with the New York state government. By describing the bank's potential to serve a public good as one that depended on them being "well regulated . . . especially in republican governments," the promoters anticipated that state lawmakers would eventually be forced to author a set of legal rules to govern and guide its operations. Of course, the bank's directors would presumably wield a heavy hand in shaping such regulations. Once codified in state law, the Bank of the State of New York would then become an institution designed to not only reflect the interests of the state's largest landholders and specie-rich merchants; it would also formally structure that interest, consolidating its membership into a corporate institution that—with shares priced at $750 apiece—would speak in the voice of its wealthiest owners.

From the start, then, it was understood that the land bank was not an apolitical entity that spontaneously sprang forth from the private market-place; instead, it was an institution that deliberately mixed interests—landed and mercantile, established aristocrats and nouveau riche arrivistes, and private citizens along with office-holding public servants—to stockpile financial as well as political capital. And there, from atop the perch of one of the only incorporated banks in the western hemisphere, Robert Livingston and his partners would be able to influence the hearts and minds of the state and nation's top policy makers by dispensing a much-desired but limited commodity: access to credit.[31]

But as they read the plans for the land bank, New York City merchants began to appreciate just how much the land bank would privilege the interests of landowners over others. Land-bank shares would have to be purchased in part with mortgaged lands, therefore merchants who did not own real estate would be ineligible to buy shares unless they first bought property to mortgage at the bank.

Here is how the math would work out:

One share would cost $750. Because an account would be credited with two-thirds of a mortgage's face value, a $750 land purchase would be worth $500 at the bank. A merchant would therefore have to top off that sum with $250 in coined money. Not including transaction costs—legal fees, commissions, appraisals, taxes, and surveys—it would therefore cost a merchant at least $1,000 in cash and property purchases to buy a bank share worth only $750.

By comparison, someone who was already a landowner would need to raise only $250 in cash to purchase that same bank share after mortgaging his or her existing holdings at the bank.

Thus, an inequity had been structured into the land bank's design: one that privileged property holders over coin holders. This distinction would be even more magnified among the bank's directors, who had to own four shares of stock. Although Robert Livingston would meet that requirement with only $1,000 coming out of pocket, a city merchant—someone like Isaac Sears, one of Livingston's and Sayre's original partners—would have to spend $4,000 to buy the same number of shares. Yet as equal shareholders on paper, both men would be eligible for the same amount of bank credit. What merchant would trade $4,000 in gold and silver coins for the same face value in less secure paper money?

The proposed Bank of the State of New York would therefore be incapable of answering the commercial credit needs of either the city's merchants or their customers. Paper notes backed by land instead of gold or silver coins would never pass muster among merchants who were accepting only two sources of domestic paper money at the time, both of which happened to be from Philadelphia: those from the Bank of North America and so-called Financier's Notes issued by Congress's finance superintendent Robert Morris.[32] City merchants came to view Livingston and Sayre's proposal as fundamentally flawed—not because it was a land bank, but because it was designed primarily to serve landowners.

The Private Bank

When Alexander Hamilton first heard that people were proposing to open a land bank in New York City, he believed it had been the brainchild of Stephen Sayre. Later, he would say that he had always known the "true father" was Chancellor Robert Livingston.[33] Either way, Hamilton was under instructions to not pay too much attention—a directive that had come from John B. Church, the wealthy British merchant who in 1783 had hired Hamilton to be his agent in America.

Although Hamilton was a relative newcomer to the city, his experience made him well suited to succeed in its commercial affairs. He had worked as a clerk in a St. Croix import-export house after being orphaned in 1768 and had run the firm's headquarters for several months in 1771 when he was just sixteen years old. He therefore knew how to contract debt, pass bills of exchange, and negotiate transactions, making him intimately familiar with the skills needed to run the portfolio of a successful trading firm.

In the early 1780s, Hamilton befriended two men who made a fortune during the Revolution: John B. Church and the merchant Jeremiah Wadsworth. When the duo left American shores for Paris after the war to buy goods and collect debts, they made Hamilton their go-to man in New York City. Being Church's agent meant that Hamilton was charged with managing his business affairs, investing his funds, and acting as his legal representative.

It also meant that he had a breathtaking amount of daily autonomy; in the fall of 1783, neither Hamilton nor John Chaloner, who, as Wadsworth's top American agent in Philadelphia, was Hamilton's counterpart, had heard from either of their principals since July.[34]

Being Church and Wadsworth's agent also meant that, by late 1783, Hamilton was already thinking like a banker. Church and Wadsworth, after all, were no ordinary merchants. Among their many assets was the largest single bloc of shares in the Philadelphia-based Bank of North America, then the only bank in the nation. Hamilton was in charge of Church's half, managing a combined investment of 202 shares worth just under $82,000. He was directly responsible for collecting dividends paid on Church's bloc of shares and held a power-of-attorney that entitled him to cast shareholder votes in Church's name, making him the proxy voice for one of the country's most important merchant-bankers and a de facto stockholder in the bank itself.[35]

Despite all their influence within the Bank of North America, however, Church and Wadsworth were unhappy with how the institution was being managed. They suspected that bank president Thomas Willing was collaborating too closely with his onetime business partner Robert Morris, the financier and merchant who had been Congress's superintendent of finance since 1781. When Willing announced in December 1783 that the bank was expanding and would put additional stock shares up for sale, it looked to Hamilton like Robert Morris was behind that plan, one that would cost his clients money and dilute their influence within the bank. Chaloner predicted the new stock would "lessen the dividend" paid to current shareholders— reducing the profitability of bank shares as an investment—and "throw it out of the power of a few individuals" to select directors and "control" the bank itself.[36]

Moments like this tested principal-agent relationships in the eighteenth century because the physical distance separating Hamilton from Church could be narrowed only by trust. Although Hamilton wrote to Church for instructions in December, his letter did not reach London until February. Church's response, penned days later, did not reach New York until later in the spring. He and Wadsworth directed Hamilton to discreetly "strain at every nerve" to buy up the new shares in the Bank of North America.[37]

But during the intervening weeks when letters were in transit, Hamilton's on-site autonomy and judgment led him to begin working on a different plan. In his December letter, Hamilton suggested to Church and Wadsworth that instead of tangling with Robert Morris and fighting a corporate structure rigged against them in Philadelphia, the partners should open a bank of their own in New York City. Such a bank would be unincorporated and have no shareholders. The only people with equity in the venture would be Wadsworth and Church; although this meant the bank would be smaller than the Bank of North America, the advantage would be that nobody else would have a say in its governance or management. The bank Hamilton offered to help set up would therefore be the partners' own private commercial bank—their own personal "engine" of regulation and power in New York City.[38]

Church and Wadsworth envisioned their bank as an avenue to extract profits and deploy leverage in New York, and to maximize this effort they intended to restrict ownership in the bank solely to themselves. Therefore, when Stephen Sayre approached Alexander Hamilton in late 1783 to solicit Hamilton's principals to join the land bank he would soon propose, Hamilton refused. Moreover, he did not tell Sayre that Church and Wadsworth were already nursing bank ambitions of their own. Recalling the encounter to Church, Hamilton seemed to not realize that Robert Livingston had partnered with Sayre; Church dismissively said he would be "sorry if Mr. Sayre should effect his Establishment" but "astonish[e]d if Men of Property are weak and credulous enough to give him their Confidence."[39]

What Hamilton and Church did not yet realize was that those "Men of Property" would soon not need to have confidence in Sayre alone. Once Chancellor Robert Livingston and merchant John Stevens became the highly visible front men for the proposed land bank, they were the authentic men of property threatening Church and Hamilton's plans.

In response, Hamilton spent much of February working to "start an opposition" to what he called the "scheme" of the proposed land bank. There was "great reason," he believed, to fear that the legislature would approve the land bankers' request for both a corporate charter and a law declaring it exclusive, which would prevent competing banks from being incorporated. "For the sake of the commercial interests of the state," Hamilton was making it his mission to "point out [the land bank's] absurdity and inconvenience to some of the most intelligent Merchants," some of whom eventually "saw the matter in a proper light" and joined in opposition.[40]

Hamilton also began a whispering campaign to "convince the [land bank] projectors themselves of the impracticability of their scheme." In this he was aided by the land-bank promoters after they raised doubts about the propriety of mortgage-backed paper money, asking if buildings could be accepted as collateral if they were not insured against the risk of fire. On 16 February—one day before their incorporation petition reached the state assembly—Livingston or one of his partners answered their own question by announcing that "some Gentlemen have it in contemplation" to form a fire-insurance company and that once "such houses . . . are insured, [they] will be of course, received as security in the Bank."[41] This statement must have shaken confidence in the land bank's backers, sparking investors' imaginations to begin asking what other risks awaited them besides fire? The land bankers had clearly not thought through the consequences of their plans and had now committed to founding and managing not one but two new institutions in the city: a bank and an insurance company.[42]

Yet even as support for a land bank eroded in New York City, its prospects nonetheless seemed robust in the state capital. According to Hamilton, Robert Livingston "had taken so much pains" to cultivate support among landowning legislators—Hamilton called them "the country members"—that he feared they were coming to see the land bank as "the true Philosophers stone that was to turn their rocks and trees into gold."

Hamilton decided he had to block the land bank once and for all, and as he peeled away supporters he hoped he could convince them to rally around the bank he hoped to found on behalf of Church and Wadsworth, who were prepared to sell their Philadelphia bank shares and reinvest the profits in New York.[43]

The Commercial Bank

Up to this point in February 1784, the one group with the most at stake in Manhattan's bank machinations had been sidelined: the city's merchants.

From the periphery, they watched as would-be land bankers sketched an institution incapable of meeting their credit and commercial needs while seeking an exclusive charter of incorporation from the state legislature. At the same time, they learned that Alexander Hamilton's elite patrons were planning to open a private bank, subjecting the whole of their community to the whims and wills of two faraway and well-connected competitors. The former threatened to place landed aristocrats at the head of the state's first and only bank; the latter would give John B. Church and Jeremiah Wadsworth a unique capacity to distort New York's political economy. In response to these prospects, New York City's mercantile community began countermobilizing by drawing up their own plan for a bank. Of the three proposals, theirs would be the only bank to actually open (and survive to the present day): the Bank of New-York.

The first public sign of the merchants' organized resistance appeared in the 23 February edition of the New York *Packet*. A letter from "A Merchant" announced that a proposal would soon be "delivered . . . for the establishment of a Bank on the most equitable and generous footing" to be called "the Monied Bank of New-York." The writer then turned to dissecting the flaws in the proposed land bank. Although he agreed with the land bankers' claims that banks in general could deliver "great benefits," he believed that "success . . . depend[ed] on the nature of [its] foundation." The Livingston-backed land bank was flawed, he explained, because it was "clearly founded" to "[add] consequence to the landed interest" in New York. "The language" of Livingston's prospectus assumed that "commerce is dependent on agriculture" and therefore proceeded as if "the landed interest must be of more consequence to the society than the commercial." In the writer's view, however, that "idea is absurd." Holland, after all, needed "no landed interest to support her." Instead it was "commerce, the first spring of the whole machine," that found a market for "the fruits of agriculture."

In addition, the writer alleged that the land bank had been designed to benefit particular landholders, including Robert Livingston. He believed that even before its subscription books were officially opened to the public, the land bank's board—"its Governor, Directors, and Cashier"—were "already in nomination." He had been told, he reported, "one gentleman has been induced to subscribe to four shares, as he is intended for a director." The mercantile letter writer hoped the land bankers' petition would "meet with the fate it merits," because "free people" had no need to show "such partiality," particularly when no "thing was known before in a Free Country." Even the Bank of England, "that source of wealth," did not have "an exclusive privilege," and the "resentment of the Public will not be less than their surprize" if the New York legislature granted Livingston's request for an exclusive charter of incorporation—one that would not only establish the land bank as a corporation but also bar any other bank promoters from receiving a corporate charter for years or even decades to come. A more equitable alternative, the "Merchant" promised, would materialize "shortly."[44]

Three days later, on 26 February, retired major general and current state senator Alexander McDougall presided over a meeting at the Merchants Coffee-House where "merchants and citizens . . . unanimously" vowed to form a bank of their own. The "Bank of New-York," as it was to be called, would be a *money*, or *commercial, bank* with paper banknotes backed by gold and silver coins. The bank would make short-term loans called *discounts* at a 6 percent interest rate. There would be one thousand shares of stock for sale, priced at $500 each—half of what land-bank shares would cost a merchant. Shareholders would be expected to pay the first half of their stock subscription at the bank's first meeting; they would have to pay the second half six months before being eligible to receive the bank's promised twice-yearly dividends. The bank's officers—a president, twelve directors, and a cashier—would be chosen by a plurality of votes cast by shareholders in elections designed to favor smaller investors. Each shareholder would receive one vote per share for their first four shares, shareholders with six shares would command five votes, those with eight would have six, and those with ten or more could cast seven. Therefore, no shareholder could cast more than seven votes no matter how large their investment. With a twelve-member board of directors (twice as many as the land bank), an electoral system that maximized the influence of smaller investors, and a set interest rate, the bank's structure explicitly discouraged the hoarding of shares by people trying to take over the institution or seek special, more favorable borrowing terms.[45]

In these ways, the Bank of New-York was designed to answer the perceived financial flaws in the proposed land bank and the elite dominance of the Church-Wadsworth private commercial bank. Although any bank that backed its paper with specie would naturally be more oriented toward mercantile interests, the Bank of New-York promised credit to a wider community of less wealthy, newly established merchants than those who dominated the city's older transatlantic trading houses. Each of the six men who cosigned the advertisement announcing the bank's details were "merchants," a label that seems superficial when one considers the varieties of political experience they brought to bear in making their proposal. Most had held public office in the provisional state government or had served on local committees during the Revolution; one was a sitting city alderman. A person who wanted to subscribe for Bank of New-York stock would have a choice to do so at John Alsop's law office, Robert Bowne's printing and stationery shop, or Nicholas Low's mercantile firm. On the whole, these promoters were younger, more directly engaged in politics, and less economically secure than many of their social and economic betters, also called "merchants"; only one of the six was established enough to have been a member of the city's Chamber of Commerce before the war—the remaining five were still climbing toward that status. The Bank of New-York was therefore a political mobilization led by political entrepreneurs seeking state support for a financial institution capable of representing the interests of a broad spectrum of the city's commercial sector.

Two interests of that commercial sector in Manhattan were Tory-Whig reconciliation and revolutionary settlement. The bank supporters' selection of Alexander McDougall as their nominal leader was meaningful on this front. He had been one of the most radical merchants in the state before war, and now at the age of fifty-two was one of the city's senior statesmen and its current state senator. McDougall therefore had political clout. More important, he had been one of the foremost advocates for postwar reconciliation in the city.

When elections were held in the fall of 1783 to choose the members of a provisional state-level government that would transition the city from British occupation to American independence, a broadside was printed to target the city's working-class mechanics—among them, blacksmiths, silversmiths, and hatters. The author, using the name "Cincinnatus," had cautioned that a hostile climate for Tories would ricochet back on the people creating it, injuring their own commercial and financial prospects and sowing chaos. "The[se] [Tory] families," Cincinnatus warned, "will go to neighbouring states, and we can expect none to come amongst us, but adventurers who delight more in tumult and anarchy, than in order and good government." Envisioning a distinctly urban collaboration between laboring mechanics and commercial merchants, the author of the broadside urged mechanics to vote for merchants in special legislative elections to be held several weeks in the future. In London, "the largest and richest city in Europe, made so by Commerce," voters had "chosen for her Representatives, Merchants, men well versed in the practical knowledge of trade." New Yorkers, Cincinnatus concluded, would be wise to follow suit by remembering that their city was no island. "Our local situation, on what the city of New-York has to rely, not only for her own existence but for that of the adjacent country" could be succinctly summarized "in one word," he wrote, before plainly declaring: "It is Commerce." The broadside was not an empty call for unity; rather, the author wanted mechanics to temporarily set aside dissatisfactions they had with merchants just long enough to elect them to office.[46]

Given the nom de plume "Cincinnatus," the broadside's author was probably Alexander McDougall. His plea, however, met with fierce dissent. One reply authored by "a battered soldier" shouted that, of all the groups in the city, merchants were the least patriotic or fit for office. Candidates "who profess themselves to be your Friends" and were "of good natured Dispositions" were plainly too ambitious to be trusted. Moreover, merchants had shown themselves to be too forgiving of Loyalists' misdeeds. "From their natural Timidity, Want of Firmness, and [the] intimate Connexions, by the Ties of Consanguinity, or Marriage" to Tories, the writer warned, merchants would naturally "feel disposed to pardon the most obnoxious Tories." "If you [mechanics] fail" to elect candidates who will firmly punish Tories, he predicted that "you may depend on it that you and your Children will soon become Hewers of Wood, and Drawers of Water, to the Tories in this State." In other words, either the Tories had to be defeated or the state's patriots would once again find themselves under British domination.[47]

Consolidating Forces

Alexander Hamilton did not attend the first meeting to organize the Bank of New-York. In steering Manhattan merchants away from the land bank, he had hoped to drive them into the arms of a Church–Wadsworth bank, but they showed little desire to trade one form of financial domination for another. Hamilton knew, moreover, that it would become harder to establish a bank for Church and Wadsworth once the Bank of New-York was organized. The shares, he explained to John Church, had "been taken up by the broad footing of the whole body of the Merchants" in the city. Under those circumstances, he continued, "it never would be your interest to persue a distinct project in opposition to theirs." Though it "embarrassed" him, Hamilton therefore "concluded it best to fall in with" the Bank of New-York before it was too late. By "employ[ing] [Church and Wadsworth's] money" to make them "purchaser[s] in the general bank," Hamilton hoped "to induce" the bank promoters "to put the business upon . . . a footing" that would "enable" Church and Wadsworth "[to combine] interests with theirs."[48]

The bank's promoters were more than willing to accept Hamilton's involvement in their institution. Even though he had no fortune of his own and would never own more than one symbolic share of the bank's stock, Hamilton's name was added to the would-be board of directors.[49] In conversations with the bank's "most influential characters," Hamilton set about convincing them to relax their restrictions on shareholder voting. Originally, he explained, "no stockholder" of "whatever amount" could cast "more than seven votes." But Hamilton convinced them to allow shareholders one additional vote for every five shares they owned in excess of ten. This, he reported to Church, was as far as the Bank of New-York's promoters would "depart" from their original limits. The change, however, gave Church and Wadsworth a greater voice within the institution and how it distributed credit. Therefore, even before the "Constitution for the said Bank" was drafted, Hamilton had made substantive changes to the institution's design.

Although Hamilton is often credited with being the bank constitution's author, the true extent of his contributions is unclear; the copy of the document found in his files was not in his own hand. It does, however, bear his intellectual fingerprints: subtle but substantial alterations to strengthen shareholder governance and security beyond what was outlined in the bank's original plan. These changes included adding one more seat to the board of directors to make it a tie-proof cabinet of thirteen, which would, in future elections, directly choose bank officers by majority votes. The new compact empowered directors to expand the bank's capital and required them to take oaths of office before a city magistrate. And perhaps most important, a provision in the constitution's nineteenth article mandated that the president and directors apply to the New York legislature for a charter of incorporation and file separate petitions seeking laws that would make "Fraud or Embezzlement" a crime and "punish the Counterfeiters of Bank Notes and Checks" as they thought "necessary and proper for the Security of the Stockholders and the Public."[50] This was not to be a bank that existed separately from the state. Rather, it depended on government for corporate privileges and statutory regulations that would allow it to function more effectively in the marketplace. The bank was asking the state for recognition and inviting it to expand its involvement in the local and regional economy by regulating transactions and banking activities.

Similarly, Robert Livingston's outline for the Bank of the State of New York had called for state "officers of the government" to "inspect [the bank's] books" and "examine their mortgages," in exchange for the bank serving as the "receptacle of public money" and having its "notes taken in taxes." In other words, the bank would welcome the intrusion of inspection if it was granted the privilege of being the official state bank and the repository of public funds.[51] New York's bank promoters therefore not only knew that the state legislature would be involved in their institution if they were granted a charter, they were counting on it; state-imposed regulations would be a necessity, as would the drafting of new laws to define and protect the bank's operations. These expansions of state power were explicitly sought by bank promoters.[52]

The Bank of New-York's petition was submitted to New York lawmakers on 12 March—three days before a shareholder meeting "officially" ordered them sent. Nearly a month had passed since Robert Livingston and the land-bank proprietors had submitted a petition for the exclusive incorporation of their institution. A state assembly committee had already drafted legislation to charter the land bank and give it exclusive privileges for two years, a law that would have prevented any rival banks from opening in the state during that time. The Bank of New-York's promoters therefore not only had to win a privilege for themselves; they also had to defeat a legislative process already underway.[53]

Former Sons of Liberty leader and merchant Jacobus Van Zandt—an advocate of specie-based money and a speculator in Tory-forfeited lands—was the first signer of record on the bank's petition. Conveniently, his nephew Peter P. Van Zandt was a newly elected member of the state assembly from New York City.[54] There were other connections, too, as Alexander McDougall was a leader in the Bank of New-York and a state senator, and Isaac Roosevelt was a city merchant and one of the bank's newly chosen directors. With the exception of Alexander Hamilton, the new board of directors was composed entirely of merchants. Bank president Alexander McDougall, more than any merchant in the state, had unassailable patriotic credentials. Two other directors—Thomas Randall and Comfort Sands—were merchants who had tried to run for political office in the recent past and had been opposed by the city's more working-class mechanics.

Yet these figures were far less controversial than three other men in the group: onetime Loyalists Joshua Waddington and Daniel McCormack, both of whom were bank directors, and William Seton, another Loyalist who was to be the new bank's cashier, conducting its day-to-day affairs. The new bank seemed to have become a vehicle for urban coalition building among Whigs and Tories, garnering its support from former Loyalists, subtle varietals of "hot-headed" and moderate Whigs, established merchants and ambitious upstarts, onetime land-bank supporters, and even some of the city's mechanics.[55]

The capacity to create common interests among onetime enemies and potential rivals had been one of the Bank of New-York's earliest and most important assets, making converts among those who might have otherwise opposed it more forcefully. Alexander Hamilton, for example, might not have wanted to undermine this burgeoning coalition in Manhattan, knowing that in Philadelphia a new bank had become a "coalition bank" composed of once-"violent Whigs" and "violent Tories."[56] Land-bank supporters, too, recognized that the Bank of New-York—more so than their own proposed bank—was an effective tool to advance Tory-Whig cooperation. Even Robert Livingston's brother-in-law Thomas Tillotson acknowledged as much when, after critiquing anti-Tory legislation, he reassured Livingston, "I wish you to understand that I mean not to adopt Genl. McDougal[l]'s plan, but mean that they should get [Senator Abraham Yates] out of the Senate." Tillotson therefore viewed the Bank of New-York and Alexander McDougall's leadership of it as evidence of its potential to advance Tory-Whig reconciliation and to frustrate Yates.[57]

In their harshest critiques aimed at each other, advocates of both the land and money banks hesitated to openly question the loyalty or motives of their rivals; public letters that can be traced back to the banks' promoters during the first months of 1784 focus almost exclusively on the merits of their respective proposals, suggesting that these were not rhetorical attacks but efforts to persuade. The land- and money-bank coalitions each believed their charter applications would be strengthened if they could expand their appeal by attracting supporters and investors from the rival cohort or by offering concessions that would consolidate the two proposed institutions into a single pro-bank effort. Even though Alexander Hamilton thought the land bank was "a wild and impracticable scheme" and had worked to array "all the mercantile and monied influence . . . against it," he did not take to the city's newspapers to attack Livingston and his allies.[58] Instead, he directly solicited the land bankers' support by carving out room for their interests within the Bank of New-York. According to notes kept by Hamilton concerning the bank's charter application, he and his colleagues considered allowing one-fifth of their bank's capital—up to $200,000—to consist of mortgaged properties.[59]

Robert Livingston's critiques were tempered by a reluctance to have the land bank seen as a divisive counterweight to the Bank of New-York. He rejected the claim that "a monied interest and a landed interest of Merchants and Farmers" were necessarily "opposed to each other, when common sense must dictate that they are members of the same body, and mutually support each other." "The Merchant" he stressed, "could not exist without the Farmer, and the Farmer without the Merchant would be a dissocial solitary animal."[60] Livingston acknowledged that the land bank could be more solicitous of "monied persons" in the future and lauded Alexander Hamilton for "sh[owing] what appears to me faulty in the constitution of the Land Bank." The quality of mortgaged lands could be improved, he conceded, and it was unfair to ask merchants to "[draw] too much of their stock from trade to vest it in lands" in order to buy shares in the land bank.[61] Livingston, therefore, exhaustively highlighted the advantages and shortcomings of both the Bank of New-York and his own land-bank proposal in the weeks when both were being considered before the legislature.

Even writing under a cloak of anonymity, Livingston's harshest criticisms of the Bank of New-York addressed only the propriety of having merchants serve as bank directors. In the process of pointing this out, Livingston showed that he envisioned a significant public role for his proposed land bank. The land bank, he said, could someday hold state government deposits, something that likely would enable it to multiply the amount of credit it offered to its clients. This prompted the chancellor to ask whether "the Government [could] lodge their money with those who afford them no security but their good characters" in a commercial bank. Could a "careful Guardian leave the money of his Ward with a Bank whose Directors must change every year," especially when it "circulates more than its capital" and its credit "depend[ed] on the opinion the world entertain of Directors who, from being in trade, are always liable to strong temptations to aid each other?" He warned that the temptations of banking would drive some "Merchants [to] change their profession and become Stockholders." Merchants, he argued, could not be trusted to oversee a stable and publicly useful bank.[62]

Both bank cohorts, then, recognized that the petitioning and charter-application process was a dynamic one. Although they did not consider combining their proposals, both offered compromises to attract new supporters and build a more persuasive case for incorporation. The petitioning process therefore not only aggregated financial capital but also encouraged the consolidation of human and political capital as well. Both bank coalitions assumed that the legislature would approve at least one bank petition in 1784. The only question seemed to be which one would clear the hurdle.

The Legislature

Within the legislature, however, that question was far less clear-cut.

As bank partisans offered concessions to each other in the hopes of building consensus around dueling proposals, state legislators—the audience for these petitions—seemed increasingly unwilling to take affirmative steps on behalf of either bank.

Despite the connections that the Bank of New-York enjoyed in the legis-lature, there remained twelve senators and sixty-eight assemblymen in the legislature who were not directly linked to the proposed bank. New laws had to win majority support not only in both houses, but also in the state's Coun-cil of Revision—a panel composed of the governor, two justices of the state's supreme court, and the state's chancellor, who happened to be Robert R. Liv-ingston, the chief supporter of the rival land bank. Only after winning sup-port in the Council of Revision could a bill be laid before the governor for his signature, making it necessary for the promoters of both the commercial Bank of New-York and the land Bank of the State of New York to lobby legis-lators using a variety of appeals—neither bank was large enough, after all, to give every lawmaker a line of credit or a seat on its board of directors.

Harnessed from across the state and crammed into the narrow quarters of City Hall, New York's state legislature reflected many of the same tensions and motivations found in the civic and economic lives of the few dozen city blocks that surrounded them near the southern tip of Manhattan. Any per-son capable of reading a newspaper or entering a tavern was acutely aware of the divisions between loyalist Tories and patriotic Whigs in the city, and ve-hement anti-Tory passions were expressed by legislators who proposed to strip former Loyalists of their rights to hold office, vote, or own property. A cadre led by Albany County state senator Abraham Yates was hostile even to the notion of reconciliation with Tories and relished questioning the patri-otic credentials of Whigs who dared to socialize or do business with onetime Loyalists. One of Robert Livingston's friends believed that the "narrowness of [Yates's] mind & the badness of his heart . . . injures this state more than ever his services will expiate." "Men of integrity & education," he fumed, indulged Yates's "pretended patriotism" and "suffer that old booby to thwart & discon-cert whatever has the appearance of wise & sound policy with impunity."[63]

The Bank of New-York steered directly into this storm once it published the roster of its managers and directors in city newspapers, making it a target for anti-Tory politicians and their allies. A letter to a New York paper soon wondered what was behind the "present confidence and audacity" of "truly detestable and obnoxious Tories" who appeared in public as bank directors. The Whig directors and bank president McDougall, one writer asserted, had become nothing more than "advocates" for these "bloody-minded villains," and it was "high time" for the state legislature to once and for all "make a proper discrimination" between "friends and foes of this country" by banish-ing "sworn enemies" who "endanger the piece of society by *parties, factions,* and *cabals.*" The Bank of New-York, the writer concluded, was nothing more than an "absurd and ridiculous system" for advancing Tory interests.[64]

Other letters made the same critique and pointed to the land bank as a preferable and patriotic alternative. In an "Appeal to the Legislature," one writer who styled himself "A Real Whig" wrote in the New York *Independent Gazette* that the most potent British threat to America was a financial one. "We never had so much to fear from [Tory] arms," read the letter, "as from their influence and wealth"; the author said the Bank of New-York was "the most dangerous and effectual engine of power that can ever be formed in a State," and lauded the land bank as the more authentically American "Whig bank." In opposing the "Whig" land bank, the writer warned, Tories had pooled "hoarded riches . . . the plunder of our citizens, the wages of death and the earnings of slaves" in order to create "influence in a Bank." There, they would "lay the foundation of power . . . [and] silence every Whig character who applies to them for aid." Referring to Alexander McDougall's leading role in the bank, the writer told readers: "Be not deceived by the names of a few Whig characters who appear. . . . The danger is the greater while the real agents are behind the curtain." The writer alleged that bank cashier William Seton was conspiring to unite New York Tories with Philadelphia Tories, and closed his letter with a threatening flourish: those who had "hitherto borne the name of patriots" would be committing "apostasy" if they failed to "withdraw their names when the cloven foot appears to men of discernment."[65] This land-bank supporter had therefore decided that the way to defeat the money bank was to ignore concerns about assets and instead scrutinize the patriotism and motivations of those aligned with the Bank of New-York. By linking Tories with money, the writer sought to raise the stakes of the approval of a charter for a money bank; such a legislative act would empower the nation's most dangerous domestic enemies and unravel the gains of the Revolution by elevating a class of unreliably loyal Americans to positions of financial and political power.

But another rhetorical thread soon developed amid these fights: a call to reject both banks' petitions for incorporation. Writers argued that neither bank should be incorporated and questioned the propriety of bank chartering altogether.

One letter, punched up with emphatic typesetting in the *Journal,* pointed to the Tory–Whig coalition and asked whether bank chartering created dangerous alliances and corrupting influences that the legislature should try to extinguish rather than encourage. As the writer understood it, new banks were "extraordinary *phenomena.*" One in Pennsylvania was composed of "*rigid* Presbyterians (who have hitherto assumed to themselves the style and character of *pure* and *untainted* Whigs), *firm* and *unshaken* Quakers, and *bigoted, furious* Tories (Churchmen and others)" who all "appear[ed] in the Fields of Politicks and controversy." Meanwhile in New York, "similar coalitions, equally destitute of public spirit, and destructive of the Whig interest, [were] now forming." The writer demanded that the legislature "guard against" the "dangerous consequences and tendency" of banks, and asked whether "either the land or money Bank, would not be more beneficial to a few money lenders and traders, than to the country at large?" Because the legislature would be vesting an important privilege in a narrowly drawn group, the writer alleged that lawmakers were creating a situation where "*Government* will be laid under obligations to *usurers*, & c. who will of course worm themselves into lucrative posts and high stations" while escaping accountability from voters.[66]

Another letter, printed a week later in the *Journal* and written by someone who wanted to be known only as "a Mechanic," echoed these concerns and raised a broader question about incorporated banking: "Where ought credit be placed for the public weal in a republican government?" According to the writer, neither a land- nor money-bank proposal was a suitable answer. Credit should rest "in government only," because allowing it to reside in the hands of bankers had "pernicious and destructive consequence." "It removes both power and credit out of the proper hands," the author said, "and fixes them into those of individuals." Because those people proposing a bank tended to "assert that government have no credit to circulate their own paper"—meaning that they opposed the emission of state bills of credit and other forms of inflation-prone paper money—the author felt that it was "a burlesque or insult on government" for those same individuals to "ask their sanction to give a credit to the property of individuals." Bank charters "advance the power of stockholders, and depreciate the power of government," creating conditions that lead to high interest rates for debtors, the political disenfranchisement of renters, and state legislatures dominated by bank shareholders. In Pennsylvania, the writer warned, "the Assembly must become Brokers for the Bankholders" because lawmakers had taken steps to protect the Bank of North America. The risk was that New York would follow suit, placing bank stockholders "in the path to acquire the same ascendancy and authority over the United States."[67]

In both letters, then, the writers' opposition to incorporated banks did not arise from a preference for a particular kind of asset or method of securing the value of paper money but from a fear that banks were far too dangerous to be entrusted to the care of elected officials. By incorporating a bank, state legislators risked diminishing their own institutional legitimacy by creating a separate, quasi-independent hostile policy-making and regulatory agency that was responsible not to lawmakers or voters but to shareholders. A bank threatened to empower a cadre of unelected financiers whose actions and behavior could not be monitored or tempered by officials or voters; it created a group of people without boundaries who were responsible only to themselves.

Although these letter-writing bank opponents might have been given to hyperbole, they offered a savvy analysis of the competition for bank charters in New York in 1784. Lawmakers were not simply evaluating competing coalitions' proposals on the basis of political connections or judging relative merits of land and coined metals as sources of bank credit. They would not be selecting one proposal, adopting an incorporation law, and letting that bank run free; any bank that opened under their watch would create an abiding interest among legislators to prevent it from turning into what the legal profession termed *imperium in imperio*: a state within a state. Because banks could shower lawmakers with credit or offer them lucrative opportunities to become shareholders, banks had an arsenal of tools at their disposal that enabled them to influence public officials in ways that would make them approach policy questions in terms of the banks' own institutional interests. And if officials became dependent on the credit or services provided by bankers, they would no longer be dependent on voters. Ultimately, banks could distort political economy by shaping policies to their liking and breaking the bonds of accountability that linked voters to their elected representatives.[68]

The Bank of *the City of* New-York

From the competing proposals put forward in the spring of 1784, only one bank emerged: the commercially focused money Bank of New-York. And it opened without a charter.

Although it is tempting to imagine that the bank proposals canceled each other out for personal reasons or political expediency specifically related to the events of 1784, lawmakers' hostility to bank chartering proved durable. A slate of Bank of New-York directors and interested allies won election to the

state assembly in April 1784, defeating a group of land-bank supporters that
included Stephen Sayre, yet the bank's petitions were denied. In 1785, a circle
of more radical merchants followed their conservative brethren to support
the Bank of New-York's incorporation but to little effect.[69] And although subsequent legislatures were not bound by their predecessors' decisions, future
legislators also refused the Bank of New-York's repeated requests for corporate privileges during the next seven years. The bank reapplied for a charter
in the fall of 1784, in the spring of 1785, and again in 1789 and 1790. Each time
it was refused. In 1786 the bank had to fend off a proposal to make all forms
of private banking illegal.[70]

State legislators, of course, had never been under any obligation to grant
all or any of the petitions for bank corporate charters, and New York's state
government did not incorporate a bank until 1791. Therefore, although a corporate charter was a valued political prize and a clearly desirable legal tool, it
was an exceedingly rare species in New York during the 1780s.

But the state legislators' decision should not be confused with inaction;
lawmakers never explicitly banished the corporate form from the state, and
petitioners continued to believe they had reasonable chances of success. By
refusing to charter a bank in 1784, lawmakers were not preventing a bank
from opening; had that been their goal, they could have adopted a law barring the creation of such enterprises or erected onerous regulatory barriers
similar to the one considered in 1786. Instead, by taking what seemed to be a
neutral policy stance, New York legislators—perhaps inadvertently—ensured
that the only bank that opened in 1784 was the merchant-backed Bank of
New-York. Without monopoly protections or corporate privileges, the Liv-
ingston-led land-bank coalition dissolved; the risks associated with using
mortgaged lands as a basis for bank capital were simply too great to attract
investors when compared to the straightforward and familiar organization of
the Bank of New-York.

Even in this instance, therefore, the state was a central agent of change in
shaping its political economy. By deferring action in 1784, legislators affirmed
that they would continue to receive and consider future petitions, creating
incentives for future mobilizations by would-be bankers and other politically
entrepreneurial projectors, and shaping the behavior of the Bank of New-
York itself. During the years when the bank lacked a charter, its directors ran
the bank as a New York City–centric institution, one that was conservative
and cautious out of necessity. Without the privilege of limited liability, shareholders were theoretically exposed to financial risks beyond the sum of their

investment. For some investors, the risk of owning shares in an unincorporated bank was simply too large to bear. When the bank opened, one investor publicly but anonymously announced that he was abandoning the bank because, without a charter, shareholders "become to all intents and purposes *Bankers* and *Copartners*, and every man is liable (however small his share may be) for all the engagements of the Bank, to the extent of *his whole fortune*." "If I wished to be a Banker," he said, "I would chuse my own partners, connect myself with one or two persons of probity and substance, and, instead of leaving the choice to others, the management of the affairs, upon the risque of my *whole* fortune depended, attend to it myself."[71] Despite these risks, however, most shareholders did not adopt this view and no further public defections followed.

During this period, some sought to exploit this vulnerability at the Bank of New-York to their advantage. Soon after the bank's charter application stalled in the state legislature, Gouverneur Morris suggested that the New York directors consider gaining a charter by becoming a branch of the Philadelphia-based Bank of North America. But Alexander Hamilton and bank cashier William Seton refused the offer. Seton told Hamilton that he and Morris "differ[ed] widely in [their] Ideas of the benefits" that would come from any formal connection between the two banks.[72] The Bank of New-York's mission was to create liquidity, enabling merchants to have short-term credit and specie-backed paper banknotes widely accepted and even desired by creditors. When it opened its doors on 9 June 1784, the bank was already developing into an intensely local institution whose directors never petitioned for an exclusive charter or arrogated unto themselves either the name or role of an official state bank. Instead they focused on serving the domestic needs of the city's commercial class; their constitution explicitly stated that the institution would not deal in foreign bills or notes, and it refused to accept mortgaged properties as collateral.[73] Once the president and directors of the bank took oaths before the mayor of New York City on 22 May 1784, pledging to "conduct the business . . . to the best of their knowledge and abilities for the interest and benefit of the Proprietors," merchants across the city began announcing one by one that they would accept the bank's notes.[74] On 3 June, Thomas Hazard & Co. signaled that the bank's notes would be welcomed along with Morris's notes, Bank of North America notes, beeswax, barrels of beef or pork, pot or pearl ash, or "cash"—meaning gold or silver. A week later, the firm of Morton and Horner's began selling printed tables calculating the rates at which British, French, and Spanish gold coins would be paid at the bank.[75] Had the bank's directors been striving for precision, they would have renamed their institution the Bank of *the City of* New-York.

Although the internal deliberations of the bank's directors are unknown during this decade, its ledgers reveal that the institution offered $1.3 million in discounts in its first year.[76] Most directors used the advantage of their positions to obtain credit; the vast majority of the money loaned by the bank went to people beyond this small circle, however, enabling the institution to attract support among onetime land-bank promoters and skeptics, along with "radical" merchants who were quickly de-radicalized by experiencing commercial banking firsthand. Mechanics, too, found the bank's directors supportive of small-scale manufacturing enterprises in the city.[77] The bank also integrated itself into the political economy of the city and state, becoming a lender to the municipal government, an underwriter for the construction of a new City Hall, and eventually a lender to the state government—all while it was an unchartered institution, the petitions of which were routinely rejected by state legislators whose financial fortunes were too geographically distant from Manhattan to ensnare them in the bank's credit network.

The founding of the Bank of New-York, therefore, inaugurated a long-term investment in the economic and political structure of New York by creating a mixed-economy institution where the dividing line separating private capital from public authority was consistently and sometimes deliberately blurred. At first, lawmakers jealously guarded their power to grant charters and print money. But as bankers begged to be recognized and regulated and as they demonstrated a capability to meet credit demands while serving as useful partners to governing institutions, it became clear that the interests of lawmakers and bankers frequently intersected. Although the Bank of New-York's coalition had initially been a hasty union of patriots and Loyalists, those distinctions gradually eroded within a matrix of credit obligations and shared dependency. The bank raised the risk tolerance of those who used its paper in commercial transactions, making them familiar with printed money, interest, and timely repayment. It demonstrated the value of coalition building and the ways in which it could fail legislatively while remaining financially viable. And most important, the founding of the bank facilitated subsequent private speculation and investments in the infrastructure of the city and state; its notes came to represent a durable financial investment in the long-term political and economic viability of the polity, which would rise or fall on the strength of the regional economy it supported. It created an incentive for citizens to maximize their geographical, commercial, political, and strategic advantages by investing money—their most mobile asset—in both short-term commerce and longer-term fixed assets of government policies and public infrastructure.

Had they solely wanted to make profits in a mercantilist system, the cadres of New York bank petitioners and promoters could have attempted to create incorporated trading companies—American versions of the British East India Company and the Dutch West India Company. Had they wanted to integrate Tory merchants into the Manhattan economy, they could have offered them partnerships in new firms. Had they wanted to speak out against anti-Tory legislation, they could have sought elected political offices. Eager to address each of these agenda items in commercial, social, and political contexts, however, the city's pro-bank promoters and petitioners—groups that included elite landowners and real estate speculators, established and neophyte merchants, and arriviste attorneys—decided, independently of one another, that their best shot at broadening the city and state's commercial horizons and settling the Revolution on acceptable terms was to start an incorporated bank. Banking, therefore, was an intensely political activity.

During the next fifteen years, Robert Livingston watched the Bank of New-York offer a stable source of credit to New Yorkers, growing its base of supporters in proportion to its capital. In that time, banking became ever more fundamental to his understanding of politics. Those who wielded credit wielded leverage. And by the time Livingston and other Republican allies were looking for a way to consolidate and discipline their rival political factions in the late 1790s, it was clear to them what kind of institution would be most useful in their quest: an incorporated bank.

CHAPTER 2

"An Enlarged American Scale"

Incorporated banking was just one activity that interested early American political entrepreneurs. The state had as its sovereign power the ability to bestow a charter, monopoly grant, or other exclusive privileges on any individual or coalition. Among politically connected would-be investors and directors with financial and political interests outside Manhattan, transportation ventures were often just as attractive as financial ones. In fact, to the extent that internal-improvement promoters from upstate New York favored the chartering of banks, it was often with an eye toward steering bank capital and credit toward the construction of turnpikes, canals, and other transportation projects that would make upstate land more desirable and salable by connecting it to marketplaces.

The scale of potential profits to be generated by transportation development in northern and western New York was large enough that contemporaries found potential profits difficult to calculate. By one measure, New York's state government in 1790 possessed $75 million in unsold public lands. Meanwhile, in the western part of the state two Massachusetts merchants headed a syndicate that either owned or owned the right to buy from Iroquois tribes six million acres of land that stretched to Lake Erie, for which they had paid $1 million in 1788.[1] For all the vastness of these expanses, however, the most valuable land in the state was concentrated along a narrow ribbon: the banks of the Hudson River. This was not because soil elsewhere was infertile or unusable but because it could not be reached. All but the most durable agricultural products shipped to New York City or Albany from faraway farms spoiled before arriving or became so expensive because of shipping costs that it was impractical to attempt such trade. The only way to render such distances irrelevant was to increase the speed, quantity, and transparency of exchanges by altering both the physical and the institutional landscape of the state.

Although people living far from cities were most directly injured by this status quo, political entrepreneurs who speculated in upstate and distant land purchases were better positioned to persuade state lawmakers to adopt remedies. In the early 1790s, a coalition of politically connected land speculators and bank promoters lobbied New York's legislature to incorporate two companies that would be charged with building canals northward and westward from Albany. At the time, the city itself had a population of just several thousand people. It was situated, however, in Albany County, one of New York's most populous, with more than 75,000 inhabitants.[2]

These canal projects promised almost immediate benefits: just the prospect of slashing shipping costs could reward land speculators with speedy profits as soon as they could unload their holdings onto ambitious upstart farmers. For some promoters and lawmakers, longer-term interests were also at stake: a desire to consolidate the vast territory of New York State by populating it with settlers, some of whom would dispossess Iroquois Indians and connect New Yorkers across the state's spanning stretches. There were also nationalist reasons to support the projects: forming commercial connections to easterly markets would speed the integration of western states and territories into the federal union.[3]

However, for all the gains, financial and political, promised by the two canal companies, both faltered. The Northern and Western Inland Lock Navigation Companies had been created alongside a new Bank of Albany, the state's second bank. The canal companies were chartered on 30 March 1792 and the bank's petition for incorporation was approved by the legislature on 2 April 1792. The bank and canal companies shared many of the same investors and sponsors, most notably Philip Schuyler, the onetime general and former U.S. senator who lobbied for all three incorporations from his seat in the state senate. When they were incorporated, the canal companies counted Federalists, anti-Federalists, and future Republicans among their directors and shareholders, including Stephen Van Rensselaer—likely the wealthiest man in the state—as well as Chancellor Robert R. Livingston. Despite having this political and financial capital at their disposal, however, the companies soon ran short on funds and repeatedly found that their charters, crafted by the legislature to restrain the powers and privileges that were inherent in state-issued grants of incorporation, hobbled them from fully executing their missions. Just months after the companies were incorporated, Schuyler and the companies' directors returned to the legislature seeking to amend their charters so that they could acquire wider rights of way—the amount of land

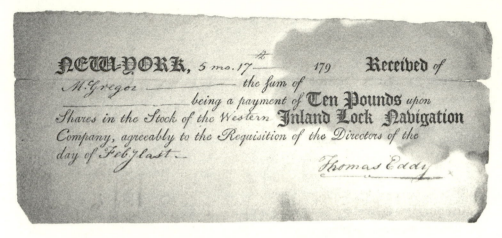

Figure 2. Stock certificate (probably 1797) issued by the Western Inland Lock Navigation Company. Note that the Northern and Western Companies shared stock certificates, leaving a blank space before "Inland Lock Navigation Company" to be filled in as needed. Source: Private collection.

bordering either side of the canal. They needed this land not only to cobble together a commercially viable route for their projects but also to have enough room to do the practical work of clearing that land of trees and obstacles while doing construction. Legislators overwhelmingly supported this request over the property-rights objections of some state jurists and residents of affected counties.[4] The companies' dependence on lawmakers turned out to be chronic. Neither corporation was able to sell enough stock shares to give it the money to complete its work, so the companies' directors repeatedly sought and were often granted relief by the legislature, both in the form of loans and as outright grants of cash.[5]

Although the canal companies' charters, in retrospect, left the companies inadequately capitalized to perform the scale of their required work, legislators were not ultimately responsible for their failure; the companies' directors and managers did more than their part to reach that end. As president of both firms, Philip Schuyler personally mismanaged the companies' operations and finances while attributing stumbles and opposition to his rivals' "corrupt motives"—a serious accusation to lodge in the early republic. In 1793 Schuyler appointed himself as the Western company's engineer even though he had no experience or expertise in the field. Two years later, Schuyler began hiring Irish convicts who were unpopular with locals; he paid them so little that they went on strike. In 1796 the Western company's already decaying wooden locks opened and began charging toll rates so high that petitions flooded the legislature in opposition. By 1797 the Northern company folded with more than $100,000 in debt, while the Western company's most important asset was the right of way it would later sell to the state of New York before construction began on the Erie Canal in 1817. By then the company was almost entirely owned by speculators from New York City.

In a book about early American political economy, it is easier to choose to write chapters about state-chartered enterprises that either were successful or collapsed after many decades of longevity. Short-lived or poorly run firms do not loom large in historiographies of business or economics mainly because of survivorship bias in the selection of case studies and also because companies that failed in the 1790s did not leave behind large paper trails of letters, account ledgers, or legal and legislative records. Failed firms never had the chance to have memoirs published commemorating their founding or subsequent anniversaries; the principals in those firms were understandably reluctant to revisit their mistakes in print or commit them to posterity, and often the papers related to those businesses were never kept, let alone archived.[6] The available source bases for examining companies like the Northern and Western Inland Lock Navigation Companies are therefore thin.

Although the companies themselves may be difficult to reconstruct in this instance, the lessons that contemporaries took away from the failures of New York's early canal policies are readily accessible. In fact, the Erie Canal that was eventually constructed in 1817 was designed, financed, managed, and organized in response to the perceived shortcomings of these two canal companies that had been chartered twenty-five years earlier. Most notably, the legislature's decision to finance the Erie Canal with debt—in the form of bonds—rather than through the sale of ownership-conferring stocks, did not arise because legislators had turned hostile to corporations or monopolies in 1817. To the contrary, most lawmakers were themselves shareholders or directors in state-chartered enterprises and were therefore familiar with the habit of structuring the state's marketplace with the use of public-private mixed-economy institutions. But this firsthand experience was also furnished with knowledge about what had happened to the Northern and Western Inland Lock Navigation Companies, enabling those later canal promoters to anticipate the problems that arose when private and public interests diverged within a transportation-infrastructure corporation.

What, then, had they learned?

One of the most high-profile writers on the political economy of canal policy during the 1790s was Elkanah Watson, the onetime director of the Western Inland Lock Navigation Company who was later ousted by company president Philip Schuyler over their clashes concerning the management of the firm. When he first joined the company, Watson was a peripatetic 35-year-old merchant who had moved to Albany from North Carolina after a series of business failures in the West India trade. Watson's memoirist proudly recalled him moving to the town when it was home to no more than five families; by the 1780s, he was known as "that paving Yankee" for initiating repairs and improvements to the city's main thoroughfare, making him one of Albany's first authentic political entrepreneurs.

Although it drew forth his enthusiasm, the idea of building a canal to stretch from Albany, which lies on the northern end of the navigable portion of the Hudson River, westward to Lake Ontario or Lake Erie was hardly an original idea when Watson began writing on the subject.

In 1724 the colonial Province of New York's surveyor, Cadwallader Colden—father of the future Erie Canal memoirist—proposed linking the Great Lakes to the Hudson River. As Colden observed, the vast, unsettled, and undeveloped Southern and Northern tiers of New York were served by waterways that were neither navigable nor oriented to boost commercial interests. Looking at a modern-day map of New York's rivers tells the same story: the Susquehanna River basin leads to the center of Pennsylvania, the Delaware and Neversink Rivers hastily leave the state to bisect Pennsylvania from New Jersey, the St. Lawrence basin carries travelers northward to Quebec, and the Finger Lakes feed the Oswego's drainage into Lake Ontario. Colden's written tour of the province envisioned joining the Atlantic Ocean to Lake Erie via the Hudson and Mohawk Rivers, followed by traveling on the Oneida, Oswego, and Seneca Rivers, which eventually leads to the fierce maw of Niagara Falls. There, a fifth of the fresh water in the world makes a 90-degree turn before falling 170 feet from Lake Erie into a churning spiral of Lake Ontario. In the eighteenth century, only the Hudson River could carry goods from the interior of New York to another in-state port or marketplace. Connecting the state's interior to the Hudson promised to direct trade inward, developing a western market within New York that could be integrated with the state's eastern portions. Without such improvements—large, sustained, and coordinated investments in the construction of artificial roads and routes—the potential for economic development and agricultural improvement in New York would remain strangled by nature. With the exception of the Hudson River, the state's rivers all seem to flow the wrong way.[7]

Drawing inspiration from Colden's vision, an Irish-born engineer named Christopher Colles in 1784 presented the New York legislature with a proposal to begin "removing the obstructions" on the Mohawk River as part of a larger plan to "promote" both the "settlement of the interior country" and "inland navigation." Submitted alongside petitions for the incorporation of banks and a Chamber of Commerce in New York City, Colles described a plan to "let a number of Gentlemen subscribe the sum of 13,000£ and let application be made to the Legislature to embody them into a Company, vested with powers to carry on the said work." In short, Colles was asking for a corporate charter. If the legislature would grant him this wish, along with 250,000 acres of "waste and unappropriated lands" from the state, Colles's new company would find "sober, honest, industrious farmers or workmen" to labor on the new water route, after which they would each take charge of 150-acre parcels of that land, turning unimproved and unused territory into "a settled neighbourhood." "Internal trade will be increased," Colles predicted, "foreign trade will be promoted . . . the country will be settled . . . the frontiers will be secured." Moreover, he continued, "in time of peace, all the necessaries conveniences, and if we please the luxuries of life may be distributed to the remotest parts of the Great Lakes which so beautifully diversify the face of this extensive continent." Urging legislators to look to British policy as a model, Colles called his proposal one "of considerable public as well as private advantage . . . to direct the stimulus of private interest to public purposes."[8]

New York lawmakers lauded Colles's proposal, but they had another idea about how to implement his planned work. A state assembly committee recommended that "if Mr. Colles, with a number of adventurers"—their term for investors—decided to undertake the planned improvements, "they ought to be encouraged by a law giving and securing to them, their heirs and assigns for ever, the profits that may arise." Thus, although Christopher Colles had asked legislators for a corporate charter to structure public and private investments on behalf of a project that would serve "both the public and individuals," legislators suggested giving him a legal privilege that looked more like a monopoly grant instead. Colles's plan "merit[ed] encouragement," but lawmakers simply had no appetite "to cause that business to be undertaken at public expense" by giving him access to public lands.[9] Without a corporate charter or those 250,000 acres, however, it was unlikely that Colles would ever be able to attract sufficient investments to complete his proposed work. The corporate form, after all, was an attractive way to organize a business because, when ideally executed, it offered a way to legally structure a coalition of financiers, lobbyists, and promoters who could capitalize a firm, allowing the company's board of directors to then hire managers who could competently run the enterprise. Without such a charter, Colles would have to instead recruit a wealthy patron or scramble to assemble less durable partnerships by promising them percentages of a monopoly privilege.

But even this less-than-ideal possibility never came to fruition. Despite a positive recommendation from one of their own committees, New York's state assembly hesitated to act on Colles's petition in 1784. He applied again to the legislature in 1785; instead of recommending a monopoly grant, lawmakers appropriated $125 for Colles to research and write "an essay toward removing certain obstacles in the Mohawk River" for their consideration. In 1786 Colles again sought aid from the legislature, this time petitioning the state senate, but he was once again rebuffed. Colles made no further petitions to the legislature with plans to finance inland navigation between the Hudson River and the Great Lakes, nor did anyone else for the remainder of the 1780s—a period one canal promoter later called a "profound silence."[10]

The idea of building a canal persisted, however. In 1791 a more state-centered vision of commercial development was outlined by New York governor George Clinton in his annual legislative address. "[O]ur frontier settlements . . . are rapidly increasing," wrote the governor, "and must soon yield extensive resources for profitable commerce." Therefore, he recommended a "policy of continuing to facilitate the means of communication with them, as well to strengthen the bands of society, as to prevent the produce of those fertile districts passing to other markets," meaning Quebec. Legislators responded by vowing to investigate "the most eligible move of effecting and defraying the expense" of improving the Hudson and Mohawk Rivers, and later adopted a bill that funded a survey to "estimate . . . the probable expense that would attend the making of canals sufficient for loaded boats to pass."

By 1792 that report was complete, and Governor Clinton again touted an Albany-to-Lake Ontario canal as a "measure, so interesting to the community" that it would "command the attention due to its importance" in part because of its "very moderate expense." His call mobilized two associations of investors to begin lobbying state lawmakers for corporate privileges to build two canals, one to link portions of the Mohawk River near Little Falls, New

York, and another to join Lake Champlain to the Hudson River. Each canal was seen as a rapidly achievable project, and because the investors assured lawmakers that they would rely entirely on private capital for construction they claimed they would need the state to bear only the expense of land surveys, for which lawmakers appropriated £100 in March 1791.[11]

Undertaking an ambitious project—or a pair of them—by handing it to a corporation was less controversial in the 1790s than it had been in the 1780s. By the 1790s, such a project seemed feasible because of a greater availability of capital and credit. In New York City, Alexander Hamilton's plans for a national bank, with the national government's assumption of state debts, was helping to make the city a center for financial transactions and exchanges: money could be borrowed or repaid, stocks and U.S. bonds could be traded, and insurance policies could be taken out on recently placed shipping orders.[12] With more brokers and bankers handling more financial instruments—stocks, bonds, banknotes, checks, and bills of exchange, to name a few—New York's microeconomy was becoming more financialized, offering political entrepreneurs more opportunities to participate in a growing economy of influence.

Yet to one New Yorker, the plans being proposed in the spring of 1792 were too modest. Elkanah Watson had personally surveyed a westward canal route in late 1791 and thought Governor Clinton's wished-for canal would—and should—be far more ambitious (and expensive). He quickly sought to convince state senator Philip Schuyler of the same. In Albany, both Watson and Schuyler had reputations for being political entrepreneurs involved with development projects that blended private capital with public authority. Schuyler, however, was a far wealthier man than Watson, and he preferred to pave routes to prosperity with paper. When Watson approached him, he was pressing colleagues to support the incorporation of the Bank of Albany, one of the pet projects Schuyler adopted after returning to the state senate once he had completed a term as a U.S. senator.

Watson tried to convince Schuyler that a lack of vision and imagination—rather than actual capabilities or capacities—was hindering state legislators from demanding more ambitious plans of petitioners seeking to form canal companies. The two proposals recently approved by lawmakers to create the Northern and Western Inland Lock Navigation companies had been passed after considerable lobbying by Schuyler, but to Watson they represented only "half the business" of canal building in New York State. "The charter[s] should stretch," he said, "to admit the commerce of the great lakes into the

Hudson River, and vice versa." Legislators had instead settled for too meager a set of proposals, and Watson felt that Schuyler agreed with his sentiments. "No one of that body," Watson wrote, referring to the legislature, and "not even the Governor," he continued, "appears to soar beyond Fort Stanwix [present day Rome, New York] except yourself."[13]

For Watson, visionary ambition in canal building had patriotic connotations. He later explained that much of his inspiration was drawn from a two-day visit he had made to George Washington's home at Mount Vernon in 1785. Four years before becoming the first U.S. president, Washington organized and became president of a canal company called the Patowmack Company, a venture jointly supported by the governors of Maryland and Virginia to improve the channels of the Potomac River, dig smaller branch canals, and build locks to traverse its waterfalls. Watson pronounced the project "worthy of the comprehensive mind of Washington" because it was to link the Atlantic Ocean with the Mississippi River and reach as far as Detroit. "Hearing little else for two days from the persuasive tongue of this great man," Watson recalled, "I confess completely infected me with the canal mania, and enkindled all my enthusiasm." It lit, Watson said, "the canal flame in my mind."[14]

Recalling this visit and seeing a need to act as boldly as the hero of the Revolution, Watson pressed Schuyler in the spring of 1792 to use his influence in the state house to block passage of the two pieces of canal legislation—bills Schuyler had lobbied to pass—on the grounds that the proposed projects would be too small to sufficiently develop the state's resources. Watson boasted that, unlike most state legislators, he had traveled through both western New York and Europe. He had seen firsthand how "luxuriance of soil, mildness of climate, and easy access to market" could be brought together with a canal, telling Schuyler,

> Perhaps no part of the world, so distant from the sea as our western country, presents such irresistible allurements to emigrants, as well from the eastern hive as from Europe. . . . Nothing will tend with so much certainty to accelerate the progress of these great events, and to open a door to the happiness of unborn millions, as to render a water communication at once cheap and easy of access. Exclusive of continuing an intercourse with the greatest chain of lakes in the known world, it will give a powerful stimulus to a new creation in the very heart of this State.[15]

Watson therefore did not believe that a larger canal would simply emulate European exemplars; he predicted it would spark transformative economic development.

From his perspective as a traveled observer, a vantage point he considered superior to that of legislators mired in institutional habits and precedents, Watson thought he had the credibility to put forth a new way of thinking about American political economy. His argument drew on the writings of two of the most prominent European political-economy theorists of the period: Emmerich de Vattel and Adam Smith. Both viewed turnpike, bridge, and canal building as a way to build links among existing commercial centers. Connecting markets in cities and towns provided opportunities for producers and consumers to engage in commercial exchanges; therefore, the cost of building a channel of commerce—a canal or road—paled in comparison to its usefulness.[16]

Some American canal promoters like Elkanah Watson—and, later, De-Witt Clinton—readily imbibed European political economists' arguments in favor of transportation-infrastructure investments while discarding part of their underlying analysis. The glaring difference between a New York canal and a British turnpike was that the former would not link a chain of already established marketplaces—it would instead plow through unsettled territory. Watson acknowledged and embraced this difference by suggesting that European ideas had to be adapted on an "enlarged American scale," writing, "If we proceed on the European mode of calculation, waiting in the first instance to find the country through which canals are to pass, to be in a state of maturity and improvement, the answer is at hand—No! But calculating on the more enlarged American scale, and considering the physical circumstances of the country in question, should the canals precede the settlements, it will be justified on the principles of sound policy." To begin building out-of-doors support for this "sound policy," Watson decided to start writing essays and sending them to newspapers in New York City under the pen names "A Citizen" and "An Inland Navigator."[17]

In those articles, Watson expanded on his idea that canal development should be seen as a catalyst to encourage territorial settlement. Building existing towns with active commerce could not be a precondition for public infrastructure investment in America; instead, that had to be the goal of such policies. To this end, constructing "channel[s] of commerce," ones more bold than the two corporate proposals before the legislature, would soon inspire transformative development. "A vast wilderness will, as if were by magic, rise into instant cultivation," Watson predicted. Canal building represented an opportunity to actively instigate commercial growth and shape the state's destiny, both to satisfy its own internal needs and to raise its profile as a state that was both a partner and a competitor with other states. Therefore, although Watson's reasons for wanting to see a New York canal reach the nation's western territories might have seemed more self-consciously cosmopolitan than Governor Clinton's professed desires to settle the interior of the state, it was grounded in a realpolitik, state-centric conception of interstate commerce in the federal union.[18]

In his written appeals to both the public and Philip Schuyler, Watson took pains to lay out his concerns that New York might lose out to competing states' commercial-development policies. By 1792 Watson looked at George Washington's Patowmack Company and saw it as well on its way toward breaching the Mississippi River, diverting the profits of western commercial expansion to Virginia. As admirable as Watson thought that ambition to be, he also feared it would deliver a devastating and permanent blow to New York's long-term commercial prospects. "[A] channel of commerce," he explained, "may receive an early bias to a different point," but "when once established in any particular direction, it is generally found difficult to divert it."

To give Washington's concern "a fair competition" and to avoid losing out on western development altogether, Watson therefore wanted New York legislators to think more boldly and imaginatively about their project. Moreover, as a political entrepreneur himself, Watson perceptively recognized that the scale of the project would forever be tethered to the sources and structure of its financing. The proposals before the legislature were to build canals by creating two corporations. Lawmakers were becoming more familiar with and supportive of the corporate form; corporations were also useful tools for attracting investors with private capital and managing their interests.

Yet Watson believed that the larger canal he wished to see built could not be financed by a corporation. To be clear: Watson was not suggesting that private interests would fail to build a sound canal or would constrict the settlement of the state, nor did he think that toll rates might become so heavy as to render the canal empty. Rather, he thought that if the canal were to ever truly be a public good, where the public reaped the benefits of the project in full, that outcome could not be delivered by a private venture.

To Watson, the proposed canal's path and utility were so self-evident that he believed it should be treated as a natural channel of commerce—similar to a waterway or river—instead of being subject to the same political-economy practices that gave protections of monopolistic exclusivity, special regulations, and private privileges to other artificially built bridges and turnpikes. He recognized that even thinking about internal-improvement projects in this way would require a theoretical and an intellectual pivot among lawmakers before it could be institutionally elaborated in changes to the way the state expected such projects to be organized, financed, and executed. At the time, no American model existed—neither in state-statute books nor in the institutional memory of legislators or out-of-doors political entrepreneurs—for how a state could directly plan, fund, and construct a project as grand as the canal Watson was proposing. Nevertheless, only "a scale of a truly enlarged [canal] policy" that involved the state funding the project "out of its own ample means" would "leave the passage free and open" for future generations. If the policy goals of canal building were settlement and economic development oriented toward the interest of the state, the state then bore responsibility for financing the project. This was the "enlarged American scale" Watson envisioned for the nation's applied political economy, one that acknowledged and departed from European political economy to better suit domestic needs.[19]

Recognizing that he was proposing something novel, Watson urged lawmakers to exercise their fiscal imaginations. "Are we advanced to a sufficient state of maturity to justify an undertaking of this magnitude?" he rhetorically asked. Moreover, he thought that if the state was focused on economic-development outcomes, it would want the canal to have as many users as possible, making hefty toll collections counterproductive. Because a New York canal would not link ready-made markets but would instead enable development along an arterial channel, Watson did not think it was viable to pay for the enterprise directly through either benefit taxation—a tax paid by the people who would benefit from living alongside the canal—or through tolls collected from the users of the canal. Because the state's interest was in seeing as much development as possible, it would not have the same interest in turning a profit from toll collection as private or incorporated owners would. "Private individuals having a toll in view," he wrote, would realize profits that "would probably be small for a few years, but the increasing benefit which will arise from this species of property, will keep equal pace with the augmenting settlement and cultivation of the country." In time, "posterity will be burthened with a weighty tax (in the article of toll) to the emolument of the successors of the first adventurers, which ought not to exist in a land of liberty, where the intercourse should be as free as the air which we breathe."

In Watson's mind, therefore, the canal was simply too important to be privately owned; its toll revenues would be far too large to be properly placed in the hands of private interests. What was needed, therefore, was for states to once again take on debt. Yet instead of paying for a war, these new obligations would fund internal-improvement investments that would pay for themselves over time. Watson thus anticipated the financial arrangements that would one day fund the canal's construction, suggesting that the state go into debt and issue its own bonds rather than delegate canal construction to privately held corporations and their stockholders. "If executed gratuitously by the public," Watson predicted that such a financing method would be low risk; "the State in effect will be retarded only a few years," he explained, before "receiving a tenfold return for all its disbursements" in canal construction outlays.[20]

For the intellectual and rhetorical energy Elkanah Watson poured into his public essays, his decision to partner with state senator Philip Schuyler proved counterproductive to his goal of seeing the state's canals become publicly financed objects of an "enlarged" policy. Watson had wanted Schuyler to block the adoption of the two proposed canal projects, which the senator did. But Schuyler's substitute proposals did not substantially change those original canal-incorporation plans; instead, they shuffled his own political allies into the companies' boards of directors, ensuring that the canal companies—and, by extension, the state's canal policy—would be guided by the private, personal material interests of Philip Schuyler and his associates.

Although a legal grant of incorporation represented one of the most aggressive forms of state-directed development available to early American lawmakers, the scale of the two companies chartered to build canals in New York was anemic. The Northern and Western Inland Lock Navigation Companies were each authorized to raise $25,000 by selling a thousand shares of stock at $25 per share. Compared to other incorporated enterprises this was an almost absurdly small figure; the Bank of Albany, which was one of the smaller chartered banks in the nation, had a capitalization of $260,000. In addition, no shareholder in one of the canal companies could own more than ten shares of its stock, meaning no one person could invest more than $500 in the state's canal programs. Under the terms of their charters, once the companies exhausted their initial $25,000, the state would give each company a "gift" of $12,500. That meant the companies would have to run out of money before they could draw on state support or seek additional outside investments.

Given these circumstances, it was notable that the legislature authorized the companies to collect canal tolls of $20 or $25 on each ton of shipped goods for a period of fifteen years. Tolls had been the scourge of Watson's missives to the legislature because they represented private profits collected at public expense. But in this case, tolls would not be used to pay dividends to company shareholders or fund canal maintenance; instead, they would likely be needed to finance the construction of the projects.

At Schuyler's urging, the legislature had worded the companies' charters to allow them to pay shareholders a dividend of at least 6 percent but no more than 15 percent per year. At the time, he was worried that the companies would fail to attract investors without the security of a dividend. Neither company, however, managed to find buyers for all of its stock shares. The Western company received an especially lackluster reception after its public offering, selling 722 shares in its first three months, followed by just 21 in the three years that followed. With $18,000 on hand in late 1792, the company paid for a survey, which informed them that only one portion of their planned work would cost more than four times that sum. In all, the estimated costs of their proposal exceeded $500,000. Even after the state contributed its "gift" and responded to the company's pleas for help by buying 200 shares to become a direct investor in the corporation, the Western company was able to construct only two very short canals. One was not quite a mile long; the other was two miles long and only functioned with the aid of nine separate locks. The company did pay a dividend—in 1798. It was a 3 percent dividend. The company would not pay another dividend until 1813. During the intervening fifteen years, the company had to devote its toll revenues toward regularly replacing portions of the canal's wooden locks, which rotted during their first six years of use.[21]

Unfortunately for Elkanah Watson, his name and reputation were chained to these sinking enterprises. Even though the legislature's actions had been at odds with the policies Watson had advocated both publicly and privately, Philip Schuyler nevertheless "rewarded" Watson with a seat on the board of directors of the Western company. Watson could have refused but opted to join the cadre of political entrepreneurs handpicked by Schuyler, including land barons, improvement promoters, and bank directors. Schuyler, too, was a director—and soon was chosen as the companies' president.[22]

This board of directors seems to have realized early on that the company was likely to be unprofitable, that their expenses were unsustainable, and that they would not achieve their intended goal of providing the state with accessible, reliable, and reasonably priced canal transportation. Yet they pressed on anyway, creating a legacy of failure that future canal promoters would have to explain away. Philip Schuyler was an able state legislator but not an engineer. Nevertheless, he persuaded the Western company's board to name him to be the company's chief engineer in addition to president. In his words, he took the job so as not to "[dim] the hopes of stockholders."[23] At least one of those stockholders was not fooled: DeWitt Clinton, a young nephew of New York Governor George Clinton then serving as the governor's secretary. Schuyler, DeWitt Clinton knew, was little more than a "mechanic empiric . . . wasting the property of the stockholders" of the Western Inland Lock Navigation Company.[24]

When the Northern and Western Inland Lock Companies were created in 1792, their supporters had asserted that even though publicly chartered corporations were financed with private capital, such institutions deserved to be differentiated from other private enterprises. The state's role in creating the companies distinguished them from mere "speculations," wrote Robert Troup, a New York City attorney and former state legislator who had once been Alexander Hamilton's college classmate. Troup thought that even to "dignify" comparisons between public-private corporations and other private ventures "would be preposterous." "The policy pursued by a State," he explained, "can only be known from the schemes adopted by its constituted authorities, and from the measures taken to carry such schemes into effect." The creation of corporate bodies "with rights to authorize, and privileges to facilitate [the] successful prosecution . . . [of] an expensive and arduous enterprise" had been the only appropriate way to structure the state's canal policy.[25]

Troup's own investments, however, told a different story. During his term as a director of the Western company he began acquiring lands along the Mohawk River where the company's work was being performed. Over the next four years, from 1792 to 1796, Troup burned through $3,000 in savings to speculate in lands, directly acquiring 81,000 acres for himself and buying a partial interest in another 112,000 acres. When canal construction began, the value of those tracts rose to an estimated $290,000, of which his own stake was worth $130,000—more than five times as large as the canal company he directed.[26]

Such dramatic price surges were not a surprise; even Elkanah Watson had predicted that a consequence of the companies' canal efforts would be an increase in land prices in upstate New York. But what Watson did not fully anticipate was that, for many of the company's investors and directors, boosting land values was their first priority. To them, the canal companies were a means to an end: turning a profit on land speculations. Some New York City merchants like Nicholas Low had invested in the companies because they were genuinely interested in enlarging the city's commercial reach, but other shareholders like Robert Morris, Robert Troup, and Melancton Smith became shareholders to aid their own land interests or those of the owners of the Phelps and Gorham Purchase, the British syndicate of investors called the Pulteney Associates, or the Dutch-owned Holland and Ogden Land Companies.[27] By one calculation, fifteen of the original thirty-six directors of the two inland navigation companies were land speculators who directly benefited from the company's work. One even placed newspaper advertisements boasting that his holdings were close to the company's anticipated construction route—a route he had helped lay out.[28] The directors used their insider information to buy up lands that would be touched by the project in the near term, and used the companies to maintain the appearance of a credible construction operation just long enough to allow them to resell their holdings. Therefore, once the Western company made surveys of the route it intended to improve, the company had fulfilled its usefulness to land speculators. They had wanted the promise of a canal more than an actual canal.[29]

It was apparent early in their existence, then, that the Northern and Western Inland Lock Navigation Companies were less focused on building canals than they were in protecting shareholders' profits and property. In their pursuit of a project with consequences that were widely acknowledged to be of a public nature and which consumed both public funds and public lands, private interests were nevertheless paramount to the companies' boards of directors.[30] The boards did not seem to be capable of making commitments that signaled a long-term investment in state infrastructure; instead, they made near-term compromises and behaved in a way that made it look like they were raiding the companies' accounts to serve their personal interests. Elkanah Watson and DeWitt Clinton both recognized these flaws and were prepared for what followed the end of the canal land boom in 1797, when many of the Western company's onetime shareholders and directors dumped the company's stock, necessitating further state bailouts that were politely called "gifts."[31]

It is easy to dismiss, as DeWitt Clinton did, these first canal ventures as a "total failure."[32] Watson's original vision of a state-supported and state-financed project seemed vindicated by the shortcomings of what had been approved in its place: the chartering of corporate institutions ill-equipped to sustain a durable canal policy. Although the legislature in 1792 had feared creating a pair of companies that would be overcapitalized, they instead had created inadequately funded companies that were incapable of executing their missions with speed or competence. Jonas Platt, a state senator who would help reanimate canal advocacy ten years after the companies slid into decline, wrote, "[I] t is a truth which ought not to be disguised that the gross errors which were committed by the advocates," of the Northern and Western companies, "in their estimates of the expense, and of the profits and advantages of those improvements, resulted in a complete failure of the benefits promised by its projectors." As a future canal commissioner, Platt would someday be asked to explain why Philip Schuyler and Elkanah Watson had so dramatically "erred" in underestimating the projected costs of the Western canal—"by more than 200 percent." He would be asked why he and his fellow canal commissioners should be thought of as any more "wise and skilful" than these earlier canal supporters. The "history and experience of the Northern and Western Inland Lock Navigation Companies," he later reflected, had presented "powerful impediments to the enterprise of the Erie Canal."[33]

For all this talk of failure, however, New York's initial canal ventures encouraged canal construction in other states. Just as New York had been inspired by George Washington's "Patowmack" canal corporation, other states followed New York's lead by chartering similar companies and policies. Well into the first decade of the nineteenth century, states handed over their canal policies to private investors by granting them corporate privileges in Massachusetts (1800), Pennsylvania (1801), Delaware (1802), Virginia (1805), and New Hampshire (1807). New York's example was in fact so influential that when President Thomas Jefferson's Treasury secretary, Albert Gallatin, proposed a package of internal-improvement projects in 1807, he included plans to spend $2.2 million in federal funds on a canal to join the Hudson River to Lake Erie.

In his report, Gallatin showed himself to be entirely familiar with New York's experiences with incorporated canal companies. He believed that "the general utility of artificial roads and canals" was so "universally admitted" that it did not "require any additional proofs" from him, and he offered none. It had long been the case, he observed, that private "individuals" in "countries possessed of a large capital, where property is sufficiently secure to induce" investments, had found the initiative to begin improvement projects on their own. "Individual exertion[s]" had taken advantage of commercial opportunities, making "direct aid from government" unnecessary.[34]

Yet the state had nevertheless played a substantial, if indirect, role in making those investments happen. In New York's case, Gallatin believed that the state had been uniquely active, channeling private capital toward public-private mixed-economy infrastructure projects. "A greater capital has been vested on turnpike roads [in New York] than in any other [state]," he wrote, detailing that "in less then seven years sixty-seven companies have been incorporated, with a nominal capital of near five millions of dollars" to build 3,000 miles of roadway, while twenty-one "other companies have also been incorporated with a capital of 400,000 dollars, for the purpose of erecting twenty-one toll bridges."

The primary tool of the state, then, had been its power to incorporate—enticing private individuals and investors to pledge their capital toward a project of public importance in exchange for receiving special privileges and rights unavailable to other citizens engaged in commerce and profit-seeking enterprises. And in Gallatin's view, this had—for the most part—been extremely effective.

But there had been stumbles, and Gallatin's *Report* noted that the Western Inland Lock Navigation Company had made "considerable progress" before running out of funds, while the Northern Inland Lock Navigation Company had withered from "insufficient" funding after first "expend[ing]" its money "without much permanent utility."

Such failures proved, Gallatin concluded, that in spite of legislators' intentions and investors' enthusiasm, the "large scale" of canal projects and long periods required for their construction "naturally check the application of private capital and enterprise." Investors might not want to tie up their capital in projects that promised returns only far in the future when more immediately profitable opportunities were at hand, or in projects that would connect far-flung points along thinly settled territory that might fail to attract capital at all. And because crucial pieces of this developing infrastructure were being built individually, they could—even if completed—remain isolated. Indeed, Gallatin observed that some "works already executed are unprofitable" and "many more remain unattempted" because their "ultimate productiveness"—their utility and the potential profit they could deliver to investors—depended on "other improvements, too extensive or too distant to be embraced by the same individuals." In short, some projects were simply too big to be executed with private capital. They were too expensive, would take too long to complete, or would depend on an even larger system of improvements and infrastructure projects that were beyond the capacity and vision of even the most ambitious state legislators and petitioning political entrepreneurs.[35]

As a remedy, Gallatin did not propose that the country abandon the practice of privately financing such projects. Instead, he proposed that the federal government should, "with the assent of the States," attempt some projects on its own while supporting "companies incorporated" by the states to construct others. Federal support could take the form of either government purchases of company stock shares or government loans. Gallatin clearly preferred the former, since the intervention of the national government would "give the most proper general direction to the work" while "effectually control[l]ing local interests." He worried that direct loan money might be misspent or wasted on petty, local concerns.

Gallatin, then, did not want to retire the practice of states chartering corporations to enact an infrastructure agenda. Rather, he saw those companies as the building blocks for any future agenda and recognized that they offered certain advantages. If it undertook a project directly, even the national government might rely on "private companies" simply because they tended to offer "a more economical plan."

In addition, the realities of congressional politics meant that among the readers of Gallatin's *Report* were many men whose careers had started at such companies and whose present-day interests—personal, public, financial, political, and social—were yoked to the layered, interlocking directorates of companies and corporations sprinkled throughout the United States. These existing road, bridge, and land companies, as well as other companies, were incumbents in the marketplace. Legislators and other investors with a stake in these companies could naturally be expected to defend these interests by deflecting competing proposals. Yet they were also just as likely to welcome and even seek out projects that might enhance their interests. Therefore, to survive the political process, new projects had to embrace existing interests and offer lawmakers and lobbies opportunities to participate in the capitalization, building, and management of those projects.

This prospect of money—federal money—reinvigorated canal promotion in New York State, giving Elkanah Watson's ideas about publicly owned and financed projects a second chance at being adopted as state policy. Although the route of the Erie Canal ended up not being much different from what was originally imagined, New Yorkers used a different means to achieve their goal. Corporations were here to stay, yet, with a growing financial capacity, lawmakers could afford to be more imaginative about how to fund new projects. And because of their experience with the Northern and Western Inland Lock Navigation Companies, there was consensus in New York on at least one basic principle: no charter, corporation, monopoly, or patent would be granted to build what would become the Erie Canal.[36]

CHAPTER 3

"A Very Convenient Instrument"

On the eve of one of the first and most important state ballot contests that would decide the 1800 presidential election, a scion of New York's foremost Republican family reached for a quill as he sought to soothe the anxieties of the faraway Virginian who hoped to be the victor.[1] "A very important change has been effected," Edward Livingston assured Thomas Jefferson, "by the *instrumentality* as Mr. Hamilton would call it of the New Bank." Called the Bank of the Manhattan Company, the "new bank," Livingston explained, had "emancipated hundreds who were held in bondage by the old institutions." "Old institutions" referred to two banks: the New York City branch of the Alexander Hamilton–designed national Bank of the United States, founded and incorporated in 1791, and the Bank of New-York, another Hamilton-influenced bank that had been founded in 1784 and incorporated in 1791.

In his letter, Edward, a brother of New York chancellor Robert R. Livingston, opined that voters "all know and understand the principles of their deliverers." Grateful for having a third bank available to them, those voters, Livingston predicted, would reward Republican candidates with their support in upcoming state legislative elections, a contest that "promises a favorable issue to our labors." Once seated, those newly elected legislators would then award the state's twelve electoral votes to Thomas Jefferson in the 1800 presidential election. The founding of the Manhattan Company, therefore, was injecting what Livingston called "republican Energy" into the federal "system thro[ugh] the State governments."[2]

Up to this point, banks as institutions and banking as an activity were understood to be political. Nearly all of the nation's major banks were shareholder-owned, publicly traded companies with state-granted corporate charters (except for the Bank of the United States, which had a charter from Congress).[3] Corporate privileges were just that: privileges. Being incorporated meant having access to a selectively distributed bundle of legal and economic advantages unavailable to ordinary firms, partnerships, and companies. To win a charter, a group of would-be bankers mobilized supporters with an eye toward filing a petition that could win support from majorities in their state's legislative houses. Furthermore, to ensure that a hard-won charter was renewed, banks kept legislators happy by plying them with loans, dividend-paying stocks, and other discretionary benefits. Thus although their financial operations might seem to the naked eye to be economically driven, a bank's shareholders, directors, and managers were constantly engaged in the care and feeding of a managed cohort of political supporters. Incorporated banks supported their dependents and were dependent on their supporters. In the political economy of early America, banks blurred distinctions between public and private; even in facilitating transactions—a bank's most basic economic function—they behaved in ways that were inherently political.

But according to Edward Livingston, banking in New York City was not merely political—it was partisan.

The new bank's partisan significance was so remarkable, in fact, that Livingston could craft a narrative in which the new bank was an essential element in enabling Jefferson's presidency. Republicans, he said, were poised to win local and national electoral victories because the Manhattan Company was generating a jolt of "republican energy" in the federal system. Arguably the purpose of his letter, sent just before one of those victories, was to explain this to the future president, reminding him that he owed no small part of his political success to the New York Republicans who had birthed and managed the new bank. In this telling, the election that Jefferson would someday mythologize as the "revolution of 1800" could not have happened without the Manhattan Company.[4]

What made this moment all the more remarkable was that the Manhattan Company was never supposed to be a bank. When it was incorporated in early 1799, the company was supposed to be a water utility.

In 1798, having suffered through recurrent summertime yellow fever epidemics, a broad political spectrum of New Yorkers—including one of the nation's most public Federalists, Alexander Hamilton, and one of its better-known Republicans, Aaron Burr—decided that the best way to alleviate the disease was to improve the city's supply of fresh water. Following a now-familiar playbook in the early republic's political economy, the coalition petitioned the state legislature to incorporate a water company in New York

City. Corporate charters had been used before to blend private and public interests by channeling private financial capital toward a public good. By selling stock shares to investors, the new water company would raise enough money to build a new supply of fresh water that would be available to subscription-paying customers in the city. With the support of New York City's Common Council, the water coalition's petition reached Albany in the spring of 1799. There it was to be shepherded through the state capital by Aaron Burr, who was then a state assemblyman.

But in Burr's hands, the proposed water company began to change. Burr amended the proposal to enlarge the company's board of directors and populate it with a Republican majority. He inserted language into the charter that would allow the company's "surplus" capital to be used with broad discretion—so broad that the directors would soon be able to operate a bank.

Most legislators never noticed these alterations before the Manhattan Company was incorporated on 2 April 1799. But days later, Federalists began accusing Burr of masterminding a swindle. Republicans responded by claiming to have endured nearly a decade of coercion at the hands of the city's two "Federalist" banks. Printed in city newspapers, these exchanges created the impression that banking in New York had always been both openly partisan and exclusively Federalist, a charge that gained currency through historiographical repetition.[5] Those claims were further bolstered when Republicans captured the New York legislature in 1800 and appointed a Republican slate of presidential electors—a victory that both Federalists and Republicans attributed to the influence of the Manhattan Company. To them, it seemed like Thomas Jefferson's election, the Revolution of 1800, had been purchased with a reservoir of Manhattan Company cash.

For historians, the Manhattan Company's founding is a story that seems to speak to everyone. It had implications for the development of political parties and electioneering, political culture, the press, and, of course, banking. Much of the focus has been on Burr's role in the chartering of the company, with many historians accusing him of duplicity. After all, how else could Burr have founded such a politically useful bank except by tricking Federalists into being accomplices? His guiding hand is congruent with perceptions of him as a self-serving and clever political lothario.[6] Several economic historians counter this narrative by suggesting that legislators, and even Alexander Hamilton, tacitly approved of the Manhattan Company's entry into banking but allowed Burr to take the credit (and blame) anyway.[7]

As compelling as these arguments are, they all tend to focus on Aaron

Burr, making the Manhattan Company's founding peculiarly dependent on the shifting ad hoc alliances and fleeting loyalties that defined his political career.[8] This is not, however, a narrow story about Aaron Burr or even Thomas Jefferson.

To make sense of the circumstances surrounding the Manhattan Company's chartering and its implications for the development of corporations and banking in early American political economy, it is instead necessary to not only understand Aaron Burr's legislative maneuvering but to appreciate why it was needed in 1799. There is little mystery as to why political entrepreneurs would want to be involved in banking: being at the head of an incorporated bank vested directors and owners with the potential to exercise broad discretion in extending loans and facilitating commerce, all from behind closed doors. Bankers could offer and deliver favors, enabling them to build support for their own interests and those of their selected allies. Plus, as chartered institutions, corporate banks enjoyed legal and economic privileges unavailable to ordinary firms.

But these privileges were not accessible to New York Republicans at the end of the 1790s. It would have been unthinkable to apply for a bank charter for a transparently partisan reason. Federalists could not support such an application if to do so meant admitting that banking in New York had become partisan, and even among Republican allies such a petition would have no political legitimacy. Moreover, Federalists had no intention of allowing any new banks to be chartered in New York City if it meant that their own institutions would face competition. Republicans therefore did not only face the ordinary skeptical opposition that came with petitioning for corporate privileges; they would have to battle the directors of a pair of banks who felt entitled to share a duopoly over incorporated banking in the state and who had had a decade to convince state lawmakers of the same. Thus the political landscape of the state was already dominated by Federalist banks that had captured the policy-making apparatus, regulating whether there would be any new entrants into that marketplace. Given these circumstances, Republicans in 1799 decided that their only viable option to gain banking privileges would be to pursue a high-risk strategy: to exploit the petitioning and incorporation process by hijacking a broadly popular water-company proposal and, using the legislative skill of one of "their" elected lawmakers, to design that institution so that it could be turned into a bank without having it be immediately recognizable as such.

Fifteen years separated the founding of the Bank of New-York in 1784 from the founding of the Manhattan Company in 1799. In that time, the day-to-day functions of banks had largely stayed the same; they still circulated banknotes, printed checks, granted and denied credit, and facilitated commerce.

Nevertheless, banking had changed. As institutions that cultivated the interests of their clients and owners, banks reflected their economic, political, and social context, all of which had been in flux since the 1780s.

During the Critical Period after the end of the Revolutionary War, anxieties abounded over how to safeguard the Revolution's gains and where to settle the extent of its transformation. Moreover, the Articles of Confederation had not given the national government clear authority to raise revenues through taxes, to conduct diplomacy, to defend itself, to mediate disputes among and between states, or to govern western territories. Delegates to the 1787 Constitutional Convention were intent on remedying these shortcomings, setting out to design a new federal union with a fiscal-military state capable of delivering, in Alexander Hamilton's words, "strength and stability in the organization of our government, and vigor in its operations."[9] In theory, the national government would be capable of mobilizing resources to address unforeseen priorities, yet it would be—in the words of one historian—"light and almost invisible in periods of peace and tranquility."[10] The writing and ratification of the Constitution was therefore an aggressive exercise in nation building and state formation that had ramifications throughout the layers of the federal union.[11]

One thing the Constitution did not build, however, was consensus. On the contrary, it stirred ambitions among the delegates and soon carved divisions between the supporters of the Washington administration, who called themselves "Federalists," and the less cohesive dissenters, who began calling themselves "Republicans." The chief animating force that helped sort and mobilize these early political factions was the French Revolution. Republicans called for the administration to support the French cause while Federalists worried that creeping French-ness threatened a second revolution at home. This dispute over foreign affairs revealed just how ambiguous the American Revolution's legacy remained in the 1790s. International crises did not only steer government policy but also colored how Americans perceived their own domestic political rivalries, heightening them to appear as more ominous threats.[12]

In New York, the Republican faction organizationally emerged out of Democratic-Republican clubs formed in support of the French cause and in opposition to the 1794 Jay Treaty between Britain and the United States. The Republican coalition was broad. Although New York Republicans supported the new federal Constitution—and claimed to favor its strict interpretation—they also drew strength and numbers from the anti-Federalist cohort once led by New York governor George Clinton. Likewise, while Republicanism embraced mechanics, middling merchants, and aspiring tradesmen, it also became the political home of Robert Livingston and other elite, estate-owning landlords. These shifts occurred as New York Federalists during the 1790s gradually became a party of established merchants and professionals, a demographic accurately (and often pejoratively) called "the monied interest."

Partisanship in banking was not particularly new in New York. When it was founded in 1784, the Bank of New-York was already a somewhat partisan institution in that it was organized and owned by a cohort of merchants and commercially oriented people who favored Tory-Whig reconciliation and a normalization of trade and diplomacy with Britain.

We can appreciate, however, that this species of partisanship is different from having the bank be seen as a vehicle that exclusively advanced the interests of an incumbent political coalition. Banking in New York might not have been as crassly partisan during the 1790s as contemporary critics would allege, but over the course of the decade the city's two incorporated banks, the Bank of New-York and the city's branch of the Bank of the United States, had become unquestionably Federalist. The banks were not merely identified with Federalists. Instead, they functioned as institutions that served and advanced the political goals of the city's Federalist faction by doing what banks did: facilitating financial intermediation on behalf of New Yorkers engaged in trade and commerce. And increasingly, those New Yorkers were Federalists.

This consolidation began in 1791 when Alexander Hamilton's proposal to launch the Bank of the United States won support in Congress and from President George Washington over the fierce objections of James Madison and others who called the plan unconstitutional. In keeping with federal design of the union, the national bank was to have branches in the nation's major commercial cities, and it was all but certain that one of those branches would be in New York City.[13]

For seven years, New York state legislators had resisted granting a corporate charter to the Bank of New-York. But with the national bank now coming to town, they changed their positions. "It is as requisite to have a State Bank to control the influence of a National Bank as of a State government to control the influence of the general government," explained Federalist assemblyman James Kent, who planned to support the incorporation of the Bank of New-York on "ground of expediency, and from a conviction of the utility of banks on general principles."[14] Although Kent's vote might have been expected, many onetime anti-Federalists joined him in backing the established bank. Members who had opposed the bank "in abstract" now were supporters. Governor George Clinton and "his adherents," said another Federalist assemblyman, "are as eager for it as they have formerly been against it."[15] The charter was adopted and signed into law by Governor Clinton on 21 March 1791.

One of the chief reasons Clinton and his supporters—many of whom would come to be called Republicans—had backed a charter for the Bank of New-York is that they expected that the state-chartered bank would be a competitor to the national bank.[16] For a time, this seemed to be a very real possibility. Rufus King, a soon-to-be director of the branch bank and one of New York's United States senators, warned his agent Nicholas Low, a Bank of New-York director and city merchant, that the "appearance of Jealousy on the part of the Bank of New-York, strengthens my apprehension of a division in the city arising from a competition." King continued, "It is very desirable that their respective interests, should, if possible, be made to harmonize. . . . [Y]ou very well know my sentiments respecting the issue of a competition—my regards for the union and this measure will give my mind a decided bias in favor of one of these institutions over the other."[17] Both men were associates of Hamilton's and both identified as Federalists. They agreed on the necessity of bank cooperation, yet their loyalties were to the institutions to which they were formally attached, which was why King referred to the national branch as "our Bank." The possibility of competition seemed to be overwhelming whatever goodwill existed between the two banks' boards of directors.[18]

Competition between two chartered institutions, however, was a frightening prospect to Alexander Hamilton.[19] Hamilton personally began mediating between the city's two incorporated banks by tugging at the multiple ties that joined their directors. The directors' identification with Federalism proved an insufficient bond on its own in this case because it competed with stronger impulses such as fidelity to Hamilton, existing business relationships, and personal financial interests, in addition to the financial health of the city and ideological preferences for federal or state institutions. Party identity, if it animated participants' actions at all, was overwhelmed by these institutional and personal imperatives. Nevertheless, Hamilton's intervention brought together a cohort of Federalists to ensure that instead of competing with one another, the city's two banks became collaborators.[20]

Soon the two chartered banks in New York were even formalizing relationships with other cities' banks as the institutions' directors drew on personal ties that bound elites regionally in this period.[21] Writing about an alliance with the Bank of North America in Philadelphia, Rufus King wrote Nicholas Low in 1792 that "if the Banks here operate with mutual confidence, and the same sentiment can be established between them & the Bank of New York, it will be in the power of the three institutions to afford accommodations, which will restore the public confidence and prevent the further & ruinous depression of the stocks."[22]

The "ruinous depression" to which King referred was the Panic of 1792, a financial panic sparked, in part, by the chartering of the national bank and the Bank of New-York, along with the opening of many other speculative banks in their wake. Hamilton's efforts to encourage cooperation among New York's bank directors could not prevent other joint-stock associations from opening unchartered banks, selling stocks, and peppering the state legislature with petitions for incorporation. At its height, the speculation was so rabid that within two hours a single bank attracted $10 million in pledged subscriptions, earning it the name "the Million Bank." Together, three upstart banks collected a phantom capitalization exceeding $13 million, far outweighing the $1 million limit prescribed by the legislature in the Bank of New-York's charter.[23] The speculative frenzy ended when a scheme to corner the market on government bonds collapsed, taking many New York financiers down with it.[24]

Alexander Hamilton called the debacle "bancomania," and it fixed in the public imagination a disreputable impression of unchartered banking and a justifiable fear of bank competition.[25] The directors of chartered banks responded by becoming an even more tightly knit group—appointing committees of correspondence to foster inter-institutional dialogue. They also began steadfastly opposing any proposals to launch a third bank in Manhattan. Earlier, in 1791, Hamilton had cautioned the Bank of New-York's cashier, William Seton, against supporting other bank coalitions' petitions for incorporation, writing that "it is impossible but that great banks in one City must raise such a mass of artificial Credit as must endanger every one of them and do harm in every view." "The joint force of two solid institutions," Hamilton continued, would be sufficient to "without effort or violence—remove the excrescence . . . the dangerous tumour in your political and commercial economy" that was speculation.[26] Having fewer banks meant having safer banks and a more stable economy in Hamilton's view.[27]

Although it never became a matter of formal policy, Hamilton's advice to Seton resonated in New York politics throughout the decade. When members of the Livingston family joined other anti-Federalists to propose a third "state bank," Hamilton drew on his influence to ensure opposition to what he called the "mad scheme."[28] He enlisted his father-in-law Philip Schuyler to oppose the bank from his seat in the New York state senate (a year earlier, Schuyler had been a key supporter of Hamilton's national bank legislation as one of New York's United States senators before returning to the state senate). Hamilton also cautioned Seton and the Bank of New-York's board of directors against imagining they could forge a "better alliance" with a third bank, one he called a "newly engendered monster."[29] The bank heeded Hamilton's call by offering a higher interest-rate payment on state deposits than what the proposed bank could match, hoping to win over any legislators who might have been inclined to support the would-be rival's petition.[30] In response, the "state bank" proposal faded into obscurity and no association launched a vigorous effort to charter a bank in New York City until the Manhattan Company opened its discount office in 1799. Even the most well-connected political entrepreneurs could not win bank charters in New York for most of the 1790s.[31]

For nearly a decade, New York City operated under this dual-bank regime, an intensely personal financial environment where connections and reputation often trumped actual wealth in regulating access to credit and capital. Governed by shareholder-elected boards of directors, banks usually employed only a manager-cashier and several clerks; directors often personally voted on whether to grant credit to specific borrowers. This structure vested bank directors with significant private financial influence through their positions of public institutional authority. Operating out of only a few rooms, the space occupied by banks reflected their elite nature. Without counters or teller windows, a bank needed only a single room for its cashier and directors to meet; often there was not even a partition between them. Of but not necessarily for the public, banks often accommodated patrons on the second floors of buildings.[32]

The clients of the Bank of New-York, however, were hardly austere. Anybody with the requisite money could buy a share in a bank, yet discounts and accommodations were primarily granted to those who contemporaries referred to as the *monied interest*—the merchants, professionals, and landed gentry whose public reputations and personal worth distinguished them from the hoi polloi of mechanics, cartmen, and tradesmen in the city. Yet even among this elite, banking was situational, discretionary, and personal; credit was extended only to those who could recruit fellow elites or patrons to cosign for their discounts and loans. Moreover, official records did not reveal how boards of directors made their decisions or who was involved or affected. Agonizing over some of the repercussions that came with such discretion, Rufus King wrote,

> By declining to endorse a note for our friend Lawrance, which a few days since he was about offering for discount, I unfortunately gave him some Dissatisfaction—and though I should in some measure have been influenced by the same consideration to decline endorsing your notes, yet in the present instance I should have endorsed them, had I not supposed that I would promote your views better if I did not endorse them than if I did. I have desired Mr. Lewis to present your not[e] for 8000 Dol. under a separate cover, and to accompany it with the information that the discount is requested on your amount. I will attend the discount, and give you all that aid in my power—I thought it better not to present the note for 2000 Dol. as there is no probability that both would be done.[33]

King refers to Morgan Lewis, a prominent anti-Federalist supporter of New York governor George Clinton; the latter signed the Bank of New-York's charter into law. Although King was reluctant to cause Lewis the "dissatisfaction" he visited on "Lawrance," this same instinct was nowhere to be found in his dealings with the scion of another of New York's prominent anti-Federalist families, H. Brockholst Livingston.[34] King gives no signal that politics guided these decisions in any way. Claims that New York's bankers denied credit to members of the opposite political party solely on the basis of party preference require one to privilege party identity above the other competing and contingent identities that bound together New York's financial coterie. Such claims presume that parties' non-electoral roles were important enough to infect banking and business and that party identity trumped self-interest and profit motives; they also presuppose that individuals' partisan commitments could be definitively and accurately made. The political elite, however, routinely ignored rivals' allegiances and alliances in matters of business and law; though they were fierce electoral opponents, for example, Alexander Hamilton and

Aaron Burr routinely disregarded their political differences to work in con-
cert on financial and civic matters, including the creation of the Manhattan
Company.[35] Therefore, although the asymmetrical power relations of banking
could seem to be motivated at times by politics, the close-knit and interdependent web that defined the monied interest was animated by many different types of alliances. Although banking offered occasions to extend
favoritism and exact retribution, participants were unlikely to deny themselves business opportunities solely because of another's political leanings or
to risk compromising their long-term financial viability by needlessly snub-
bing fellow elites.[36]

Thus there is little evidence to support the claim that banking was exclusively Federalist prior to the founding of the Manhattan Company. Political
opponents did not deny each other membership in networks of credit in the
1790s, and being a Federalist did not guarantee banking privileges.[37] Bank
directors lacked a financial incentive to deny discounts to willing clients and,
given the dignity accorded corporate directorships, might have nursed reser-
vations about the development of adversarial political parties.[38] And with
both partisan rank-and-file membership and leadership rosters still fluid
during the 1790s, it remained difficult to determine who was a Federalist and
who was a Republican without explicitly asking.

However, in a city where the ballot did not replace voice voting until 1804
and where merchants were permitted to stand by at the polls and suggest
votes to employees, it was certainly possible for Federalists to have both the
motive and the opportunity to cultivate votes among the monied interest and
their dependents.[39] The secrecy of banks' operations added plausibility to Republicans' suspicions and allegations of partisanship. Moreover, in explaining
the reasons for being denied credit, politics provided a convenient and face-
saving cover; in the vacuum of bank directors' silence, snubbed borrowers
could allege partisan bias in situations where past irresponsibility or unac-
ceptable risk was the actual reason for the denial. The banks' Federalist ties
provided a handy excuse to spurned clients, but they inflamed suspicions
about their anonymous and opaque decision-making process. And the banks
themselves—as institutions—were created under controversial circumstances and had always been a part of political rhetoric.[40]

More important, banking need not have been conducted explicitly for or
exclusively among Federalists for it to be perceived as "Federalist." From the
1790s onward, the ownership of the city's two incorporated banks was concentrated among Federalists—and not just any Federalists but a small circle

of financiers and political entrepreneurs with personal ties to Alexander Hamilton. Indeed, the boards of the two banks seemed to be an interlocking directorate of Hamiltonian devotees.[41] Moreover, because membership in an extra-institutional credit network was essential to participate in New York banking, the city's credit network was a web of discretionary dependency that could easily enforce a rough social and political conformity among its members. With such intimate and dependent connections, it would be surprising if political alliances and rivalries did not affect access to credit. Nor is it difficult to recognize that conformity could be expected from second-tier members of the monied interest who were dependent on elite patronage. Jabez Hammond, writing his political history of New York in the mid-nineteenth century, explained the "Federalism" of one of New York's banks by writing, "[T]he stock and direction of the Bank of New York was in the hands of federalists . . . it had, no doubt, fallen into their hands, not in consequence of any political maneuvering, but by the natural course of trade and traffic among the citizens."[42] Borrowers would be hesitant to attend meetings of their patrons' political rivals, and even if those patrons had no expectations of partisan loyalty, borrowers might nevertheless associate with Federalists to gain access to bankers and their cohort, establishing a social basis for a future credit relationship. To the extent that New York banking became Federalist, in some individual instances that partisanship might have been inadvertently coerced.

Even if the city's banks were not behaving as overtly Federalist institutions, they nevertheless were under the control of Federalists, and their influence in the city grew with each day as the 1790s wore on. Manhattan's two banks had a total capitalization limited to $1.6 million; as the city expanded, however, the power that came from the sum became ever more concentrated in the hands of an increasingly elite cabal that reshaped the financial geography of the city.[43] These concentrations of wealth not only shaped the city's commercial life but also laid out its political topography. Tradesmen, cartmen, and laborers—the poorer trades—lived on the northern frontier of the city, while more established merchants and professionals tended to live near Manhattan's southern tip, where the banks' offices were located.[44] Wealth was concentrated in these southern wards; according to one calculation, the average freeholder in the centrally located Third Ward had three times the assets of the average freeholder in the Fifth Ward. In addition, the ratios of property-owning residents to renters varied wildly among the wards. In 1795, there were 1.5 renters for every property-holder in the Third Ward, but 5.8 renters for every owner in the Sixth, the area that became the electoral stronghold for the Republicans.[45] In city elections, freeholders were allowed to vote in each ward where they owned property worth at least $100; renters, however, were ineligible to vote. The requirements for state elections were more relaxed, with a £20 property or a $5 annual rent qualification (which would have been roughly £1.5). Thus, the city government was firmly in the hands of property-owners, but state and federal elections were more competitive, with twice as many renters as property owners. Throughout the 1790s, anti-Federalist and Republican votes were concentrated among these laborer and immigrant renters, who lived in a "poverty belt" north of the city's commercial areas; more rural wards tended to swing for either party. Republicans carried the heavily rented Sixth and Seventh Wards by 60, 70, and even 90 percent, while Federalists produced similar margins in the wealthier First, Second, and Third Wards.[46]

It is problematic to link party membership to wealth, occupation, or status—a Republican-identifying mechanic would not necessarily prefer a Federalist mechanic to a Republican elite. Yet, both Republicans and Federalists voted for candidates from an elite stratum of merchants and attorneys selected by both parties' leadership. Among the rank-and-file voters of the city, evidence reveals situational correlations between party preference and wealth. In this context, mercantile finance, banking, and wealth in general were linked to Federalism. Although the city underwent substantial demographic and commercial growth during the decade, there remained only two banks throughout the 1790s. Faced with an institutional stasis in banking, the city itself stepped in to act as a petty lender. By 1799, a rising demand for credit and currency grew so dire that the city's Common Council was repeatedly forced to reassure the public that it would continue to print and circulate its own "small change" notes, quashing panic-stirring rumors to the contrary.[47]

Finances were foremost on the minds of New York voters in 1799, particularly after Aaron Burr, the Republican former U. S. senator who had been elected to the New York Assembly in 1798, sponsored a bankruptcy reform bill in the legislature. The proposal drew fire from city merchants who viewed it as a bid to curry favor with debtors. The city's burgeoning presses, which acted as partisan rallying points between election seasons, made strident arguments for and against the proposal.[48] A Republican-leaning newspaper scolded the merchants' hostility, charging that "ignorance and prejudice" against debtors drove some "to ascribe all the evils our Country experiences, to the Democrats."[49] Responses to the bankruptcy bill reified the notable, though not exclusive, links between credit and Federalists; financial success was frequently linked to electoral success, and Federalist newspapers repeatedly claimed that the Washington and Adams administrations were responsible for the mercantile growth of New York.

With Federalism and merchants linked in print and rhetorically juxtaposed against a backdrop that associated failure and insolvency with Republicans, it was essential for Republicans to conspicuously play the role of financial patrons in the city, reversing this reputation by showing leadership while simultaneously forging political alliances through economic dependence. To be perceived as financial equals, Republicans had to overcome not only Federalists' rhetorical claims but also the documented anti-Federalist suspicions of banking on which they were based.

Individual Republicans might have been able to escape these associations with financial failure and anti-bank hostility, but the Republican label as a whole could not be rehabilitated on individual bases. DeWitt Clinton, for example, later in life lamented that he drained his wife's inherited fortune by making himself into a one-man bank by routinely endorsing the notes of "republican young men."[50] Therefore a bank was an ideal institution for Republicans to control. A bank would be able to answer the depth of the capital required to create subsidiary networks of credit that could later be mobilized to build partisan electoral support among elites and aspiring merchants.

Yet if Republicans sought to use financial patronage to aid their party's development, New York presented a particularly inhospitable environment. No banks had been chartered in the state since the "bancomania" of 1791. With Alexander Hamilton as the de facto leader of the Federalists and the architect of the nation's banking system, it was unlikely that the city's two-bank regime would be voluntarily broken; Hamilton's reputation carried enough weight to start or stop any proposed bank. Nor could Republicans openly petition for a bank or corporation of their own; with obligations to serve the public good, such institutions had to be at least nominally nonpartisan.

In this environment, the Federalism of New York City's banks not only made it difficult to be a Republican party leader but also frustrated the ambitions of political entrepreneurs who happened to be Republican. During the 1790s, New York Republicans had no meaningful way to participate in corporate banking because the institutions that controlled access to bank credit—the banks and the legislature that could charter and regulate them—had been captured by Federalists and a Federalist way of thinking about banking. Hamiltonian Federalists owned and ran the city's banks and, by extension, made state policy when it came to banking by swaying legislators and shaping public debates. According to them, bank competition was not inconvenient or illegitimate—it was dangerous. Access to banking in New York—and in any American city where there was a bank—had always been limited to the elite and their dependents and associates. But once this socioeconomic barrier became partisan, a broader cross-section of the city's elite found the city's banks to be off-limits. Party became yet another discretionary reason to deny a limited supply of credit to those who might be competitors in business or politics, or both. Republicans could not gain access to credit because they did not control any banks, and they would not control any banks until they won electoral majorities in the state legislature—a feat that control of a bank would make far easier to accomplish.

Although this combination of ideology and *realpolitik* made the chartering of a bank—partisan or otherwise—nearly impossible, the legislature regularly considered petitions for public works proposals. Proposals that answered an urgent need and carried broad political support were most likely to meet approval. And a coalition of the city's political entrepreneurs soon found a proposal they could support—one that would aid their political futures and their own material ambitions.

In 1799, New York City needed clean water. Yellow fever epidemics had paralyzed the city during previous summers, causing acute health crises in the late 1790s. The city's Common Council solicited advice from physicians, who blamed stagnant water, narrow streets, and crowded residences for creating an unsanitary water supply. The city's main water source, the Collect, warmed to a bacteriological brew during the summer months.[51]

Yet even with dire disease at its doorstep and the legal authority to take action, the city's Common Council considered itself incompetent to unilaterally address the problem without authorization from the state legislature. As an incorporated city created under the pre-Revolutionary Montgomerie Charter, New York's city council insulated itself against charges of being monarchical or antithetical to republicanism by frequently suborning itself to the popularly elected state legislature.[52] When the Council solicited proposals for a new drinking-water source, it was receptive to a proposal to tap the Bronx (East) River through the use of an independent incorporated water company.[53]

Legislators in the early republic, fascinated by constitution-making, devoted much attention to the petitioning and corporate-chartering process.[54] This assertion of legislative prerogative alleviated concerns that corporations could become unaccountable or dangerously influential permanent entities.

On its face the proposed water company, called the Manhattan Company, was a bipartisan idea. Six citizens—three Federalists and three Republicans—were chosen by Alexander Hamilton and Aaron Burr, recruited to recommend that the Common Council seek a legislative charter for an independent water company, rather than a public entity to be run by the city, and to be the lobbyists in charge of seeing the proposal come to fruition, using their reputations and influence in the city and with lawmakers.[55]

Hamilton's design for the company, however, had a more Federalist cast. The company was to have a seven-person board of directors. The city—a corporation itself—was to own a third of the stock in the company, giving it a one-third share of control over the company and its profits. Hamilton also recommended that the city recorder be an ex officio director of the company, ensuring that the Common Council could monitor and influence its management.[56] Although each of these provisions might be unremarkable in isolation, Hamilton—a veteran charter writer—could not have missed their implication: his original design for the Manhattan Company would have produced a company that would have been bipartisan at first, but which would gradually have fallen into Federalist hands as the Federalist-controlled city government exercised its influence over its operations and Federalist stockholders accumulated controlling stakes in its publicly traded shares. Then the Manhattan Company would have become, like virtually every other chartered company in the city and state, an outlet for Federalist favoritism and for the advancement of Federalist political entrepreneurs' interests.

When Hamilton's proposal reached the state legislature, Burr offered—as one of New York City's assemblymen—to shepherd it to passage.[57] On the surface, Burr was collaborating with Hamilton to win approval for a plan to serve the public good. But privately Burr had other plans. Burr quietly began amending Hamilton's proposal to make the Manhattan Company charter look like those used when the state had incorporated the Northern and Western Inland Lock Navigation Companies earlier in the decade. He doubled the company's proposed capitalization to $2 million; granted it legal powers of eminent domain, perpetual life, and the freedom to set rates without outside approval; and exempted it from obligations to provide water used in fighting fires. In return for these privileges, the company was required to "furnish and continue a supply of pure and wholesome water sufficient for the use of all such citizens dwelling in the said City" within ten years. If it failed to meet this goal, the company would forfeit its charter.[58]

These amendments to the Manhattan Company's charter were substantial, but none fundamentally altered the institution's trajectory as much as a seemingly innocuous sentence added by Burr shortly before the legislation's passage. Since at least 1796, Burr had been investigating the form and design of bank charters. By 1799 he was well versed enough to know that the barrier distinguishing a water utility from a bank could be smashed with a sentence.[59] Hours before the Manhattan Company's charter was up for a final vote, Burr inserted a clause into the charter to give almost unlimited latitude in how the company used its "surplus capital." The draft language said: "It shall be and may be lawful for the said company to employ all such surplus capital as may belong or accrue to the said company in the purchase of public or other stock, or in any other monied transactions or operations, not inconsistent with the constitution and laws of this State or the United States, for the sole benefit of the said company."[60] As one of Burr's protégés later wrote, the clause "intended [that] the directors use the surplus capital in any way they thought expedient and proper." They would be able to open "a bank, an East India Company, or anything else that they deemed profitable."[61]

Therefore although it was to be a publicly chartered and traded company created for the purpose of solving a public problem on behalf of and at the behest of public authorities, the Manhattan Company's own charter would—in plain language—liberate it from having to serve only the public good. Instead, the company could pursue its own interests—interests that in a shareholder-owned and director-managed firm would be inherently private and oriented toward producing material, financial gains for those owners and managers and to serving whatever other interests those owners deemed to be a priority. As long as the Manhattan Company devoted at least part of its resources to supplying water to the city, it was free to become a bank, a trading company, or both—even a multiunit conglomerate if its board so desired.

In spite of the unique financial flexibility vested in the Manhattan Company, few seemed to notice Burr's handiwork, probably because nobody had ever tried it before. Burr was exploiting his reputation and his colleagues' trust in order to bend the petitioning and chartering process to let him create a bank out of a company being incorporated for another purpose. Most elected legislators in this period were inexperienced, serving year-long terms in chambers with high turnover rates.[62] Most lawmakers were therefore inexperienced at making laws and unfamiliar with the relay of formalities—committee meetings, amendments, and readings under the rules of order—that led to the passage of new laws. Although legislators may have been interested in corporate charters, they were fundamentally unfamiliar with the finer mechanics of how those institutions were designed. And because corporations were public-private mixed-economy institutions, lawmakers did not engage in corporate chartering as disinterested gatekeepers and regulators; they often saw the petitioning and chartering process as an opportunity to extract rewards that would enrich themselves and their colleagues.

Never at risk of believing men to be angels, Aaron Burr did not treat this aspect of lawmaking as a defect; it was instead an opportunity, and one he exploited to his advantage. In the crucial hours before the Manhattan Company's amended charter was put to a final vote, Burr enlarged the company's board of directors from seven to twelve members. With more slots to fill, Burr would be able to include enough prominent and influential elites on the board to all but guarantee the charter's passage.

Part of Burr's motivation was partisan: by changing the charter's form he could turn the Manhattan Company into a bank, and by adding directorships he could make it a Republican-controlled bank. The three Federalists originally selected for membership on the board could now be outnumbered—and outvoted—by seven Republican counterparts whom Burr chose from among the state's three Republican factions: the Burrites, Clintonians, and Livingstonians. Because party loyalty was contingent and often unrecognizable among elites, it may not have been apparent to the legislature that the Manhattan Company was so stealthily politicized. Few of the proposed directors were elected officials; most had never appeared on past partisan electoral tickets. The lack of past cohesion among the three factions made it difficult to determine who was a Republican leader on any given day, and with parties' rank-and-file membership in flux during the 1790s, it remained difficult to determine who was a Federalist or a Republican without explicitly asking. Therefore because the nominated directors were elite men of reputation with ties to other prominent New Yorkers and because many were already directors of other corporations in the city—including its banks—it was unlikely that they would have been accused of cooperating in Burr's scheme or that their participation could even have been detected.[63]

Despite its partisan nature, however, the Manhattan Company's principal function was not to provide an institutional architecture to the state's Republican Party. Rather, the company was going to be a bank operating from within a water company that happened to be governed by Republicans. Much of the partisan benefit for Republicans would therefore come from the fact that banking itself was an already inherently politicized activity that formed durable institutionalized interests among borrowers, lenders, shareholders, and directors. Banks built interests, so by gaining access to bank stocks, directorships, and credit, Republicans would be able to exercise the same leverage and discretion that Federalists had long enjoyed in the state's incumbent banks. As Chancellor Livingston recognized, a lack of unanimity within Republican ranks had long prevented them from channeling public disaffection into electoral coalitions.[64] Republicans had captured seats in previous legislative elections, but they had never produced majorities in the legislature or statewide elections.[65] Burr therefore used the chartering process to compel cooperation among a board of directors that looked like an executive committee of party leaders who would be rewarded—financially and politically—for breaking the Federalist-dominated duopoly over the city's banking sector.

Aaron Burr did not have to approach the chartering process with an eye toward making the Manhattan Company an exclusively Republican bank. If the company was to thrive it would need both financial and political capital, necessitating that Burr build cross-bench and out-of-doors alliances with Federalists and Republicans for whom partisanship was just one of many competing motives. Most legislators and political entrepreneurs were eager to cooperate with him because the Manhattan Company's business model offered profit opportunities—even if they were not aware of the "surplus capital" clause in the charter. In addition to distributing directorships among Republican factions, Burr strategically structured the company's stock ownership to reflect a similar pattern: the three largest subscriptions were held by representatives of the state's three Republican factions.[66] Yet Burr also engaged Federalists in the company, enabling him to win votes from ten upstate Federalist legislators who supported the Manhattan Company's charter in the Federalist-dominated Assembly. One Federalist lawmaker later claimed to have been ignorant of the "surplus capital" clause until after the measure reached the floor for approval, suggesting that Burr's outreach may have been designed to distract lawmakers from the charter's contents.[67] Other Federalists, however, were more supportive. Nicholas Low, a director of the Bank of New-York and an assemblyman, said he bought one hundred shares "on Condition of my approving the Charter."[68] In the Senate, Burr could have relied on Republican senator DeWitt Clinton, who represented New York City, to manage the floor vote on the charter. But he instead recruited two Federalists and a Federalist-turned-Republican senator for the job; the latter was permitted to subscribe for one hundred shares of Manhattan Company stock.[69] That move brought over two other prominent Federalists: Samuel Jones, the state comptroller and so-called Father of the New York Bar, and Thomas Morris, who assuaged Jones's financial concerns about "surplus capital" by warning him that the Manhattan Company's costly task would require a "profitable" ancillary enterprise to attract stock subscribers.[70] Burr also made sure to offer stock subscriptions to other Federalists who were not in the legislature, giving them the chance to buy Manhattan Company shares before they were offered to the general public. Among the new shareholders were New York City's Federalist recorder and an illustrious list of mostly Federalist merchants. Federalist lawyer Robert Troup, a close friend of both John Jay and Alexander Hamilton, confidently predicted that "the company will make its way into full business as a bank & that in time its stock will be the best amongst us."[71]

As evidence of how effectively Burr managed this process, the only meaningful legislative opposition to the incorporation of the Manhattan Company came from a Republican member of the state's Council of Revision. Vested with executive veto powers, the council was composed of the governor, the chancellor, and Supreme Court judges. Judge John Lansing, a Republican, disapproved of the "speculative and uncertain" powers granted by the "surplus capital" clause but found himself alone in his opposition to the law. Chancellor Robert R. Livingston, the largest shareholder in the Manhattan Company, was joined by a Federalist in overriding Lansing.[72] Thereafter, on 2 April 1799, the state's Federalist governor, John Jay, signed the act incorporating the Manhattan Company.

Soon after the charter became law, observers began to reconstruct the scale of Burr's legislative maneuvering. As a politician known for his ambition and an all-but-declared contender for the presidency in 1800, Burr was already under suspicion by some Federalists who skeptically viewed his involvement with the Manhattan Company as a sign of trouble. Even one of Burr's Federalist allies noted weeks after the company's creation that, "[Burr] governs everything by a decided majority among the directors ... he is acquiring much influence."[73] Federalist director John Coles wondered about the Manhattan Company's true purpose when, at a 12 April meeting with two Republican directors, they discussed abandoning the company's original plan to divert water from the Bronx River in favor of a less costly alternative: constructing a reservoir near the Collect. The goal, admitted one of the Republican directors, was to prevent "any immediate demand for money, which might of course be applied to other speculations." This strategy, however, risked raising public ire; the same director noted that it was "incumbent on [the directors] to convince our fellow Citizens that we are truly earnest in the business. . . . [S]hould we do nothing we shall raise a violent clamor ag[ainst] us." Therefore, although the Manhattan Company's water operations and bank were each intended to be useful additions to the city's political economy that boosted the stature and popularity of the company's Republican directors, the actual conversion of the company from a water utility into a hybrid bank was going to be challenging for the company's directors to manage. The company would have to constrain its water plans and postpone construction in order to have enough surplus capital on hand to open a bank, a move that risked alienating Federalist directors and shareholders as well as the city's press.[74]

Even before the Manhattan Company took overt steps toward forming a bank, Federalist-leaning newspapers routinely induced merchants and other commercially involved citizens to support Federalist candidates for office. "Commerce," one paper editorialized in early April 1799, "is the primum mobile which gives action to every part, and forces the vital current thru' every artery . . . it is by means of commerce that every portion of the globe becomes our tributary and is made to contribute to our prosperity."[75] Couching political pleas in the rational, scientific language of economics imbued it with authority, enabling writers to engage in partisan combat without seeming to be simply partisan. Therefore, a fruitful avenue to discredit the Manhattan Company was by charging that it posed a threat to the city's economic development and violated accepted norms of political economy. If Burr had manipulated the chartering process, the Manhattan Company would represent a usurpation of the legislature's—and, by extension, the people's—will. Corporations, after all, were slivers of sovereignty temporarily granted by the legislature.

Thus it was in the press that Federalists—editors and newspaper contributors—began a coordinated, full-fledged attack on both the Manhattan Company and Aaron Burr. Seeking to maximize their advantage in the upcoming legislative elections to be held at the end of April and in early May, New York City Federalists made their 1799 campaign a referendum on the Manhattan Company. The election, wrote John Jay's son, was driven by "a full Knowledge of the Manhattan Scheme & by some well written Publications which appeared in the Papers."[76]

As a prominent Republican, Aaron Burr would have already been a target in the Federalists' campaign, but his public reputation and legislative role in

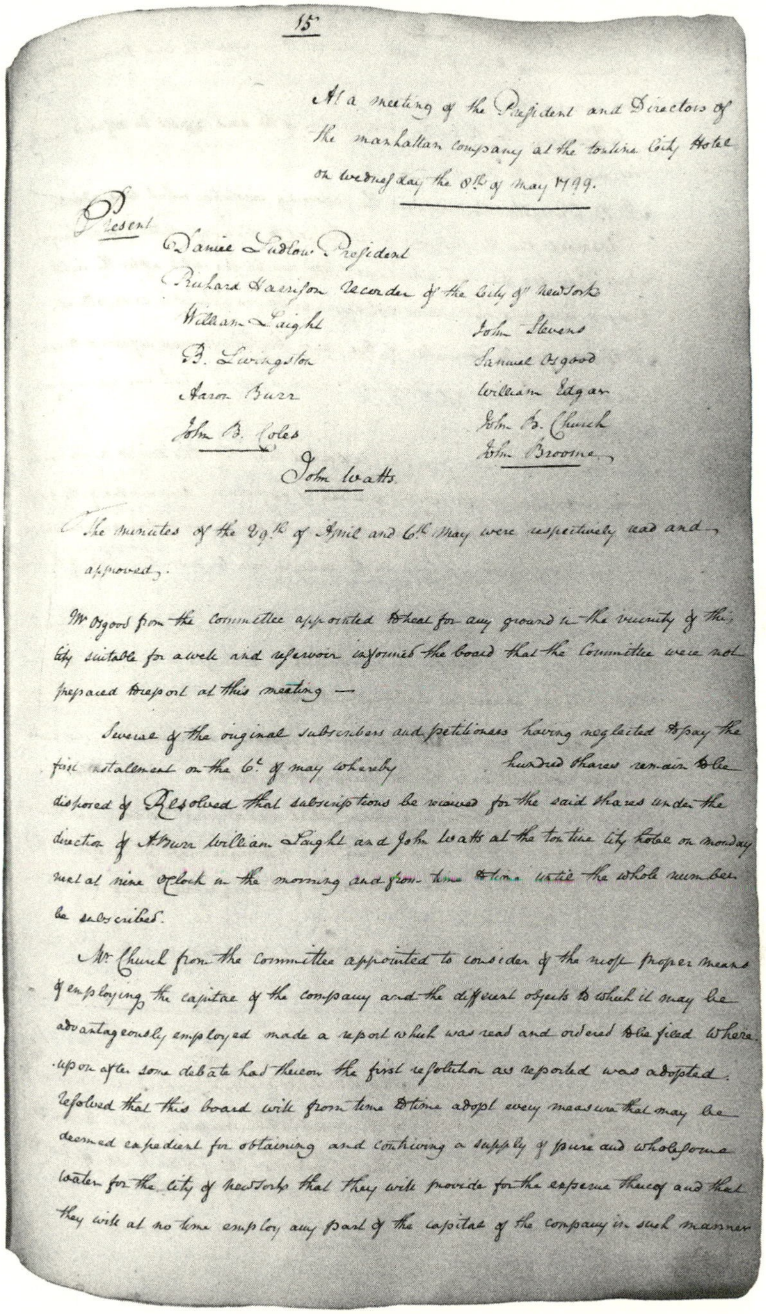

At a meeting of the President and Directors of the manhattan Company at the tontine City Hotel on wednesday the 8th of may 1799.

Present

Daniel Ludlow President

Richard Harrison recorder of the City of newYork

William Laight

B. Livingston

Aaron Burr

John B. Coles

John Stevens

Samuel Osgood

William Edgar

John B. Church

John Broome

John Watts

The minutes of the 29th of April and 6th May were respectively read and approved.

Mr Osgood from the Committee appointed to treat for any ground in the vicinity of this City suitable for a well and reservoir informed the board that the Committee were not prepared to report at this meeting —

Several of the original subscribers and petitioners having neglected to pay the first installment on the 6th of may whereby _____ hundred shares remain to be disposed of Resolved that subscriptions be received for the said shares under the direction of A Burr William Laight and John Watts at the tontine City hotel on monday next at nine oclock in the morning and from time to time until the whole number be subscribed.

Mr Church from the Committee appointed to consider of the most proper means of employing the capital of the company and the different objects to which it may be advantageously employed made a report which was read and ordered to be filed Whereupon after some debate had thereon the first resolution as reported was adopted. Resolved that this board will from time to time adopt every measure that may be deemed expedient for obtaining and continuing a supply of pure and wholesome water for the City of newYork that they will provide for the expense thereof and that they will at no time employ any part of the capital of the company in such manner

Figure 3. Corporations like the Manhattan Company were required by law to keep a record book with the minutes of the meetings of their boards of directors. Pictured is the page from the 8 May 1799 meeting in which directors voted to begin running a bank by "discount[ing] debentures at lawful interest." Courtesy JPMorgan Chase Corporate History Program, 2003.

the company's founding became a useful narrative hook for stories that connected his troubled personal finances to warnings about a third bank in the city. One writer warned merchants that Burr, "a bankrupt politician," was "repairing his fortunes by 'monied transactions,'" inducing others in the city to "sport" with money.[77] Even among the Federalist elite, this critique gained currency; Fisher Ames privately reported to Rufus King that "Burr is out of credit, tho' his water or bank scrip has turned reputation into the ready."[78]

It was a challenge, however, for the Federalist press to discredit the Manhattan Company when so many Federalists were its directors and shareholders. On paper, the Manhattan Company was the most politically integrated corporation in the city of New York. Nevertheless the Federalist press began insisting that the company was "Republican." Focusing on its "surplus capital," the press drew attention to its potential to be a third bank in the city, one owned and managed by a "Republican" majority of shareholders and directors. One writer alleged that the company's board of directors had been assembled to have "the right complexion in politics."[79] Federalist newspaper editors—not the Federalist elite—were, in fact, the first to publicly connect the Manhattan Company to a partisan agenda.

Federalist writers took pains to absolve their fellow partisans of willingly—and, in some cases, knowingly—participating in the chartering of a water company they knew would be converted into a bank. Instead, they charged legislators with negligence and alleged that Burr had misled his colleagues. One writer lamented,

> [T]he late house enjoyed, till near its decease, the reputation of being Federal—but sense may be requisite, as well as honesty and Federalism—and in the hands of such a man as Mr. Burr, dupes are more dangerous instruments than knaves. . . . The Bronx is made a pretext for selling you the putrid waters of the Collect at discretionary prices. The Collect is made the foundation of a Bank—the Bank is to overflow you with a deluge of notes—to depreciate and discredit paper currency—to raise while it exists an anti-federal monied interest—then to break, and make the fortune of Mr. Burr—Thus the natural course of all such schemes . . . Mr. Burr would disorganize this state in a single winter.[80]

The same writer even ventured that Federalist legislators might have been absent from Albany on the day that the charter was approved.[81] Calling himself "A Merchant," another writer professed, "I am willing to believe that the legislature was not aware that a bank could or would be created under that charter."[82] A week prior to the election, the same newspaper accused "Mr. Burr and a junto of Directors of whom three quarters are antifederalists" of "pursuing an entirely different object, by a kind of Politico-Commercial-Financial-Bronx-Operation." "Fellow-Citizens! This is a dangerous man in any situation," the writer warned, "let the merchant, the mechanic, the lawyer, and the labourer—let the rich and the poor, and all classes unite, come forward and exert themselves—they have a common interest in the prosperity of the country." Federalist electoral victories would therefore ensure that the "important commercial interests of this city" would "not again be misrepresented by any person from the slough of the Democratic Society."[83]

Even some in the Federalist elite began to buy into this narrative, convincing themselves that they had been ignorant of the Manhattan Company charter's "surplus capital" clause or its implications. Robert Troup, who in April had praised the charter and (accurately) predicted the company's evolution into a bank, was by June privately accusing Burr of "lull[ing] [the legislature] into a profound sleep by his arts and misrepresentations."[84]

Amid these attacks on Burr and the company, Federalists reportedly began doing something explicitly that they had long been accused of doing quietly: denying Republicans access to credit and capital on the basis of their partisan affiliation. According to the New York *Journal and Patriotic Register*, both the Bank of New-York and the New York branch of the Bank of the United States systematically refused to discount Republicans' "unexceptionable commercial paper" in the days before the 1799 election.[85]

Discounts were simply loans made in which the interest—called a "discount"—was collected up front, and for nearly a decade the city's Federalist-controlled banks had been suspected of denying credit in the form of discounts to their political rivals. Although these decisions might have seemed partisan, they likely reflected the reality of an urban economy where there were only two incorporated banks. Those banks' charters capped both their size and the interest rates they could set, and under those circumstances bank credit would gradually become restricted to all but the most secure borrowers: major merchants—usually Federalists—and uncommonly wealthy landowners like Chancellor Livingston. Livingston had been a Federalist before becoming a Republican, but his personal wealth would have always overridden any partisan considerations in deciding whether he should be allowed to borrow money from a bank.

Amid all of this partisanship, even while banks were controlled by Federalists and allied to Federalist state legislators, borrowing had never been exclusively Federalist, which is why a move to deny credit to Republicans before the 1799 election represented an unprecedented escalation in the use of bank privileges as political leverage. And although the impact of this tactic was largely confined to the elite, it evidenced a newfound willingness to use state-chartered mixed-economy institutions to enforce party discipline. More than any printed jeremiad could, this act firmly established a "Federalist" character to banking by making it undeniable that the Bank of New-York and the New York branch of the Bank of the United States were, at least temporarily, Federalist banks. By forcing patrons to declare or recognize previously ambiguous party affiliations, the banks grafted themselves onto an existing culture of partisanship.

The tactic worked as a part of the Federalists' overall electoral strategy. In early May 1799, Burr and his cohort were defeated at the polls by landslide 5:1 margins in swing wards and even by a 3:2 margin in what had been their Sixth Ward stronghold in the city.[86]

It was a short-lived victory, however. Within a year, Republicans would point to this event to justify the Manhattan Company's founding and its turn toward becoming a Republican-friendly bank. Now, just a week after the election, the company's board voted to begin to "discount debentures at lawful interest"—their words for opening a bank.[87] That move prompted director William Laight, who also served as a director of the New York branch of the Bank of the United States, to resign from the Manhattan Company's board. Laight was not openly Federalist, but he was a member of the city's Chamber of Commerce and one of Alexander Hamilton's longtime associates.[88] Though neither board asked him to choose between the two, Laight had decided to remain loyal to the national bank. He was quickly replaced on the Manhattan Company's board by a Republican.[89] Therefore the Federalists' electoral tactics and their political commitments to the city's existing banks were pushing the Manhattan Company toward becoming an even more Republican corporation after the 1799 election.

Federalists responded to the Manhattan Company's move toward banking by warning that it would lead to speculation. They echoed Alexander Hamilton's notion that the city could not sustain more than two incorporated banks. "A Merchant" wrote, "[I]t would have been deemed worthy of a very mature consideration whether a rival should be encouraged by the state of New-York, against the bank of New-York. . . . The danger of giving too much power to one set of directors may be an argument for having two banks . . . but the same reasoning by no means applies in favor of a third."[90] Another raised objections to the company itself, asking, "[A]re not all corporations unwieldy machines, with difficulty made amenable to the laws, and attended with many inconveniences?"[91]

In the Federalist press, hostility toward corporations grew strident throughout the summer, to the surprise of some Federalist leaders. After publishing an article titled "On Canals and Turnpike Roads," which lauded corporations' efficiency and compared charters to constitutions, one Federalist editor was compelled to publish an apology:

> In the Commercial Advertiser of Saturday is an extract . . . in favor of incorporated companies. . . . I am at a loss to account for the insertion of this extract, at the present time, unless it was for the purpose of turning aside the stream of public odium which is every day accumulating in force, and promises to overturn the late incorporation of the Manhattan Company. No man has yet . . . to attempt, in any of our public press, to support or justify, in any direct manner, that incorporation. . . . [L]et us have no sideway attempt to give it popularity.[92]

That the Manhattan Company's existence would lead to anticorporate critiques in a Federalist newspaper speaks to the alarm provoked by its entry into banking. One letter writer asked Robert Livingston, "[D]o you believe that while any remembrance of the Manhattan Company remain, either yourself or Mr. Burr will be considered as proper persons for governors," of what the writer called "the State of Manhattan"—plainly a reference to the British East India Company, a state within a state.[93]

The Manhattan Company had neither opened its bank nor acted in an overtly partisan way during its first months, but Federalists could nevertheless see the outlines of Burr's vision: a bank ruled by Republicans, meeting demands for credit that Federalist banks were incapable of answering. Some Federalists were content to demonize the company in print, but others plotted action in the form of a hostile takeover. Nicholas Low, who had supported the company's charter in the legislature, wrote, "[S]ome of our Friends support it not because it is right in itself but because it has been granted & then say that if the Legislature have given birth to a monster it is their Duty to strangle it."[94] Calling the company "a greater Pestilence than the Yellow Fever," Low said, "some of our wise ones recommend that federal men subscribe & endeavor to get the management into their Hands."[95] By concentrating company stock shares in Federalist hands, Low hoped to change the Manhattan Company's board of directors during the next annual shareholder election. "Our friend [Nicholas] Low," wrote Robert Troup, "would annihilate the charter in an instant if he could and the temper he possesses is common."[96] But to Low's frustration, only a few seats on the board of directors rotated each year, making his strategy somewhat impractical. Recognizing that such a takeover was all but impossible, other Federalists simply opted not to buy Manhattan Company stock shares.[97]

Proposals to amend the Manhattan Company's charter arose during the next session of the Federalist-controlled legislature. Seeking to prevent the Manhattan Company from opening a branch bank in Albany, the Bank of Albany's directors petitioned the legislature to curtail the "extent of the rights vested in" the Manhattan Company "to prevent any injury to incorporations of a similar nature, or to the public."[98] Rather than force a confrontation with hostile legislators, the Manhattan Company directors turned again to Aaron Burr, who preempted the company's enemies by asking the legislature to clarify the company's powers as a water utility and a bank; the move was approved by the assembly but left to languish in the senate.[99]

Thus, despite their public fulminations, there was no coherent Federalist response to the Manhattan Company's founding and no formal action taken against it. Some Federalists, in fact, seemed ready to move on. Rather than join the Bank of Albany's petitions to restrict the charter or the Manhattan Company's own petitions to reopen its charter, the Bank of New-York's directors sought parity by asking the legislature to revise their charter to grant them certain advantages of capitalization and board rotation enjoyed by their new rival.[100] Referred to an assembly committee, however, the Bank of New-York's petition was rejected because the Federalist committee chairman, William Woolsey, reported that he could not "advise the House to correct a great existing evil by creating a new one." (Woolsey, who owned 150 shares of Manhattan Company stock, did, however, eventually support allowing the Bank of New-York to retain directors indefinitely as the Manhattan Company could, which would permit a continuity of political representation on the board.)[101] For his part, Nicholas Fish, who had originally supported the company's charter before seeking to launch a hostile takeover of its board, soon wished he had more cash on hand to invest in the company's stock, which he predicted "promises to be a profitable fund."[102] So many Federalists, in fact, were lured by visions of dividends that writers in the Federalists' own

Commercial Advertiser newspaper wondered aloud why "respectful men and even the corporation of the city itself have been drawn in under an inconsiderate and utterly mistaken policy to subscribe their names for Bank shares."[103]

Federalist opposition softened for one simple reason: despite predictions, the Manhattan Company was both reliable and profitable. Even as it prepared to enter the banking sector, the company's board took visible steps to fulfill its civic water-related obligations. Joseph Browne, architect of the Manhattan Company's water plan, wrote to Burr, "I expect and hope that enough will be done to satisfy the Public and particularly the Legislature that the Institution is not a speculating Job, but an undertaking from whence will result . . . incalculable advantage to the City of New York."[104] Burr and his allies were determined to show that a bank—even one with a partisan agenda—could perform the essential functions of a bank while also building a public reputation as a responsible civic institution.

As anticipated, the banking terms offered by the Manhattan Company were more liberal than those offered by the other banks in the city. The bank's very first loan was highly partisan—to the Cayuga Bridge Company, helmed by Burr's lieutenant John Swartwout.[105] As a Republican pamphleteer recalled years later, "[In 1800] the bank . . . had the power of conferring favors, and was an object to be courted by all those whose situation or business required pecuniary aid."[106] As a Republican institution, the Manhattan Company could build loyalty among merchants and a cadre of debtors and investors who previously had neither the freedom nor an incentive to cultivate a Republican identity; it could materially reward its converts, creating Republican identities among New York elites and their dependents.

Yet the company's directors remained sensitive to public perceptions. For the sake of long-term political viability, they entangled themselves in the finances of other institutions.[107] In that spirit, the largest loan made by the bank in its first year was to the city of New York.[108] The company's two remaining Federalist directors continued to serve on its board despite the fact that one, John Coles, had won election to the assembly on the ticket that opposed the company's creation.[109] The presence of these Federalist directors allowed the company to pursue an agenda that was predominantly but not exclusively Republican, all while being monitored in the event that the company strayed too far from its chartered purpose or into financial instability. By year's end, the Manhattan Company's stature rivaled that of other New York corporations. A Federalist partisan reported that "the stock of the company is on the rise. The company does a great deal of discounting business—and is gaining ground in public esteem."[110] The directors even marched in the funeral procession mourning George Washington's death on the last day of 1799, heading a column of directors from the city's other chartered institutions, including its banks.[111]

In the weeks before the 1800 legislative election, the Manhattan Company dramatically increased its discounting activities in ways to benefit Republicans. In the seven months prior to 30 March 1800, the bank collected $42,755.90 in interest on its bills, but from April through June 1800—the three months when the election occurred—it collected even more in less than half the time: $45,720.86. The bank was therefore loaning three times as much money as it had done during all of the prior year—about $762,000. In fact, there was so much activity that the directors had to order more bills to be printed to keep up with their business.[112]

Rather than hide this activity, the company and its allies celebrated it. Republican editor James Cheetham spared no effort to portray the Manhattan Company as a Republican institution performing a public good, distinguishing it from Federalist banks that had used exclusivity to coerce votes. Prior to the polling in 1800, "A Merchant" reminded voters, "at the last election, each of you were threatened with ruin, if you did not vote for the federal ticket."[113] Another writer crafted the Manhattan Company's founding as a liberation narrative, addressing "the Cartmen of New-York":

> The establishment of the Manhattan bank has rendered the merchants independent. They are no longer afraid that the avowal of republican principles, can deprive them of discounts. A necessary competition has annihilated the despotism of banking monopoly. This happy circumstance has strengthened the republican interest, at the expence of their opponents. It has detached many from them, whom timidity had joined to them, no impudent combination to deprive any of you of employment can now be formed with the least prospect of success. The law places it in your power to punish the man who shall dare to influence your vote, by the threat of depriving you of bread.[114]

During the election of 1800, therefore, the Manhattan Company served as a rhetorical rallying point for New York City Republicanism. It was also a site of party consolidation, as reflected in the Republicans' legislative ticket. Knowing that his association with the company had been a liability in the last election, yet still harboring ambitions for national office, Aaron Burr opted not to campaign for the Assembly from Manhattan. Instead, he engineered his nomination in nearby Orange County and handpicked a slate from New York City that, like the Manhattan Company's board of directors, mirrored the three dominant Republican factions in the state. At a late-night meeting at Burr's home, thirteen men—including George Clinton, Brockholst Livingston, and John Swartwout—formed a ticket. Of the thirteen, four were Manhattan Company directors; all the others also had direct ties to the company.

When the ballots in the 1800 election were counted, Republicans had won the city with 52.7 percent of the vote, only a year after the Federalists had garnered 59.4 percent. Federalists attributed the Republicans' strength to the Manhattan Company.[115] Assessing the Federalist defeat, "Portius," wrote to the "friends of the present Government and particularly to the Merchants" that the Republicans

> do not confine themselves to three days exertion and an ill-digested, ill-concerted arrangement of two or three evenings; they devote weeks, months, even the year itself to secure their purposes. Two days had scarcely elapsed after the determination of the last year's election when measures were begun for ensuring that success which they have now obtained. They planned and immediately began to execute. They discriminated throughout this city between their partisans, and those opposed to them, and they soon knew to a man the name of every doubtful character.... Among other things, all the influence of the Manhattan Company has been enlisted in their service; and it is here that we are to look for the great loss of votes which we met.... In all their transactions in private life they have acted with an eye to the same object; was a cartman to be employed or a mechanic to be hired, the first enquiry made was—What are his politicks?[116]

Logistical innovations implemented by the Republicans' exertions in 1800 have been detailed by other historians, including Burr's creation of a round-the-clock campaign headquarters, complete with cots and coffee, and his sophisticated door-to-door, get-out-the-vote effort. Burr did not campaign to voters directly but instead relied on the mediation of a "league of energetic young lieutenants."[117] In the same vein, the Manhattan Company encouraged Republican leaders to cooperate first with each other and then provided them with an institutional basis to create expansive, durable, partisan networks of patronage that were based on material, rather than ideological, interests.

Republicans, too, attributed their success to the Manhattan Company, having broken the Federalists' monopoly on institutional finance. One partisan reflected that the company had ended years of "coerc[ing] the mechanics and cartmen to prostitute their most important and inalienable right, the elective franchise," through financial sanctions.[118] "You had to contend with powerful and insidious foes," another Republican wrote, "a host encompasses you on every side—Federal, State and Corporation Officers, took the field against you."[119] According to James Cheetham, the Manhattan Company was the Federalists' death knell: "Federalism retained its domination until the establishment of the Manhattan Company; after that event its empire became dissolved."[120] That sentiment was shared by Republican chieftain DeWitt Clinton, who in 1808 told Manhattan Company cashier Henry Remsen, "[T]he cause of republicanism . . . is intimately connected with the prosperity of our institution."[121]

Much of the energy driving the 1800 state elections had to do with the presidential election to follow. The legislature would be choosing the slate of electors who would cast ballots for president and vice president. New York City, Aaron Burr believed, was the keystone to a national Republican victory, a view shared by other national Republican leaders. As Thomas Jefferson wrote James Monroe on 4 March 1800,

> In New-York all depends on the success of the city election, which is of twelve members and of course makes a difference of twenty-four, which is sufficient to make the two houses, joined together, republican in their vote. . . . In any event, we may say that if the city election of New-York is in favour of the republican ticket, the issue will be republican; if the federal ticket for the city of New-York prevails, the probabilities will be in favour of a federal issue, because it would then require a republican vote both from New-Jersey and Pennsylvania to preponderate against New-York, on which we could not count with any confidence.[122]

Thus, when Edward Livingston wrote to Jefferson about the "very important change" put in motion by "the instrumentality . . . of the New Bank" it was in anticipation of this national election. For his part, Alexander Hamilton rued the day that Burr, "by a trick established a Bank, a perfect monster in its principles, but a very convenient instrument for profit and influence."[123]

Republicans concurred in the bank's instrumentality. Moreover, in the

wake of the Jeffersonian Revolution of 1800, Republicans justified their partisan use of a bank by concocting political histories that labeled the Bank of
New-York and the New York branch of the Bank of the United States as banks
that were and always had been exclusively Federalist. They aided "aristocratic
influence among the poor but industrious classes of society," according to
one writer, and enforced a "system of terror which was acted upon at the election in '99," when the city's two incorporated Federalist banks behaved like
"bullying menaces . . . to intimidate the weak and dependent."[124] "Banks in
this City, prior to the Manhattan establishment, were notoriously as much
subject to the influence of party, as the purse of an individual," wrote James
Cheetham in 1801. "To pursue their aid," he said, "it was necessary to be of the
same political color as themselves."[125] Incorporated banks, in Cheetham's
words, were "weapons of faction."

Considered in its totality as an institution—as a Republican-governed incorporated water company and bank—the Manhattan Company represented
a new chapter in the development of American corporations and political
economy.

As legally privileged state creations, corporations had long been political
entities. But in the light of the formation of organized political parties, it was
an open question concerning how such useful instrumentalities of the state—
incorporated financial and transportation ventures as well as grants of
monopoly—would become integrated into the increasingly partisan political
system. Would the practice of political economy constructively coexist with
partisanship, or would the political and economic interests that germinated
within corporations instead challenge institutional political parties?

New Yorkers' experience with banking provided an answer. As a third
bank in the city that served as an alternative source of credit for people restrained or rejected by its counterparts, the Manhattan Company's creation
and Republican-ness directly challenged Federalists' often repeated claim to
best represent the commercial class in the city.[126] The company shattered the
exclusivity of the links among federalism, banking, and commerce forged by
Alexander Hamilton and perpetuated both in the Federalist press and
through the interwoven connections of Federalist bank directors and office-
holding Federalists. Departing from the Federalists' restrictive, and therefore
increasingly elite, vision of banking, Republicans answered the monetary
needs of merchants and tradesmen by offering broader access to credit while
aligning the political and economic interests of New Yorkers with a partisan
electoral agenda.[127] Unlike the Tammany Society or Democratic-Republican

club, the Manhattan Company was not merely a setting for party meetings where people plotted "paper wars" in city newspapers and handbills. Instead, the Manhattan Company's founding signaled that Republican leaders wanted to participate in the distributive politics of early America's political economy.[128] Deliberately designed to advance the personal and political fortunes of Republicans, the Manhattan Company's bank empowered Republican leaders to integrate themselves into the financial and civic lives of New York City voters. By offering patrons and clients access to bank credit and by becoming an investor in fellow Republicans' enterprises, the company attached a material benefit to Republican Party membership that could not be replicated by existing Democratic-Republican societies. The integration of banks and their political entrepreneur directors and clients into early American political parties, meanwhile, vested those parties with permanence and stability. Bank directors—instantly ushered into the city's so-called monied elite— each headed multiple subsidiary networks of credit through which capital reached middling merchants and tradesmen; the establishment of the Manhattan Company enabled republicanism to politically consolidate itself within a highly capitalized financial institution in which the investors were also invested in the electoral success of Republican candidates for office. Manhattan Company shareholders voting for Republicans, as both shareholders and civil voters, were thus voting in support of the longevity and success of their company.[129] In a period before parties could rely on state patronage networks or autonomously fund and staff their own organizations, corporations like the Manhattan Company served as poles of profit and opportunity around which partisanship was encouraged, maintained, and even incentivized.

Moreover, the Manhattan Company's dual roles as a water utility and a bank offered directors, clients, and shareholders a material stake in the civic life of the city, signaling that as political parties emerged in early America, their demand for state-sanctioned enterprises to structure the marketplace and facilitate commerce would only accelerate. By virtue of its institutional form, the Manhattan Company aggregated political, financial, and social activities under the aegis of a civic project. As the company dug wells and laid pipes, observers saw physical evidence that banking had augmented rather than supplanted the directors' original charge. Through a purchase of stock shares as an owner or a payment of interest as a debtor, those who channeled money to the company became participants in a project to improve the health and quality of New York City itself.[130] The company's partisanship did not detract from this mission; rather, the Manhattan Company's engagement in both commercial and infrastructural improvements meant that an association with the company—as a depositor, borrower, contractor, or client—could confer partisan and civic identities that were complementary. Put simply, partisanship provided a path to becoming enmeshed in the commercial, civic, and ceremonial life of the city.[131]

Political entrepreneurs could therefore welcome the development of political parties as coalitions that would continue the habit of outsourcing internal-improvement projects to mixed-economy enterprises. In addition to being a useful tool for aggregating financial, human, and political capital, the corporation could now also satisfy the increasingly sophisticated electioneering needs of officeholders and the ambitions of constituents who sought favorable consideration for their pet projects. Before parties matured enough to fund their own organizations and patronage networks, corporations like the Manhattan Company modulated the voter-party-legislator relationship by providing leaders and voters with common interests, encouraging partisanship by offering opportunities for personal profit and public responsibility. Six years after the election of 1800, Republican pamphleteer James Cheetham pronounced that "Federalism retained its domination until the establishment of the Manhattan Company; after that event its empire became dissolved."[132] To the extent that Federalism dissolved in the waters of the Manhattan Company, it did so in a shower of paper—the Manhattan Company stock certificates, banknotes, checks, and charter that Republicans used to build their Revolution of 1800.

CHAPTER 4

"To Occupy All Points"

In 1809 Robert R. Livingston started keeping an account book. As one of the richest men in the United States and one of the largest landowners in New York State—not to mention a judge, diplomat, bank director, and promoter of merino sheep—Livingston kept many account books during his lifetime. But this was the sixty-three-year-old Livingston's first account book tied to his new transportation business. Two years earlier, in 1807, he and the engineer Robert Fulton had launched a steamboat that mastered the Hudson River's current and won them a monopoly: the exclusive right to run steamboats in New York State for twenty years. After spending nearly a decade and untold thousands to build and berth this first boat, the *Clermont*, the duo was soon at work on a second vessel.

Livingston probably picked up the account book at T. B. Jansen & Co., a stationer and bookseller on Pearl Street in lower Manhattan, steps from the boat slips on the north-south lane that traced the city's original eastern banks. Jansen stocked everything a New Yorker would need to keep business records: "ledgers, waste, blank, and receipt books of every size . . . ruled to any pattern, and bound on the shortest of notice" as well as quills, ink, sealing wax, and penknives. In addition to books on "history, divinity, law, physic, novels, & c." and "the most useful of School Books," the shop sold manuals concerning how these different species of account books should be used.[1]

Livingston's new codex was blank, and it was technically called a *waste-book*: a palm-sized notebook that could be tucked into the waist of one's breeches or plucked from a coat pocket. According to John Mair's authoritative *Book-Keeping Modernized, or Merchant-Accounts by Double Entry, according to the Italian Form*, first printed in 1736 and sold in its eighth edition at Jansen's shop, the waste-book (if not a book title) was supposed to be marked by brevity. It was to be a comprehensive yet simple record of agreements, prices, and information, recorded plainly and chronologically. Properly used, it would provide a record of "every occurrence that affects [the owner's] stock, so as to impair or increase it," spanning anything from most formal arrangements to word-of-mouth wagers. Before a contract was drawn up, a receipt issued, or a statement calculated, it went in the book. Gradually, a waste-book was filled with contemporaneous records of both mundane and momentous transactions and events that marked the daily life and monetary mindset of the book's user. Yet as a historical source, the waste-book is more than a timeline of deals and contacts. It is a record of priorities, revealing what the user believed to be not only useful in the moment but also important over the long term.[2]

Robert Livingston may have bought and started this account book, but it had two users: he shared it with Robert Fulton, his partner in the steamboat enterprise. More than two hundred years later, it is available for inspection at the New-York Historical Society. The library's catalog calls this leather-bound volume, with its elegantly marbled Florentine endpapers, an "account book"—either out of simplicity or because the "waste-book" label does not suit the book's upholstered dignity. Yet it was undoubtedly used as a waste-book. In both men's hands, Livingston and Fulton recorded that their venture purchased fire insurance, used iron forged in Connecticut's Litchfield County, deposited money in the Manhattan Company bank, ordered copper plates from Paul Revere, and spent a total of $15,176.14 to build their second steamboat, called the *Car of Neptune*. From these notes and figures emerges a portrait of how much coal, wood, and cash a steamboat consumed.[3]

But from those numbers and across its pages, the book also reveals a striking divergence within this partnership: Robert Fulton wanted the recognition of a federal patent and the validation of his countrymen for being the "inventor" of the steamboat, while Robert Livingston sought to make a return on his investment. In Fulton's hand are recorded legal fees for depositions and filings and lawsuits against other steamboat designers and builders; in Livingston's hand are expenses for lobbyists and notes about rival steamboat operators. And within an account book that recorded not just transactions but priorities, the most striking evidence of this divergence is found on the inside cover, where Livingston clipped and pasted a portion of the New York Senate's journal of 27 March 1811, when members approved a law that gave broad powers to the steamboat monopoly run by him and Fulton. It directed state courts to issue injunctions against illegal rival boats on Fulton and Livingston's behalf, prescribed $2,000 fines and yearlong prison terms

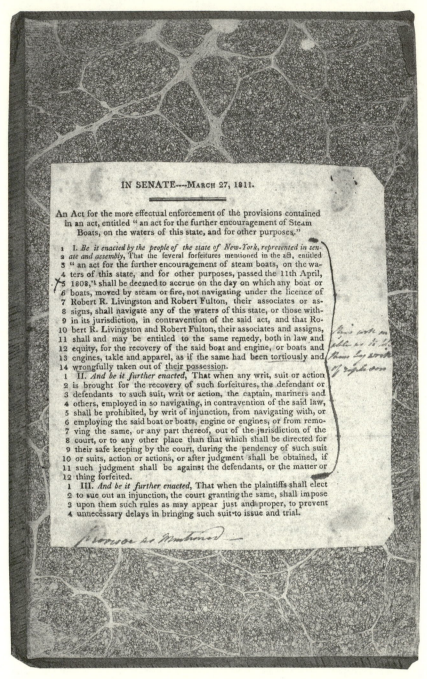

IN SENATE----March 27, 1811.

An Act for the more effectual enforcement of the provisions contained in an act, entitled " an act for the further encouragement of Steam Boats, on the waters of this state, and for other purposes."

1 I. *Be it enacted by the people of the state of New-York, represented in sen-*
2 *ate and assembly,* That the several forfeitures mentioned in the act, entitled
3 " an act for the further encouragement of steam boats, on the wa-
4 ters of this state, and for other purposes, passed the 11th April,
5 1808," shall be deemed to accrue on the day on which any boat or
6 boats, moved by steam or fire, not navigating under the licence of
7 Robert R. Livingston and Robert Fulton, their associates or as-
8 signs, shall navigate any of the waters of this state, or those with-
9 in its jurisdiction, in contravention of the said act, and that Ro-
10 bert R. Livingston and Robert Fulton, their associates and assigns,
11 shall and may be entitled to the same remedy, both in law and
12 equity, for the recovery of the said boat and engine, or boats and
13 engines, tackle and apparel, as if the same had been tortiously and
14 wrongfully taken out of their possession.
1 II. *And be it further enacted,* That when any writ, suit or action
2 is brought for the recovery of such forfeitures, the defendant or
3 defendants to such suit, writ or action, the captain, mariners and
4 others, employed in so navigating, in contravention of the said law,
5 shall be prohibited, by writ of injunction, from navigating with, or
6 employing the said boat or boats, engine or engines, or from remo-
7 ving the same, or any part thereof, out of the jurisdiction of the
8 court, or to any other place than that which shall be directed for
9 their safe keeping by the court, during the pendency of such suit
10 or suits, action or actions, or after judgment shall be obtained, if
11 such judgment shall be against the defendants, or the matter or
12 thing forfeited.
1 III. *And be it further enacted,* That when the plaintiffs shall elect
2 to sue out an injunction, the court granting the same, shall impose
3 upon them such rules as may appear just and proper, to prevent
4 unnecessary delays in bringing such suit to issue and trial.

Figure 4. This is Chancellor Robert R. Livingston's waste-book, in which he kept notes on his steamboat monopoly's business and legal expenses. Pasted inside the cover is a copy of the law that the New York legislature approved to help Livingston and Robert Fulton defend their exclusive rights. Courtesy New-York Historical Society.

for those boats' owners, and enabled the two monopolists to take possession of the boats. It was presumably Livingston who cut out and mounted the text of this last portion of the law—the police powers he and Fulton now held—because next to it is scribbled in his angular, hurried penmanship: "this will enable us to [stop] them by writ of injunction."

Between 1809 and 1812, Robert Livingston invested more than $24,000 in steamboats. That was in addition to what he spent to win a monopoly grant—along with subsequent extensions, enforcement provisions, and legal privileges—from the state of New York. Every dollar that passed through the enterprise affected him materially. Livingston invested in steamboats because the state offered him a monopoly, and the viability of his enterprise depended on his ability to attract future investors and customers without being forced to race to the bottom in what he charged for passengers and freight. He saw to it that every additional steamboat that he and Fulton put into service stretched the lifetime and reach of their grant, offering a better chance at profitability.

Unrestricted competition threatened their enterprise with ruin, and even limited competition—if tolerated—would make any "monopoly" privileges little more than a legal fiction. Therefore, what Robert Fulton was willing to spend on attorneys in courts fighting for his patent, Robert Livingston would spend on lobbyists in legislatures fighting for his investment. A state monopoly is a creature of law and politics, and the New York steamboat monopoly depended on the enforceability of those laws and the good relations Livingston and Fulton maintained with the authors of those laws. Livingston did not consider the monopoly he held to be something that was static, nor was he content to accept the original laws New York passed on his and Fulton's behalf. Instead, he convinced legislators to deputize him and Fulton as state agents, giving them two separate yet equally important powers: the authority to police their own monopoly law and the access to courts where they could prosecute the offenders. Therefore, the 1811 enforcement law pasted on the inside cover of the waste-book was part police badge and part trophy. As much as any monetary transaction, agreement, or contract recorded in the book, it was a financial asset held by the monopoly: it illustrated that Livingston and Fulton not only had exclusive rights over steamboats in New York but also had enough influence—within a broader economy of influence—to sway the state government to enlarge, modify, and reaffirm these rights in spite of pressure from competing interests.

A clipping in a waste-book offers a momentary glimpse into the mindset

of one of its owners, but it also reveals some of the financial context and economic implications of New York's steamboat monopoly laws. To be sure, the
monopoly was a creature of statutes, but it functioned as a business. Political
wrangling over the wording of those laws may have taken place and been
documented in the chambers and journals of the state legislature, but that
was a proxy fight: the real clashes were happening on the rivers and in the
harbors of the northeastern United States. What appears in the law books is
there because of what happened in the account books. And the laws governing the steamboat monopoly, as expansive as they were on paper, were neither applied in the ways that opponents had feared nor were as fearsome as
monopolists had hoped.

Yet this rich context eluded even Fulton and Livingston's contemporaries,
who could trace a line through more than a decade of steamboat legislation
and find themselves led from Albany to Washington, D.C. There in 1824, the
Supreme Court's decision in *Gibbons v. Ogden* set a precedent for how the
Court would interpret the Constitution's prohibition on state interference in
interstate commerce.[4] Chief Justice John Marshall ended the monopoly's
meddling beyond New York's borders and capped the end of its narrative
arc.[5]

Because the monopoly's legal history ascended from parochial begin-
nings to such a momentous conclusion, it is understandable that the focus
has primarily been drawn to law books instead of waste-books. But historians' fixation on the *Gibbons v. Ogden* case transplants the steamboat monopoly from its native New York to the federal soil of Washington, D.C.,
inadvertently ignoring its commercial and political contexts. Although the
judiciary's evolving views of interstate commerce and its own constitutional
role surely merit the interest of historians, examinations of the steamboat
monopoly that aim to explicate *Gibbons v. Ogden* often must start with a pre-
sumption that the monopoly was inherently dysfunctional, leading research-
ers to scour statutes in search of evidence to support that view.[6] Likewise,
studies of Fulton and his steamboat—cognizant of the veneration he showed
toward his patents and the rhetorical efforts of his legacy's guardians—are
drawn toward analyses of the deficiencies in federal patent laws, the contested meaning of the title "inventor," and Americans' immature understanding of intellectual property in the nineteenth century.

Neither of these aforementioned approaches—legal or intellectual—to
the history of steamboats confronts how the monopoly functioned day to day
as a transportation enterprise. Although the monopoly repeatedly sought

protection in laws, it nevertheless operated as a commercial concern. Amid a political economy in which money and influence could not be monopolized, Livingston and Fulton dealt with the reality that the laws protecting their enterprise were compromised from the start. First, their rivals—though operating illegally—had investors, assets, and allies of their own. This meant that, no matter how many police powers the monopolists wielded, they were limited by what they perceived to be politically possible and publicly acceptable. Seizing the wrong boat from the wrong owner risked prompting backlashes from the owners' and investors' allies in Albany, not to mention the customers of the seized boat. Second, while Robert Livingston lobbied to win police powers from the state of New York to strengthen his monopoly claim, he was running a passenger and freight business—not the Coast Guard. Just as the state of New York lacked the capacity to design, test, and launch steamboats, it had little ability and even less desire to physically seize illegally operated steamboats. Even though the state legislature could direct state courts to issue injunctions, fines, and prison terms on the monopolists' behalf, it still fell to the monopolists to file legal briefs and do the dirty work of prying a steamboat out from under the feet of its captain and owners. Vessels powered by coal-fired boilers, capable of ramming speeds, and larded with iron parts and sharp-edged tools are not easy to seize from territorial mariners; the monopolists would be lucky if pilots fought back only with withering verbal assaults.

In the face of such pecuniary, political, and practical obstacles, the monopolists often asked themselves two questions before lodging complaints against rivals: was it in their financial interest to win, and was it in their political interest to try? More often than not, the answer to both was no. In fact, Livingston and Fulton mounted legal challenges to rivals only as a last resort, preceding such cases with bargaining and offers to compromise. The monopolists' conflicts erupted into public view only when those private negotiations faltered, often because rivals saw an opportunity to politically weaken the monopoly or challenge its legality. Even then the monopolists held off from filing actual lawsuits; instead, they pointed to the statutes in their favor to scare their competitors back to the table. Resistance was futile, yet they were ready to deal.

Thus the paradox of New York's steamboat monopoly was that although its laws were written to forbid competition, those laws instead encouraged competitors to collaborate with the monopoly. This monopoly, such as it was, was never able to escape challenges from illegal rivals because the New York legislature existed in an economy of influence. The state assembly and senate was a marketplace of proposals and counterproposals, and steamboat competitors repeatedly tried to build coalitions to defeat the monopolists' coalitions, while the monopolists responded by seeking ever-stronger statutes in Albany. Once they won those laws, Livingston and Fulton and their successors used them to co-opt their competitors, absorbing rivals and declining to punish when they could instead persuade.

The explanation for this paradox is revealed in Livingston and Fulton's account books: steamboats were expensive, but monopolies were not designed to attract new investment capital. New York's legislature already understood the utility of the corporation: the state could draft a charter that granted specific legal privileges to a set of shareholders who were charged with engaging in a particular task, thereby encouraging investors to pool their capital to produce a public good. But the state did not start out by giving Robert Livingston and Robert Fulton a corporate charter. Instead, they were given an exclusive right to operate steamboats. When they did incorporate a steamboat company, its operations were conducted under the monopoly privileges individually held by Livingston and Fulton.

Thus the *Gibbons v. Ogden* case, an epic moment in the legal history of interstate commerce and constitutional law, was not simply about a monopoly run amok and colliding with neighboring states. Rather, it was sparked by an intra-monopoly conflict that happened to take place on interstate waters claimed by New York: an unintended consequence of democratizing a monarchical and an exclusive privilege to conform to the economic and political imperatives of a federal republic. The case did not end the monopoly itself, which continued until the late 1830s, nor should it signal that the steamboat monopoly itself was a failed experiment.[7] Given that the initial goal of the New York legislature was to encourage the experimentation and deployment of a fleet of steamboats on state waters, the monopoly would likely have to be judged a success based on the scores of boats operating in New York by 1824.[8] *Gibbons*, then, is one of several moments of conflict that reveal a broader story: the utility and shortcomings of state-granted monopoly privileges in the early republic, and the costs and benefits incurred by the people who possessed them. And before Gibbons and Ogden, or Livingston and Fulton, that story begins with the New York legislature and John Fitch.

New Yorkers were aware of the immense opportunities afforded by the state's expansive territory, having commissioned surveys during the 1780s and 1790s to assemble an inventory of potentialities.[9] Although the public could at times be wary about the viability of experiments and inventions, there was an enormous appetite for lectures on the natural sciences and news of new inventions.[10] The steamboat was understood to be an invention—or innovation—that combined existing technologies: the steam engine and the paddle wheel.

In a state as vast as New York, the prospects of such a development were boundless. Not only did the state's chief port, New York City, afford access to Atlantic and interstate coastal trading, but the city's western border, the Hudson River, was a 325-mile-long ribbon that ran past the state capital at Albany to Lake Champlain. For legislators who braved uneven, splattering roads to reach the state capital, the prospect of making the journey by boat may have presented an immediately attractive alternative. But the far larger potential to sail against winds, tides, and current was promising enough to justify the encouragement of steamboat inventors.

But even if New York State had the capacity to fund such a venture (it did not), it lacked the requisite expertise to evaluate the technological merit of particular experiments and projects. This was also the case for most private investors. The multiplicity of inventive enterprises in early America thus not only precluded direct state investments but also militated against aggressive private investments.[11]

Yet the political economy of New York in the late eighteenth and early nineteenth centuries embraced active state intervention in economic development. The state and city of New York regulated the activity of the city's trading houses, appointed auctioneers, established weights and measures, levied import duties, and founded a Manufacturing Society to which the state subscribed the first one hundred shares.[12] Economic issues were decided not merely by privatizing particular enterprises or favoring particular interest groups, but by defining the scope and rules of the market as a whole.[13] State policy was pragmatic, predicated on an assumption that governmental involvement in economic and mercantile activity was a regulatory mechanism beneficial to the common good.[14]

To mobilize capital toward useful ends and promote useful improvements and enterprises, states dispensed legal privileges and tools to incentivize experimentation and encourage capital formation. This came in the form of franchises, licenses, tax exemptions, corporate charters, and grants of exclusive rights for inventions or rights-of-way.[15] Revolutionary and postwar rhetoric were hostile to monarchical institutions and privileges, and few legal creations were as closely associated with monarchy as monopolies and corporate charters. Paradoxically, however, both thrived in the post-Revolutionary era. From the 1780s onward, New York and other state legislatures enthusiastically embraced charters.[16] Advocates of such legal instrumentalities argued that their publicly sanctioned activities reconciled them to republican ideals.[17] Thus the corporate charter and exclusive grant could mobilize idle capital and tame the threat of speculation by directing funds toward the public good, rationalizing speculation by subjecting it to a modicum of state regulation and direction. A guarantee of exclusive rights could enable entrepreneurs to attract a pool of investors among the risk-tolerant speculators, while also giving the state the option to shift its favor from one entrepreneur to another. Speculators, long blamed for destabilizing the city's economy throughout the 1790s, could be encouraged to be innovative and congruent to the public good; speculative capital, invested in inventions, became republican.[18]

It was in this environment that New York first offered exclusive steamboat privileges to John Fitch in 1787. An inventor born in Connecticut and living in Pennsylvania, Fitch tried to duplicate the steam engine designed in Britain by James Watt but that was unavailable to Americans because its export was prohibited. In late 1787, Fitch publicly launched a steam-powered boat on the Delaware River before members of the Constitutional Convention. Several states offered Fitch a monopoly if he could replicate the efforts in their waters—New York's was for fourteen years—and in 1791 he was granted a federal patent. But John Fitch delivered no boats to New York. Another federal steamboat patent was given to James Rumsey, narrowing the scope of Fitch's claim to steamboat technology. After losing both pride and investors after years of successive failures, Fitch committed suicide in 1797.

New York's steamboat grant did not lie dormant for long. Steam's prospects captured the imagination of the patriarch of the state's wealthiest family, Robert R. Livingston. Following Fitch's death, Livingston entered into an agreement with two inventors—John Stevens and Nicholas Roosevelt—to build a steamboat, and petitioned the New York legislature to reassign Fitch's grant to him, which they did in 1798.[19] Fitch had died before producing a boat in New York, therefore New York's legislators owed his heirs nothing and were free to reassign his monopoly privileges to Livingston.

Livingston's grant gave him the exclusive right to operate steamboats within the state for a limited, decade-long period, providing that he demonstrate a boat publicly before a group of New York politicians by 1806. The potential profits of a statewide monopoly would more than make up for the expenses he would incur along the way, encouraging Livingston to push on even after costly and repeated failures.

Robert Livingston fancied himself a technological and an agricultural improver, yet within a few years he seemed prepared to let this steam dream slip quietly away. His boats were failures. And his relationship with Stevens and Roosevelt faltered under his insistence that the two engineers continue to use his sketches, despite their doubts about the functionality of his designs. Livingston treated them as employees rather than partners, believing that if it was his money being put at risk, Stevens and Roosevelt owed labor instead of opinions. Livingston's enthusiasm for steamboats was rekindled, however, when he met Robert Fulton in Paris in 1801. Sent by the Jefferson administration to negotiate the purchase of the Louisiana Territory, Livingston, then fifty-five years old, was introduced to Fulton by the American poet Joel Barlow.

Fulton proposed a different boat design than Livingston's and envisioned dodging the import restrictions that had dogged John Fitch. With an engine bought in Britain and a hull crafted by Parisian shipwrights, Fulton put Livingston's capital to work. Despite Fulton's use of side-mounted paddle wheels—contradicting years of Livingston's insistence to the contrary with his original steamboat partners—Livingston had no hesitation about signing a partnership with Fulton. He told his brother-in-law, New York attorney general Thomas Tillotson, "You know my passion for steam boats & the money I have expended on that object." He continued,

> I am not yet discouraged & tho all my old partners have given up the pursuit I have found a new one in Robert Fulton a most ingenious young man. . . . We are now actually making experiments upon a large scale upon the Seine[.] Sh[oul]d they succeed it would be mortifying to have any other competitor for the advantages—I have therefore drawn a short petition which I hope you will reduce to the form of law[,] copying the old one only substituting Fulton's name & mine & reducing the size of the boat to one of twenty tons instead of thirty.[20]

Part of an influential family that included Tillotson, Governor Morgan Lewis, and a cousin named H. Brockholst Livingston—the recorder of New York City–Robert Livingston could touch the center of New York's political structure even from a European capital. As Livingston requested, Tillotson drafted a revision of Livingston's original steamboat grant that replaced Nicholas

Roosevelt and John Stevens's names with Robert Fulton's, and added two years to their experiments. It passed the legislature in 1803.

Later that year, both in a bid for patronage from the French government and to test for an eventual New York model, the duo launched their first boat.[21] Even before the boat sank, French elites scoffed at their demonstration, but Livingston was delighted to return to technological tinkering. The one-time bank director had no intention of being remembered as one of the people he warned his brother-in-law about in 1803: "monied men" with "no home, no country" who bred "extravagance" among noble "farming citizen[s]."[22]

Livingston was likely also anxious about damaging his reputation by abandoning his prior experiments before achieving success. In the four years between Livingston and Fulton's Parisian and New York steamboat launches, Livingston was able to self-finance most of his and Fulton's work. He also appealed to relatives and assembled a small cadre of outside investors, but they were only willing to lend him their money if they could remain anonymous, lest they be embarrassed by being associated with a boondoggle so seemingly destined for failure as the steamboat.[23] Fulton lamented that he and Livingston "made [an] offer to several gentlemen . . . no one was then willing to afford this aid to [the] enterprise." Not even the offer of a silent partnership was enough to persuade some investors who "feared their folly would become a matter of public ridicule" should the experiments fail.[24] Like a corporate charter, the promise of exclusivity made the monopoly grant somewhat useful for attracting early investors; it fostered the exploratory partnerships that matched well-funded investors to able engineers. By bestowing a vote of confidence first on Livingston, and then including Fulton, the New York legislature provided a rationale for other investors to lend capital to their experiments. At the same time, these investors (unlike those who owned shares of a corporation) could remain anonymous; the monopoly privilege, as an ad hoc tool for raising capital in high-risk investments, offered creditors cover. Their identities and reputations were shielded from some of the economic damage that would follow if the steamboat enterprise went bust. Thus, when Livingston noted that it would be "mortifying" to suffer competition if his steamboats were successful, he was not merely referencing financial risks. Competition would be potentially ruinous for a steamboat enterprise, but what would be truly "mortifying" would be the collateral damage to the reputations of Livingston, his family, and his associates—especially those who, like Livingston himself, were publicly known to be indebted to their experiments.

Functional steamboats had been launched before, and with hindsight Livingston and Fulton's eventual success seems nearly inevitable. Yet they were not expected merely to produce a boat that would float or work for a few hours. Livingston had until 1808 to build a twenty-ton steamboat that could overcome the current of the Hudson River to reach at least four miles per hour in the presence of the governor, lieutenant governor, and surveyor-general of New York.[25] Twenty years passed from the time John Fitch first received a grant from New York's legislature before Livingston and Fulton's boat, the *Clermont*, was launched in August 1807. It took Robert Livingston nine years and three engineers to achieve that goal.

Only one of those engineers, however, was named in Livingston's grant: Fulton. For a man sensitive to mortification, the chancellor's removal of Stevens's name from the New York grant was curious; Stevens was an able engineer who lived across the Hudson on the edge of New Jersey. He was also Robert Livingston's brother-in-law. Seeking reconciliation—and perhaps money—Livingston went back to Stevens years after having him removed from the monopoly grant before the *Clermont*'s launch. Livingston made him an offer, explaining that his and Fulton's experiments during the winter of 1806–7 were expected to cost $5,000. For one-third of that sum—Fulton later called it "just" $1,666—Livingston was willing to offer Stevens one-third of their future steamboat business. Fulton recalled, "My partner, Mr. Livingston, proposed to Mr. Stevens to be a partner with us, to the amount of one-third of every advantage which might accrue from our United States patent and state grants, on condition he would pay one third of . . . our experiments. . . . He declined this offer."[26] Livingston's terms seemed generous, allowing Stevens to buy a one-third share of the monopoly for "just" $1,666 after he and Fulton had invested more than $15,000. Stevens's rejection of this offer from his kin points not only to hurt feelings but also to the perceived weakness of Livingston's position. Before launching a boat, there was nothing that Livingston and Fulton controlled; their exclusive right to operate steamboats in New York was provisional and temporary, and it gave them no authority to prevent others from launching a boat first and lobbying to have the state's exclusive rights reassigned.

Stevens had already constructed and briefly operated a steamboat on the Hudson River in 1806, months before Livingston's offer. The boat, called the *Phoenix*, broke down and was being repaired that winter; Fulton insisted to Stevens that their offer was not made from "motives of generosity . . . but from a sense of equity and justice."[27] Just months away from the planned launch of their own boat, the *Clermont*, Livingston and Fulton recognized that if they were successful, it would thereafter be illegal for Stevens to operate the *Phoenix* in the Hudson River. Instead of dismissing Stevens's achievements—the *Phoenix* was likely a superior engineering feat—and causing Stevens financial hardship, they sought to incorporate him into their enterprise. Stevens's previous investments would be protected under the monopoly grant and his talents would be channeled toward the further development of the steamboat, rather than wasted on a competing and illegal enterprise.

Rejecting Livingston's proposition, Stevens counteroffered: he invited Livingston and Fulton to join *his* enterprise, expressing wishes to "avoid collision" with their grant. Together they would "set all competitors at defiance" while "contribut[ing] mutually toward bringing to perfection one of the greatest works for the benefit of mankind that had ever yet been effected." Although Stevens said it was his "sincere wish to unite upon equitable principles," he warned Livingston and Fulton that he felt no obligation to respect their monopoly grant. He remained "at liberty, upon liberal principles," willing to run his boat illegally if it was mechanically superior to or faster than the New Yorkers' vessel.[28] This mutual refusal of offers and counteroffers reveals that although Livingston and Fulton and Stevens were confident in each other's shipbuilding skills, they had divergent opinions about whether New York's exclusive grant was legally and politically sound. The legislature's grant to the New York duo was contingent upon the successful demonstration of a steamboat, but it did not specify that Livingston and Fulton's boat had to be the best, the fastest, or even the first to navigate the Hudson River. The grant was a prize only one team could win.

Although this might have dissuaded others from undertaking steamboat experiments, Stevens believed this exclusivity was open to challenge because he had been a partner with Livingston before Fulton's arrival in New York, giving him a public platform and legal grounds to contest the monopoly grant based on the technical merit of his work. He believed that if his boat was superior and protected by a federal patent, it would be incumbent on the state to nullify the Livingston-Fulton grant. What Stevens did not realize, however, was that state law need not privilege federal patents over state grants; federalism permitted the federal and state governments to make parallel declarations about the provenance of intellectual property.[29] Furthermore, federal patents were notoriously difficult to defend.[30] Unlike a patent, the state grant was premised on neither originality nor superior speed; it was intended to foster the development and deployment of steamboats by conferring a right to operate free from competition. Thus it was incumbent on Stevens, as a competing inventor, to either partner with the grantees or risk losing the thousands of dollars and hours invested in his steamboat; Livingston and Fulton's offer of $1,666 for a third of the monopoly was therefore both underpriced and likely made—as Fulton indicated—out of "equity."

Stevens's counteroffer to Livingston and Fulton, by comparison, undervalued what they brought to his enterprise: a commercially viable future of competition-free operations. Once the Livingston-Fulton boat was in the water, Stevens's bargaining position would be weakened. New York's grant required no additional technological innovations beyond the original terms, so Stevens's engineering knowledge would be of less value to the monopolists. And as the sole entity entitled to deploy steamboats on the waters of New York State, the monopoly would probably be too expensive for Stevens to afford a share as new investors emerged and old investors came out of hiding to call in favors. At that point, the monopoly would have no legal obligations to recognize or reward the innovations of a one-time competitor—even if he had a stack of federal patents to his name.

For Livingston, that day could not come too soon. Having spent more than $40,000 developing the *Clermont*, Livingston and Fulton's accounts were tapped.[31] The boat launched at last on the morning of 18 August 1807, with spectators gathered along the Hudson River to catch sight of the machine. One who saw the smoking boiler and turning paddle wheels said it looked as if "the devil had gone up the river on a saw mill."[32] Shortly after dawn that day, Livingston wrote, "[The boat] leaves town this morning, & will be here by daybreak tomorrow. It now only remains to see whether she will have such a number of passengers as to defray our expenses, & make the proffit we expect. If it does, I shall now have nothing left to wish for."[33] The *Clermont*'s voyage was a public triumph for Livingston and Fulton; starting at New York City, the boat ended its trip at Livingston's Hudson River estate at Clermont, where Livingston (still called "the Chancellor" in family correspondence) announced Fulton's engagement to his niece, Harriet Livingston. In one day, Robert R. Livingston's long labors came to fruition: he launched his boat, took possession of the monopoly grant, and brought his partner into the family.

In some ways, this was the easy part. Now they had to turn a profit.

The New York law granting Livingston and Fulton the exclusive right to operate steamboats in New York gave them twenty years—until 1827—but little else. It offered no structural means to make steamboats a sustainable business venture. It neither encouraged improvement nor contemplated what form and framework a successful steamboat-ferry enterprise might require. It provided no specific legal remedies for the monopolists to use against illegal competitors, nor did it include any mechanisms for the monopolists or state authorities to use when enforcing their exclusive right. In this vacuum, Livingston and Fulton took the initiative in 1808 and petitioned the state legislature for an extension and expansion of their rights.

The resulting legislation, passed with the broad support in both chambers of the capital, created the elastic and expansive monopoly that outlived both men.[34] It fundamentally enlarged the scope of persons eligible to be a part of the enterprise, creating an incentive for Livingston and Fulton to add people to the monopoly and put boats on the water. The law's first section referred to "Robert R. Livingston and Robert Fulton, and such persons as they may associate with them" and later mentioned people who had "license of the persons entitled to an exclusive right to navigate the waters of this state, with boats moved by steam or fire, or those holding a major part of the interest in such privilege." Together these three clauses gave Livingston and Fulton permission to share their exclusive right with others—creating co-monopolists— and signaled the potential for them to sell licenses to subordinate steamboat operators, granting temporary permission for boats to use specific routes or run in particular territorial waters.

The provisions of this 1808 statute, therefore, could be interpreted as mirroring some of the privileges normally embedded in a corporate charter: perpetual life and the right to divide ownership among associates (persons who held an interest) and to grant property rights to licensees. Unlike a corporation, Livingston and Fulton were not given liability limitations; their expenses and debts, like their profits, would be theirs alone. Nor did they gain a formal corporate identity; they would have to personally defend their rights in court. But with a monopoly grant that would last until 1838, it might as well have been perpetual life because it was well past the expected lifetimes of the already elderly Livingston and the middle-aged Fulton. The monopolists' new law envisioned an expanding and complex organization of partners, associations of interested persons, dependents, and licensed franchisees that could collectively exercise police power on behalf of the state through their "exclusive" privileges. The monopoly could exist without its two original grantees, through descendants and associates who would be able to inherit and purchase shares of the monopoly, and who had the option of being jointly represented in court.

The new monopoly law resolved a problem with the original grant under which the steamboat was developed. That first law, in 1798, was a monarchical relic, lightly adapted to serve a republican purpose; it was, however, static. Once the monopoly was active, the law did not allow the grantees to recover debts or pursue illegal rivals, nor did it give them incentives or means to improve their machinery and build new boats by raising capital or hiring engineers. By contrast, the new 1808 statute allowed the monopolists to raise capital by bringing in investors and partners, enabled them to improve their technology by recruiting engineers and associates who could be repaid with rights and licenses, and created incentives for the monopolists to put more boats on the water piloted by licensed would-be competitors who would otherwise have their boats seized by the state and face a year in jail and a $2,000 fine. Thus the monopoly would not be the end of steamboat development but the beginning of a business capable of mobilizing capital and channeling ingenuity toward the improvement and multiplication of steamboats throughout the state's navigable waters. As conceived by Livingston, Fulton, and the legislature, the monopoly would not suppress the talents and resources of the state or become a source of political division; rather, the 1808 law was the most inclusive exclusive grant possible.

Quieting enemies was no small challenge for Livingston and Fulton early after the *Clermont*'s debut. The boat was targeted several times by saboteurs, forcing Fulton to install metal fenders that would protect the *Clermont*'s paddle wheels from damage. Although the new law rewarded the monopolists for recruiting allies, it punished people who "combin[ed]" to destroy a monopoly steamboat. Therefore, for all their flexibility, the monopolists knew they might not be able to fully satisfy critics and co-opt rivals, even after targeting their most recalcitrant competitors with their coercive powers.

Not surprisingly, John Stevens intended to be the first to test this law.

In a series of letters exchanged with Robert Livingston, Stevens insisted that his federal patent gave him the right to navigate a steamboat anywhere in the United States, including New York. He observed that Livingston and Fulton held no such patents, expressed skepticism about the merits and originality of Robert Fulton's engineering, and was dismissive of the idea that Fulton would ever be eligible for a steamboat patent.[35]

Then he re-invited his brother-in-law, the celebrated chieftain of the steamboat monopoly, to become a business partner and notified him that his boat, the *Phoenix*, was scheduled to rise again and resume operations on the Hudson River.

This was a schoolyard dare. Stevens hoped to lure Livingston into a legal trap, believing that the scissors of his federal patent could cut the paper of the New York grant. He also thought the monopoly's popularity could be out-flanked by the faster *Phoenix*, charging that "were it not for the monopoly there might be 500 steamboats navigating occasionally upon the waters of this state."[36]

Livingston's reply was legalistic; he would neither condescend to consider the offer nor respond to Stevens's taunts. Livingston offered a defense of monopoly law and asserted that he was committed to technological improvement. He rebutted Stevens's claims about the deficiencies and unoriginality of the *Clermont*'s paddle wheels (the *Phoenix* was propelled by screws), and reminded his wife's brother, "You refused to come into partnership with us, though we repeatedly requested it, & communicated to you the result of our experiments at Paris[,] because you believed our propelling power more defective than your own."[37] Although Livingston accused Stevens of abandoning him over an 1802 dispute about the steamboat propulsion design, he was in fact revising the record to minimize the circumstances of their falling out, which began well before Livingston left for France. Livingston's goal was not to isolate or insult his onetime friend but to force Stevens to work with him (and for him) in expanding the monopoly. He continued, "I sincerely hope the proposition we have made you may be agreeable. . . . I am satisfied it is more advantageous than the one you propose. . . . Still, I think if you should upon a fair trial succeed so as to run a mile or two faster than we do, that we might make a better plan."[38] If Livingston's courtesy and flexibility arose from a reticence to test the monopoly's rights in court, he did not betray that in his letters. Instead, he was willing to concede the *Phoenix*'s superior speed, make an offer more generous than his prior olive branch, and move forward in a united family-held monopoly. He matter-of-factly warned Stevens that "the penalty [of violating the monopoly] is the forfeiture of [your] boat and engine and £100." And he added that although he was disposed to be generous toward his brother-in-law, his partner, whom Stevens seemed bent on insulting, might tolerate no such deal. "Howsoever much I might be disposed to [offer a deal]," Livingston warned, "I doubt whether the same disposition would be found in Mr. Fulton."

Livingston was rhetorically attempting to play the good monopolist to Fulton's bad monopolist. Even though they initially hoped Stevens would go elsewhere, "considering how large a field the U.S. open[ed]" to steamboat development," they remained willing to deal with him "out of mere friendship."

Even though he mentioned the possibility that Stevens would forfeit his boat under New York law, Livingston said this only to entice Stevens's cooperation. After all, Livingston and Fulton only hoped to convince Stevens of their "undisputed right to navigate with steamboats all waters belonging to [New York]" so that he would realize just how generous an offer they were enclosing.

Livingston told Stevens that he and Fulton were willing to "abandon . . . a portion of [their] rights" that would be "more advantageous to [Stevens] than the partnership [he] propose[d]." Their offer had two parts. First, they planned to run two boats on the Hudson River in New York City and were willing to let Stevens buy a one-fifth share in one of the boats. If it was sufficiently profitable, clearing $15,000 per year, Stevens would see a fifth of that: $3,000. Second, the monopoly was willing to allow Stevens to operate steamboats along two routes: from New York to New Brunswick, New Jersey, and from Trenton, New Jersey, to Philadelphia. Livingston had not been offered a monopoly by either New Jersey or Pennsylvania, but nevertheless considered it in his power to dispense those routes to Stevens. Their arrangement would enable Stevens, Livingston assured him, to "benefit by our invention from New York to Philadelphia" while being "secure . . . against all risque."[39]

Recall that Robert Livingston began this offer by musing that he and Robert Fulton had once wished that John Stevens would take the *Phoenix* elsewhere in the United States, far away from their monopoly. Yet that was exactly where Livingston now proposed to send Stevens, if possible, as a newly minted associate and agent of the monopoly. If he accepted, Stevens would be claiming two interstate steamboat ferry routes for the New Yorkers: between New York and New Jersey and between New Jersey and Pennsylvania. And the first licenses issued by the monopoly would be for travel to out-of-state waters, all because the route originated in the Hudson River and New York Harbor, where Livingston and Fulton claimed exclusive rights to operate steamboats. By dealing with Livingston, Stevens would therefore not only be surrendering his opposition to monopolies in general; he would also be agreeing to become the lead agent for this monopoly's regional expansion into states where they had no actual legal rights to claim any exclusive privileges.

Not long after he dispatched this offer, Livingston sent his brother John R. Livingston to New Jersey, where he offered to buy a share of the *Phoenix* from Stevens. This would permit Livingston and Fulton to license the *Phoenix* to run from New Jersey to New York, so that even if Stevens rejected Livingston's offer, he could escape a confrontation with the monopoly.

But Stevens rejected both offers. This left the chancellor with two options: he could seize his brother-in-law's boat, testing the monopoly law itself by embarking on a legal fight over the superiority of state grants to federal patents, or he could try to force Stevens's compliance, testing the monopoly law's ability to mobilize capital and influence on his behalf.

Livingston chose the latter. Perhaps a court injunction might draw unwanted public attention in New York and legal scrutiny in a federal court, raising concerns about the intended scope of the New York monopoly. Stevens could testify, after all, to both Livingston's effort to concentrate the monopoly among relatives and his expansionist ambitions. Therefore, Livingston decided to hold back from using the forfeiture clause of the 1808 law as a weapon. Instead, he decided to teach John Stevens a lesson about the dangers of competition by threatening to drive him out of business.

The chancellor directed his brother John to begin building a steamboat on the Raritan River in New Jersey, where Stevens was then running the *Phoenix* as a passenger ferry to New York. A second ferry would guarantee that neither boat would be profitable, and John Stevens knew that John Livingston could suffer a deeper and longer loss than he.[40] At a time when banking was still a personal business and credit was granted by way of reputation and references, Stevens was in no position to outspend the Livingston family.

Before the boat could be completed, Stevens folded. He signaled to Livingston and Fulton that he would agree to a deal, forming a "joint concern" as soon as his latest boat was completed. He remained steadfastly opposed to the monopoly's claims, but he said that although he could wage "a vigorous attack," he thought it "unnecessary." Stevens also teased Livingston for not agreeing to his earlier offers, writing, "[Y]ou have as little confidence in my success this season, as I had in yours, last season. So be it."[41]

In the end, neither Stevens nor Livingston was willing to test the superiority of their legal claims. Too much was at stake, particularly because each side was willing to offer settlement terms that he considered generous. So, using the broadest possible geographical interpretation of his grant and exercising the 1808 law's licensing and partnership structure, Livingston forced John Stevens to bargain with him for his commercial survival.

The scope of Livingston's victory was stunning. First, Stevens surrendered his interests in traveling New York's waters, granting his assent to the territorial integrity and legitimacy of the monopoly. Second, he promised to construct a boat with his own money, giving the monopoly five years of additional life for deploying a new boat. Third, the monopolists acquired access to both Stevens's patented mechanical designs and his future work, affirming their active engagement in the discovery and improvement of steamboat technology. Finally—and perhaps most important—they recruited John Stevens to become an agent for the monopoly's expansion. Barred from the interior waters of New York, Stevens was given a seven-year-long license to operate steamboats in places other than New York State.[42] Without filing a lawsuit or seeking permission from neighboring state governments, the Livingston-Fulton monopoly had issued licenses for New Jersey and Delaware River ferry routes, claimed jurisdiction over the entirety of New York Harbor, and asserted that its privileges extended to inland rivers and coastal waters stretching from Rhode Island to Maryland. No courtroom verdict could ever have yielded such riches.[43]

Buoyed by this success, the monopolists began attracting outside investors. Fulton and Livingston were the first to add their names to a subscription sheet for Stevens's steamboats; shares were $1,000 each, and Stevens sought to raise $75,000 to fund three steamboats that would travel on the Delaware River and the Chesapeake Bay. John Livingston, former New York City recorder John Watts, and New York Republican leader DeWitt Clinton were among the first investors.[44] Of the thirteen initial subscribers, all but one were from New York City, and most were directly linked to the two most prominent factions within the New York Republican Party—the Livingstonians and Clintonians.[45] Many in the group, like Stevens, had been involved with the founding of the Manhattan Company.[46]

Able to direct an initial $13,000 toward the Stevens franchise, the monopolists were more financially secure in 1810 than three years earlier. The daily public demonstrations of Fulton's boats, the public enthusiasm for the steamboat, and the security of monopoly privileges made steamboats an attractive investment. In a moment of self-congratulation expressed to his new partner, Fulton told Stevens that "the reputation of the North River Boats stand very high and will give confidence in the Chessapeak establishment." He was certain, he continued, "such notice will be of use in filling your subscription."[47]

With the power to issue licenses and recruit agents and with access to both the criminal and civil courts of New York, the Livingston and Fulton steamboat monopoly was undoubtedly a state institution. Yet it was privately managed and privately funded; its proprietors determined who could operate a steamboat, where it could be operated, and what standards of technology were used. And it operated without regard for federal patents and without competition, enjoying a first-mover advantage that enabled them to define the landscape by which steamboats could operate throughout the northeastern United States.[48]

But how would the monopolists' powers of persuasion work on competitors who were not related by marriage? In the case of John Stevens, Robert Livingston was able to use family connections to intimidate and woo Stevens into cooperating with the monopoly. But Stevens was an out-of-state competitor and never tried to leverage political support among Livingston's political opponents or foment antimonopoly sentiment in the state legislature.

Fulton had long worried about the consequences of in-state competition on the monopoly's vulnerable financial position. In 1807 his co-monopolist calculated that, even if they made three trips per week to Albany with fifty to seventy passengers per trip, their annual profit would clear only $7,000; that was hardly enough to cover the many thousands they had borrowed from the Bank of the Manhattan Company during the prior decade to fund their experiments with the *Clermont*.[49]

Despite having attracted a bevy of investors among New York's financial and political elite, Livingston and Fulton were struggling to achieve solvency. Their only hope for expansion had to come at others' expense. To that end, they absorbed and quieted Stevens, and in 1809 they founded the unincorporated North River Steam Boat Company to manage and fund the construction of their first new boat, the *Car of Neptune*.[50]

But a threat lurked to the north. Beginning in 1808, Livingston frequently began mentioning in his letters an association of engineers and investors from Albany who were interested in steamboats; they were not, however, interested in joining the monopoly or buying a license. That summer, just a few months after the legislature granted Fulton and Livingston the power to seize rival boats, Fulton feared that "unthinking men who had not calculated the expense or profit of the undertaking" would flood the harbor with steamboats.[51]

Livingston already had a label for these "unthinking men": "Albanians." He thought they were an immoral cabal who had been "laughing at his folly" during his decade of experiments and were challenging his exclusive rights by launching a boat modeled after the *Clermont*.

But in truth, although the twenty-one Albanians planned on competing with the steamboat monopoly, they initially hoped to avoid a legal collision. Early on, they anticipated neither needing a license nor risking the forfeiture of their boats because they were building only an ersatz "steamboat," which was to be propelled by a motorized pendulum rather than a steam engine.[52]

The trouble with this plan was that this pendulum motor did not work, so the Albanians decided to directly take on the monopoly by building a near-exact replica of the Fulton-designed *Clermont*. It is unclear whether they posed as passengers aboard the steamboat to copy the design or simply requested a copy of the schematics from the Patent Office in Washington, D.C., where they were on file along with the other documentation Robert Fulton submitted in his 1809 federal patent application.[53]

Using Fulton's patented innovations, the Albany partners in the winter of 1810–11 built a replica of the *Clermont* and began operating it as a ferryboat between Albany and New York City on 1 May 1811. They named the boat the *Hope*. Outraged, Fulton fired off a letter of complaint to Stevens that urged action. "The Albany pendulum geniuses," he wrote, "are proceeding with madness in attempts to evade and oppose my patent." He continued, "[W]e are come to a point when we must lay aside all unnecessary feelings of ambition . . . and combine to oppose our enemies."[54]

Fulton had good reason to be angry. The Albanians had begun diverting passengers from the Livingston-Fulton boats to their own by dispatching agents into the city's taverns and bribing Albany's coachmen to deliver passengers only to the *Hope*. On one occasion, Robert Livingston was traveling on one of his monopoly's boats with a state senator when the Albanians' boat passed by; it was crowded with one hundred people, while his was carrying only eighteen. Even though the *Hope* was "better fit for a coffin than to sleep in," the captain of a monopoly steamboat lamented, "we have all Albany against us."[55]

But the Albany partners' campaign against the Livingston and Fulton monopoly was about more than playing pranks and paying bribes to stock the *Hope*'s inferior berths with passengers. Commercial competition was only the opening salvo in what was actually the Albanians' political war against the monopoly itself. The investors in the *Hope* were drawn from Albany's political and financial elite—including the clerk of the state Assembly. In the words of a Livingston and Fulton defender, the Albanians "made it their business not only to seduce" passengers but also "to traduce Mr. Livingston and Mr. Fulton by the most wanton misrepresentations . . . [making Fulton] looked upon . . . as a vile impostor." The Albany cabal accused Fulton and Livingston of holding back the march of technological progress with their exclusive grant. They even blamed them for boosting the price of wood at Albany's marketplaces.[56]

In response, Fulton called for "combination," his term for a mobilization of the monopoly's political allies, and Livingston began mapping a strategy to defend the monopoly as a public good. Livingston told John Stevens, "[S]omething *must* be done, because the public is complaining that we will neither exert ourselves nor let others do it, without ourselves or our connections having all the boats."[57] Fulton and Livingston, therefore, planned to publicly argue for their monopoly's technical superiority and its ability to meet the growing public demand for access to steamboat service. In that context, Livingston and Fulton could make a case for the monopoly as a positive good and point to its supporters and associates as evidence of its legitimacy and utility in New York's political economy.

By attacking Fulton and Livingston for running a well-connected enterprise, the Albany partners' might have made it seem counterproductive for the monopolists to retaliate by mobilizing their allies. That strategy would only confirm the Albanians' narrative. Yet in Livingston and Fulton's experience, the monopoly's most precious asset was its ability to attract—and even compel—people to ally with them. The revisions Livingston sought in the enabling legislation adopted in 1808 had transformed their enterprise; what started as an experimental boat involving two principals and several employees and equipment suppliers had ballooned into a broad network of partners, associates, agents, investors, licensees, and lawyers linked to the monopoly directly, as well as many more who were shareholders, board members, engineers, agents, and employees of the North River Steam Boat Company. All of them had a stake in the survival and prosperity of the New York steamboat industry. Thus, although it is possible to imagine "the monopoly" as an inventory of steamboats, the proprietors of the monopoly—Livingston and Fulton—saw it as an aggregation of human capital. When the Albany partners asserted that this network was evidence of the monopoly's corruption, they were attacking the essential function and nature of the monopoly itself.

The Albanians were also ignoring their vulnerability to the same charge they were leveling at the monopoly. Their own association existed, in part, because of the Livingston-Fulton monopoly. Their twenty-one investors coagulated a reciprocal network of shareholders and partners who mobilized political allies, agents, mechanics, boat crews, newspaper editors, carriage drivers, tavern owners, and various henchmen of their own. And it was only because the Albanians were so well-connected in the state legislature that Livingston and Fulton were unable to compel their obedience to state law. Although the monopoly had proven itself flexible in absorbing John Stevens, it lacked the critical mass of political capital necessary to avoid this fight, forcing both steamboat associations to leverage their political and financial influence and seek favorable outcomes in the legislative and judicial branches of New York's state government.

The monopoly already had a head start. Even before the *Hope* sold its first ticket, Livingston and Fulton started to lobby the legislature for another law—this time to let them directly seize illegally operated steamboats. They filed their petition in March 1811, two months before the *Hope* set sail from Albany. Both Livingston and Fulton personally trekked to Albany to lobby legislators for stronger legal protections and a more robust method to seize rivals' boats. A judge could make them wait months, they argued, before issuing an injunction against an illegal steamboat, and in the meantime the violators would profit at the monopoly's expense. Livingston and Fulton wanted a "summary mode" to enforce their exclusive grant, and asked the state for the power to directly seize violators' vessels.[58]

The state capital in 1811, however, refused Livingston and Fulton the warm reception they saw in 1808. The glow of the *Clermont*'s launch had faded; they were also on the Albanians' home turf. After procedural delays, Livingston and Fulton were forced to accept a modification to their requested legislation: an exemption for the Albany steamboat and for a second boat then running on Lake Champlain. This new act barred Livingston and Fulton from seizing those boats, forcing them to seek court injunctions under the 1808 law.

They had little choice but to accept this outcome. In Albany, Livingston and Fulton discovered firsthand just how much resentment their exclusive rights excited among certain legislators. With each successive reading in the state assembly, their bill's margin of approval dwindled; on a third reading it was approved with a vote of 45 to 40, and the final vote soon after delivered just a two-vote margin, 44 to 42.[59] The Senate, to Livingston and Fulton's relief, approved the bill later the same day, and without controversy.

Having been unable to defeat the Albanians in the legislature, Fulton and Livingston opted to take their fight to the judiciary. They requested an injunction in what they perhaps expected would be a friendly venue—the federal chambers of Robert Livingston's nephew H. Brockholst Livingston, a former New York state judge who in 1806 was appointed by President Thomas Jefferson to be an associate justice of the Supreme Court of the United States. Much to their disappointment, Justice Livingston dismissed their suit on the grounds that a federal court lacked jurisdiction to hear a case when both parties were from the same state.

The monopolists next tried a familiar venue—the New York Court of Chancery. There Robert Livingston had served as New York's first chancellor following the adoption of the state's constitution. Yet even in that venue he and Fulton found no victory; Chancellor John Lansing refused to grant them an injunction because the monopoly, he claimed, violated the rights of New Yorkers to freely travel on their state's waterways.[60]

Left with one last legal option, Livingston and Fulton filed an appeal in the state's Court for the Trial of Impeachments and the Correction of Errors. During the winter of 1811–12, Livingston drafted many of the monopoly's legal briefs. "I was compelled," he wrote, "to rub up the law which for the past twelve years I have been forgetting & to be counsel to my counselors."[61]

But Livingston did not limit himself to legal tactics alone; he executed a parallel political campaign, hoping to lay the groundwork for a successful outcome before this peculiar court. The Court of Errors was both a legal and a political venue, composed of five judges and five state senators, making it subject to many varieties of influence. Thus, while Livingston worked on his legal filings, he and Fulton also made their case to the public by publishing a pamphlet that refuted Lansing's opinion and reminded readers that their steamboats had been constructed "at the hazard of their fame and their fortune." Their Albany opponents, by contrast, took no such risks, and schemed to "combine, and club their purses" in an effort to "turn [Livingston and Fulton] out of possession" of hard-won privileges.[62]

Behind the scenes, Robert Livingston was counting votes and putting his deep knowledge of the state's institutions to use. Because Chief Justice James Kent had supported the 1808 monopoly law when he was a member of the state's Council of Revision, Livingston assumed they could count on Kent's support again.[63] But Livingston wanted to leave nothing to chance, and to that end he made sure that his most sympathetic allies on the court would be eligible to hear his case. He made sure that people with ties to the Livingston-Fulton monopoly divested themselves of their financial holdings before his appeal was heard. Had they not, they would have been forced to recuse themselves from his case. In one instance, Livingston advised an associate that a state senator named William Taylor was an investor in the Albanians' boat and had not anticipated that their case could come before him, creating a conflict-of-interest necessitating his recusal. The monopoly would have to avoid Taylor and the Albanians' oversight, Livingston observed. "Judge Ingbert thinks there is a possibility of the [steamboat case] coming before the Senate," Livingston continued, "he should not disqualify himself from deciding . . . by holding any similar property." Therefore, Livingston instructed an associate, John Yates—who was himself related to one of the judges on the Court of Errors—to act on Judge Ingbert's "application to strike his name from the [monopoly steamboat] subscription list and . . . repay him his advances."[64] By privately coordinating the divestiture of monopoly holdings among his judicial and legislative connections, Livingston avoided public accusations of impropriety, all the while trying to rig the outcome in his favor.

Livingston's effort paid off. Of ten possible votes on the Court of Errors, four judges and three senators supported the monopoly. In this instance, those seven votes were a unanimous decision; one judge and two senators with financial interests in the Albany steamboats—who almost certainly would have voted against the monopoly—were forced to recuse themselves from the case.[65] The monopolists now had an injunction empowering them to seize the *Hope* from the Albanians.

Livingston was more relieved than elated. He complained that legal expenses and political tiffs got in the way of the business of steamboating. "I begin to tire of all these expenditures, & indeed I have not the means of working with hazardous plans of a boat on the Sound," Livingston wrote to John Stevens, "unless I can get something for our state and patent rights."[66] The chancellor later told his brother, "[I]f you can conveniently spare the money, I should be glad of it" because the steamboats "brought little last year owing to the opposition, & our expenses in law suits & new boats."[67] And although Fulton thought the triumph over the Albanians gave the monopoly "not only the best works but the best prospects in the United States," he too was less sanguine about the finances of the enterprise, admitting, "I am as poor as Jobe pressed by my Bills in the Bank and the children looking for bread."[68] Yet even under these clouds, the monopolists had one last move planned: to offer a deal to the defeated Albanians. After the Court of Errors' decision, the Albany partners made one more trip to the state legislature where they hoped that the state might take custody of their steamboat and its profits, rather than surrender to the monopolists. Livingston traveled to the state capital to confront his "Jacobinal" opponents, but he was conciliatory once they met. He offered a carefully crafted compromise. Instead of seizing the *Hope*, the monopolists located a buyer for the Albanians' boat in Virginia. In exchange for allowing the proceeds from the *Hope*'s sale to defray the monopolists' legal bills, they offered to the Albanians a twenty-six-year license to operate a second steamboat on Lake Champlain, called the *Perseverance*.[69]

The monopolists were pursuing a new goal: "popularity." According to

Fulton, they intended "to occupy all points by which to create support."[70] Never again did they intend to enter into such a costly and bruising competition with rivals. Although John Stevens's challenge offered Livingston and Fulton an opportunity to demonstrate their flexibility, the Albany episode exposed a weakness: even with police powers to seize rival boats, the monopolists could not deter competitors from contesting their exclusive privileges. And the illegality of a challenge would not prevent New York elites—investors, legislators, and judges—from publicly wagering against the monopoly's survival, nor would it carry weight among passengers who resented the monopoly's favored position. Because the very existence of a monopoly inspired opponents and competitors, it became necessary for the monopoly to become as universal as possible, rendering personal and partisan animosities obsolete by "occupying all points" and co-opting rivals as often and early as possible.[71] In the end, the monopoly existed for itself and had to devour rather than defeat its opposition.

Like the corporate charter—many corporations were created to administer monopoly rights—the unincorporated monopoly was a monarchical form reintroduced by state legislatures to post-Revolutionary America. But in contrast to the corporation, there was no easy way to make a monopoly conform to the ideological imperatives of the early republic. Legislators could tinker with the language of corporate charters, using different clauses to liberate or regulate as they saw fit; the steamboat monopoly, however, had no charter or constitution detailing its ownership structure, capitalization limits, and obligations of its managers. New York's steamboat monopoly laws offered little guidance on how the business was to be structured and function. Had it been a bridge or turnpike, this would have been less problematic; in those instances, a petitioner won the right to build a bridge or road on a specific route, and the privilege to collect tolls in exchange for financing and maintaining the infrastructure. Steamboats, however, were a different business. There was no fixed place of commerce or single route that Livingston and Fulton were obligated to service; there was no set of criteria to which they could be held to account that would encourage future innovations and improvements in steam technology. Thus the steamboat monopoly was given a broad privilege for a long time with few strings attached, and its proprietors were thrown into an already competitive market for waterborne freight in which they could travel nowhere that could not already be reached either by carriage or other wind-powered sailing vessels. In some ways, winning the monopoly was the easy part; surviving as a business required different skills.

Holding a monopoly privilege to steamboat technology was valuable so long as there were customers. But to gain more customers, one needed more steamboats traveling more routes, ensuring that passenger and freight tolls were competitive with other transportation methods while being able to exploit the advantages of steam power: speed and distance. And building boats was expensive; it cost nearly $40,000 to build a steamboat in 1810.

The most significant shortcoming of a monopoly, when compared to a corporation, was that it was not an inherently useful tool to attract steady and sustaining streams of investment capital. Corporate shares, traded in exchanges with transferrable ownership, paid dividends; corporations were assigned limitations on the amount of capital they could raise. The monopoly faced no such limitation because it had no moderately priced shares to sell in a stock market that attracted investors seeking dividends. On its face, New York's monopoly laws offered Livingston and Fulton myriad ways to spend money but few ways to raise it. Capital formation was simply not contemplated in the statutes that initially defined the extent of their exclusive privileges.

Recognizing this problem, the monopolists responded in two ways. First, they petitioned other states—neighboring and distant alike—for similar exclusive privileges, citing their New York monopoly rights as evidence of their competence to construct and operate steamboats. Second, they sought modifications and enhancements of New York's laws from the state legislature on two fronts: the newer laws enabled Livingston and Fulton to confront illegal competitors, and offered them incentives—more years added to their monopoly grant—as a reward for launching more steamboats. These alterations added dynamism to what was otherwise a static privilege. And although they appeared to strengthen the degree to which steamboats would remain exclusively controlled in New York State, the laws—in ways not anticipated by legislators—offered Livingston and Fulton the flexibility to confront and co-opt competitors, rewarding their willingness to absorb rivals.

The monopolists responded by turning rivals into allies. Competitors who challenged the monopoly found themselves on the wrong side of the law; instead of taking their boats and making enemies, however, the monopolists offered deals. In exchange for not seizing their boats, the monopolists sold would-be competitors a license to a specific route; Livingston, Fulton, and successor proprietors came away with cash in their accounts, more years added to their exclusive privilege (for adding a boat), and a new set of one-time opponents who were now co-monopolists. The New York steamboat

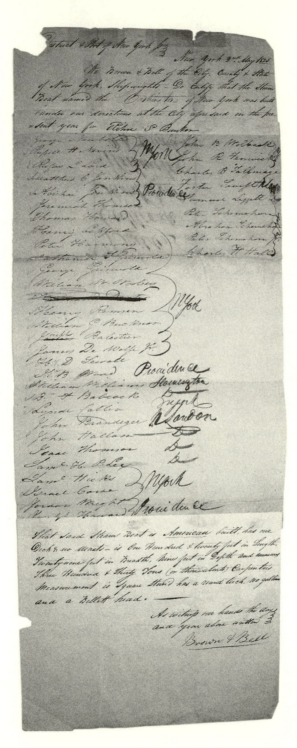

Figure 5. Revealing just how many people were needed to financially support the construction of a steamboat, this 1824 contract for the building of the steamboat *Washington* features the names of thirty-eight investors, hailing from New York, Providence, and London. Source: Private collection.

monopolists repeatedly used their exclusive steamboat privileges to dilute the exclusivity of that privilege, turning rivals into both partners and dependents. Now stakeholders, these licensees lent capital toward extending the reach of New York's steamboats and exerted influence in Albany toward protecting their fellow monopolists.

In Livingston and Fulton's minds, absorbing and appeasing competitors fulfilled an obligation to the public good in addition to these urgent imperatives. Livingston, in fact, long resisted calling his exclusive right a monopoly at all. "It is then to what has falsely been called a monopoly," he wrote in 1811, "that the state owes the incalculable advantage & honor of steamboats."[72] Because the steamboat monopoly was willing to incorporate new partners and improve its technology, routinely making large capital investments in new boats and engines, Livingston did not believe that his privilege shared any similarity to the older, pre-Revolutionary construct. Although rigid on paper, the steamboat laws lobbied for by Livingston and Fulton were used to turn a static and an unstructured privilege into a dynamic and persuasive interest capable of attracting investment capital that it bundled with human and political capital. In their equation, more boats meant more votes.

Gradually, however, this democratization of monopoly privileges unleashed a problem: within an infinitely divisible monopoly that evolved to have separately licensed point-to-point steamboat routes, there was no superintending authority. The state's reintroduction of the monopoly into the nation's post-Revolutionary political economy put a burden on the steamboat monopolists; they possessed a legal privilege without an institutional form capable of addressing their capital and political needs. In response, they improvised statutes and applied them toward sharing their privileges in exchange for economic and political longevity. This made the monopoly accessible to outsiders and consolidated the New York steamboat industry. By picking off rivals one-by-one, however, the monopoly's proprietors inadvertently created competing interests within the monopoly itself. Conflicts inevitably erupted among its members. But without a board of directors, a shareholder election, or a central office with a manager, the proprietors and licensees of the steamboat monopoly had no internal governance structure capable of resolving disputes. In that vacuum, steamboat operators reached out to attorneys who turned to law books. There they found the statutes Livingston and Fulton labored to adopt, written to give the monopoly rigidity and access to courts but never applied in that literal way by their users.

Therefore, five years into its operations, the New York steamboat monopoly remained economically fragile. Its political strategies and tactics were dictated by the numbers in its account books, and as much as Livingston and Fulton's daily lives were their steamboat enterprise, they found that being at the head of a state monopoly required a good deal of political entrepreneurship.

Since first granted a monopoly privilege in 1798, Robert Livingston handled most of the enterprise's political and legal legwork, along with its banking and finances. And since 1802, Robert Fulton handled most of the engineering—boat construction, maintenance, repairs, and specific orders from suppliers and vendors. Like all partnerships, it was not without conflict. Yet it united two diverse skill sets in ways neither partner anticipated.

Therefore, although Livingston's death on 26 February 1813 at the age of sixty-six brought more than a thousand mourners to his estate at Clermont, it left Robert Fulton with a broad and unfamiliar portfolio.

It also invited a significant political challenge. Almost exactly one year after Livingston's passing, Aaron Ogden, the former governor of New Jersey, petitioned the New York legislature to repeal the forfeiture and enforcement provisions included in its 1808 and 1811 steamboat monopoly statutes so that he could legally operate a steamboat between New Jersey and New York.

Prior to becoming governor in 1812, Ogden had been a member of the New Jersey Assembly and had persuaded his colleagues to give him the exclusive right to operate steamboats in that state. As governor in 1813, Ogden lobbied the legislature to strengthen his right by adopting a law that mirrored New York's 1811 law.

New Jersey's law was intended in part to halt John Stevens from using his New York monopoly-granted steamboat license in New Jersey. But its larger purpose was to create parity between the two states' steamboat monopolies. New York's territorial claim made it impossible for Ogden to legally operate his boat in the Hudson River or New York Harbor. Although not endorsing this claim, Ogden had been willing to recognize the New Yorkers' claim to have the exclusive right to land a steamboat in New York. Ogden's ferry line ran from Elizabethtown, New Jersey, to Manhattan, but his steamboat did not make the entire journey. Instead the pilot and crew of Ogden's steamboat, the *Sea Horse*, stopped once they were halfway across the Hudson River, pulled up alongside another boat, and directed their passengers onto that ship. Then the second vessel, powered by actual horses and called a *horse-boat* or *team-boat*, completed the journey and docked at New York. By 1814, Aaron Ogden—and likely his passengers—were impatient with this awkward compromise. Early that year, well before the spring thaw, Ogden sought the right to land his steamboat directly and legally at New York, and asked New York to repeal its monopolists' enforcement powers.[73]

There was no good reason for New York to entertain this request. After all, three years earlier a group of New Yorkers, most of whom lived near the state capital, challenged the monopolists and lost. Aaron Ogden was not particularly well-connected in New York nor did he have favors to call in or partisan support to count on: he was a New Jersey Federalist. And unlike the New York monopolists, he did not spend years cultivating allies and investors with crafty compromises and dispensed favors. Even without Livingston, the monopoly continued to be integrated into the institutional ecology of the state's political economy. On 24 January 1814, one day before Ogden sent his petition to Albany, Robert Fulton and a new partner, William Cutting, signed a twenty-five-year-long, $103,000 lease with the city of New York to run a ferry across the East River from Beekman's Slip on Pearl Street in Manhattan to Brooklyn's "Old Ferry Slip"; they anticipated launching the newly built *Nassau* in May, agreed to the city's demand that they add a second boat to the route by 1819, and formed the New York and Brooklyn Steamboat Ferry Associates Company to raise capital for the enterprise. The New York monopoly hardly seemed weak.[74]

Yet Ogden's petition found a friend in William Alexander Duer, a freshman member of the New York legislature. The son of disgraced Federalist William Duer, who had been Alexander Hamilton's assistant Treasury secretary and whose speculation in U.S. bonds in 1792 triggered a financial panic, Duer the Younger was no stranger to the Livingston family. He became a close ally of Edward Livingston's while the latter was the U.S. attorney for New York; after Livingston was swept from office by a financial scandal and relocated to New Orleans, Duer followed him there to study Spanish civil law. Though Livingston was nominally a Republican and Duer would later be elected as a Federalist, both were thought to be Burrites. However, although Thomas Jefferson merely suspected Edward Livingston of working against him in Aaron Burr's favor after the election of 1800, Duer had actually done so as a contributor to the pro-Burr newspaper *The Corrector* with a group of other Burrites that included Washington Irving. Duer eventually fled Louisiana's heat for New York's mild climes and the moderating warmth of marriage in 1806. He opened a law practice in Rhinebeck, New York, and was elected to the state assembly in 1814. He was sworn in on 25 January, starting his legislative career on the day Ogden submitted his petition.[75]

For a monopoly that absorbed competitors and offered licenses to its most motivated opponents, Duer was probably a nonentity: he was in his first term, he was a Federalist in an era of Republican ascendancy, and he had no financial interest in *any* steamboats—outwardly he maintained that he had "no selfish purpose."[76] Yet Duer was a Federalist in a state assembly controlled by Federalists, vesting him with a measure of influence simply because he was in the majority; he was also one of five assemblymen from Dutchess County, of whom one—James Emott—was elected assembly speaker. In that context, William Alexander Duer was as well positioned as a freshman state legislator could be at the opening of the New York Assembly's thirty-seventh session in 1814.

When Aaron Ogden's petition arrived at Albany, it was not referred to a veteran legislator but instead passed to Duer, who was charged with chairing a special committee for its consideration. Although Ogden might have timed his petition to coincide with the opening of a legislative session run by fellow Federalists, the leadership's choice of Duer to hear the petition all but guaranteed that Ogden would be treated not only fairly but deferentially. After all, when Duer was born in 1780, he was named for his grandfather, William Alexander, Lord Stirling, a major-general in the Continental Army. Stirling gained fame for his bravery at the Battle of Monmouth in 1778, and afterward he singled out for praise the twenty-two-year-old captain who served as his aide-de-camp during the clash: Aaron Ogden.

Ogden's petition was referred to Duer's committee on 25 February 1814; the chairman set a hearing for the following day. In it, Ogden attacked Fulton's inventions, questioning their originality and the provenance of his patents, and suggesting that the only "novel combination" Fulton had discovered was one of "intrigue and powerful connections."[77] Fulton's lawyer, Cadwallader Colden, happened to be in Albany that day lobbying for a charter of incorporation for the York and Jersey Steamboat Ferry Company, Colden's monopoly-licensed ferry route between Manhattan and Jersey City.[78] He learned at noon that a hearing on Ogden's petition was scheduled for six o'clock that evening. Colden corralled another lawyer who had represented the monopoly in the past, former New York attorney general Thomas Addis Emmet, and the two arrived to find Ogden not only in the room but prepared to speak at length. He had with him drawings, exhibits, and even "pretty tin machines and models." Instead of challenging monopoly laws—which he benefited from in New Jersey—Ogden focused on discrediting Fulton's federal patents. Colden recorded that Duer "paid particular attention to [Ogden's] performance...with great satisfaction, and seemed particularly pleased with the moving of his models."[79]

Four hours into Ogden's presentation, Colden pleaded with Duer to allow Robert Fulton, then in New York City and unaware of the proceedings, to come to Albany so that he could personally answer Ogden's charges and defend his patents. Colden stressed that neither he nor the other attorney were engineers or qualified to assess the mechanics of steamboats and the merit of Fulton's federal patents.[80] Their client was being sandbagged; even worse, they did not know why a New York assemblyman seemed so intent on destroying New York's steamboat monopoly on behalf of the former governor of New Jersey.

Resuming his committee's hearings the following day, without Fulton yet present in Albany, Duer gave Ogden broad latitude to continue his attack. In addition to miniature models, Ogden had human props in Albany as well. Two of Robert Livingston's former partners—Nicholas Roosevelt and Benjamin Latrobe—testified that Fulton's steamboat designs were unoriginal. Roosevelt, who had been included in Livingston's original 1798 steamboat plans, was embittered by Livingston's later successes with Fulton. The monopolists tried to make amends and buy his cooperation with a $600 payment to seek out new steamboat opportunities along the Mississippi River. However, once the money ended, so did Roosevelt's silence. He wrote that he volunteered to aid Ogden's cause so that he would "still come in for a share of the payments, after the loaves and fishes have so long been feasted on by Messrs. Livingston and Fulton."[81]

Listening to Aaron Ogden's charges, Duer professed shock and amplified the criticism of Fulton. It was unjust, Duer claimed, that the monopoly had for so long enjoyed privileges when it was headed by an unoriginal engineer who not only "exclude[d] all future improvements by others" but also "prohibit[ed] the use, even by the inventors, of all prior discoveries."

Unable to produce witnesses or evidence on such short notice (clearly Duer and Ogden had planned and possibly rehearsed their colloquy), Fulton's attorneys rejected the charge that Fulton had pirated others' work to help Livingston obtain their monopoly grant. During several committee sessions, they defended the propriety of the legislature's grants and argued that the 1808 monopoly statute was as unbreakable as a contract.[82] They also dismissed Ogden's claim to be a champion of intellectual honesty. Colden wrote that Ogden was little more than an opportunist: one of many "artful speculators . . . with patriotism on their tongues, and selfishness in their hearts, who may mislead some future legislature by false and crafty declamations against the prodigality of their predecessors."[83]

Duer's panel finished its hearings before Fulton had the opportunity to defend himself, concluding in its report that the Livingston-Fulton monopoly had been granted under false pretense because Fulton was not the original inventor of the steamboat. In his report to the Assembly on 8 March, Duer opined that the boats "built by Livingston and Fulton [we]re in substance the invention of John Fitch" and that the expiration of Fitch's federal patent made the monopoly's boats "common to all the citizens of the United States." Although Aaron Ogden's steamboats, Duer continued, were also built "upon the principles invented by . . . John Fitch," they were distinguished by virtue of being "improved" and merited protection. Therefore, Duer rejected Fulton's claims of having improved the steamboat, dismissed the authority of Fulton's federal patent, and further concluded that in 1798 the state legislature's reassignment of John Fitch's monopoly rights to Robert Livingston— the basis of the Livingston-Fulton monopoly—was based on reasoning that was "not true in fact" because Fitch possessed a federal steamboat patent while Livingston did not.[84]

Duer also ventured that the state of New York lacked the authority to "interfere with or prevent the navigation of a vessel in any of the waters of this state, and more especially in any waters lying between this and a neighboring state" when the offending vessel's owner has a federally issued coasting license. Duer told the assembly that the section of the 1811 monopoly law that dealt with enforcement—the clip Livingston pasted in his account book—was unjust because it "shuts the courts of justice" to anyone "who may be desirous of bringing to a legal test the rights claimed by Livingston and Fulton" and could cause even a successful plaintiff to forfeit his steamboat to the monopoly. This was, in Duer's words, "a manifest injustice" and merited the legislature offering Aaron Ogden "relief" under the principles of "faith, honor, and justice."

When confronted with the fact that New York's chief justice James Kent upheld these same laws in the monopoly's case against the Albanians several years earlier, Duer dismissed the jurist's judgment: "[T]he reasoning of the learned Judges . . . stood opposed, upon some points, to the opinions entertained by the Committee." He insisted that any legislation that "vested in individuals, rights hostile in their exercise to the general interests" was an "error."[85] Duer was equally unmoved by observations that Aaron Ogden was neither an inventor nor in possession of a federal steamboat patent, and that Ogden's home state of New Jersey in 1811 and 1813 granted him forfeiture powers that mirrored—and were retaliatory toward—the New York laws that both men were now trying to repeal.

Duer followed his report by introducing legislation in the assembly that would repeal the forfeiture and enforcement provisions of the 1808 and 1811 monopoly statutes. Even as he did this, he claimed to support the New York monopoly, indicating that Livingston and Fulton deserved "gratitude and bounty" in recognition of their "successful introduction of steam boats upon the waters of this state." [86] What they did not deserve, in Duer's view, was any way to protect such a grant.

After Duer made his report to the state assembly, Colden requested a delay on further action until Fulton could offer testimony; he was expected in Albany within a week, and Colden pleaded that Duer's bill would be Fulton's "entire ruin" along with "many who have purchased rights from him under the laws of this state." [87] Fulton finally had an opportunity to address the legislature on a mid-March evening, when the assembly met and invited the state's thirty-one senators to watch from the chamber's gallery.

Duer and his allies tried to use the event to embarrass Fulton publicly. A witness reported that Duer, "with skilful management and usual eloquence," eulogized Fulton "to his face," drawing tears from the engineer.[88] Not to be outdone, Thomas Emmet sketched a sympathetic portrait of Fulton as a publicly minded genius, besieged by an "antagonist" whose motives were "interest and avarice," and concluded his rising encomium by comparing Fulton, successively, to the "light of Heaven," the French revolutionary martyr Marat, and *Macbeth*'s King Duncan.[89]

Duer was unmoved. However, his colleague, assembly speaker James Emott, tried to negotiate a compromise between Ogden and Fulton after the hearing. Emott suggested that narrowly tailored legislation could preserve the monopoly's powers and give Ogden the right to land at New York; Fulton agreed, but Ogden—overestimating his strength—wanted a full repeal of the monopoly's enforcement laws.[90] Two weeks later, on 30 March, the assembly sharpened Duer's proposed legislation and voted to do just that; they voted to repeal parts of the 1808 and 1811 laws by a vote of 49 to 42. But by the time this vote was over, the act was little more than symbolic. Fulton had declared victory ten days earlier. Knowing that their enterprise was gravely threatened, Fulton, Colden, Thomas Emmet, and John R. Livingston, the deceased chancellor's brother, lobbied the state senate, bringing to bear the full weight of their political and financial connections. After expressing support for the 1808 monopoly law's enforcement powers by a margin of 19-to-8, the senate rejected the assembly's legislation by a narrower 15-to-13 vote on 19 March.[91] Fulton declared victory and left Albany for New York City. "I came to defeat Aaron Ogden's projects," he said the following day. "[I] exposed his fallacious pretensions and established my priority of invention and my state rights on a base more secure than formerly because [they are] now better understood."[92] Duer complained that the "splendid eloquence of Counsel at the bar" had been outdone by "the acrimonious effusions of the agents in *the lobby*."[93]

Although Fulton professed to appreciate this high-stakes opportunity to explain the monopoly to a group of legislators who seemed intent on killing it, he did not appreciate Aaron Ogden's gratuitous insults. After its past challenges—with John Stevens and the Albanians—the monopoly usually reconciled with opponents, repeatedly demonstrating its elasticity and enhancing its position by acquiring competitors' capital, talents, and vessels.

But the bitter saga with Ogden and Duer was the monopoly's most serious challenge to date; it barely survived. Livingston and Fulton largely ignored public opinion during the first years of their monopoly; the chancellor resented the "monopoly" label and published two pamphlets on the subject in 1811 to educate and shape opinion. They had never before been forced to sway hearts, minds, *and* votes in the face of open hostility. After the Duer-Ogden challenge, the monopoly was a more politically and publicly engaged organization in Albany. Duer and Ogden forced hostile legislators into the open, making it essential that the monopoly not only finesse its friends but also identify and intimidate its opponents.

The monopoly's subsequent pursuit of Aaron Ogden reflected this new aggressively political, and partisan, reality. Ogden had originally sought an agreement with Fulton before he instead filed his anti-monopoly petition with the New York legislature. Ordinarily he might have expected to receive an offer to join the monopoly after his defeat. But no offer came.

Instead, John R. Livingston, who operated a competitor to Ogden's steamboat and had assumed a comanagerial role in the monopoly after Robert Livingston's death, asked the New Jersey legislature to repeal the former governor's exclusive steamboat grant. Livingston's petition accused Ogden of using "*unbound influence* [to create] an invidious distinction between the citizens" of New Jersey and New York, and of "materially injur[ing]" both his and John Stevens's steamboat businesses, even though—they reminded the legislators—they were "citizens of your own state." They further pointed to defects in

Aaron Ogden's steamboat, starting with its size: compared to Livingston's boat, the *Raritan*, Ogden's steamboat *Sea Horse* was only a third as long.[94]

The New Jersey Legislature granted Fulton and Livingston a hearing, and in mid-January 1815, they and their attorneys descended on Trenton. Albany had been a rehearsal. This time, Ogden was in the hot seat, forced to defend monopolies while the New Yorkers argued that the New Jersey statute infringed on Fulton's federal patent rights and constrained the talents of New Jersey's own steamboat operators. In the end, the outcome was transparently partisan: Ogden, a Federalist, saw his monopoly grant repealed by a 21-to-17 vote. Republicans had gained control of the General Assembly during the previous election; all of them voted against Ogden and in favor of their fellow Republicans from New York.[95]

Fulton had spent years pursuing lawsuits to win respect for his patents. According to Livingston's account book, Fulton had even spent $8 on a mahogany box to house them, making his victory in New Jersey all the more poignant. On their return to New York, Fulton and his party were walking across the frozen surface of the Hudson River to reach Manhattan when Thomas Addis Emmet, their attorney, slipped through the fractured ice and into the gelid slurry. Fulton plunged in and rescued his friend, but he spent several minutes in the water before being pulled to safety. He had a sore throat by the time their party reached the edge of Manhattan. It progressed to pneumonia and then to consumption. Fulton died at his home at One State Street in Manhattan on 24 February 1815. He was buried in Trinity churchyard, immediately adjacent to Alexander Hamilton's grave and in the same cemetery where William Alexander Duer's grandfather, General William Alexander, had been laid to rest.

With the original monopolists deceased, control of the exclusive grant passed to their heirs and associates, as envisioned by the 1808 law. Cadwallader Colden, the lead monopoly attorney, assembled a syndicate of investors who bought the Hudson River steamboats and their routes from Fulton's widow for nearly $100,000.[96]

In addition to taking on partial management of the monopoly and its branches, Colden took it upon himself to become the custodian of the monopolists' legacies as well. This was not merely a historical exercise; Fulton and Livingston's reputations affected contemporary perceptions of the New York steamboat monopoly, then commonly called the "Livingston-Fulton monopoly" even though both men were dead. In 1816, Colden produced a laudatory biography of Fulton that coincided with the renaming of the street that linked the piers of the Hudson and Brooklyn ferries on the west and east sides of lower Manhattan: the name changed from Ferry Street to Fulton Street.[97] Colden's biography was written out of admiration, but it was also plainly commercial and political. And it drew a reply from none other than William Duer.[98] In a public letter to Colden, published as a pamphlet in Albany, Duer resumed his attack on the monopoly and Fulton; he believed that his prior campaign in the legislature had been, if anything, insufficiently aggressive. Colden replied in 1817, and Duer replied again the following year.

Duer's pamphlets offer an antimonopoly perspective of the monopoly's history, resting in part on the (false) claim that the profits of the enterprise were "ascertained to be immense." [99] Duer wrote that there was little "distinction between laws passed to favor *the accumulation* of money, and those enacted for *the security of property*"; the monopoly grant had never been about protecting property rights or steamboat technology. Instead, Duer contended, the monopoly was a machine designed to accumulate and concentrate wealth.[100] It is entirely plausible that Duer was writing this with sincerity. With new articles of incorporation given to Colden and his associates and a small flotilla of steamboats plying the state's waters, the monopoly must have seemed successful to an observer. But because it had been tightly controlled and managed by a consolidated group of Livingstons related by blood, marriage, and attorney-client privilege, few knew what the monopoly's finances actually looked like, or could have guessed that the profits were as lean as they had been in many years. Fulton spent many of his last months engaged in building what he called "new enterprises": steam-powered floating batteries and frigates for the U.S. Navy that would be deployed in New York Harbor. Even as he was at Albany defending his monopoly in 1814, Fulton was updating President James Madison on the project.[101] To Duer, this may have looked like another benefit of patronage and privilege, but to Fulton it was a way to collect a salary amid health and financial setbacks. Even as Duer and Ogden painted Fulton as a rich steamboat mogul in late 1814, Fulton privately worried about how his wife and children would fare if he should die.[102]

Duer's antimonopoly essays were published in 1817, prior to his chairing a second inquisition targeting steamboat privileges in New York. His hero remained Aaron Ogden, whom Duer maintained was a "public spirited vindicator of rights common to every Citizen of the United States" and who "seemed to regard his private interests as identical to those of the Community."[103] Ogden earned such praise when, Duer recalled, he "generously refused a compromise" that would have forced him to "bow down" to the monopolists in exchange for a material gain.[104]

Shortly before Duer initiated a second attack on the monopoly, however, Aaron Ogden decided to become a fellow monopolist. Ogden purchased a franchise for $600 from John R. Livingston to run a ferry from New Jersey to New York.[105] Surprised and disappointed, Duer abandoned his effort to modify the laws protecting the monopoly and instead convinced legislators to tax steamboat fares and steer the proceeds toward the construction costs of the newly started Erie Canal.[106] Duer mounted a challenge to the monopoly again in 1822, but no legislation from his committee received consideration in the assembly.[107]

The monopoly's most dangerous enemy was no longer William Duer or even the state legislature. Rather, it was the monopoly itself. Whereas the steamboat enterprise had once been a partnership of two and then grew to become a secretive and quasi-fraternal organization of Livingstons, invited Republicans, and co-opted rivals, the monopoly in Livingston and Fulton's absence had become a network. After 1817 no significant attack on the monopoly took place because there was no reason to spend the effort when licenses could be purchased from Cadwallader Colden, Thomas Addis Emmet, John R. Livingston, or someone who already had a steamboat license and wanted to share or subdivide the ferry route. Fulton's goal to "occupy all points" became a reality after his death. Although Cadwallader Colden was the public voice of the monopoly, returning fire against William Duer's paper war, Colden was not a manager or controlling owner of the enterprise. He was merely a spokesman for an amorphous collection of franchises, licenses, ferry routes, boats, and stock shares.

Even as New York's regional economy grew, fueled in part by the steamboat, newer steamboat owners and operators had a diminishing dependence on direct routes to and from New York City. Most franchise licenses were owned by the North River Steam Boat Company and the York and Jersey Steamboat Ferry Company, which were incorporated under licenses from the Livingston-Fulton monopoly. These aggregated licenses were the companies' principal assets and not for sale to other private investors—and even if they had been, they would have been unaffordable.

The corporations brought order only to their particular licenses within the larger monopoly because no larger governing authority was managing the monopoly as a whole.[108] Thus steamboat-licensing schemes grew increasingly complicated once the enterprise's hub, Manhattan, became dominated by corporate-owned Hudson River licenses. And because the monopoly lacked a structure to provide for a continuity of governance in the absence of the original grantees, it suffered two other codependent problems that created intractable conflicts of interest among the unincorporated owner-operators of steamboats in and around New York Harbor. First, they held licenses that were narrowly tailored to make them affordable but could nevertheless conflict with existing routes and licenses. Second, although these licenses were haphazardly issued and uncoordinated, they were valuable assets supported by aggressive state laws. Even though this disorder might appear to be the result of political decisions made in the New York legislature, the fault lay with Livingston and Fulton; the state government approved the laws they sought, protected them from attack, and incorporated ferry lines upon request. All told, the legislature was extraordinarily responsive to the monopoly's proprietors, despite the fast pace of turnover among members of the legislature's two houses, changes in the government's partisan composition, and an economic and political environment that was ever more dynamic and competitive.[109]

In this environment, unregulated chains of ownership led to unlikely partnerships. Aaron Ogden in 1816 purchased the right to operate a ferry between Staten Island and Manhattan from the heirs of a deceased partner of Daniel Tompkins. Tompkins, a onetime New York governor, had signed the 1808 monopoly law that Ogden sought to undo in 1814. Two years later, Tompkins and Ogden were in business together as partners in the monopoly. A year later, in 1817, Tompkins was elected vice president of the United States.

The Ogden-Tompkins "partnership," however, existed only in that the men co-owned a ferry route. Theirs was not an official relationship based on contractual obligations, transparency, and bylaws, or even tempered by partisan affiliations or the simple social graces of friendship or decency. Thus, nothing but sober judgment stopped Tompkins from making a separate, private arrangement with another steamboat operator that undermined his "partner" Ogden. And Daniel Tompkins was not known for temperance. In 1818 he sold such a ferry route to a former Georgia congressman named Thomas Gibbons, then living in New Jersey.

Gibbons was a hard-drinking, short-tempered man who invested in banks, roads, farms, hotels, and whatever else seemed profitable. He was thought to have stolen a congressional election in favor of former Revolutionary War general Anthony Wayne in the 1790s and later dueled with the loser of that election. In 1801 he bought a getaway home in Elizabeth, New Jersey, formed alliances with other Federalists in the region—including Aaron Ogden—and established other varieties of connections that drew him into a paternity suit and made a fierce enemy of the painter John Trumbull. Gibbons's career was later described—perhaps charitably—as "a scene of political corruption."[110]

In 1819 Gibbons unsuccessfully tried to run a steamboat ferry parallel to a route owned by Aaron Ogden (who once had Gibbons arrested after he challenged Ogden to a duel for trying to collect a debt on the Sabbath). Ogden sued him under the 1811 law, and New York chancellor James Kent issued an injunction against Gibbons's boats. Gibbons then bought a monopoly-backed ferry license from Vice President Daniel Tompkins that enabled him to bring passengers from New Jersey to Staten Island, where one of the Ogden-Tompkins boats subsequently took them to Manhattan.[111]

What Livingston had called "mortifying" competition had become the de facto norm in New York. Because the monopoly statutes did not provide for anything other than the defense of the rights themselves, the plural economic interests competing within the monopoly had only one political entity to which they could appeal when resolving a conflict: the courts. With fewer barriers to entry in the steamboat monopoly, conflicts increasingly were between people already associated with it. Access to the state judiciary was a privilege the monopoly had been given in 1808 to protect it from competitors. Now in the late 1810s and early 1820s, it became the weapon of choice for dueling monopoly members; the injunction was the chief legal remedy that governed the steamboat industry. Therefore, every time a steamboat operator sought an injunction from the New York Chancery it put the entire monopoly at risk.[112]

Thus, when Vice President Daniel Tompkins, who shared a steamboat license with Aaron Ogden, made a secret arrangement with Thomas Gibbons allowing the latter to compete with one of Ogden's ferries, Ogden had only one place to seek relief: the New York Chancery court. Amid a flurry of lawsuits among Gibbons, Tompkins, and John R. Livingston, Ogden defended his slice of the monopoly rights against Gibbons's incursion. Gibbons appealed the case to the Supreme Court, where he was represented by Daniel Webster and U.S. attorney general William Wirt. They argued that James Kent's injunction was unconstitutional because Gibbons was a New Jersey resident who had a federal coasting license that should give him access to any coastal waterway in the United States.[113]

Ogden, represented by longtime monopoly consigliere Thomas Emmet, argued for the right of New York to encourage inventions and improvement by using its sovereign authority to grant monopoly rights. John Marshall and his colleagues, however, were more concerned with the "war of legislation" they saw among Connecticut, New Jersey, and New York; "[I]f there were no power in the general government to control this extreme belligerent legislation of the States," Marshall wrote, "the powers of the government were essentially deficient."[114]

The common story of the *Gibbons v. Ogden* case is that the Supreme Court settled a dispute over interstate commerce by ending nearly a decade of discord between New York and its neighboring states over the development of steamboat transportation. However, the federal constitutional implications of the Court's sixty-six-thousand-word decision (three times the length of this chapter) are of limited use in illustrating the implications of reintroducing the monopoly privilege in the early republic. Excavating layers of licenses and their chains of custody yields a colorful narrative but one centered on just two overlapping steamboat routes within a monopoly brimming with potential internal conflicts.[115]

As an institution designed to reflect political and legal assumptions about political economy in the wake of the Revolution and ratification of the Constitution, the Livingston-Fulton monopoly was designed to be inclusive rather than exclusive. The 1808 and 1811 statutes expanding and extending the monopoly enabled the grantees to mobilize capital, attract broader participation in the enterprise, and widely distribute its risks. This allowed the monopoly to have the flexibility to both confront and appease its competitors and opponents, responding to problems as they arose with the freedom to pragmatically confront challengers. Thus, the monopoly was maximizing its capacity to be embracing—and disorganized—when John Marshall penned his opinion in 1824.

The vast scope and national scale of the Court's decision overwhelm what was in reality a more parochial intra-state and intra-monopoly dispute, misdirecting attention from a critical shift in New York's political economy that became evident in the years after Robert Fulton's 1815 death. William Duer's multiple challenges to the steamboat privilege were not merely rhetorical exercises, and Cadwallader Colden's biography and subsequent defenses of Fulton were not written to establish a historical record. Rather, they were attempts to, respectively, redefine and defend the political economy of the state and the republic by examining the propriety of granting exclusive monopoly privileges to political entrepreneurs.

The monopoly proprietors responded by intensifying efforts to form alliances, quiet rivals, and overwhelm critics. They protected their privilege by taking advantage of the bonds of partisanship and advancing institutional party discipline in legislative caucuses and among other state agents while manufacturing interest—and conflicts of interest—within municipal governments, in New York's and other states' legislatures, and among governors, judges, and two U.S. presidents.

But William Duer and his allies did not merely counterattack with pamphlets and legislative hearings. Duer's successful push to levy a tax on steamboat-ferry passengers—and direct that revenue toward the newly started Erie Canal—was not intended to be a symbolic victory over the monopoly. Rather, it was a signal that although Duer and many legislative colleagues grudgingly accepted the monopoly's longevity, they intended to consign such privileges to the past and craft future policies to be more accessible, accountable, and moral. Emerging from the crucible of the War of 1812 and the most strident defenses of the monopoly, the state's canal policy deliberately departed from internal improvement and transportation programs based on private advantages and corporate privileges. They were informed by the legislators' experiences with the steamboat monopoly, and they can be read as a rebuke to a steamboat interest that was seen as an agent of corrupting monetary persuasion, partisan influence, and commercial racketeering during a period of rapid peacetime economic and territorial expansion.[116]

Even before the first hearings Duer chaired on the monopoly in 1814, opponents of the steamboat privilege from both New York and other states voiced—across a series of petitions and letters to the New York legislature and the U.S. Congress—strikingly similar objections to and arguments against the Livingston-Fulton enterprise. First, they questioned the legitimacy of Robert Fulton's federal patents on the grounds that his "invention" was only a novel "combination" of prefabricated parts driven by an imported British steam engine.[117] In later years, they also occasionally lampooned Fulton's torpedoes, naval experiments, and canal ideas, before returning again to steamboats and comparing Fulton to John Fitch, the original holder of New York's exclusive privilege. One pamphleteer writing under the nom de plume "Friend of John Fitch" said that Fulton had only a "talent for business" and that if he deserved a "statue"—as Cadwallader Colden suggested in his *Life of Fulton*—then so did the Revolutionary War financier Robert Morris. It particularly irked the writer that Colden's biography had been delivered before the Literary and Philosophical Society of New York, where authentic inventors "should [have been] pitied" until "some other great and fortunate genius discover[s] and overturn[s] 'crank' power again."[118]

A second line of criticism was of the monopoly's police powers, particularly the 1811 law allowing the monopolists to seize boats even before New York courts judged whether injunctions were justified.[119] In contrast to Livingston's waste-book notation, "Friend of Fitch" thought that the law was a sign of weakness: the "unstable ground whereon rests the colossal statue of [a] monopoly" unwilling to test its privileges in court.[120] Months after winning the 1811 New York law, Fulton and Livingston sought a congressional extension of and protection for their patent rights, but both the Albanians and Aaron Ogden petitioned the United States Senate in protest. The Albanians pointed to the New York law and their own pending lawsuit as a reason for Washington to avoid "legislation in particular cases" that could introduce "an odious and oppressive favoritism, in subversion of justice and right." Delaware senator James Bayard, a Federalist, found this argument so compelling that he had the Albanians' petition printed and distributed to fellow senators; soon after, Fulton's bill found no Federalist votes, lost the support of one of New York's own senators, and received no action when it reached the House of Representatives.[121]

For Livingston and Fulton, this was a rare defeat. Following their triumph over the Albanians in the New York Court of Errors, the duo was not shy about flexing political muscle in state capitals. Fear and revulsion at the monopoly's use of interest and intimidation constitute the third, and most potent, line of antimonopoly critique during the paper wars of the 1810s. Recalling the monopoly's narrow victories in courts and legislatures during the decade, a Connecticut observer wrote in 1819: "*It is remarkable that every petition presented to the assembly of New-York has been reported upon it in terms the most decisively favourable, and the bills to repeal the obnoxious laws lost by the least possible majority.* Sometimes in committee of the whole they have passed; when soon after by the *accidental* absence of a few, or the *happy* arrival of one or two more the scale has been turned." Once the monopoly directed "aggression" toward individuals, the writer concluded, it was "unresisted," despite the fact that "the acts of New-York are looked upon by half their legislature and by three-fourths of the people with indignation."[122] This narrative of political seduction was one that the monopoly's defenders, and Cadwallader Colden in particular, sought to refute. In an address similar to the *Life of Fulton* Colden presented to the Literary and Philosophical Society, DeWitt Clinton told the American Academy of the Arts in 1816 that Robert

R. Livingston was an "eminent arbiter elegantiarum, or judge of propriety" who valued "mutual dependence, and reciprocal benevolence" and tried to "do the greatest good to the greatest number . . . [within the] extent of his own powers, and the plentitude of his own resources." Similarly, Clinton pronounced Fulton "a genius" and concluded that they both would be remembered as "benefactors of the world . . . the Castor and Pollux of antiquity . . . stars of excellent light and of most benign influence."[123]

To most potential competitors and onetime opponents, however, Livingston and Fulton's influence hardly seemed "benign." Years earlier, Livingston himself laid out a vision of the monopoly far more sweeping than contemporary biographers readily admitted. Anonymously writing an "Examination of the Chancellor's Opinion" in his 1812 case against the Albanians, Livingston asserted that although the "public good [should] *direct*" the monopoly's actions, "nothing *limits* its powers." In response to the often-raised charge that the steamboat privilege had been invalidated by New York's ratification of the Constitution's commercial and patent clauses, Livingston maintained that state's "legislative power [was] absolute," even in a federal republic. According to Livingston, the "legislature had, doubtless, a right to bind their citizens" by a monopoly agreement during the pre-constitutional confederation period of the 1780s, and—because this grant preceded the Constitution—no citizens of New York or any other state had a right to challenge its validity. Furthermore, because the legislature was composed of "*the people themselves*" represented by "the attornies who act for them," any shackles on the legislature's power were "a diminution of that people."[124] Therefore, Livingston's belief that national patents were inferior to his monopoly grant (a position shared by James Madison) was actually informed by a far more absolutist position on the sovereignty of states in the federal union. Although the Connecticut pamphleteer of 1819 wrote, "It is not to be believed that Chancellor Livingston foresaw the extremes to which his project is carried . . . to enrich his already rich posterity," Livingston's own words confounded that assertion.[125]

Even if William Duer had read Livingston's "Examination," his own initial writings about the monopoly reveal less concern about the monopolists' views of federalism and political economy than about Livingston and Fulton's willingness to harness state power by capturing legislators' interests. Duer in 1817 may have presumed too much about Fulton's family finances, but he understood the monopoly's structure and the influence wielded by its entangling alliances. In his first pamphlet, he pointed to the reconciliation of

Livingston, Fulton, and the Albanians as a cautionary tale of private interests comingling with public influence. "A compromise was effected," Duer wrote, and the monopolists "paid to the association *against whom they prevailed*, a considerable sum of money [to] purchase [the] boats which had already been declared forfeited, . . . and gratuitously ceded . . . the exclusive privilege of steam navigation upon Lake Champlain."[126] The implications of such a development spoke to the true danger of monopolies; because the enterprise could offer its enemies lucrative licenses and partnerships, "the original proprietors rel[ied] for [their] protection . . . upon the strength of their association, [instead of the] conviction of their right."[127]

Although Duer saw the monopoly's ability to absorb opponents as a threat to the public good, Robert Livingston and Robert Fulton could have argued that such elasticity was essential to their enterprise. They used the monopoly's structure as a tool to manufacture interest, attract investment, and protect themselves from competitors by grafting themselves into the state's institutional ecology of banks, parties, insurance companies, manufacturing, municipalities, and courts. While alive, they were accountable for such decisions. But after their deaths the monopoly nevertheless continued. And it was in Livingston and Fulton's names that the new monopolists sought corporate charters and further enhancements of the rights they either inherited or bought. In 1816, Harriet Fulton, Robert's widow, asked Congress to extend the terms of her husband's federal patents. Her case was made before the Senate by Rufus King, the aging New York Federalist lion; the dire state of Harriet Fulton's finances was confirmed by Supreme Court associate justice H. Brockholst Livingston. And she was represented by Cadwallader D. Colden, her late husband's attorney and an owner of his monopoly rights.

There was, however, opposition. The owner of John Fitch's patent rights— a Virginian named Ferdinando Fairfax—protested Mrs. Fulton's request. Rather than pay homage to the widow and her children, Fairfax accused "able gentlemen of the bar" of exploiting the "popular plea of relieving the widow and orphans of a public benefactor." He asked the Senate whether "the purchasers of Mr. Fulton's claims [were] necessarily interested in its success." New York's laws, he argued, "deter prudent men of moderate capital" from inventing and investing in steamboats because "the combined force of this odious monopoly, wealthy and influential companies formed under it, (embracing gentlemen of the greatest talents, and the highest legal abilities,) and the strong tide of popular favor" stood in their path. Any enlargement of the Fulton patents would merely boost these monopolists' "general influence" at a time when they already "carry matters with so high a hand."[128] The proposed legislation was never brought up for a final vote in the House of Representatives.

William Duer was disgusted by Colden's use of Harriet Fulton to strengthen a monopoly he already considered too strong. Reflecting on the episode three years later, Duer accused Colden of using "the ashes of the dead to inflame the passions of the living." Colden, he wrote, tried to "solicit the pity of the community, in favor of [a] private bargain" rather than "manfully appealing to reason to uphold [his monopoly] rights."[129]

After learning that Colden and four other partners each paid Robert Fulton's estate $100,000 for the late inventor's monopoly privileges (for a total of $500,000), Duer tried to calculate what the monopoly rights themselves could be worth. Valuing the five boats then traveling the Hudson at $200,000, Duer determined that the monopoly privilege itself cost $300,000. Although he believed that sum was "arbitrary," it was nevertheless made more valuable because of the monopolists' assurance that the "dissolved and irresponsible" legislature, of which Duer had been a part, would not interfere with the monopoly right.[130] Thus Duer saw Colden and "a combination of wealthy associates" scheming to maintain their privileged rights out of greed, and succeeding because they had used their "odious" monopoly to securely capture the interests and votes of legislators who had betrayed the public trust. And Colden, Duer believed, was sufficiently compromised by the enterprise that concern for his "professional reputation" would never stop him from "gallant[ly] . . . 'venturing any assertion' which the interests of the Monopoly may require."[131]

In the light of these revelations, Duer was motivated to resist the monopoly by forces "stronger than the ties of legal obligation." He came to believe, he wrote, that the "the common rights of our Citizens—not only the ordinary rules of Justice—but the fundamental principles of our government are prostituted and sacrificed, that [the] Monopoly may be guarded."[132] In a "Republic of Letters," Duer believed, knowledge and progress were supposed to be diffused. The monopoly, however, denied "future prosperity" to yet-unborn Americans. Although the State of New York might have crafted the monopoly privilege in "good faith and honesty," Duer observed that "good faith and honesty are of no kindred, or party, or particular connection."[133] In contrast to monopolists like Colden, who profit from "unrewarded service" and believe that monopolies "ought to be common," Duer thought they were fundamentally incompatible with a healthy and virtuous American political economy; it was his hope that "the purity of republics is such, that in them a monopoly will not be endured." Monopolies, Duer continued, were "at variance with the principles of political economy, and the liberal spirit of the common law; they are regarded with an evil eye by both, as unfriendly to the great rule of *Public Utility*." Even when monopolies were created in the public interest to serve a public good, Duer doubted whether a monopoly's "great end" could be "effectually served by laws"—perhaps because lawmakers were so easily influenced by the monopoly itself. He continued, "[W]hether they be the gifts of a monarch or the fruits of a blind bargain with a republic; whether conceded to court favourites, or obtained by the management of intriguing demagogues; whether their object be the private emolument of an iron-crowned tyrant, or the gratification of a brawling tribune of the People: PUBLIC UTILITY is equally violated."[134] Therefore, Duer's conclusion was as sweeping as it was simple: monopolies were inherently incompatible with moral and effective republican government, and they had no place in the political economy of the federal union. Monopolies were a mercantilist relic, a special privilege created to demonstrate sovereignty but which in turn degraded the independence of lawmakers and diminished the free flow of ideas and free trade of goods long valorized by so many of Duer's Federalist forbearers, and which more recently were embraced by Democratic-Republican contemporaries following the War of 1812.[135] Monopolies might have been justifiable during a period when states enjoyed more absolute sovereignty, but the ratification of the Constitution had rendered the monopoly obsolete and made the state authority supporting it inferior to the national regime. And as long as the steamboat monopoly persisted, Duer warned, it would both fail to live up to its intended purpose and corrupt all that it touched.

Although Duer could not convince his fellow legislators to repeal the monopoly grant, he continued his pamphlet war with Cadwallader Colden. And when the opportunity presented itself, Duer ensured that the steamboat monopoly helped pay for a new chapter in the state's political economy, one that did not involve the awarding of private privileges or grants or charters of incorporation, and that was instead a state-owned and publicly financed open channel of commerce intended to unify, rather than divide, the state and nation: the Erie Canal.[136]

CHAPTER 5

_____

"If We Must Have War or a Canal,
I Am in Favor of the Canal"

Construction of the Erie Canal was completed at ten o'clock on the morning of 26 October 1825. From Buffalo, New York, Governor DeWitt Clinton boarded a slender and crowded packet boat and began traveling east. Trailed by a flotilla of other vessels, Clinton's party floated along the canal's 363-mile-long route to Albany, pausing in towns along the way for local celebrations. As the boat departed, a cannon fired off a celebratory shot in Buffalo, initiating a chain of booms that raced eastward along the canal and then turned south, tracing the Hudson River until ending at Sandy Hook in New York Harbor. It took an hour and twenty minutes before the first echoes reached Manhattan, some 544 miles away. Then, after ten minutes of silence, the exercise was repeated in reverse, with guns firing along a path that led northward to Albany, then westward back toward Buffalo.[1]

Elaborately choreographed, this sonic boomerang was the opening act of a canal celebration that, for DeWitt Clinton, was a week of valedictory validation. The Erie Canal was constructed in just over seven years, and for all but two of them Clinton had been both the governor of New York and the president of its Canal Board. He had been a canal commissioner since the body was first formed in 1810, and his fingerprints covered the promotion, planning, execution, and early operation of the Erie Canal. Clinton's rivals suspected this advocacy was motivated by self-interest. He was nominated as the Democratic-Republicans' candidate for governor during final negotiations over canal legislation and was elected in the same month the state legislature gave the project its final approval. On 4 July 1817—just three days into his first term—Clinton traveled to the town of Rome and—with his bare palms—stirred the first handfuls of earth to begin the canal's construction. It was no

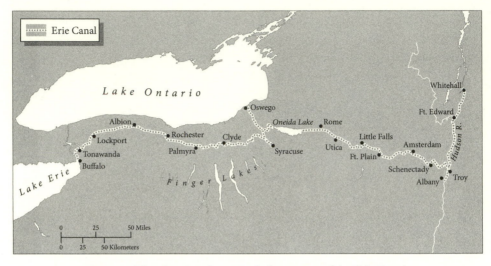

Figure 6. Map showing the 363-mile-long route of the Erie Canal.

wonder, then, that Clinton's detractors saw his political career and the canal's birth as one and the same; the public's "desire of having the canal made" had kept Clinton "continually in the public eye, without an opponent," said one.[2]

Now, eighty-eight months later, days of festivities lay ahead for the governor. Once his squadron reached Albany they entered the Hudson, bound for New York. At daybreak on 4 November, a fleet of steamboats towed them past the city's west-side wharves, dry docks, and the Battery, turning the corner of Manhattan's southern tip and heading up the East River toward the Navy yard. Pilot boats, barges, a U.S. Navy frigate, and two British Navy sloops crowded the water to render honors to Clinton's flagship, the *Seneca Chief*. At the head of the line, a group of "aborigines from Lake Erie" paddled canoes. Cannons fired, then fired again, following a specific rite prescribed by a city committee's official "Regulations for the Grand Aquatic Display."[3]

Once Clinton's boat reached the "monarch of the deep"—the committee's name for the visible ripple where the harbor's protection sweeps into the deeper currents of the Atlantic's might—the governor emptied two ornate casks of water over the side of the *Seneca Chief*, comingling Lake Erie's water with that of the wine-dark sea. A moment later, Clinton's friend, the canal promoter and former congressman Dr. Samuel Mitchill, added vials of water taken from the world's great rivers—the Thames, the Seine, the Elbe, La Plata, the Columbia, the Neva, the Tagus, the Amazon, the Ganges, and the Nile— into the marinade. Clinton was then presented with a memoir the city had commissioned only days earlier, after asking Cadwallader D. Colden to assemble it on short notice as a souvenir. Colden's hasty work, running more than a hundred pages, was a comprehensive but politically partial narrative: he buffed the canal's legislative record, settled scores with naysayers, and distributed credit for the work among almost a century of New York's political leaders. Printed just in time to be handed to Clinton in the harbor, the book was eventually gifted to local patrons and politicos along with a medal, also struck at the city's behest, befitting a triumph they saw as something on par with the conquest of Gaul or the pyramids at Giza; it was an event that would, in time, punctuate the recorded history of the human species's earthly career.[4] On one side, the coin featured an eagle perched on top of the state seal in the harbor; on the obverse sat Pan, god of the land, with his arm wrapped around Poseidon, god of the seas. The medal was presented in a round wooden case made from a piece of maple carried on the *Seneca Chief*'s voyage. Gold versions were sent to the last surviving signers of the Declaration of Independence and the nation's four living presidents.[5]

From this point on, the ceremonies moved ashore. Church bells rang for three hours and a parade composed of representatives of every conceivable trade and profession—horsemen, trumpeters, bakers, brewers, millers, tillers, coopers, butchers, furriers, hatters, masons, soap makers, tanners, upholsterers, potters, smiths, shipwrights, sailmakers, riggers, caulkers, carvers, foresters, painters, priests, bankers, doctors, senators, artists, and engineers, along with "strangers of distinction"—marched across the city towing floats and waving banners before watching fireworks cast shadows over vast feasts.[6] The day's only disappointment came when a planned hot air balloon ascent, guided by one "Madam Johnson," was abruptly canceled and an "enraged populace committed some excesses upon the garden fence and shrubbery."[7] Such was the reception and after-party that followed the morning's "Wedding of the Waters."

Amid all this fuss, it is worth asking: what exactly were New Yorkers celebrating?

As a work of engineering, the Erie Canal was the first successful large-scale American canal venture. It dwarfed in audacity, cost, and scale any internal-improvement project then contemplated in North America.[8]

In interrogating this project's political and legislative origins, however, it is important to understand that "the Erie Canal" was not really a single stand-alone construction project, a ditch started at one end and finished at another. Instead, the Erie Canal was a compilation of three smaller sections—middle, western, and eastern—built separately, along with a Champlain Canal linking Lake Champlain to the Hudson River. The first of these three sections to be built, the middle, partially opened in 1819. By building the easiest, middle, section first and opening it to traffic, the commissioners enabled the canal to begin collecting tolls to fund construction costs and the interest due on state loans well before the larger project was scheduled to be finished. In 1820 and 1821, 94 miles were put to use, netting more than $28,000 in tolls; in 1822 that total rose to 116 miles and $60,000, followed in 1823 by 160 miles and $126,000 and in 1824 by 280 miles and nearly $300,000. Each time an additional section or part of a section was finished, it too opened to begin carrying traffic and collecting tolls.

The project had intentionally been designed this way by the authors of the state's 1817 canal law, who structured the project so that its political fortunes would flow from its demonstrated economic viability. Canal proponents had little confidence that the plan's obvious merits would simply propel the project to completion. By leveraging the popularity of easily completed canal segments and attainable revenue goals on behalf of their plans, DeWitt Clinton and his allies built broader pro-canal constituencies who demanded the project's completion while insulating the canal from legislative interference. The policy was therefore intended to actively recruit, engage, and align out-of-doors interests in favor of the canal during the seven years it took to construct the project. Each time a canal section was opened, the occasion was celebrated with ceremonial boat launches and local festivities. By the time the entire length of the canal was linked in 1825, canal-themed parties had become almost routine spectacles in upstate New York.

But the building of the "Grand Canal" had been about more than just construction. It had taken Clinton and his fellow canal commissioners almost as long to develop and win legislative approval for the Erie Canal as it took engineers and laborers to execute the work. And even as negotiations over a canal law drew toward a close in 1817, it remained unclear whether state legislators would even bring the bill up for a vote until the final hours of that year's session of the New York legislature.

From seemingly technical wrangling over the legislative language of that 1817 law, a canal policy emerged that did not merely enable a construction project. Instead, it reoriented the institutional habits and applied political economy of the period by creating a project with an institutional structure unlike anything in the now-familiar armamentarium of the state. Haunted by the ghosts of failed past attempts to build canals in New York, legislators refused to part with the Erie Canal's public character as a down payment on its construction. Their choice to finance the Erie Canal with debt, appoint commissioners to oversee its construction, and retain ownership and regulatory authority over the canal and its tolls ensured that it would be an undeniably public project. Thus the 1817 plan was not merely ambitious in envisioning a "Grand Canal" across the entire northern tier of the state of New York, it was also a radical departure from past practices and assumptions concerning how public works were to be financed, constructed, and operated. In form and function, the canal legislation reflected the growing capabilities of the state and the aspirations of its policy makers. It signaled the dawn of a new set of assumptions about the proper relationship between the state, its banks and corporations, and the development of its infrastructure and commercial interests. And it inaugurated a regime change in the political economy of the early American republic.

In 1806 Jefferson's message to Congress on the state of the Union had been a narrative of peril and promise. Hostile relations with Britain and Spain and the first hints of an armed insurrection in the West led by former vice president Aaron Burr were first and foremost on the president's agenda at the midpoint of his second term. The territorial expansion he inaugurated with the Louisiana Purchase and the exploration he commissioned by sending Meriwether Lewis and William Clark to the Pacific had been meant to celebrate the nation's breadth, catalog its potential, and provide opportunities to unborn generations of yeomen farmers. Yet the union instead seemed to be spread thin, with only the faintest illusion of control at its western border.

Still, there were remedies at hand. A budget surplus was waiting to be spent, and Jefferson suggested that "patriotism" would "prefer . . . its application to the great purposes of the public," such as "education, roads, rivers, canals, and . . . other objects of public improvement" contemplated by the Constitution. "By these operations," the president imagined it would be possible to open "new channels of communication" between the citizens of far-flung states, knitting them together as they discovered commonalities and "identified" their "interests." "Lines of separation will disappear," Jefferson predicted, and the nation would be "cemented by new and indissoluble ties."[9]

Seeking a path toward transforming this rhetoric into reality, in early 1807 the U.S. Senate asked the administration's Treasury secretary, Albert

Gallatin, to prepare a memo outlining what a comprehensive set of infra-structure projects—called "internal improvements"—might look like.

Presented a month later, Gallatin's report—officially titled the *Report of the Secretary of the Treasury on the Subject of Public Roads and Canals*—surveyed routes for turnpikes and sites for canals in every region of the country, laying out a comprehensive vision that would weave inland waterways and roads from Maine to Georgia. If undertaken as a package, the plans laid out in the *Report* would cost more than $16 million to complete, $2.2 million of which would come from a New York canal joining the Hudson River to Lake Erie.

As Gallatin well knew, crafting comprehensive congressionally designed internal-improvement packages was a politically complex project. Identifying just which interests to mobilize or satisfy was made difficult by the fact that the nation's institutional landscape was crowded with the legacies of state and local governments that had been individually pursuing uncoordinated agendas since the founding of the republic.

In New York, state lawmakers had briefly resisted empowering political entrepreneurs from using politics to advance their economic agendas. But that impulse was quickly overwhelmed when select coalitions and interest groups began petitioning legislators to enact an ambitious agenda by granting incorporation privileges and other exclusive rights. For any comprehensive system of internal improvements to be financially practical and politically possible, therefore, it would have to preserve and consolidate those existing institutions and the coalitions of interests backing them—investors, owners, managers, and users—into a layered, federal status quo.

Those interests began stirring even before Albert Gallatin's *Report* was printed. Soon after Jefferson's annual message was circulated in local newspapers, two Federalist assemblymen in the New York legislature proposed a bill to resurrect the proposal to build a canal that would connect the Hudson River to Lake Erie. An opportunity to steer federal revenue toward New York was at hand, and the duo wanted the state legislature to commission a survey to plot an achievable route. It would become an off-the-shelf plan that could be handed to Congress and to the administration as soon as funds became available.

Compared to the state's past commitments to canal building, approving a survey was a minor gesture. However, some of the assemblymen's colleagues in the New York legislature were skeptical about reviving canal visions, even if no state funds would be put at risk.

In contrast to Treasury secretary Gallatin, steamboat promoter Robert Fulton better recognized how such roadblocks were obstructing an ambitious infrastructure program of publicly financed and coordinated internal improvements. In a letter to members of Congress that was included in Gallatin's *Report* as an addendum, Fulton cautioned Washington readers that some states' electoral politics and legislative leadership were downright hostile to such projects. Like Gallatin, Fulton believed that canals and turnpikes each had relative advantages that should be carefully weighed—and after apologizing for having lately been distracted by "private concerns," Fulton went on to extol the virtues of deploying fleets of steamboats throughout the country's waterways. On balance, Fulton was optimistic that the benefits of internal improvements would eventually become self-evident to "every intelligent American." But many citizens, he continued, were "not yet . . . aware of their best interests." If elected officials delayed acting until there were public roars demanding comprehensive plans, Fulton believed they would be in for a long wait. Such choruses would not materialize because voters could not "be expected . . . [to] perceive at once the advantages of those plans of improvement which are still new in this country." In the meantime, "[T]he most useful works have sometimes been opposed" and—likely in reference to New York—Fulton added, "we are not without examples of men being elected into the State legislatures for the express purpose of preventing roads, canals, and bridges [from] being constructed."[10]

To Fulton, then, the politics of internal improvements were even more complex than Gallatin's *Report* let on. Embracing existing interests was the easy part.

Fulton's larger concern was that there were elected officials in New York and other states—with voters backing them—who evinced blanket opposition to any improvement project. Out of either or both principle and interest, they pledged to block new plans from being considered and adopted, playing the role of permanent skeptics whose questions could not be answered and whose doubts could not be satisfied. Their agenda was to block the formulation of an improvement plan, a stance that placed them beyond the reach of promoters and political entrepreneurs who routinely distributed stock shares, corporate directorships, and salaried sinecures to legislators in order to build voting majorities in favor of particular proposals. These legislators resisted such incentives, which in Fulton's mind made them a somewhat unreachable and unpersuadable opposition.

But in reality—in ways Robert Fulton failed to appreciate in the

administration of his own steamboat monopoly—opposition to improvements from one legislator or even a small cabal of confederates did not usually stop such projects from moving forward. Instead, by making it more
difficult for these initiatives to be state-financed, they ensured that they
would be funded with private capital by private investors who were organized
under a public grant of state privileges and exclusive rights.

Being "anti-improvement," then, did not necessarily result in the creation
of fewer improvements. Instead, it merely motivated and rewarded political
entrepreneurs who sought to use the state as one more tool to advance their
personal economic interests. By blocking projects from being publicly funded
and by preventing legislators from even imagining such a possibility, opponents of improvements prolonged and intensified one of the more controversial institutional legacies of the Revolution: the persistence and proliferation
of corporations and other exclusively held competitive advantages that were
unavailable to ordinary entrepreneurs, firms, and enterprises.

When the two Federalist assemblymen who proposed a canal-route survey wrung a $600 appropriation from the New York legislature, they congrat-
ulated themselves for overcoming opposition and doubts, convincing enough
of their colleagues that the expense "could do no harm and might do some
good."[11] But the man responsible for conducting the work, state surveyor-
general Simeon De Witt, scoffed at the sum. It was laughably small, he said,
as if "it was expected that something would be done for nothing, or that a
good deal of what ought to be done must be left undone." Instead of performing the job himself, the state surveyor sent out a deputy to survey only some
sections and merely visit others; even then, expenses exceeded his allotted
budget by $73.[12]

Although he might have held a lofty title, De Witt was very much a dependent. His annual budget and salary—$1,250—were set by the state legisla-
ture, his resources were constrained, and on occasions such as this he had no
choice but to rely on private resources to fulfill his public duties. To complete
his task, Simeon De Witt sought counsel from a better-funded and more
knowledgeable source: Joseph Ellicott, the Holland Land Company's resident
agent in the state.[13]

Since 1800 it had been Ellicott's job to sell the Holland Land Company's
most recent purchase: a 3.25-million-acre tract in western New York. Formed
in 1795 by a consortium of six Dutch banks, the company had been buying
land in upstate New York and western Pennsylvania as a way to find a home
for funds they otherwise would have invested in France had the French

Revolution not threatened private property.[14] Iroquois land cessions made under the 1797 Treaty of Big Tree cleared the way for the company to take possession of tracts west of the Genesee River, which were eventually acquired from Robert Morris. The company soon began surveying the lands—both because a federal law required it, and because they could not be resold unless divided into sections and townships. Joseph Ellicott was hired to perform the task, dubbed the "Great Survey," and set off on a two-year-long errand into the state's western wilderness, taking 150 men with him. By the time it was complete, the "Great Survey" had cost $70,921.69½, more than a hundred times what New York State appropriated to its surveyor-general ten years later.[15]

No wonder Simeon De Witt turned to Joseph Ellicott for help.

But in so doing, De Witt was not merely seeking professional courtesy from a fellow surveyor. As a reward for his efforts, Ellicott had been given the job of selling the territory he had surveyed, one that paid a $1,500 salary plus a 5 percent commission on all transactions. He set up an office in Batavia—named for an ancient Germanic tribe that lived in what became the Netherlands—and began looking for people to settle the six-mile square towns he had mapped out. The job came with a good measure of personal discretion; he could adjust prices higher or lower, and he could require buyers to build improvements such as mills or inns—anything that would increase the value of surrounding lands—in exchange for leniency on rents or in lieu of interest. He accepted payments of livestock when cash was not available and used company funds to build schools and churches. On occasion, he simply gave land to particular tradesmen, such as blacksmiths, if they would settle in the company's territory. For this, Ellicott earned $11,500 per year during most of his first decade as resident agent.[16] And for all these reasons, Joseph Ellicott did not read Simeon De Witt's plea as a request to simply borrow a few maps. He received it as an agent for an exclusive group of Dutch bankers whose sole job was to open up to settlement 5 million acres of land that covered two-thirds of western New York.

When Joseph Ellicott responded to Simeon De Witt's request after six weeks, he offered the state surveyor more than just maps; his reply was a detailed argument in favor of a particular route, with explanations for why some paths were superior to others, predictions of how many locks would have to be constructed, and estimates of labor and materials costs. De Witt had offered Ellicott a platform to state his case in favor of a canal, and Ellicott delivered, aware that his reply to the surveyor-general would be included in a report to the legislature and would likely be forwarded to Congress. Ellicott was in favor of a single canal from one end of the state to the other, arguing that the project was both physically and financially achievable. "I profess to have a pretty accurate knowledge of this tract of country," he wrote, "as far as it extends through the Holland Purchase . . . and it appears to me, that nature seems to have pointed out this route for a canal, not only in consequence of the little labor, comparatively speaking, that would be required in digging it, but because the necessary materials for the construction of locks are close at hand." His detailed commentary, he knew, would add credibility to the surveyor's report. His inclusion in the preparation of the 1808 survey empowered him to shape the canal discussion to reflect the interests of the Holland Land Company. And his endorsement of the project sustained the idea that it was a project suitable for federal funding; he even pledged $2,500 toward a state-chartered canal company "in case the United States should think the object inexpedient" and pass up so obvious an opportunity.[17]

If it seems like Ellicott had been waiting for an opportunity to make this case, he had. Scarcely two months later, he and the Holland Land Company's principal American agent in Philadelphia, Paul Busti, agreed that if either a federal or a state canal project got underway, the company would support the effort by donating half the land that touched its path. And in the way they sketched out this imagined offer, they intended to maximize their influence over canal policy: a Holland Land Company donation would be generous—half the land!—yet it would conditionally include every other lot along the route. Therefore you could not find a way to knit the route together without satisfying the company's demands.[18]

In Simeon De Witt's mind, his eventual 1809 report "satisfactorily established, that a canal from lake Erie to Hudson's river was not only practicable, but practicable with uncommon facility." He credited it with casting such a "favourable light" on the project that "after encountering prejudices from various sources, and oppositions made for various reasons, [the report] induced the legislature, in 1810, to organize a board of commissioners, with powers and means to prosecute the business."[19]

But despite the financial interests and ambitions larded in Ellicott's responses to De Witt, the Holland Land Company's fingerprints were barely visible on the finished product the surveyor-general delivered to the legislature. Only one explicit reference is made to "Judge Ellicott," while the rest of his observations and opinions were seamlessly integrated into the report alongside those of De Witt's $673 deputy surveyor. By inviting the agent of

the Holland Land Company to contribute to the state's official canal documents and then quietly blurring evidence of his influence, the state surveyor-
general subsidized his office's budget by compromising its independence.[20]
The state had, in effect, put its own seal on a report paid for and written by
the Holland Land Company.[21]

Therefore, although the canal survey commissioned by the New York assembly looked like a state-driven initiative to steer federal dollars toward a
long-contemplated infrastructure project in the state, it actually created an
opportunity for out-of-doors interests like the Holland Land Company to in-
sert themselves into the process of shaping a canal program. When Simeon
De Witt coped with his office's insufficient funding by relying on Joseph Ellicott and his survey, Ellicott recognized that he could exploit that relationship
to smuggle his company's plans into a state legislative document—a source of
supposedly impartial information—with the tacit cooperation of the surveyor-general. Legislative opposition to both the public financing of internal
improvements and to the adequate funding of studies and surveys of such
projects could lead them to be crafted and drafted to suit the agenda of the
companies and interests that provided officials with information and advice.

Even in its relaunch, then, the new "public" Erie Canal was not a complete departure from the past practice of deputizing private interests to accomplish public goals. Rather, instead of tapping private capital by chartering
two companies to build canals, the state was quietly—almost invisibly—
mobilizing private interests and capital on behalf of a canal by intimately involving them in the earliest germination of state planning and policy design.
Thus it was possible for legislators to look toward recent history and recognize that certain institutions such as corporations or monopolies were ideally
suited or ill-suited for particular applications while not questioning the propriety of a mixed economy that comingled private capital and public authority. Such an outlook allowed lawmakers to separate specific institutional
forms and arrangements from the larger context of a political economy that
encouraged and empowered private participation in public policy making.

The tension between this change and continuity was especially evident in
the creation of the state's first canal commission. In response to the publication of the state surveyor's report in 1809 and enthusiasm kindled by Albert
Gallatin's *Report* on improvements, landowners and townspeople in Albany,
Madison, Oneida, Onondaga, and Schenectady counties began sending petitions to the New York legislature calling for the construction of an upstate
canal.

One of those who took notice was Federalist state senator and gubernatorial candidate Jonas Platt. Canal advocacy was in his bloodline; his father Zephaniah, once a member of the Continental Congress, had also spoken in favor of a Hudson-to-lake canal.[22] As Platt was likely to support such a project, the senator was approached in the winter of early 1810 by Thomas Eddy, the treasurer of the Western Inland Lock Navigation Company.

For twelve years, Eddy had held the thankless job of presiding over the finances of a deteriorating set of partially completed river improvements. The company had not declared a dividend since 1799, the state was now its largest shareholder, and in 1808 the company all but gave up on its future by ceding back to the state its rights to build anything west of Lake Oneida. But with De Witt's survey and Gallatin's *Report* in hand, Eddy sought out Platt, his friend and state senator, hoping to convince him to rekindle a canal plan that would place his company once again at its nexus.[23]

On a mid-March evening in 1810, Eddy asked Platt to introduce a bill appointing a commission to explore expanding the Western company's improvements from Rome, New York, to the Seneca River, some forty miles away. Platt supported the idea of creating such a body, but he "startled" his friend by suggesting that the commissioners evaluate a larger possibility: a "complete canal" from Lake Erie to the Hudson River.[24] He also told Eddy that he believed their proposal should omit any references to the Western company, a detail Eddy neglected to include in his memoir but that Platt recalled quite clearly in 1828. "I also expressed to [Eddy] my decided conviction, that no private corporation was adequate to, or ought to be entrusted with, the power and control over such an important object," he remembered, "I also told him, that the Western Inland Lock Navigation Company had disappointed public expectation; and that it would be inauspicious to present any projèt which should be subject to that corporation."[25] Platt, therefore, not only dismissed Eddy's suggestion that the Western company build the canal but also rejected the notion that any privately held corporation could, or should, do the work. His foremost objective was to tie the Gallatin *Report*'s concept of federally financed infrastructure development to the conclusions of Simeon De Witt's (and Joseph Ellicott's) can-do survey, hoping that a panel of state-appointed commissioners would be able to convince Congress to throw their support behind the project.

Like De Witt, then, Jonas Platt was willing to allow, and even invite, Thomas Eddy—a corporate officer in the Western Inland Lock Navigation Company—to influence canal policy. After all, the idea of a canal commission was Eddy's; Platt only unveiled his own canal ambitions after scoffing at Eddy's more modest and corporate-centric proposal. Subsequently, Platt introduced Eddy to other state legislators, let him coauthor the bill Platt introduced in the state senate, and gave him a hand in selecting canal commissioners. "We agreed in the necessity of selecting persons equally from the two great political parties" in the state, Eddy wrote. "According to the best judgment [they] could form," they selected three Republicans—state surveyor Simeon De Witt, state senator and Republican leader DeWitt Clinton, and Buffalo, New York, congressman Peter B. Porter—and four Federalists—former U.S. senator and statesman Gouverneur Morris, land baron Stephen Van Rensselaer, former Albany congressman Benjamin Walker, and Thomas Eddy himself. This group, Platt explained, "combine[d] talents, influence, and wealth."

The following morning, Eddy met Platt at the capital to seek DeWitt Clinton's support for their measure. Platt thought Clinton was of "primary importance" because he "possess[ed] a powerful influence over the dominant party in the state." The two men had Clinton "called out" from the senate chamber, as Eddy was not a member and they hoped to make their proposition in private. In an adjoining room off the senate floor, they laid out their resolution, with Platt flattering Clinton by observing that the designated commissioners were men of "wealth and public spirit" likely to serve without pay. Clinton agreed to second the motion so long as Platt introduced the resolution without the commissioners' names.

Heading to the state assembly chamber, Platt and Eddy approached two Federalist assemblymen, Stephen Van Rensselaer and state attorney general Abraham Van Vechten. Like Platt, both men represented the Albany area. Van Rensselaer, in fact, owned much of it, having inherited the 1,200 square-mile Rensselaerswyck Manor on his twenty-first birthday. Platt shared his resolution and the proposed commissioners' names with the two, and they agreed to support it on the condition that Van Rensselaer's friend, retired general and former assembly speaker William North, either be added to the commission or replace one of the other commissioners. Platt and Eddy substituted North's name in place of Benjamin Walker—an interesting choice, given that North and Walker were intimate friends, having been aides-de-camp to Friedrich Wilhelm, Baron von Steuben during the Revolution and the heirs to his estate following his 1794 death.

On 12 March, Platt's blank resolution passed the state senate with Clinton's support. The following day, Platt unveiled the seven commissioners' names, winning his colleagues' votes; that afternoon, Van Rensselaer and Van

Vechten did the same in the assembly. The bill passed both houses unanimously and appropriated $3,000 for expenses.[26]

Thomas Eddy had gone to Albany to get a canal commission, and he left as a commissioner.

But Eddy had not won a favored place for the Western Inland Lock Navigation Company in the construction of a future canal. Although Jonas Platt and other legislators had no problem with offering Eddy an outsized voice in shaping state canal policy, Platt was unwilling to blindly continue the past practice of vesting control and execution of transportation projects in state-chartered and shareholder-owned corporations. Instead, he believed that the construction and management of this particular canal was simply too important to be left in the hands of such a corporation. And even if his colleagues did not share his outlook about the (im)propriety of a corporation-built canal, Platt suspected they would remember the Western company's lackluster record and conclude that no single enterprise was capable of amassing the expertise, labor, and capital needed to complete the project successfully.

With regard to canal policy, then, Jonas Platt was prepared to alter the way the state practiced political economy by explicitly limiting corporations' role in the public sphere. Despite having internalized the habits of a political economy in which possessing "influence and wealth" merited a seat on a canal commission, he nevertheless recognized that the institutional configurations that organized such arrangements were flexible—and could even be improvised. Thus although he opposed neither improvements nor the use of corporations and other privileges to mobilize private capital and structure the marketplace, he nevertheless recognized that there were limits to what corporations could do and should be expected to achieve. Therefore Platt could help invent a commission, reject the idea of an incorporated canal company, and leave unanswered the question of how a future canal might be financed—all while essentially preserving the economy of influence, which enabled connected interest groups, financiers, and other "people without boundaries" to have both formal and informal roles in the crafting of state economic and transportation policy. Even in its earliest iteration, the Erie Canal was less a rejection of the status quo than a set of modifications to and a maturation of long-standing practices and habits.

Furthermore, Platt believed that his colleagues in the legislature and in the policy-making circles of New York State—his fellow political entrepreneurs—shared the same views. This suspicion was vindicated by the report that the canal commission filed in March 1811 following their storied summer sojourn through the taverns, boardinghouses, and backcountry of western New York.[27] Perhaps predictably, they wholly endorsed the building of a canal, boldly proposing that, rather than struggle to make some river sections passable, a canal instead be carved through the ground to parallel existing waterways; Lake Erie could be tapped to flood the trench and float boats to the Hudson River. Although conceding that their $5 million cost estimate was large, the commissioners did not recoil. Instead, they insisted that the state finance the project directly. "Too great a national interest [was] at stake," they wrote, for the project to become "a grant to private persons or companies." Like Jonas Platt, they too thought that the project was too large—and too important—to be undertaken by a single corporation or company. "Few of our fellow citizens have more money than they want," they wrote, "and of the many who want, few find facility in obtaining it." There were, in other words, credit constraints and competing investments that prevented so much capital from being pooled.

By contrast, they noted, "the public can readily, at fair interest, command any reasonable sum." The public—through the state—could borrow cheaply. And "such large expenditures can be more economically made under public authority, than by the care and vigilance of any company." The state's offices and officials were sufficiently mature, sophisticated, and responsible to administer a $5 million fund effectively. By contrast, they feared that under the management of a private entity or a public-private mixed-economy corporation, the canal funds would be gambled away by shareholders who wanted to reap short-term profits and abandon the long-term mission of their charter. Veering from its intended use, the money would soon "become the subject of a job or a fund for speculation" once its custodians acted on the whims of stockjobbers and speculators.

Although the canal commissioners wanted to make this conclusion seem blandly self-evident, they were also going on record in a public way that Jonas Platt had not. So out of defensiveness or self-justification, the commission—speaking in the voice of their president, the wordsmith Gouverneur Morris—chose to preface their opinions about corporations and private companies by resurrecting a rhetorical theme raised by canal promoter Elkanah Watson twenty years earlier.

At that time, Watson had written of the viability of European political-economy practices and ideology imported into the United States, arguing that according to European models a canal through upstate New York was impractical because that area was not already populated with settlers. This meant, Watson had argued, that a new *American* political-economy model was required to anticipate future settlement and economic development.

Now the canal commission wanted to frame a similar contrast, only this time in relation to the institutional design of the canal. They therefore labeled corporations, monopolies, and exclusive franchise rights as *European*, prefacing their discussion of canal funds and state financing by saying that "the reasons adduced for grants to individuals in Europe"—the previously mentioned legal instruments—"apply inversely here" in New York because of the scale of the contemplated canal.[28]

The commissioners, of course, had little standing to label such grants as *European* when they were in fact the day-to-day manna of the state's political economy: corporate charters, monopoly privileges, exclusive rights and licenses were all practices that had been introduced to North America via the British Empire and continued voluntarily, albeit not without controversy, after the Revolution. And they were not only American; New York was at the forefront among its peers in creating corporations and monopolies to carry out transportation projects, construct a financial infrastructure, and erect the institutional supports for a market economy. There was nothing particularly European about these practices in 1776, let alone in 1810, yet the commissioners were sufficiently uneasy with proposing a publicly financed canal that they could only join Jonas Platt's dismissal of a corporate model if it was premised on the notion that there was something inherently foreign about the most commonplace political-economy institutions of the day. By painting corporations and monopolies as alien in origin, the commissioners created rhetorical space for themselves to exempt the canal from having to fit within such models. And as a body that represented both legislators and political entrepreneurs, the commission seized an opportunity to liberate state lawmakers from the constraints of past habits, inoculating them against the temptation to hand over the canal to a set of favored petitioners, a company, or a wealthy patron.

However bold some commissioners might have considered this recommendation, it was made from the comfortable position of being theoretical. Although a publicly administered fund of borrowed money would be a useful way to finance the canal, the commissioners' report makes clear that this option would only be necessary "if the state stood alone." And even if federal funding were not available, the commissioners believed that "those who participate in the benefit, should contribute to the expense." In the most narrow sense, they meant that even if the state constructed the canal on its own credit, it could extract payments from neighboring states along the Great Lakes that would benefit from it.

But in 1810, none of the commissioners believed this would be necessary. Despite their professed confidence in the practicality and utility of a canal, the commissioners had no intention of goading the state into directly funding this multi-year, multi-million-dollar project. They understood that if the legislature had wanted an excuse to build a canal, it could have fallen back on the corporate model used in the 1790s or acted on the state surveyor's 1808 feasibility study. Had Jonas Platt and Thomas Eddy merely wanted to provide the legislature with a study affirming that a canal could be built, they could have appointed engineers from America and abroad with canal- and road-building expertise. Or they could have asked Joseph Ellicott to repurpose the Holland Land Company's survey in favor of the canal project. Instead, the commission was created by the legislature because New York shared a "federal band with her sister states," which state lawmakers hoped to exploit. The commissioners represented the best chance of obtaining federal funds because they were expected to leverage their reputations and connections to negotiate favorable terms with Congress. Therefore, the only "solution" that the commissioners truly deemed "proper" and based on "principles of distributive justice" was federal funding from the "national legislature." The entire nation would benefit from the canal's consolidation of western territories and newfound commercial advantages over British Canada; therefore, it was only reasonable to expect the entire nation to contribute to its construction. The terms and conditions of this federal support—"the proportion, the conditions, the compact in short"—would be "the result of a treaty" between the national and New York State governments.[29]

The commission had been conceived of as an agency of political experts who would bolster the credibility, standing, and stature of the canal project. As Platt explained to DeWitt Clinton a year earlier, he and the other commissioners possessed "talents, influence, and wealth." They could be effective lobbyists with the new Madison administration and Congress because, except for Thomas Eddy, they were veteran politicians of regional or national stature and reputation.

Yet although in 1810 the commission told lawmakers what they wanted to hear, the canal commission's future activities were not similarly constrained. Regardless of whether they realized it yet, legislators had created an institution that would be free to discover and pursue its own interests. For, although the seven commissioners were selected to represent a bipartisan sample of the state's power structure, they had never been an ordinary cabal of partisans. Indeed, the political balance between Federalists and Republicans was an optical distraction, behind which lay a far more interesting and deliberate combination. The men were all cosmopolitans with financial contacts throughout America and Europe; nearly all of them had held leadership positions in either the state government or the state militia, and also served in the U.S. or Continental congresses. In addition, they represented some of the largest landowners and speculators at the eastern and western ends of upstate New York, along with merchants and urbanites with interests in banking and finance in New York City. The geography of these interests perfectly overlaid the Hudson-to-Lake route of the proposed canal itself. When they toured canal country for themselves, the commissioners therefore did not merely study it as disinterested advisers, they assessed it as stakeholders who had varying degrees of political and financial interest in seeing a canal built. When they subsequently vouched publicly for the project's viability and affixed their signatures to their report, they endorsed the canal regardless of whether Congress provided funds. And once the legislature voted to print and distribute five thousand copies of that report throughout the state, lawmakers gave the commissioners and their allies in New York's land, banking, and mercantile interests a stake in seeing the project become a reality. A successful canal commissioner, after all, was one who successfully won approval for a canal. It was definitional.

Lawmakers intensified this transformation by expanding the commission's membership, portfolio, and budget at the suggestion of DeWitt Clinton. The body was given the authority to apply to the federal government for canal funds, to meet with the president and Congress on the state's behalf, to hire an engineer, to accept grants and cessations of land along the canal route, and to seek aid from other states. The commission was given a budget of $15,000 and two new members who were then familiar faces in Albany: Robert Fulton and Robert R. Livingston. Both men had experience in petitioning other states for exclusive steamboat privileges by using their New York monopoly grant as a claim to both technological and legal superiority, and if New York successfully linked the Hudson River to Lake Erie, New York steamboats would dominate the commerce of the Great Lakes. By uniting the steamboat monopolists and their allies with canal promoters, the legislature further expanded the coalition of canal partisans: now those invested in steam also found themselves with a stake in the completion of the canal and with two of nine seats on the canal commission.[30]

More important, however, the addition of the steamboat monopolists to the canal commission added leverage to the state's application to Congress, implicitly signaling that if other states and Congress refused the state's request and forced New York to build a canal on its own, New York's legislature could make sure that they suffered for it. Because New York claimed jurisdiction over waters that touched the coasts of neighboring states, monopoly privileges on New York's waters naturally had an impact on the external and internal commerce of those states. The legal rights of steamboat grantees— which would be maintained and enhanced by the state legislature throughout the decade—therefore could disrupt other states' commerce and trample their capabilities to encourage steam navigation within their own borders.

Moving forward, the canal proponents would need all the influence they could muster.

Representing the renewed and expanded commission, DeWitt Clinton and Gouverneur Morris in late December 1811 traveled to Washington, D.C., to seek the aid promised three years earlier in the Gallatin *Report*. In advance of this visit, canal commissioner and congressman Peter Porter met with both President James Madison and Treasury secretary Gallatin. But it was all to little avail. Morris and Clinton were crestfallen when President Madison, reportedly "embarrassed by scruples derived from his interpretation of the constitution," suggested that instead of seeking federal funds the commissioners should first try to amend the Constitution to explicitly authorize Congress to support internal improvements. But the commissioners, many congressmen, and even cabinet officials in the Madison administration believed such support was already constitutional.

Despite his objections, Madison was willing to recommend the canal proposal to Congress on the grounds that "the utility of canals . . . was universally admitted" and that this project specifically spoke to concerns about "general security."[31]

Yet despite this introduction, the commissioners' reception in Congress was even cooler. Morris and Clinton had to wait sixteen days before the House of Representatives granted the proposed New York canal bill a preliminary hearing. The House then asked the commissioners to prepare a more comprehensive omnibus bill: "a general system" of nationwide improvement projects like the one laid out in Gallatin's *Report*. "Unless something was done for many of the states," one congressman advised, "the consent of a majority of the House of Representatives could not be obtained."[32]

As Clinton and Morris, visitors to the city, struggled to craft a package to benefit more and more states, it became obvious to them that many members of Congress from other states believed that the canal was of "superior benefit" to New York alone; they did not see its potential to promote the prosperity of "the whole union," and it was unlikely they would ever offer a vote in its favor.

The commission had faced this resistance before; months earlier, Morris, Clinton, and Robert Livingston cosigned petitions that were sent to the governors of neighboring states and newly formed territories, seeking partnerships and financial cooperation in the construction of a canal. Massachusetts and Ohio responded with offers of moral support and vague promises to consider future aid. Connecticut, New Jersey, and Vermont firmly, if politely, declined. Michigan offered support only if the commissioners would reroute the canal to serve its interests. Tennessee was the only state that offered to instruct its congressmen to support the canal commissioners' bid.[33]

In the House, Morris and Clinton encountered similar refusals. When a subcommittee delayed the proposed bill, they reported that "it was obvious that an opinion of [the canal's] superior benefit to this state was sedulously inculcated."[34] Soon after, they were handed defeat in a 4-to-9 vote, and they left Washington with the impression that the canal bill had been drawn into the politics of national bank rechartering and fears of a looming conflict with Great Britain.[35]

Upon returning to New York in early 1812, Gouverneur Morris began composing the commission's summary to the state legislature. They had a statutory duty to report on their work and, according to the 1811 law that authorized their work, the commission had another avenue left to exploit. In addition to directing the board to seek financial support for a canal from Washington and other states, Jonas Platt's statute creating the commission authorized them to "ascertain" whether the state could borrow on its own credit and on "advantageous terms" enough money to build the canal independently.

The nine commissioners seized this mandate to strike a bold note. Referring to themselves in the third person and with a tone of false modesty, they reminded the legislature that the canal's potential for commercial development was of a scale that contemporaries could not contemplate. "The commissioners will not dwell on the advantages which the commerce of this state must derive" from a canal, they wrote. Nor would they "hint at the political influence which must result from holding a key to the commerce of our western world." The "subject," they said, was "too delicate for discussion," and out of "prudential respect" for "legislative intelligence" they believed it should not be discussed by the state's "subordinate agents."[36]

But after obligatory throat-clearing pledges to "speak with caution," the commission laid out the case for a canal program. In a text that alternately coached and bullied legislators, Gouverneur Morris—writing for the nine members—declared it impossible that "an expenditure of five or six million, in ten or a dozen years, can be a serious consideration to a million men, enjoying one of the richest soils and finest climates under heaven" when "there is scarcely a spot on the globe which possesses such advantages for commerce."[37] The cost of a canal, even with unforeseen increases and complications, would pale in comparison to its long-term utility. "If a calculation were made on principles of compound interest," Morris wrote, "it would appear that the sum to be expended, with interest, until the canal shall yield sufficient revenue, will not exceed what that income would discharge in a reasonable time."[38]

Moreover, the commissioners added that, according to their statutory obligation, they had considered whether the state's credit was sufficiently strong to allow it to borrow funds for canal construction. Their answer was affirmative. "Notwithstanding the scarcity of money" brought on by continental wars, they believed $5 million could be borrowed from European bankers at an annual interest rate of 6 percent for a period of ten or fifteen years. And despite their recently failed efforts in Congress, they also thought that the federal government would grant New York land for the canal—some 4.4 million acres.[39]

Beyond laying out an apparently self-evident argument for the canal's economic and commercial practicality, Morris deployed his most persuasive rhetorical energies when discussing the state legislature itself. Riding to the rescue of an institution besieged by straw-man arguments and hampered by perceptions of its own limitations, the commissioners—as Morris depicted them—were speaking as advisers to the legislature who wanted to guard its prestige and the reputations of its members. Although naysayers were "triumphantly declar[ing] that the legislature has not the spirit and intelligence" to build a canal, Morris dismissed them as people who wanted to make sure that "the envied state of New York will continue a supplicant for the favor and a dependant on the generosity of the Union." He and his fellow commissioners, by comparison, wanted to make to New York and its government "a manly and dignified appeal to her own power."[40]

Therefore, there was no sense in waiting for a future generation of legislators to act. Would successors be better equipped or more patriotic? Would land become cheaper after being "planted as an orchard, tilled as a garden, or covered by a house . . .?" Even in the future, men with "fertile imaginations" might "invent" reasons to postpone the project. But taking the state out of "its corporate capacity" and imagining it as a person, Morris observed that no man would "hesitate to double the value of his property, and increase his revenue threefold, without labour, without expense." "Or suppose this individual to be an infant," he continued, "would his guardians do their duty should they let slip the golden opportunity so to promote the interest of their ward?" Predicting that a canal would outlive the republic itself, Morris envisioned a future when "by the flow of that perpetual stream which bears all human institutions away . . . our constitution shall be dissolved and our laws be lost," yet "the same mountains will stand, the same rivers run . . . after a lapse of two thousand years . . . this national work shall remain." Lawmakers were not inferior to the task at hand and not "so cold as not to feel the dignified sense of immortalizing [their] name, by contributing to a monument of national magnificence, unequalled by any thing on earth." The state legislature was "the guardian of the state," according to Morris and his fellow commissioners; all they had to do was say yes to the project. It was simple: "[I]f therefore the Legislature say, let it be done—it will be done."[41]

Although Gouverneur Morris was careful to describe the members of the canal commission as the state legislature's subordinate agents, the tone and content of his 1812 report told another story. The nine commissioners had assumed the role of independent canal advocates who legislators could rely on for practical and political expertise, policy recommendations, and even unsolicited counsel.

   As a body that had studied the canal route, the canal commission offered to professionalize the work of canal construction and finance. The commissioners offered to remove minute planning and construction details from the legislature's portfolio by hiring engineers—"professional" men—to plan and supervise day-to-day operations. They also volunteered to do the legwork involved in procuring a loan offer, a move that would obviate the need for new taxes and remove an immediate obstacle to the legislative support.[42] The commission, then, was working to make an ambitious policy seem more prudent than precarious. They clothed their recommendations in the language of civic republicanism and boosterism to provide political cover both to the legislature as a whole and to individual members. Realizing that the canal commission had become a valuable political asset that had filed a report too important to be ignored, state lawmakers ordered five thousand copies of Morris's brief printed for members to distribute throughout the state.[43]

Yet even as these leaflets fluttered in all directions from the state capital, the War of 1812 halted all official discussion of canals in Albany. In 1813, a motion in the legislature to request an update from the commission was rejected. The following year, the commissioners took the initiative to make their own report, admitting that the war had foiled their attempts to raise a foreign loan but announcing success in obtaining grants of land along the proposed route.

This time, they exercised even more independence by going on the offensive, firing back at a state senator named Erastus Root who was pushing legislation to disband the commission and arrest its work.

A Republican, Root hailed from Delaware County, deep in the state's middle district and far from where a canal would reach. He was a ferociously sarcastic and persuasive politician and a major-general in the state's militia; except for a three-year gap, he had been either a state legislator or congressman continuously since 1798. Since 1812 he had made himself a nemesis of DeWitt Clinton; more than any New Yorker, he consistently tried to link Clinton to the canal, coining the moniker "Clinton's big ditch" and leaving the impression that opposition to the man inspired opposition to the plan.[44]

Root roused the canal commission from its silent slumber by moving quickly in 1814 to repeal three sections of Jonas Platt's 1812 statute that empowered the body to pay surveyors and engineers and submit reports to the legislature. In the state senate, no dedicated canal partisans were present to raise an objection; neither Platt nor Clinton was a senator anymore. Platt was a judge and Clinton had been reduced to holding only the mayorship of New York City—payback from New York Republicans for his being the Federalists' presidential candidate in 1812.

Yet few members of the New York senate were as ardently anti-canal as Root; legislators agreed that the war made it an inopportune time to build the canal, but only Root spoke of suspending the commissioners' work indefinitely. Colleagues supported his legislation only after changing it to preserve contracts, agreements, and commitments already negotiated by the commission. And even then, senators approved this measure only by a voice vote; nobody wanted to go on record as a canal opponent, and would-be supporters saw no advantages in forcing them to do so. Even Root soon softened his tone, conceding that in peacetime it "might or might not be proper" to allow the state to borrow an "immense sum of money" for a canal.[45]

In the intervening weeks, the canal commissioners rushed to issue a report on their past year of activities. But in it they made two missteps, which reinvigorated opposition to their project. First, they announced the hiring of a British engineer in an environment in which an antiwar Federalist-controlled assembly was incessantly at odds with a pro-war Republican-dominated state senate, plunging the commission's work into the capital's partisan divide. Second, the commissioners abandoned their can-do rhetoric in favor of a combative stance toward canal critics. Noticing "attempts to excite opposition" to their work, the commissioners dismissed dissenters like Erastus Root as "sanguine men" who "make facts as they go along." "Whatsoever they think proper to approve of is sublime," while "whatsoever they think proper to dislike is absurd."[46]

After the canal commissioners submitted their report on 8 March, members of the New York assembly pounced, seeing no downside to speaking in favor of Root's legislation publicly and repeatedly. Canal commissioner Stephen Van Rensselaer, still an assemblyman after briefly (and poorly) commanding the United States Army during the first year of the war, tried to salvage a future for the commission by trying to amend Root's bill to suspend the body's work only until peacetime. His motion was defeated, and the assembly eventually agreed by a 45-27 vote to repeal parts of the 1812 commission bill without breaking existing contracts and agreements. When the state senate took up this version of Root's repeal bill, the commission's friends demanded a recorded vote to force their opponents into the open. Root, Martin Van Buren, and twelve other senators voted to suspend the commissioners' work; seven voted against the bill.[47]

In isolation, this episode might have looked like a win for Erastus Root and a loss for the canal commission. Yet in its larger context, it spoke to the durability of what was quickly becoming an entrenched institution in the state's political and economic landscape. If the commissioners were concerned about a permanent swing of opinion against them, they did not betray it. With the exception of Stephen Van Rensselaer, the assemblyman, no other canal commissioner visited Albany to lobby against Root's proposals. At the outset, Root hoped to convince colleagues to never again consider canal legislation; in the end, he retreated to questioning only the timing of the project while leveling no counterclaims against the canal's practicality and utility. Thus Albany had not suddenly turned against the canal or even the commissioners. Even enemies of the commission resisted unraveling its accomplishments; the economic interests entangled in canal development were sufficiently strong to merit protection.[48]

In addition to importing a British engineer and signing contracts for surveys, securing land was an activity in which the commissioners had broad latitude to act without much legislative oversight. Between 1812 and 1814, they tried to buy out the Western Inland Lock Navigation Company's land holdings and negotiate a donation from the Holland Land Company. When the Western company treasurer Robert Bowne demanded a $190,000 payment for the company's only substantial assets, Robert Fulton and DeWitt Clinton rejected the sum out of hand, presuming they would someday be able to pay less. The commission, after all, was gaining leverage, prompting a far more cooperative Joseph Ellicott to waste no time inking a Holland Land Company donation of 100,000 acres along the proposed route in 1813.[49] Canal commissioners—not the legislature or "the state"—were parties to these contracts; even lawmakers with the authority to rewrite state law could not abrogate certain binding arrangements. By confirming the legitimacy of its agreements and contracts, therefore, the repeal bill made permanent both the commission and its work.

More important, as legal formalities such agreements were evidence of long-term commitments to canal building on the part of interests, institutions, and organizations that had been recruited and mobilized to support the project. Contracts and even conditional promises were not handshakes; they were the work product of a commission engaged in building durable political and economic coalitions. Even in the absence of a settled state canal plan, land cessions and donations represented a virtual canal. By consolidating acres and miles of territory through interdependent and contingent land deals, the canal commission was quietly but steadily herding New York's upstate landowners toward a pro-canal consensus, creating alliances that elected politicians crossed at their peril, and deliberately isolating holdout legislators by casting them as the sole remaining obstacles to the project. Therefore, even as they professed to be seeking federal funds, the commissioners were making it more likely that a canal would eventually be carved through New York regardless of what happened in Washington.

For this reason, the canal commissioners kept their distance from both their state and national capitals during the years that followed. As a committee of political entrepreneurs, officeholders, and land developers, they conceived of their lobbying effort as something akin to the petition drives that had steered state policy since the founding of the republic. Taking the lead for the group were DeWitt Clinton and Thomas Eddy. By late 1815, Clinton had no public office aside from being a canal commissioner; Eddy had regained the treasurer post at the Western Inland Lock Navigation Company and had risen to public prominence as a member of the state's public school and prison reform societies, a proponent of a newly created state asylum, and—like Clinton—a founding member of the New-York Historical Society.[50] Basing their operations in Manhattan, the two began running a sophisticated but low-profile effort to align the state's landed, monied, mercantile, and agricultural interests and engineering a campaign to sow a visible and vocal harvest of petitions that would eventually be sent to Albany to demand the construction of a canal.

In the fall of 1815, Eddy visited New York City to call on Jonas Platt, his onetime ally in creating the canal commission five years earlier. Platt had left the state senate after being appointed a judge on the state Supreme Court, and, sitting in Platt's Manhattan chambers, Eddy persuaded him to call a public meeting of the city's canal supporters to draft a memorial urging the state legislature to resuscitate the project.[51]

But this would be more than a mere meeting and no ordinary memorial petition. In a city where canal support had been tepid at best, the men plotted to use the summit to build something far more durable, using it as an occasion to reconcile old foes and leverage connections to build a bloc of canal enthusiasts. Although the physical evidence—the work product—of the meeting would apparently be a pro-canal document, the canal memorial would represent a treaty among intra-party and interparty factions to cooperate on this single issue. The meeting itself would publicly unveil these alliances, rolling them into citywide and statewide momentum on behalf of the project.

Thomas Eddy's meticulousness in assembling this coalition is revealed by his actions in advance of the meeting. After his visit with Platt, Eddy sought Clinton's blessing for the public meeting. Then he visited John Swartwout, a merchant and a retired state militia general who had been the federal marshal in the city during Thomas Jefferson's first term as president.

But Swartwout was no ordinary political entrepreneur. In 1802 he and Clinton had both been members of the Manhattan Company's board of directors, but after Vice President Aaron Burr's falling-out with the state's Livingstonian and Clintonian Republican factions, DeWitt Clinton helped push Burr and Swartwout from the bank's board. Swartwout eventually landed a directorship at the Burrite Merchants Bank as a reward for his loyalty, but Burr nursed a grudge and disparaged Clinton, who responded by challenging the vice president to a duel. Burr did not decline the challenge, but instead of appearing in person had Swartwout stand in for him. And so, one day in Hoboken, New Jersey, DeWitt Clinton shot John Swartwout in the leg—twice—first in his thigh and then in his ankle, making him the only prominent New York businessman to have been shot by a canal commissioner.[52]

The symbolic weight of getting Clinton and Swartwout to appear together on the same platform on behalf of the same cause would be incalculable, and Thomas Eddy believed that their schism could be mended by the balm of common interest. Like any city merchant, John Swartwout stood to gain from trade along the canal. But he also had a far more specific and immediate stake. After being purged from his federal marshal post and alienated from New York's Republican factions, Swartwout had moved to upstate New York to start a saltworks. Within eleven years, he and his two brothers had become rich, and their salt marshes at the north end of Cayuga Lake were immediately adjacent to the proposed canal route.[53] There the canal's projected path would briefly jog south to tap the lake before returning north and resuming an east-west heading. Swartwout's lands were therefore centered on a location that could become one of the canal's first and most easily completed sections.

Soon after these meetings, about one hundred cards went out, inviting the city's "most influential" citizens to a gathering at the City Hotel to discuss the proposed canal; they were signed by Jonas Platt, Thomas Eddy, DeWitt Clinton, and John Swartwout. On the evening of 30 December 1815, the "large and respectable" body met and as their first act nominated merchant William Bayard to chair the proceedings. Bayard, a Federalist, was a principal in the transatlantic mercantile firm of LeRoy, Bayard, and McEvers. In 1814 his firm donated 2,500 acres of upstate lands to the canal commissioners, and his brother Samuel, an agent of the six-million-acre Pulteney Estate, pledged a donation as well. Both land cessions were among those protected by the legislature's repeal bill.[54]

The first speaker at the meeting was Jonas Platt, who rose to extol the generic virtues of a canal and speak to the specific benefits it would deliver to New York City. Platt also used the moment to argue against Gouverneur Morris's long-held idea of having the canal be a single inclined plane; he preferred instead a system of locks that would feed water to the trench, an opinion shared by several canal commissioners who kept silent lest they

publicly cross their president. Clinton spoke after Platt, followed by Swartwout. Some in the room weighed in against the canal, but the meeting
agreed to present a pro-canal petition to the state legislature later that spring,
and deputized Clinton, Eddy, Swartwout, and Cadwallader Colden to draft
the document.[55]

The resulting petition—considered so important among contemporary
canal antiquarians that it is simply referred to as "the Memorial"—was produced so quickly by DeWitt Clinton that it likely was written well before the
meeting. As a technical document, it contained little new information, revising familiar themes in canal-promotion literature: creating commerce, binding territory, and decreasing the cost of shipping.

But as a petition intended to identify, recruit, and mobilize constituents
for the canal and to extend the sphere of political entrepreneurship throughout the city and state, Clinton's work was a rhetorical masterpiece. Instead of
leaning on promises that a canal would bring "cheapness, celerity, certainty,
and safety" to transportation, the memorial flattered New York merchants
with assurances that a link between the Hudson River and the Great Lakes
would "render [New York] the greatest commercial city in the world." "The
whole line of canal," Clinton wrote,

> will exhibit boats loaded with flour, pork, beef, pot and pearl ashes,
> flaxseed, wheat, barley, corn, hemp, wool, flax, iron, lead, copper, salt,
> gypsum, coal, tar, fur, peltry, ginseng, bees-wax, cheese, butter, lard,
> staves, lumber, and the other valuable productions of our country;
> and also, with merchandise from all parts of the world. Great manu-
> facturing establishments will spring up; agriculture will establish its
> granaries, and commerce its warehouses in all directions. Villages,
> towns, and cities, will line the banks of the canal, and the shores of the
> Hudson from Erie to New-York.[56]

The canal, Clinton stressed, would therefore benefit both the city and the agricultural counties along the Hudson River—places that had been a principal
source of objections to the project. Neutralizing that opposition would trans-
form the terms of the canal debate, tipping a balance of legislative votes in the
canal's favor.

In this vein, three of the seven points listed in the canal's favor addressed
specific interests in New York: merchants, land owners, and investors in other
internal improvements. "Our honourable merchants" did not deserve to be

"robbed of their legitimate profits" because "dishonest smuggling" had made Montreal a more attractive shipping point to the western frontier than New York City or Albany; investors in New York's turnpikes and other internal improvements deserved "dignified impartiality and paternal affection" and a statement of "intentions" from the legislature since "turnpikes, locks, and short canals have been resorted to, and . . . villages have been laid out and towns have been contemplated." Clinton did not merely want to say that a canal would do no harm to investors and stakeholders in the state's existing internal-improvement institutions; he wanted to color the project as a positive addition to the state's institutional ecology. Therefore, he wrote, the canal would "encourage the cultivation" of "extensive and remote" lands and "create new sources of internal trade" by "augment[ing] the old channels" of commerce. Therefore, even if they had not realized it before, investors in existing and even potentially competing projects were already stakeholders in a would-be canal. And to add urgency to the matter, Clinton cautioned that "the longer this work is delayed," "the greater will be the difficulty in surmounting the interests that will rise up in opposition to it." By deferring its decision on whether to pursue the canal, state legislators were creating conditions for "injurious speculation" in improvements and "violent opposition" toward the interests behind them.

As a call to action, then, the *Memorial* therefore sought to extend Thomas Eddy's alliance-building exercises beyond the palatial ballroom of the City Hotel out to New York City and state, creating momentum for the kind of political consolidations that corporations had accomplished since the days of the Bank of New-York and the Manhattan Company. But this time, instead of creating and distributing financial interests to foster unity and discipline among rival factions in immature parties, Thomas Eddy launched the petition from a public meeting intended to demonstrate that established and settled partisan divisions could coexist with new common interests. Squabbles over patronage, party divisions, and even past duels could be overwhelmed by the relational bonds of shared commercial and financial interests that were capable of prodding shareholders to cooperate as citizens. Therefore, although its construction could not erase the past, the canal—as a kind of super-institution in the state's political economy—could temporarily reset party politics by spawning a sufficiently large number of material incentives to create a cross-bench consensus in its favor that transcended typical geographical and occupational boundaries. The commission, then, saw its role in canal promotion not merely as an advisory board but as a body that could actively interest people in its construction and completion by teasing the different valences of personal, private, material, and civic aspirations and obligations that were held by the citizen-shareholders of the early republic.

On practical and ideological fronts, this reflected the experiences of the members of the canal commission itself and the résumés of DeWitt Clinton and Thomas Eddy in particular. Both men had spent much of their careers as shareholders, directors, and officers of some of the state's public-private corporations and had leveraged those positions to gain and exercise political power within the state's economy of influence. As the nephew of a governor, Clinton began as an operative in the Manhattan Company and later took a role in founding institutions on his own in New York City while also serving as the city's mayor; Eddy had been a merchant and an insurance broker chosen by Philip Schuyler to become treasurer of the Western Inland Lock Navigation Company; he used that platform to become a canal commissioner to further advance the company's interests, and then he used his position on the commission to reestablish his social standing in the institutional hierarchy of New York City. Both men were fully incorporated into the state's institutional environment; their positions within those institutions defined their current position and future potential on the landscape of political opportunity. No wonder they and the commissioners they represented conceived of the canal project in terms of how it could both mobilize the state's existing institutionalized interests and identify and organize new interests.

In thinking about the mobilization in favor of the Erie Canal, then, it is essential to recognize that while it was a state-driven project, its origins lie in the hybrid mixed economy of New York's public-private marketplace. The public proposal for this "public" project was explicitly framed in terms of how it would augment private interests and use private capital while also serving a larger public good. And even that "public" good was in fact a vast collection of private goods and benefits—too numerous to catalog but all sharing one common trait: they were located within the territorial boundaries of the state of New York. Therefore, although it represented a new frontier in state-directed economic and infrastructure development, the proposal to have the state of New York construct a canal was not a challenge to the existing institutional order but a different way of organizing those interests.

No aspect of pro-canal mobilization better illustrated the subtlety of this shift than Clinton and Eddy's proposal to finance the project using bonds. Although the canal commission's past official reports had proposed public financing for the project, they had never been specific about just how that might be accomplished—whether through loans (as envisioned by some law-makers); through legislative appropriations directly from the state's coffers; or through lotteries, stocks, or other means.

In this vacuum, Clinton's *Memorial* began outlining a more specific proposal.

The state certainly had the right, he observed, to erect a set of new capital-gathering institutions to build the canal: corporations that would build "particular sections of the route" or even a new bank to exclusively service the canal's needs. But this option had risks. New corporations, like the Northern or Western Inland Lock Companies before them, could fail to raise sufficient capital; or they might discover and pursue a different project, veering away from the vision of a unified and publicly oriented canal. And even if a corporation did successfully complete the project, "high tolls" could "certainly injure if not ruin the whole enterprise." Bonding therefore could avoid the demonstrable pitfalls that arose in past canal initiatives.

There were other benefits, too. As described by Clinton, bonds could structure the finances of canal building in a way that made the project more practically achievable. He and Eddy estimated that the state government would have to sell $6 million to finance the entire route; if it borrowed at 6 percent per year, for every $500,000 the state raised it would be required to pay only $30,000 in interest annually. That sum, Clinton wrote, could easily be found by tapping revenues generated from the state-owned saltworks and through land sales, in addition to the "many shapes" of taxes that could be levied without being "burdensome to the community."

Beyond these practical advantages, there were also political and economic reasons to support public bonding. Although such bonds would technically be issued by the state of New York on behalf of the public, the investors and brokers in those bonds would be private investors and firms—the same cadres of merchants, bank shareholders, corporate directors, and financial houses that presently constituted the state and region's financial infrastructure. By avoiding the well-trodden trail of creating corporations to build infrastructure, the state would not be denying private investors an opportunity to profit from canal finance. Quite the opposite. Because public bonding would not "advance the views of individuals . . . foment the divisions of party . . . [or promote] the interests of a few," it promised widely shared participation in the goods and gains of a canal. Thus, public financing was in fact a wide invitation to the state's political entrepreneurs to join in pro-canal boosterism. By avoiding the creation of any new institution, the state would not only prevent a corporation from repeating past construction failures or raising toll rates so high as to render the canal off limits; it would also avoid vesting a cabal of corporate directors or monopoly-holders with the power to use the canal's awesome scale to distort the state's marketplace. Issuing public bonds would not threaten existing institutions and constituencies or challenge the state's political economy practices; instead, it would draw on the financial and transportation infrastructures that had been created by incumbent institutions during the prior three decades. And in so doing, it would harness private investors' capital, tap directors' expertise, and mobilize the state's political entrepreneurs—monopolists, licensees, patent-holders, shareholders, patrons, subsidiary dependents, and partisans—into a bloc of supporters who could be relied on to lobby Congress and the state legislature on the canal commissioners' behalf. Bonding was therefore a way for the state to develop its own capacity for action, but to do so in a seemingly decentralizing way. By integrating competing interests to advance one project, Clinton and Eddy could marshal the "deep state" power of New York's many public-private mixed-economy institutions without having it appear to be a particularly statist exercise.

And although it did not mention them by name, the framers of the *Memorial* clearly intended to use this financing proposal to target one specific, overwhelmingly powerful constituency present at the City Hotel in Manhattan as well as in the most commercially developed municipalities of the state: its banks.

New York's bank directors and shareholders were so influential over the affairs of state that it was impolitic to invoke them by name yet also unnecessary to do so. When the canal meeting was held in New York City, eight banks were already there and twenty others were sprinkled throughout the state in places like Poughkeepsie, Troy, Waterford, Ithaca, Utica, Schenectady, Newburgh, and Kingston. And although the Manhattan Company's $2 million capitalization had been scandalously large in 1799, the legislature had since created far larger firms, including the audaciously partisan and transparently corrupt $6 million Bank of America in 1812. By 1816—a boom year in charter requests—the available capital in the state's chartered banks already exceeded $24 million. State lawmakers chartered two more banks that year—one of them in canal-interested Buffalo; they created another four in 1817, and yet another four in 1818.[57]

In proposing to finance the canal with bonds, Clinton and Eddy showed an appreciation for the role the state's banks had played in organizing and mobilizing New York voters since the end of the Revolution. Politicians across the state were already indebted to banks, which routinely offered them loans, directorships, and favorable stock offerings, and which also mobilized voters on their behalf. They were centers of party formation and partisan discipline, blending money and authority to ensure that disloyalty would be more than socially inconvenient, and occasionally reminding hesitant voters that they were also dependent debtors. By holding a canal rally in the ballroom of the City Hotel and having former bank directors invite current bank directors to a meeting chaired by officers of the city's Chamber of Commerce, Thomas Eddy and DeWitt Clinton enlisted on their behalf an unseen network of shareholders, borrowers, and subsidiary dependents who had a multitude of subtle and sharp tools available to them to influence public officials and policy makers, and to penetrate even the state's most insulated chambers of power.

Moreover, in the post–War of 1812 economy, those banks and their patrons were eager to find safe, interest-bearing investments in which to park their capital. Although an incorporated canal construction company could never provide that kind of security, a state-guaranteed bond—one that paid a 6 percent interest rate—would be an attractive asset in not only the boardrooms of New York's banks but also in the markets of Amsterdam and London. Therefore, instead of creating a stock-issuing entity that would compete with the state's incorporated institutions, Clinton's *Memorial* promised the state's banks an opportunity to buy for themselves and their clients one of the most secure and productive investments available anywhere in the nation, as well as a chance to make Manhattan the epicenter of finance capital in North America.

Bonding was one practical way to take a step toward resolving long-acknowledged tensions that were inherently embedded within state-created mixed-economy institutions without making a grand ideological statement about political economy. Because they straddled the public and private spheres, privately financed state-chartered corporations would forever be tempted to prioritize short-term profits over the long-term public good. Although legislators could limit the lifespans of state-created corporations or mandate that their directors meet certain requirements before their charters were eligible for renewal, such mechanisms were only ways to check this problem; they could not, however, eliminate it. But by proposing that the state of New York—the public—retain ownership of a canal and that the same public finance it through private investments, some of which would be channeled through state-created public-private banks, public bonding would make it possible to safeguard the canal's utility as a public good while fundamentally preserving the contours of the state's mixed-economy marketplace. In this way, the state could keep its economy of influence in place while fencing off the new canal from privileged individuals' desires to privatize its purpose.

As Clinton and Eddy's *Memorial* gained signatures in Manhattan in early 1816, other meetings were held throughout the state that deliberately emulated the first in order to build local political momentum for the project and channel pressure toward Albany. The *Memorial of the Citizens of New-York* arrived at the statehouse on 16 February, bearing more than a thousand signatures. Then other petitions began arriving: first from the western parts of the state—Buffalo, Seneca, Reading, and Geneva—all on 21 February. Five days later they were from Junius, Geneva, Lyons, and Genoa—all near Cayuga Lake—and Caledonia. Two days later, on 28 February, former New York chancellor John Lansing and other signers from Albany presented their own memorial. The following day, 29 February, more signatures arrived from Albany and Lenox. On 1 March, support came in from the alderman and corporation of the City of New York; on 9 March, from Oneida County; on 11 March, from Ulysses in Seneca County and from Genesee. One day later, the citizens of Troy made their case, followed by Onondaga County on 15 March, Avon in Ontario on 21 March, Paris in Oneida on 22 March, and the towns of Chautauqua, Hartland, and Ridgeway on 30 March, and Russia, German-Flats, Newport, and Schuyler in Herkimer County on 3 April. Within a span of six weeks, more than one hundred thousand New Yorkers' signatures headed toward the state capital on pro-canal petitions.[58]

Behind the scenes, DeWitt Clinton and Thomas Eddy were still busily consolidating support for the canal by confirming support from past allies and making new appeals. Much of this work involved renewing, reviewing, and finessing past agreements. For example, rumors that Lake Ontario—not Lake Erie—was being considered as the terminus for the canal had "occasioned much anxiety" among landowners whose properties it would bypass, according to a warning passed on to Clinton by Holland Land Company agent Joseph Ellicott. Ellicott feared that unless Clinton intervened to clarify the canal commission's intentions, those disaffected might send a "remonstrance . . . against" the canal to the state legislature.[59]

In other cases, however, would-be canal opponents merely sought reassurances that the *Memorial* authors had already anticipated. Uri Tracy, a past sheriff and clerk of Chenango County, accepted that a canal would not traverse his county. Rather than seek to alter that fact, he wanted DeWitt Clinton's word that turnpikes in which he and his allies had invested would not be rendered obsolete once the canal opened. If that was the case, he would support the canal; he even told Clinton that he "presume[d] funds can be raised, by creating stock, or some other way," such as using bonds, "to obtain the object [the canal], if the State will take it up."[60] If Uri Tracy had had access to the canal petition then circulating in New York City, he would have found his question answered and discovered that he and Clinton were already in broad agreement on questions of canal financing.

Well before canal petitions began flooding the state legislature, it is likely that DeWitt Clinton had made up his mind about the practicality of having the state finance the project. But the same was not true of Thomas Eddy and an unknown number of other members of the state canal commission who worried that the state would never be able to sell enough bonds to fully fund the project. Eddy warned against approaching the legislature for authorizations exceeding $500,000 or borrowing at more than 6 percent interest; "[I]f more is asked," he wrote, "we shall get nothing." He even contemplated offering the Holland Land Company a sweetheart deal just so the commissioners could avoid seeking legislative funding altogether. If Joseph Ellicott's superiors could be persuaded to loan the state money at 4 percent interest, Eddy proposed to Clinton that the commission promise to begin canal construction near sites chosen by the Holland Land Company. Eddy had even worked out all the details, telling Clinton that "it may be advisable to begin at Lake Erie, on account of the probability of the Holland Company being induced, in that case, to give us something very handsome towards affecting a Canal from Erie, passing Genesee River, to the Seneca, at the Cayuga outlet." This would allow the commissioners to "commence on such part of the line as . . . may be productive of the greatest immediate advantage." By doing a favor for the Holland Land Company, then, the commissioners would be able to build a demonstrably successful first portion of the project, receive preferential financial backing, and command the company's political influence. Eddy was so enthusiastic about this plan that he was even ready to hire an engineer—one "of the very first talents—a practical man"—and had only one caveat: "he ought not to be a French Man—he must be a man we can confide in fully—we can't do this in any French Engineer."[61]

Perhaps Eddy had been scarred by his experience as treasurer of the Western Inland Lock Navigation Company, but Clinton disagreed with the plan. He was confident that the state's financial markets were strong enough to support canal construction and could look to the recent past to see that a wartime state loan had raised nearly $650,000 from the public, most of it from smaller investors.[62] Clinton thought that regardless of whether his colleagues realized it, the commission had at its disposal a deep reservoir of capital. In New York City alone, Clinton wrote, "centers 1/3 of our [national] commerce and from her is derived 1/3 of our [national] revenue. There are ten times more goods purchased here by Southern & Western merchants than in Philadelphia." "Philadelphia may eventually be the seat of manufactures," Clinton continued, but New York "is the centre of commerce & the focus of the monied operations of the union."[63] And because of this, there was no economic need to make deals like the one Eddy proposed with the Holland Land Company.

In Clinton's view, then, the fate of the proposed canal turned on political considerations—a situation he was trying to remedy with mounting stacks of petitions arriving in Albany. There remained good reasons to fear inaction, however. Robert Troup, the veteran Federalist Manhattan attorney who had speculated in land three decades earlier when the inland lock navigation companies were incorporated to build canals, was still a canal supporter in 1816. As the legal agent for the multi-million-acre Pulteney Estate, in fact, Troup was a diehard enthusiast for the project.

Yet when New York governor Daniel Tompkins omitted any mention of the canal in his January speech before the legislature, Troup worried that the state government's neglect of the project might lead its leaders to repeat old mistakes. He was "more & more convinced," he told DeWitt Clinton, that if the canal was "dependen[t] . . . on the operations" of the Northern and Western companies or "any other company, like incorporated" that the state would "discover, to our future loss, that we had depended on a broken reed." Although corporations were useful vehicles for capital formation, in Troup's view they simply lacked the organizational and financial capacities to fund, construct, and operate such a large-scale project. And because the state did not seem to be making canal building a priority, Troup was anxious that lazy policy makers might be tempted to revert to old habits and kick the project over to an incorporated effort that he saw as destined to fail. In Troup's view, this possibility only strengthened the case for the "absolute necessity of resorting to the patriotism of the Legislature, and to the resources of the state alone for opening a practicable navigation between the Western Lakes and the tidewaters of the Hudson."[64]

But although the petition movement orchestrated by Thomas Eddy and

DeWitt Clinton had the power to persuade, the state's legislative calendar was rapidly drawing to a close. Writing to an Albany-based correspondent in late February, Clinton hastily noted in a letter, "I shall not neglect this opportunity of promoting the Erie Canal." "If you have not seen the New York Memorial in its favor it will give me great pleasure to forward it," he added, asking whether the recipient could "leave . . . [in Albany] a small package containing two or three pamphlets?"[65]

However relentless an advocate he was for the canal in print, however, DeWitt Clinton kept his distance from the state capital in 1816. Critics close to Martin Van Buren, a state senator and leader of that house's Republican Bucktail faction, alleged that Clinton did not want to write tax laws because he intended to run for governor the following year. Certainly Clinton had no friend in Van Buren, and Clinton partisans conflated Van Buren's opposition to Clinton with opposition to the canal, amplifying this charge when Van Buren called for a year-long delay in the legislature of any consideration of canal policy. Yet in reality, Van Buren's proposal strengthened both Clinton and the canal commission, reauthorizing their work and directing them to elect a president and secretary from among their members, spend $20,000 on a detailed mile-by-mile survey of the route, hire engineers, and seek aid from landowners within the state, neighboring states, and the federal government. It also gave the commissioners the statutory authority to "consider, devise, and adopt" whatever measures were necessary to build the canal, leaving it to them to report back with a specific plan and cost estimates in 1817.[66] Postponement therefore reflected a lack of information rather than a lack of interest, and it reified the commission's role as a source of expertise and the center of gravity in New York canal politics.

With the new law, the canal commission divided the project into three sections—eastern, middle, and western—to make their work more administratively manageable.[67] Clinton began hiring engineers and recruiting staff, offering some positions to past friends of the project. Top engineering posts went to political allies with backgrounds in surveying. James Geddes, the former New York assemblyman who had performed the fieldwork in 1808 for the state's underfunded canal study, had maintained his connection to the project by organizing an upstate canal rally in 1817; he was awarded oversight of the western section. Judge Benjamin Wright, who had cosponsored the 1808 survey as a freshman assemblyman from Oneida County and been hired by Thomas Eddy as a surveyor for the Western Inland Lock Navigation Company, was made chief of the middle section. Charles T. Broadhead, a former sheriff and deputy state surveyor who had worked for the Castorland Company (or Compagnie de New York), which was formed to resettle French aristocrats who had fled the guillotine amid the safe anonymity of the Adirondacks, was given the eastern section.[68]

Critics howled over some of these hires, with one assemblyman demanding to know "Who is this James Geddes, and who is this Benjamin Wright, that the Commissioners have trusted with this responsibility—what canals have they ever constructed? What great public works have they accomplished?" But in making such politically sensitive appointments to technical and bureaucratic positions, Clinton evinced an ongoing concern for the canal's political prospects in Albany. He was not simply engaging in patronage for the sake of his career or party. Rather, this was a deliberate effort to prolong the political mobilization that he, Thomas Eddy, and other commissioners had begun years earlier. Each appointee's résumé married technical skills with political capital, each had deep organizational ties to regions and institutions that would benefit from the canal, and each was a plausible local agent who could function as an emissary for the commissioners—a political entrepreneur who represented a committee of political entrepreneurs.[69] The "easy and cheap execution" and "practicability" of the canal, Clinton believed, was supposed to offer it insulation "beyond the reach of cavil" from other quarters of the state, and his choices of appointments were clearly intended to buttress this claim.[70]

Thus, when Clinton and the other canal commissioners returned to the state capital in early 1817, they did so in an even stronger position to begin lobbying on the project's behalf. Clinton had even more at stake than a year earlier, having become the presumptive Republican nominee to succeed New York governor Daniel Tompkins, the longtime canal doubter who would shortly become James Monroe's vice president.

As requested, the commissioners presented the legislature with a mile-by-mile tour of the canal route—a document that ran ninety-six pages—outlining the topography, engineering challenges, and costs for each dam, lock, and turn of the proposed project; in all, they calculated the expenses would be $4,571,813. They also reported that the Holland Land Company had renewed their 1814 agreement to donate land to the project, and they presented this alongside other statements testifying to the canal's feasibility from the most accomplished canal engineers they could find in North America, a small pool of talent with one standout: John L. Sullivan. Sullivan had built the twenty-seven-mile-long Boston-area Middlesex Canal—in Clinton's view, the "best in the country"—and was asked on short notice to evaluate the New York commission's report. Immodestly introduced to the legislature as the seven-year-veteran supervisor of the Middlesex Canal, someone who "personally examined the most celebrated canals in England, France and Holland, [and] has had the charge of constructing several short canals with locks, dams, &c.," Sullivan said he did not know enough about the project to offer a "decisive opinion." But based on comparisons to his firsthand experiences, he advised lawmakers that the proposed canal was being built on "peculiarly favorable" territory and that the commission's estimates, "made from the best sources of information in the country," "appear[ed] to be high enough."[71]

The commission presented legislators with similarly supportive statements from any prominent New Yorkers they could find who could credibly claim experience in canal building. State senate president Philetus Swift, who had built mill races for his home in Phelpstown in Ontario County, was among this group. So was Augustus Porter, who owned a gristmill and land near Niagara Falls with his brother, former canal commissioner and congressman Peter B. Porter. Brothers Francis and Matthew Brown, who were then slicing through a quarter-mile-long stretch of bedrock to bring water from the Genesee Falls to their twenty-five-foot-diameter water wheel, also testified to the practicality of the commission's plan. Another affirmation distributed to legislators came from Colonel Wilhelm Mynderse of Seneca Falls; like Joseph Ellicott, Mynderse was a resident agent for and partner in a land company, the Bayard Land Company, and was weeks away from becoming a director of the newly chartered Bank of Geneva along with Pulteney Estate agent Robert Troup.[72]

When DeWitt Clinton and the canal commissioners decided to exhibit these particular written endorsements by having them printed and delivered to lawmakers, they did so not only to furnish them with technical details but also to provide them with physical reminders of the influence that commissioners had marshaled behind the project by recruiting political entrepreneurs who met three criteria: they had held public office, they had been involved in banking, and they had been involved in land speculation. Such were the common elements that linked the Porters, Robert Troup, Wilhelm Mynderse, and William Bayard, the land company head and New York City merchant who had been a past director and president of the Bank of New-York in the 1790s, along with any number of signers of the Manhattan and other canal memorials. Bayard, in fact, had been tasked with soliciting foreign loans for the canal commission several years earlier, illustrating just how important a role land-investing bankers had played in canal promotion. When the commissioners presented these reports to the legislature, therefore, they were showing them evidence of a pro-canal consensus that had been built over years by micro-targeting and motivating constituencies throughout the state, using every conceivable lever to mobilize interests and institutions in order to move legislators' votes.

When the New York legislature took up the canal commissioners' 1817 report, some members were exuberant about what they read. Assemblyman Jonathan Olmstead of Hamilton was so eager to share it with his constituents that he had two thousand copies printed at public expense.[73] To coordinate the assembly and senate's work, a joint ad hoc committee was formed with four senators and five assemblymen. Many, like committee chairman assemblyman William D. Ford—who hailed from the pro-canal Herkimer County—had been on the same committee a year earlier and remained staunchly in favor of the project.

Legislative consensus seemed so consolidated in the project's favor, in fact, that when President James Madison unexpectedly vetoed a bill that would have provided partial federal funding for the canal, there was no sign of panic in Albany among canal supporters. Clinton and his fellow commissioners had been hoping for federal money and had issued a memo to the state's congressional delegation estimating that the canal would cost $6 million to construct. Using a "fair and unexceptionable standard" of a population ratio, they claimed that the state was entitled to $85,000 annually, and $140,000 if the interests of Ohio and Vermont were taken into account. But when the bill was vetoed, there was hardly a ripple in the state capital. Chairman Ford merely sent a calmly worded note to DeWitt Clinton to ask for guidance on a plan of finance.[74]

Clinton answered two days later, on 10 March, with a funding formula far more comprehensive than could have been produced in just forty-eight hours. In all likelihood, much of his reply had been written by a member of Ford's committee: state senator George Tibbits of Rensselaer County. Tibbits had been discussing canal-finance details with Clinton since the winter, trying to convince the canal commission president that legislators would eventually need a specific plan. If lawmakers had to improvise such technicalities on their own, Tibbits feared for the canal's viability.

After all, in legislating, nothing is agreed to until everything is agreed to.

In their private sessions, Clinton favored having the state borrow money in the form of a general loan that would be guaranteed by revenues collected through several different taxes. But Tibbits warned that such a plan would "requir[e] the annual interference and aid of the legislature," creating potentially unstable funding sources that could cripple canal construction in the future. The senator instead suggested a plan he had been formulating since 1812: to have the state borrow money on its own credit, levy a new set of taxes, and pledge—by law—that the money raised from those taxes would be used to pay interest on the debt. To the greatest extent possible, Tibbits wanted to place the canal's finances beyond the reach of ephemeral party politics; he convinced Clinton that the state needed to create a separate commission to oversee canal financing, partitioning canal construction from canal fundraising and accounting. Tibbits was convinced that these ideas, taken together, would place canal financing on a "more substantial basis" by making the shares of the loan—called bonds—an attractive investment at home and abroad.[75]

Drawing on this colloquy, DeWitt Clinton advised chairman Ford to have the state issue $1.5 million in bonds that would pay 6 percent per year for twenty years. Guaranteed by the state itself, the bonds' interest payments could be drawn from auction duties collected in New York City, sales of public lands throughout the state, taxes on salt and steamboat passenger fares, and a newly created property tax levied on counties along the canal route. Clinton recommended that the state create a canal-fund board composed of the attorney general, treasurer, comptroller, surveyor general, and secretary of the state. He suggested that the state buy out the Western Inland Lock Company before beginning construction to avoid having the company try to extort the state for more money once its lands increased in value. He also recommended that canal construction begin in the middle section of the canal on a section that would be easily completed and profitable once it opened, generating toll revenues that would quiet any remaining canal skeptics. These proposals, Clinton summarized, would create a "wise and economical system which shall conciliate the affections, and secure the favorable opinion of those who are the source of legitimate power."[76]

As a collection of canal promoters originally deputized to offer policy advice and expertise, the state canal commissioners had prosecuted a two-front effort. First, they mobilized and organized out-of-doors voters to petition and lobby legislators on behalf of the project. Second, they created similar pressures *within* the legislature by drafting reports and crafting recommendations to provide lawmakers with reasons to build not just any canal, but *this* canal. Recognizing that a state's interests are defined by its capabilities, the commissioners prodded legislators to expand their fiscal imaginations by proposing that they adapt a familiar tool—the bond—to serve a new purpose. They tried to anticipate lawmakers' anxieties and potential objections by providing a blueprint detailing how the costs of bonding could be offset, laying out specific ways and means that could be quickly written into resolutions, sped through committee hearings, passed, and signed into law. This holistic approach to canal promotion therefore tethered high-minded appeals to civics, virtue, and ideology to more earthly concerns about interests, votes, money, and the legislative process.

It took only seven days for William Ford's committee to consider Clinton's proposals before returning a recommendation that they be adopted as soon as possible. Citing the testimonials assembled from John L. Sullivan and other luminaries—including senate president Philetus Swift, a member of Ford's committee—the chairman remarked that "benefits of actual experiment, in regard to most of the expenses . . . is far more extensively furnished by our own country than is generally imagined." In short, Clinton and the canal commission had convinced Ford that the canal should and could be a state-financed project.

These arguments took on new urgency during the week Ford's report was being drafted when legislators were presented with a last-minute offer to privately finance the canal—an offer they rejected out of hand, despite the fact that the person making the offer, Jacob Van Rensselaer, was a former state assembly speaker and a familiar, even respected, veteran of New York state politics. As the joint committee prepared its written recommendations, Van Rensselaer had misinterpreted their silence as uncertainty. He hurried to Albany hoping to extract favors, privileges, and benefits from the state government by exploiting avenues of influence long familiar to political entrepreneurs.

Van Rensselaer brought a breathtakingly audacious proposal to DeWitt Clinton and his colleagues on the canal commission: an offer to build the project himself through three possible arrangements. In the first, Van Rensselaer would build the canal for a $10.5 million fee. In the second, he would build it for $7.5 million and have the exclusive right to collect tolls on the project for the next two decades. In the third, he would build it for just $5 million and refund $2.5 million back to the state at a later date, but he would retain the right to collect tolls forever. Supposing that legislators were wavering on the utility of the project itself, Van Rensselaer added that he hoped they appreciated the benefits that could come from an "undertaking of this importance." If they were "governed by a spirit of great liberality" and avoided "[indulging] sectional interests," he was confident that at least one of his proposals would be "deem[ed] proper" and could be paid for with a "general tax" levied on the state as a whole.[77]

Jacob Van Rensselaer was no political novice. The Federalist attorney had been a longtime member and former speaker of the New York assembly and the state's secretary of state until 1815; he was also a cousin of canal commissioner Stephen Van Rensselaer.[78] He could see that canal policy was being drafted by a commission determined to collaborate with existing state interests and institutions, and whose own members had overlapping interests. Western Inland Lock Navigation Company treasurer Thomas Eddy frequently acted on behalf of both his company and the canal, seeing the two as intertwined; deceased commissioners Robert Fulton and Robert R. Livingston's steamboat monopoly would surely benefit from a canal. And no one person in the state had more conflicts of interest than canal commissioner Joseph Ellicott, who in February and March 1817 provided his boss— Philadelphia-based Holland Land Company agent Paul Busti—with a steady stream of information about canal legislation. Months earlier, Ellicott said he had accepted a seat on the canal commission but declined a bank directorship because he "conceived it might be beneficial to accept the [canal] appointment" to "giv[e] such a direction to the site of the Canal within the Holland Purchase as appeared to me not only the most advantageous to the public convenience, but the most to the interests of our Principals." Although Ellicott "believ[ed]" that the interests of the company and the public intersected, he had also calculated that the canal would increase the value of company-owned lands by as much as 1,000 percent.[79]

Two decades earlier, Jacob Van Rensselaer could have bought both the Northern and Western companies and dictated terms to Albany lawmakers and Manhattan merchants. But those days were over. What Van Rensselaer had failed to recognize was that by 1817 lawmakers—and even the ethically challenged political entrepreneurs on the canal commission—had no intention of vesting that much power in a single individual simply because of his wealth and connections. Legislators proved their determination to protect the canal's "public" qualities by publicly slapping down Van Rensselaer's offer without delay or mercy. Even though it had been conveyed to Van Rensselaer quietly, Ford decided to print Van Rensselaer's letter in the joint committee's report, revealing it for all to see and ensuring it would forever be included in any official record of the legislative history of the Erie Canal. Then the chairman explained that his committee was "entirely opposed" to Van Rensselaer's

"propositions" because they had been "persuaded, for a variety of considerations, that the state should retain the perfect control of this canal, in every
period of its construction and future regulation."[80]

Ford and his colleagues might have been genuinely offended by Jacob
Van Rensselaer's brashness, but there was a reason they used their report to
humiliate him as they took a stand on canal policy: they could afford to. With
$21 million in bank capital available in the state, the first canal loan in 1817
raised $200,000 through bond sales. That year the two largest subscriptions—
a total of $74,000—came from London. In 1818 a second loan was made for
the same sum and attracted a far more economically diverse group of sixty-
nine investors, twenty-seven of whom purchased portions smaller than
$1,000.[81] That loan was also subscribed by the New York Bank for Savings,
incorporated in 1819 to serve modest tradesmen laborers who ordinarily
would have lacked the means to participate in such transactions, but whose
collective deposits were repeatedly used to buy canal bonds.[82] Even during
the economic downturn following the Panic of 1819, canal bonds remained a
salable investment, proving in the words of one observer that an "immense
capital" was "laying dead" for want of use.[83]

That availability of capital meant that legislators needed neither Jacob
Van Rensselaer's money nor the strings that would come attached to it. In
fact, lawmakers did not need any Van Rensselaers or cadres of privilege-
seeking investors; they had found a way to fully fund the canal while shield-
ing it from the influence-seeking sources of that capital.

Following the publication of Ford's joint committee report, the canal bill
went to the New York assembly. There, William A. Duer won support for a
tax to be levied on all lands within twenty-five miles of the canal route; lawmakers also decided to set a 12½ cent tax on a bushel of salt, and tinkered
with a steamboat passenger tax of one dollar on any trip over one hundred
miles.[84] In the state senate, Martin Van Buren and George Tibbits led a cohort
of senators to amend the bill, adding the lieutenant governor to the canal
fund board. Both houses approved the bills by 3:2 margins.[85]

Yet after clearing these hurdles, one threshold remained: the state's Council of Revision.

Composed of the governor, chancellor, and three Supreme Court justices,
the council had the power to veto the entire package.[86] At first, the members
seemed split; justices Jonas Platt, the longtime pro-canal activist, and Joseph
Yates both favored the canal, while justice Smith Thompson was opposed.
Thompson's onetime law tutor, Chancellor James Kent, was an unknown. And

while acting governor John Tayler opposed the canal, he could not cast a vote unless the judges were tied. Tayler had succeeded Daniel Tompkins after the latter resigned to become James Monroe's vice president; he was due to leave office in July after the inauguration of governor-elect DeWitt Clinton.

The council's deliberations began just hours after the legislature approved the final canal bill, but they were interrupted when a surprise visitor arrived: vice president of the United States Daniel Tompkins. Jonas Platt watched, appalled, as Tompkins took his old seat and joined the discussion. He opposed the canal, he explained, because he believed that the peace treaty between the United States and Great Britain that had ended the War of 1812 was only temporary, "a mere truce." The nation, Tompkins predicted, would "undoubtedly soon have a renewed war with that country." "Instead of wasting the credit and resources of the state in this chimerical project," Tompkins said, he believed lawmakers should shove "all the revenue and credit of the state" toward building arsenals, militia arms, and fortifications.

Chancellor Kent asked the vice president if he was serious. "Do you think so, sir?"

Tompkins replied, "Yes, sir. England will never forgive us for our victories." He predicted war within two years.

Kent then stood and declared, "[I]f we must have war or a canal, I am in favor of the canal, and I vote for this bill."[87]

James Kent had long used his seat on the Council of Revision to temper what he saw as legislative overreach, issuing opinions that his critics—including Martin Van Buren—considered more politically motivated than legally reasoned. As a Federalist judge, he spent his career trying to smooth out variations among states' laws; he saw his *Commentaries* as a tool to help strengthen the federal union by bringing common-law-like coherence to a patchwork of state, county, and municipal jurisdictions.[88]

In this instance, Kent opted to use his seat on the council to defend the actions of New York lawmakers. But more important, he did so as the swing vote in the final veto point at the end of a long legislative process. At that moment, James Kent had been presented with a choice: a war or a canal. It was, of course, a false choice. Nevertheless, by recalling and retelling the council's deliberation in this way and with these outcomes at stake, Kent made clear that he understood his vote in favor of the canal as one that clarified distinctions between the roles that the national government and state governments played in setting foreign and domestic policy agendas within the federal union.[89]

Under the federal Constitution, war and foreign affairs were national issues; powers to declare war and negotiate peace resided in Congress and the
president. Therefore, while New Yorkers could follow Daniel Tompkins's advice and make preparations for war with Britain, their state government was
nevertheless at the mercy of events beyond their control.

But by contrast, congressional inaction and presidential vetoes had made
it clear that the national government's ability to plan and finance internal-
improvement projects was on shaky political and constitutional ground; it
would be contested long into the future. In this vacuum, Kent thought it entirely appropriate to stake out space for New York's and other states' governments to actively and aggressively promote their commercial interests. If the
nation was to have a legally coherent common marketplace—a necessity if it
was to be a true union—it was essential that some entity in the federal regime
be able to take meaningful steps to build infrastructure and regulate commerce, encouraging citizens to create networks of interest and affective bonds
of trust to knit together the geographically expanding republic. James Kent
thought it entirely appropriate that this happen at the state level.

Ultimately, therefore, the long and often bruising process of proposing,
considering, and finally adopting a law to authorize the construction of the
Erie Canal was not just about one single project. Instead, it redefined both
the state and the concept of what was "public" by rebooting the state government's relationship with institutions it had chartered and political entrepreneurs it had long empowered. The adoption of the bond for state use—a
practice considered routine and even mundane in modern political
economy—created fiscal flexibility for states in the early republic, allowing
legislators and canal promoters to formulate new political-economy practices
that seemed ideologically inspired but were nevertheless grounded in the
very real, practical capacity of government to directly commission ambitious
programs. By thinking about incorporated banks, turnpikes, bridges, and
other entities as institutions that together constituted "the state" and whose
collective interests were "public," it was possible for canal commissioners,
lawmakers, and even the shareholders and directors of those companies and
monopolies to see themselves as having a constructive role in state-directed
canal building even as they acknowledged the pitfalls and perils that could
arise if the government followed its old playbook of chartering a new institution every time citizens petitioned for a new project.

As a financial instrument, therefore, the bond freed policy makers to
imagine new institutional arrangements and articulate a new vision of

political economy in real time. And as they understood it, policy makers were revising European ideas to suit an American context. Thus, canal promoters could credibly claim to be tossing aside older philosophies of political economy, which insisted on population settlement as a precondition for investment; instead, they were actively creating economic opportunities by encouraging commercial and population growth throughout the howling wilderness of western New York, linking the state to interstate markets along the Great Lakes and into the West by transforming dormant lands held as speculative investments into productive farms and towns that would draw fleets of boats and millions in capital from metropolitan centers toward the hinterland.

Early on, New Yorkers recognized that the Erie Canal was a turning point. During the first two years of construction, they began publishing document collections and narratives that anticipated Cadwallader D. Colden's later, magisterial *Memoir*.[90] What New Yorkers were toasting was in large measure the political triumph that the physical Erie Canal represented. Moreover, the Erie Canal, feted across New York State in 1825, proved to be just the first phase in constructing a more elaborate canal network that expanded until the 1850s and was maintained well into the twentieth century.[91]

By the time DeWitt Clinton sailed from Buffalo to New York Harbor aboard the *Seneca Chief* to pour buckets of Lake Erie into the Atlantic Ocean, kicking off the reception that followed this "Wedding of the Waters," the Erie Canal's success was unquestionable. But of course no single person—not even Clinton himself, who was elected governor in 1817 by a 43:1 margin and owed his career to the canal—could be credited with securing approval for the canal law of 1817. By that year, thirteen men had served as canal commissioners. Their recommendations were advanced by more than 100,000 supporters who signed petitions and sent lobbyists to the capital where a 123-member state assembly deputized a pro-canal caucus to negotiate with like-minded members of the 28-person state senate. Eleven meetings later, after considering more than a dozen amendments, they overcame local pockets of resistance and the opposition of the state's sitting governor to adopt a final bill by a 64-36 majority in the assembly and a 18-9 victory in the senate. Then they had to hope to overcome a 2-2 split in the Council of Revision—a body abolished just years later in the state's new constitution—in which the nation's sitting vice president directly intervened to block action.

In that moment, the fate of the canal turned on one question: what is the role of the state in a federal union of states? In that context, James Kent's decision was not his alone; it was cast at the tail end of a long series of choices and decisions, which had helped formulate an answer. If the choice was whether to invest in an optimistic vision of the future or to turn inward in preparation for yet another European-initiated war, New York would choose the canal. And it was this series of choices and that mythologized outcome that was cause for cannon fire and naval flotillas in 1825. Not to launch a war, but to toast a victory.[92]

Corporate Political Economy

When the 1825 opening of the Erie Canal brought the water of Lake Erie to New York Harbor, decades of promises made by promoters were soon made manifest. Of all the canal's benefits, the most immediately measurable one was the fall in shipping costs for goods; that cost dropped so dramatically that by one calculation it was as if New York City and Buffalo had been brought to within forty miles of each another.[1] Of course, the canal was not celebrated by contemporaries and studied by historians because of something as mundane as carriage rates. The Erie Canal affected New York and the nation in such myriad ways—culturally, socially, economically, and politically—that it is difficult to contemplate what New York would look like today had the canal not been constructed.

From a political-economy viewpoint, the most important thing to appreciate about the canal was that it changed the landscape of political opportunity in New York by not only empowering individual political entrepreneurs but also by affirming the very concept of political entrepreneurship. As De-Witt Clinton described it in 1828, the canal's purpose was to "augment the general opulence, to animate all the springs of industry and exertion, and to bring home to every man's door an easy and economic means of access to the most advantageous places of sale and purchase."[2] There was, in other words, simply more civic, financial, and political capital available in the state because of the Erie Canal.

Generating more than $1 million per year in toll revenues, the canal easily paid for the interest due on canal-fund bonds and created surpluses that could be steered to all manner of policies and priorities, giving state lawmakers and canal commissioners discretion to encourage different kinds of transportation and financial projects and experiments. Revisions to the state constitution in 1821 may have been intended to insulate the canal board from legislative interference, but the board was, by definition, an agency of government that did not operate in a vacuum. It was therefore an inherently political institution, and it responded to the same stimuli as other political institutions did in a federal union packed with municipal, state, and national bureaucracies, as well as legislative bodies, courts, political parties, interests, and other civic, financial, and social institutions.[3]

Partisanship in this period is often described as a novel innovation, but political parties were not new to New York nor were they holistic ways of organizing politics.[4] Instead, parties were tools used to steer the state's policy-making apparatus by capturing and managing legislative caucuses. After all, people do not support candidates for office simply because they want a particular candidate to win an election; rather, electoral victories pave the way for using government to do particular things. To the extent that partisanship affected the state's political economy in the era of the Erie Canal, the question of whether the state's two major parties embraced the Erie Canal was settled (they both did). Parties had moved on to debating what should be done with the resources generated by the canal, and to that end different administrations eventually pledged money toward the state's common school system, to commit the state to a canal enlargement plan, and to fund a bank-deposit insurance and inspection regime called the Safety Fund—an innovation in bank regulation created during the last three months of Governor Martin Van Buren's tenure to encourage more citizens to make bank deposits while creating conditions for bankers to extend credit.[5]

Beyond these applications, canal funds were also used to float loans and make direct investments in other internal-improvement projects, making the impact of canal surpluses something that could be felt both directly and indirectly by the state's political entrepreneurs. Some directly profited from canal funds when they sought and won financing for proposed projects, while others indirectly benefited from the surpluses when they received credit from New York banks that had augmented their lending because of canal-fund deposits or in response to canal-driven gains. By intertwining the interests of market-savvy merchants and farmers with those of financial speculators, and increasing the amount of capital in the state in both money and real estate, the canal was helping to make New York City the financial nexus of the eastern United States, leveraging the fruits of its natural and institutional landscapes in the expanding federal union.[6]

With these resources at their disposal, state policy makers were understandably eager to expand the Erie Canal by building additional feeders and branches to its original corridor. To some out-of-doors internal-improvement promoters, the question of whether these projects would even generate revenue was irrelevant in the light of their larger, less tangible benefits. Philadelphia-based political economist Mathew Carey argued in 1831 of tolls and revenue that "the interest to be derived on the capital invested" was "a consideration befitting a mere merchant, or trader, or capitalist." However, "incomparably more important," according to Carey, were "the happiness, the independence, and the comfort of our citizens—the general prosperity of the state, and the increase of its population. . . . These are the views to be taken by statesmen worthy of being intrusted with the destiny of nations."[7] The opportunities and developments enabled by building markets and extending commerce, to Carey, always trumped state-centered concerns about tolls and budgets in the construction of public works. Carey believed that even without toll revenues a canal was worth building because it knit urban merchants and consumers together with hinterland producers in one common marketplace.

New York canal officials took some of Carey's advice to heart in pursuing expansions that did not add to the state's toll collections, but which nevertheless extended the canal commissioners' own jurisdiction and influence by delivering more consumers to the state's marketplace. These new users, it was expected, would subsequently become canal advocates and allies, further enhancing the political clout of the commissioners and agents who administered the project. The canal therefore functioned as a self-sustaining, surplus-generating, voter-recruiting, market-making, and policy-making enterprise; as long as it was profitable and popular, it was a perpetual machine. Once set in motion, the possibilities seemed endless.[8]

For more than a decade, canal surpluses meant that New York lawmakers rarely had to choose between favoring the Erie Canal and funding a project that might divert traffic from its waters. Although other states grappled with choices over whether to fund canals or railroads, New York had enough money to do both.

In theory, this should have been a windfall for all of the state's political entrepreneurs, but there was a catch: political entrepreneurs looking to exploit canal surpluses by winning corporate charters faced a pair of new hurdles put in place by the convention that had drafted New York's 1821 state constitution. Under the new rules, special acts of incorporation and direct subsidies from the state had to receive the support of two-thirds of the members of the legislature, a bar that had previously been a simple majority. This change did not diminish the underlying usefulness of a corporate charter nor did it remove chartering from the realm of politics. In fact, it did the opposite. When incorporation acts became more politically difficult to obtain, political entrepreneurs mounted ever more elaborate lobbying efforts to win them—the kind of mobilizations that had pushed New York Republicans to restrict chartering in the first place.[9] Because only the most politically connected interests stood a chance of commanding supermajority support in the state legislature, these new rules put winning coalitions in a strong position to maximize their advantages; any interest that could assemble enough votes to win a charter probably also had enough clout to win financial support, too. After 1821, the corporate form was therefore endowed with greater political significance that conferred weightier economic advantages over less privileged, unincorporated partnerships and firms.

The industry that most benefited from the new arrangements were the state's railroads. Although this was supposedly a period of restrictions on charters and state aid, 108 new railroads were incorporated in New York before 1840; they received more than $7 million in public loans and support. The state also loaned funds to turnpike roads, plank roads, and canal-lock construction projects during this period, with most of the money coming from the state's seemingly endless canal-revenue surpluses.

In the face of aggressive lobbying and tempting opportunities, however, state legislators and policy makers overextended the state's credit during the 1830s, racking up nearly $40 million in state debt by 1844. Nearly $15 million of that debt had been accumulated through canal-enlargement projects, while another $5 million had come from direct loans to corporations. The cost of serving this debt dramatically increased during the Panic of 1837 and the six-year-long depression that followed, prompting New York Democrats to call for a state constitutional convention to be held in 1846 to reorder the way the state government collected taxes, spent money, and chartered corporations.[10]

Historians of political economy who examine the product of the 1846 convention frequently conclude that it marked a significant turning point in the development of a hands-off, laissez-faire economic policy in New York and the nation as a whole.[11] According to L. Ray Gunn, a historian who studied the document more than anyone else in the modern era, the new constitution's restrictions on certain kinds of direct state investments in internal improvements and its call for general incorporation statutes were intended to "rationalize" American commerce by making the corporation "an essentially

Figure 7. Although canal enlargements eroded New York State's finances, legislators embraced such projects because they were popular and were supported by influential citizens. This petition was sent to the state capital in Albany from Jefferson County in 1827. It is nearly 5 feet long when fully opened. At right is the full document; above is a detail. Source: Private collection.

private instrument of economic organization." Curtailing the state's economic interventionism secured the legitimacy of the state legislature and restored the utility of the corporate form as a way to aggregate capital by ensuring that the laws governing incorporation—the "rules of the game"—would be fairly and uniformly applied, stripping the corporation of its political and partisan implications and returning it to what was seen as its original purpose: a useful legal tool to structure businesses and organize capital. For these reasons, the emergence of laissez-faire economic policy was a change worth celebrating. "With the passage of general laws," Gunn tells us, "the corporation's ties to the state were effectively severed," finally clarifying distinctions between public and private (capital, initiative, interest, power, and so on) in the nation's antebellum political economy that paved the way for industrialization and the creation of specialized and diversified economies of scale later in the century.[12]

Gunn's views are not an anachronism imposed by a scholar after the fact; contemporaries who analyzed the 1846 constitution came to some of the same conclusions. Yet something is different about the ways that historians and contemporaries write about the origins and purpose of these changes. In 1853 Erasmus Peshine Smith, a mathematics professor at the University of Rochester, penned what he called *A Manual of Political Economy* to lay out the ideal way of arranging and regulating the marketplace. Smith was well acquainted with the Erie Canal's impact on New York's economic development and the millions of dollars it had generated in toll revenues. But for Smith this was not a debate about numbers; it was about ideology. In his opinion, private management and private capital were always superior to their public counterparts no matter what the circumstances, even when those private entities were worse performers. Thus, even though "a single corporation" built a railroad in New York during the 1830s that cost twice as much as the Erie Canal, there was still no "sufficient reason for the State's undertaking an industrial enterprise." In general "the vigilance of individual supervision" combined with "the keenness of private interest" contributed to an economic environment that "secured" companies against excesses, waste, and inefficiencies of "neglect." Management failures in private companies fell to a "guilty party"; in public enterprises it was "divided among a multitude." Even in cases where a public agency could build a transportation project for less than a private company could, Smith thought that the potential public goods generated by tolls would be outweighed by their potential to be levied with "partial[ity]."[13]

In disqualifying the state legislature or other public agencies from participating in public works projects, Smith was willing to push his argument even further. There was, he wrote, a "general inability of government to work with the same economy as individuals." Government lacked the consent of citizens that was needed to be able to properly engage in projects directly; past activities had therefore been based only on a "supposition of free consent." As such, the only proper role for the state was to encourage individual citizens to discover and pursue mutual interests. As one of the convention delegates put it in 1846: "[I]f a capitalist chooses to loan money to a manufacturing or railroad corporation, why should we step in . . . ? Let him look after his own interests."[14] According to Smith, the true "most general purpose" of government was to "facilitat[e] and encourag[e] association among individuals" in order to "exten[d] the power of private competition with the State, and diminis[h] the temptations for it to attempt any operation for pecuniary profit." One of the highest callings of citizenship was to "to unite and contribute . . . capital to be employed for a common purpose."[15]

Although Smith thought that the state had impeded the formation of profit-driven associations by directly engaging in infrastructure development, he made it clear that he also saw extensions of state credit to certain favored enterprises as equally damaging. The practice of making loans to corporations—something seen since the 1790s—had been "impeding private association" by denying individuals the "liberty to contract with each other." By even dangling the possibility that it might offer loans to a corporation, the state had inadvertently put its finger on the economy's scale and disrupted a corporation's ability to internally calibrate its interests to create trust among its directors, shareholders, and agents. As Smith described it:

> If a thousand persons combine to build a railway or a factory, they must entrust the management of their property to a few agents. The stake which each, has in the skill and fidelity of those agents is proportionate to the amount he contributes. It would be the most natural arrangement in the world, that the partners should agree that their power, in regard to the selection of those agents, should be proportioned to their several risks, and that they should divide the profits resulting from their operations, or contribute to the loss in the same proportions.[16]

In this telling, profit-seeking business associations and corporations seemed to be rational and almost perfectible instruments, capable of distributing risks and allocating rewards in ways that were congruent to the contributions and investments of shareholders, partners, managers, and agents. Smith viewed things that he considered to be "private" as inherently superior to things he saw as "public," partly not only because he thought that shareholder-owned companies were more accountable to their investors than publicly run or publicly supported state enterprises but also because he thought that the purpose of government was to encourage its citizens to become entrepreneurs and shareholders. "Government," Smith wrote in his concluding paragraph, "is successful in the degree to which it becomes unnecessary." And had it not been for the Erie Canal, he suggested, more people would have realized that by now. The canal had been "an enterprise of such magnitude as to strain the powers of the State of New York." And looking back, Smith could not help but think that the decision to make it a public project had not only been a momentary mistake, but a missed opportunity in the nation's political economy. If the state had instead used a "private corporation" to undertake the work, DeWitt Clinton and his cohort of canal promoters "would then have been regarded as visionary to the last degree."[17]

In a way, it is understandable that Smith could take such a dim view of the state's involvement in the economy because the corporate chartering process seemed hopelessly corrupted by the 1830s. As banker A. B. Johnson recalled in 1850 with regard to bank charters:

> To resist the creation of new banks, or to assist in procuring them, came, at length, to be a regular mercenary employment, by men, who, like the straw bail in courts of law, attended the halls of legislation, to be hired, and were sarcastically called lobby members. They disguised their venality by feigning to possess a reputable interest in the projects they undertook to support; or to be patriotic promoters of the measures for merely an alleged public benefit; or if they were hired to oppose the measures, they feigned to be disinterested exponents of an alleged hostile public sentiment. Some of the persons thus engaged, were otherwise respectable; and some were even distinguished as men of station, talent, and wealth. But the practices to which they resorted in secret, were worse than their open acts, . . . so threatening to public virtue.[18]

Free banking had long been held out as a potential solution to the problem of corrupt bank-chartering practices, making free incorporation the next logical policy for those looking to reform the state's political-economy habits.[19]

Looming even larger in the political lives of New Yorkers in the 1840s and 1850s were its railroads, and briefly examining just one shows how problematic the state's incorporation policies had become.

When the New York and Erie Railroad was chartered in 1832, it had $200,000 on hand to cover an estimated $6 million in expenses. Soon it began hunting for public aid. Samuel Ruggles, a member of the board of directors, first looked to Washington, D.C., for assistance. "I am railroad mad," he confessed to his brother, who was also an investor in the venture. Ruggles hoped to win exclusive carriage contracts with the Post Office to carry the mail to the west. "I have been to Buffalo—am just returned—am going to-morrow to Washington to help petition for some land in Michigan where-with to pay our Company for promising to carry the mail in 40 hours from N.Y. to Lake Erie," he wrote.[20] "We hold," he proclaimed, "a thing which [the Postmaster General] must have and cannot do without." Indeed, Samuel reported that the postmaster later said that "the very rapidity" of the New York and Erie Railroad would "suck in all the lateral mails and that he d[id] not doubt he will send his great mail up from Washington . . . over our N.Y. & Erie railroad to the West." Samuel hoped this would merely be the beginning of a fruitful partnership with the federal government, from which he hoped to eventually borrow $3 million. "The recognition of the absolute necessity of rail roads for the legitimate & clearly constitutional object of carrying the mail must lead out into a general system throughout the Union," he explained, "and compel the Government to aid in every railroad established or to be established on any great leading mail route—and thus their aid will & must be afforded to the construction."[21]

Ruggles was so certain he would win a postal contract that he dismissed the idea he might need to turn to New York State for aid.[22] "Several big wigs (who [we]re also big Whigs)" of New York City told Ruggles that such aid would be available, but Ruggles maintained that "even without the aid of the State" a railroad through Susquehanna territory in the Southern tier of New York would bring 350,000 "good customers" and that west of Utica they could reach 900,000 "souls." Passengers, New York chancellor James Kent told Ruggles, would rise "10 on and 10 on," enabling the railroad to use its postal revenues as a fund to maintain their rails and equipment.[23]

But when the postal funds did not materialize, the railroad in 1836 petitioned for a loan from the New York legislature, arguing that portions of its route were so sparsely populated only because they were correcting previously inequitable distributions of internal improvement resources. The company again bid for support when William Seward was elected governor in 1838.

At that time, Seward asked Samuel Ruggles for his views on internal improvements and Ruggles promised "sincerity and truth." By then, in addition to having been a shareholder and director of the railroad, Ruggles was also the chairman of the New York Assembly's Ways and Means Committee, the committee charged with writing tax and revenue policy.[24] Envisioning an expansive field for state action, Ruggles told the governor-elect,

> The people expect much, very much from their new Governor in the way of Internal Improvement but I think that what they expect is *action* rather than argument—deeds rather than words. The time has gone by when it is necessary seriously to sit down and demonstrate by argument that works of intercommunication are beneficial & necessary. Their value & importance are now admitted as a matter of course in all hands, and any extended discussion as to their benefits which have now become all but self evident.

Explaining that although he had personally engaged in "speculations" with an "uncertain Future," Ruggles felt that Seward, as a Whig governor, had to take "prompt confident and decisive" action to support internal improvement corporations. "Instead of stealing timidly along, watching any puff and breeze of popular sentiment," he believed the governor-elect would be better served by emulating the "great prototype" of DeWitt Clinton, who "march[ed] boldly & fearlessly . . . [to] manfully create the public opinion which [wa]s to sustain him." The state stood at a new point, Ruggles believed: "The canals are all dug or nearly so. . . . The Aqueous branch (so to speak) as a thing of this system of improvement is thus disposed of—but the land remains—and the locomotive engine has come into existence just in time to offer a new and wider field of renown. The governor of New York if he seeks to live hereafter must cover its surface with rail roads."

In Ruggles's view, to promote "popular confidence" it was necessary to have the state spend whatever was needed to construct a system of railroads as extensive as the Erie Canal. State funds were "perfectly sufficien[t]" to "accomplish every work" in this regard. Furthermore, Ruggles thought that this kind of spending should be "a cardinal point" of Whig Party doctrine. "No man should be deemed loyal to our party, or fit in any degree to influences its counsels," he wrote, if he "shall entertain the slight[est] doubt or misgiving" about its propriety. In stark contrast to what Erasmus Smith would write a decade later, Ruggles told Seward,

> In truth the very idea of employing a *private* company to construct and manage a *public* work involves a political absurdity and a paradox in terms. I view therefore as inadequate and reprehensible the partial model in which the present expiring administration of the State Government has hitherto attempted to discharge this portion of its duty by means of the contrivance of loaning the public funds to private companies to aid them in building the public works.

Seward's administration could not "afford to share the honor" of constructing railroads with "any individual or company of individuals however meritorious." "From this view of the subject," he wrote, "it will necessarily follow that all the public works of the state, must be built by the State . . . [it] is a matter of the clearest public duty" and the state had "no right to share" this "duty" with "any individual or association of individuals, not directly subordinate to the austerity of the state."

This rejection of corporate railroading was a curious position for a corporate director of the New York and Erie Railroad to take. Yet Ruggles said that his privileged vantage point led him to have little faith in his company's ability to prosecute its work. The railroad, in Ruggles's view, could not provide "adequate security" to the state in exchange for a loan. State credit was therefore too precious to be extended to a board of directors "not appointed by the Government & in no way amenable to its authority or supervision." Ruggles also disclosed to Seward that although he was a director of the company, he had sold his shares after becoming Ways and Means chairman; thus, he no longer had a personal stake in the company, freeing him to also say that the company's other directors could have invested more in the company but had fallen short in their "pecuniary ability" because they had assumed they would soon be rescued with state funds. Therefore he cautioned Seward, "[I]f you rely on the company effectually to prosecute the work with their present means, or wish any aid which the state is likely to afford to them, you will expose the Whig Party to serious hazard." The expectations set by the railroad in advance of its previous loan meant that any future suspension of work on the railroad would be "disastrous" for the Whig Party.[25]

Ruggles's ardor for state sponsorship of improvements—and his railroad in particular—did not result in the takeover of the railroad by the state. Instead, New York opted for a half measure, albeit an expensive one, that put public funds at financial risk without demanding either control over the railroad or a share of its future profits. The legislature offered a loan to the railroad of unspecified value—equal to whatever sum the directors could raise and spend. By 1842 the state was owed more than $3 million from the New York and Erie Railroad.[26]

Writing as a political entrepreneur, Samuel Ruggles could see that this kind of lending to corporations was precipitating a crisis in both the corporate form and state policy making. By treating railroads as monopolistic enterprises—like a turnpike company—and extending credit to them as if they were state-controlled—like a canal—both the directors of the railroad and the state legislature were encouraging behavior that they knew was unwise. Corporations had long been privileged institutions engaged in pursuits that were ostensibly public, but never before had they become so reliant on public funds to enable private profits. And although those funds should have bought state officials greater transparency and control over those incorporated enterprises, the opposite seemed to be true.[27] It was no wonder, then, that the 1846 convention spent much of its energy addressing corporate chartering and debating how best to restrict state aid to internal improvement projects.

In thinking about this account offered by Samuel Ruggles, however, consider again Erasmus Peshine Smith's *Manual of Political Economy* that would be published just fifteen years later. Like many historians of political economy, Smith stands back to look at a period where corporations dominated banking, transportation, manufacturing, and all manner of other industries, and he concluded that it was a more correct way to organize an economy and civil society than the messy, conflicted, partial, and partisan arena in which Samuel Ruggles seemed all too happy to operate. Where Ruggles offers vexing complexity, Smith wrote with legalistic confidence and ethical clarity to lay out strict bright lines between What Is Public and What Is Private as a way to elevate the latter and question the propriety of the former.[28]

For historians, paying down debt and enacting general incorporation laws—the political-economy focus of the 1846 constitutional convention—are seen as a pair of imperatives that arose from the corrupt debt-generating corporatism of the 1830s. But among some of the document's contemporaries like Smith, the problems had begun even earlier when the state had decided to publicly finance and construct the Erie Canal. For them, one of the most celebrated moments in their state and nation's recent history, the "Wedding of the Waters," had come to be seen as a lost moment—a failure. They did not read the 1846 constitution as a mere set of adjustments to fix temporary lapses in the way state government financed certain projects or responded to influential interests; the document was instead seen as a wholesale refutation of the public-private partnerships and mixed-economy institutionalism that had defined both the canal and the period. Scrutinizing the "Erie Canal" was therefore rhetorical shorthand for questioning the applied political economy of the early republic.

Despite its professed clarity, there is a blind spot in Smith's critique: power. In imposing public and private categories on an institution that straddled both spheres, Smith hoped to make the corporation's artificiality seem like the natural order. This conflation of free incorporation with freedom of association may be one of the most important and challenging legacies of the supposedly laissez-faire period in American history. By viewing corporations as mere associations, historians, political theorists, and present-day citizens all risk forgetting that the corporation's origins had been contested and controversial, or that there was something inherently statist about permitting associations to organize themselves around privileges that only two generations earlier had been seen as monarchical—even by corporations' supporters. Freedom to form partnerships in business is not the same as the freedom to incorporate for the purposes of gaining legal privileges within institutions that harness financial and political capital. Aggregations of capital, as early American political entrepreneurs and legislators well knew, are inherently powerful. The decision to grant coalitions the ability to incorporate, even on a temporary basis, introduced potentially dangerous and destabilizing concentrations of power and influence into the young nation's political economy. While legislators tinkered with charters and empowered themselves to approve or deny requests for incorporation, political entrepreneurs found ways to win privileges and mobilize supporters on their behalf. In the face of such influences, the way lawmakers and out-of-doors observers monitored, and even regulated, corporations and other useful instrumentalities in the early republic was by remembering that they were mixed-economy hybrids that combined public authority and consent with private capital.

For decades state government had encouraged and channeled what one canal-era legislator had called "the enterprising spirit of [the] people" by chartering institutions for worthy applicants, offering slices of state sovereignty and public authority to entrepreneurs who had amassed financial,

human, and political capital to build a mixed economy of public-private institutions—incorporated banks, bridges, dams, harbor improvements, and
ferryboats that serviced a host of mercantile firms, farms, land companies,
mills, and mines. New York was "favorably situated for the encouragement of
every public interest." Quoting (but not by name) Alexander Hamilton's 1791
Report on Manufactures, a state legislative committee that provided crucial
last-minute support to the canal wrote that the project would be a "confirma-
tion of public order, and an augmentation of public resource." By crediting
Alexander Hamilton—named only as a "perspicacious statesman"—as an inspiration for Republican-backed canal legislation, the committee was not
merely trying to strike an air of cooperative bipartisanship on the eve of a
vote; rather, it was downplaying and even erasing past differences over how
the nation's political parties had approached questions of political economy.
If the intellectual origins of the canal project lay in the nation's founding, and
New York "State" was defined in a way to embrace a vast institutional legacy
accumulating since the end of the Revolution, there were no meaningful reasons for canal policy to remain a partisan issue.[29]

In this telling, Hamilton's call for aggressive state intervention in American economic life a generation earlier had not instigated controversy and
contestation with the likes of Thomas Jefferson and James Madison. Instead,
by adopting and adapting imperial and monarchical instruments and institutions for use in the new republic, Hamilton had helped to structure New York
State itself by setting it on a path where it would one day have the capacity to
build a project as ambitious as the Erie Canal. The fact that New York's first
banks had been the brainchild of an über-Federalist was therefore irrelevant;
factional divides over the use of corporations to construct a financial and
transportation infrastructure had largely collapsed once those institutions
became incubators for nascent political parties. Owned, financed, and led by
an army of petitioners, directors, and shareholders, those institutions had
been created by voluntary acts of the state's elected legislature, and as extensions of the state's sovereignty, they deepened the government's ability to perform one of its most basic functions: to be an energetic catalyst for commerce
and market regulation. Therefore as pro-canal legislators understood it, those
institutions—comprising the shareholders, directors, license holders, franchisees, and monopolists who exercised authority with the permission of the
legislature—were what collectively constituted "the state" itself.

In such an environment the lines separating public from private—lines
never clear to begin with—were hopelessly blurred. Yet there was a way to

order this messy story: even if corporations, monopolies, and other legal instrumentalities were hybrid mixed-economy creations that comingled private capital and public authority, they were components of the state that existed because they had proven useful. There was no reason that corporate participation in canal finance had to detract from the authenticity of the canal's public-ness.

What had made the canal a public project was that it was accomplished by the state directly. In the past, such an effort would have been performed by investors organized into a state-chartered corporation or a monopoly-privileged partnership. But canal promoters came to view those options as impractical and dangerous, arguing that no corporation could ever raise the $6 million necessary to build the project, and that even if it could, the institution would then become too dangerous to tolerate. Its legal privileges would allow it to run roughshod over legitimate sources of state authority and co-opt forces that might be tempted to hold it accountable for its actions.

For the canal's promoters, the project was the next logical chapter in the trajectory of American political economy. Corporate chartering was an exercise in sovereignty splitting, lending a group of individuals a portion of state authority for a period of time. Bonding was the opposite: it buttressed state government while binding the state, its institutions, and its people to the future. Because the state would not be selling ownership shares of the canal itself or chartering a corporation to do so, the canal would be protected from temptations to privilege short-term profits over long-term commitments, a problem endemic in all corporations and firms. Bondholders would not be able to select canal commissioners or demand favorable toll rates or discounts for friends and allies. If the canal languished, bonds would be difficult to sell; if the project went bust altogether, bondholders might never be paid at all. But if it was a success, the buyers of canal debt would have participated in a civic project that promoters believed was of world historical importance. By constructing the canal under state authority, with contractors hired and supervised by state employees, to be owned by the people of the state and controlled by their government, generating tolls that would be collected at rates set by state officials and then flow into state-government accounts at state-chartered banks, the legislature would continue to perform its traditional, fundamental role of aiding commerce but without subordinating itself to a new institution or alienating power from the apparatus of the state government.

The decision to jettison the corporate form for the canal, therefore, was not merely inspired by concerns about a scarcity of money; lawmakers and canal promoters, even those who were political entrepreneurs, were equally if not more concerned about power—a subject that merits barely a mention in Erasmus Smith's criticisms of the Erie Canal or his praise of the business corporation. Canal promoters had been profoundly uncomfortable with the notion of concentrating the power and ownership in one board of directors or one cadre of investors. The potential political and economic implications of unleashing so much influence and capital on the body politic could not be dismissed, as it would surely threaten to throw out of balance the separation of powers between branches of government and within the layered regime of the federal union. Thus, even as canal policy makers affirmed the status quo by including privileged political entrepreneurs in their definition of "the state," they were simultaneously using the legislative process to contain the influence that mixed-economy institutions and individual investors would have over future legislators.

These arrangements defied "public" or "private" categorizations, but they did not lack for clarity. Corporations, early Americans understood, were powerful economic and political instruments. They were not people. There were no such things as private corporations. And to leave them to their own devices in a democratic republic invited peril.

NOTES

Introduction

1. "On the Improvements Made by Corporations," [n.d., prob. 1784], Reel 3, Robert R. Livingston Microfilm Papers, 57 reels (Sanford, N.C., 1980). Hereafter abbreviated as RRLM.

2. For a biography of Robert Livingston, see George Dangerfield, *Chancellor Robert R. Livingston of New York, 1746–1813* (New York, 1960). For more on the family-based politics of colonial New York, see Alan Tully, *Forming American Politics: Ideals, Interests, and Institutions in Colonial New York and Pennsylvania* (Baltimore, Md., 1994), ch. 6.

3. Robert R. Livingston to John Jay, 25 January 1784, Reel 3, RRLM. Hereafter abbreviated as RRL.

4. Livingston thought about trying to win back his foreign-affairs job only to learn from allies James Madison and Alexander Hamilton that the internal politics of the Confederation Congress were no friendlier than those of the New York legislature. The chancellor was thought to be too cozy with Philadelphia financier Robert Morris, and they would be unable to whip up enough votes to support his reappointment. See RRL to James Madison, 15 July 1783; Alexander Hamilton to RRL, 23 July 1783; and RRL to Alexander Hamilton, 30 August 1783, all Reel 3, RRLM. See also Dangerfield, *Chancellor Robert R. Livingston of New York*, 177–80.

5. For more on the Livingston family's work as political entrepreneurs, see Cynthia A. Kierner, *Traders and Gentlefolk: The Livingstons of New York, 1675–1790* (Ithaca, N.Y., 1992), ch. 1.

6. All quotations drawn from RRL, "On the Improvements Made by Corporations," [n.d., prob. 1784], Reel 3, RRLM. For more on the Tea-Water Pump, see Gerald T. Koeppell, *Water for Gotham: A History* (Princeton, N.J., 2000), ch. 4.

7. See Dangerfield, *Chancellor Robert R. Livingston of New York*, 218 n. 7. Dangerfield posits that the letter was written to James Duane based on a different letter from RRL to Duane cited at 217, n. 6. There is, however, no indication in RRL's manuscript that this essay was ever sent or included with other correspondence. Based on his interpretation of the evidence, Dangerfield believes Livingston is merely attacking the "fruity subject of the Corporation's courage" while weighing in against improvements. My view suggests another reading: given that the essay was not published and seems to have never

been sent to anyone, I believe the essay—and the opening and closing paragraphs in particular—are systemic criticisms of the city and state's political economy as a whole rather than jabs aimed at any one individual.

8. RRL to John Jay, 30 July 1784, in Henry Johnston, ed., *Correspondence and Public Papers of John Jay*, 4 vols. (New York, 1893), 3:129.

9. The period was first defined in historiography by John Fiske, *The Critical Period of American History, 1783–1789* (New York, 1888). See also E. Wilder Spaulding, *New York in the Critical Period, 1783–1789* (1932; repr., Ann Arbor, Mich., 1969).

10. See John Kaminski, *George Clinton: Yeoman Politician of the New Republic* (Madison, Wis., 1992), 77–80; Kierner, *Traders and Gentlefolk*, ch. 5 on "Aristocratic Republicans." For more on this cohort and their ideological commitments, see Edward Countryman, *A People in Revolution: The American Revolution and Political Society in New York, 1760–1790* (1989; repr., Baltimore, Md., 1981), 196–202. My thinking on the big-picture post-Revolutionary divide between "demo and aristo" has been informed by John Brooke's *Columbia Rising: Civil Life on the Upper Hudson from the Revolution to the Age of Jackson* (Chapel Hill, N.C., 2010), which persuasively establishes the tension between democratic and aristocratic impulses and interests amid a granular examination of civic institutions and habits in post-Revolutionary New York. On this subject, see also Bernard Bailyn, *The Ideological Origins of the American Revolution* (Cambridge, Mass., 1967); Gordon S. Wood, *The Creation of the American Republic, 1776–1787* (Chapel Hill, N.C., 1969); Gordon S. Wood, *The Radicalism of the American Revolution* (New York, 1991); Richard H. Buel Jr., *Securing the Revolution: Ideology in American Politics, 1789–1815* (Ithaca, N.Y., 1972).

11. On the development of governance in the city of New York, see Hendrik Hartog, *Public Property and Private Power: The Corporation of the City of New York in American Law, 1730–1870* (Chapel Hill, N.C., 1983), chs. 3–4. See chs. 7–9 in the same for more on the more activist government that emerged in the new republic, which aligns with some of the public functions outlined in the introduction of William J. Novak, *The People's Welfare: Law and Regulation in Nineteenth-Century America* (Chapel Hill, N.C., 1996). See esp. Novak, ch. 3, for a discussion of the common law origins of the police powers and market regulations mentioned by Robert Livingston, and their implications for a government that made efforts to protect the *salus populi*, or people's welfare.

12. For more on New York's Revolutionary constitution, see Alfred Young, *The Democratic Republicans of New York: The Origins, 1763–1797* (Chapel Hill, N.C., 1967), 17–22.

13. RRL to Robert Morris, 20 December 1783, Reel 3, RRLM.

14. For the purposes of this book, the field begins with the publication of Adam Smith, *An Inquiry into the Nature and Causes of the Wealth of Nations*, 2 vols. (London, 1776), see esp. Book IV. See also Jean-Baptiste Say, *A Treatise on Political Economy* (Philadelphia, Pa., 1803); John Taylor, *Tyranny Unmasked* (Washington, D.C., 1822); Mathew Carey, *Essays on Political Economy; or, The Most Certain Means of Promoting the Wealth, Power, Resources, and Happiness of Nations: Applied Particularly to the United States*

(Philadelphia, 1822); Karl Marx [Frederick Engels et al., eds.], *Capital: A Critique of Political Economy* (1867; Chicago, 1906); John Stuart Mill, *Essays on Some Unsettled Questions of Political Economy*, 2nd. ed. (London, 1874).

15. Historical scholarship that explores this subject and influenced this book begins with John Lauritz Larson, *Internal Improvement: National Public Works and the Promise of Popular Government in the Early United States* (Chapel Hill, N.C., 2000), and Andrew Shankman, *Crucible of American Democracy: The Struggle to Fuse Egalitarianism and Capitalism in Jeffersonian Pennsylvania* (Lawrence, Kans., 2004). See also Richard Bensel, *The Political Economy of American Industrialization, 1877–1900* (New York, 2000); Thomas K. McCraw, *Prophets of Regulation: Charles Francis Adams, Louis D. Brandeis, James M. Landis, Alfred E. Kahn* (Boston, Mass., 1986); Robin L. Einhorn, *Property Rules: Political Economy in Chicago, 1833–1872* (Chicago, 2001); Robin L. Einhorn, *American Taxation, American Slavery* (Chicago, 2008); John R. Nelson Jr., *Liberty and Property: Political Economy and Policymaking in the New Nation, 1789–1812* (Baltimore, Md., 1987); Harry L. Watson, *Liberty and Power: The Politics of Jacksonian America* (New York, 1990).

16. Here I owe a debt to Robert A. Caro, *The Power Broker: Robert Moses and the Fall of New York* (New York, 1975).

17. New York has been a rich landscape for political-economy studies. See Robert G. Albion, *The Rise of New York Port, 1815–1860* (New York, 1939); Clifton Hood, "Robert G. Albion's The Rise of New York Port, 1815–1860," *Reviews in American History* 27, no. 2 (June 1999): 171–79; Charles W. McCurdy, *The Anti-Rent Era in New York Law and Politics, 1839–1865* (Chapel Hill, N.C., 2001); Sven Beckert, *The Monied Metropolis: New York City and the Consolidation of the American Bourgeoisie, 1850–1896* (New York, 2001); Nathan Miller, *The Enterprise of a Free People: Aspects of Economic Development in New York State During the Canal Period, 1792–1838* (Ithaca, N.Y., 1962); Steven E. Siry, *DeWitt Clinton and the American Political Economy: Sectionalism, Politics, and Republican Ideology, 1787–1828* (New York, 1990).

18. More than a decade of recent scholarship has made it clear that the state and its subordinate institutions matter; this book takes that proposition as a given. And a cohort of historians—many of them in business, economics, or political history—has built a persuasive argument for the essential importance of institutions in state formation and the socioeconomic and political lives of Americans. Their continuing work demonstrates a nuanced sensitivity for detecting the pressures of the state's presence and the influence of its institutions, which we can now define broadly on a spectrum that stretches from formal organizations at one end to informal habits and painstakingly documented norms at the other. Richard R. John, "Governmental Institutions as Agents of Change: Rethinking American Political Development in the Early Republic, 1787–1835," *Studies in American Political Development* 11 (1997): 347–80. See also Stephen Skowronek, *Building a New American State: The Expansion of National Administrative Capacities, 1877–1920* (New York, 1982); Stephen Skowronek and Karen Orren, *The Search for American Political Development* (New York, 2004); Theda Skocpol, "Bringing

the State Back In: Strategies of Analysis in Current Research," in Peter B. Evans, Dietrich Rueschemeyer, and Theda Skocpol, eds., *Bringing the State Back In* (New York, 1985), 3–43; Ira Katznelson, "Rewriting the Epic of America," in Ira Katznelson and Martin Shefter, eds., *Shaped by War and Trade: International Influences on American Political Development* (Princeton, N.J., 2002), 3–23; Brian Balogh, *A Government Out of Sight: The Mystery of National Authority in Nineteenth-Century America* (New York, 2009).

19. Peter S. Onuf, *The Origins of the Federal Republic Jurisdictional Controversies in the United States, 1775–1787* (Philadelphia, 1983); Douglas Bradburn, *The Citizenship Revolution: Politics and the Creation of the American Union, 1774–1804* (Charlottesville, Va., 2009); Daniel J. Hulsebosch, *Constituting Empire: New York and the Transformation of Constitutionalism in the Atlantic World, 1664–1830* (Chapel Hill, N.C., 2006); David C. Hendrickson, *Peace Pact: The Lost World of the American Founding* (Lawrence, Kans., 2006); Max M. Edling, *A Revolution in Favor of Government: Origins of the U.S. Constitution and the Making of the American State* (New York, 2003).

20. Christopher Tomlins, "Law's Empire: Chartering English Colonies on the American Mainland in the Seventeenth Century," in Diane E. Kirkby and Catherine Coleborne, eds., *Empire's Reach: Land, Law and Cultures* (Manchester, U.K., 2001), 26–45.

21. For work that celebrates the emergence of a vigorous public-private mixed economy, see Louis Hartz, *Economic Policy and Democratic Thought: Pennsylvania, 1776–1860* (Cambridge, Mass., 1948); Oscar Handlin and Mary Flug Handlin, *Commonwealth; A Study of the Role of Government in the American Economy: Massachusetts, 1776–1861* (Cambridge, Mass., 1969). See also Harry N. Scheiber, "Government and the Economy: Studies of the 'Commonwealth' Policy in Nineteenth-Century America," *Journal of Interdisciplinary History* 3, no. 1 (Summer 1972): 135–51.

22. My interest in this subject was originally kindled during conversations with Wilson Carey McWilliams, who, as a visiting professor of history at Haverford College, pointed me to Bertrand de Jouvenel's essay "Thoughts on a Theory of Political Enterprise," which can be found in Dennis Hale and Marc Landy, eds., *The Nature of Politics: Selected Essays of Bertrand de Jouvenel* (New Brunswick, N.J., 1992), 119–32. I am forever grateful to Carey for his early guidance and kindness. For his take on competing interests and their place in a democratic republic, see Patrick J. Deneen and Susan J. McWilliams, *The Democratic Soul: A Wilson Carey McWilliams Reader* (Lexington, Ky., 2011), 21–43. Thanks also to Johann Neem for his suggestions on how to approach this topic.

23. In this way, I see the so-called Second Party System of Andrew Jackson's era that followed three decades later as a more mature manifestation of institution-bound and interest-based politics that had always animated and legitimized American government—a continuation of practices that began under the colonial administration of the British American colonies and traced its origins to the British Empire and Prime Minister Robert Walpole's administration in the early eighteenth century. See Richard McCormick, *The Second American Party System: Party Formation in the Jacksonian Era* (Chapel Hill, N.C., 1966); Michael Kammen, *A Rope of Sand: The Colonial Agents, British Politics, and the American Revolution* (Ithaca, N.Y., 1968); John Brewer, *The*

Sinews of Power: War, Money, and the English State, 1688–1783 (Cambridge, Mass., 1990).

24. See James Taylor, *Creating Capitalism: Joint-Stock Enterprise in British Politics and Culture, 1800–1870* (Rochester, N.Y., 2006); Robert E. Wright, "Rise of the Corporation Nation," in Douglas Irwin and Richard E. Sylla, eds., *Founding Choices: American Economic Policy in the 1790s* (Chicago, 2011), 217–58; Andrew M. Schocket, *Founding Corporate Power in Early National Philadelphia* (DeKalb, Ill., 2007); Joseph S. Davis, *Essays in the Earlier History of American Corporations*, 2 vols. (Cambridge, Mass., 1917); Edwin M. Dodd, *American Business Corporations Until 1860* (Cambridge, Mass., 1954); Morton J. Horowitz, *The Transformation of American Law, 1780–1860* (Cambridge, Mass., 1979); James Willard Hurst, *The Legitimacy of the Business Corporation in the Law of the United States, 1780–1970* (Charlottesville, Va., 1970).

25. For more on economic rhetoric and the Revolution, see James A. Henretta, "The War for Independence and American Economic Development," in Ronald Hoffman et al., eds., *The Economy of Early America: The Revolutionary Period, 1763–1790* (Charlottesville, Va., 1988), 45–87; Edward Countryman, "The Uses of Capital in Revolutionary America: The Case of the New York Loyalist Merchants," *William and Mary Quarterly*, 3rd ser., 49 (January 1992): 3–28; Edward Countryman, "'To Secure the Blessings of Liberty': Language, the Revolution, and American Capitalism," in Alfred Young. ed., *Beyond the American Revolution: Explorations in the History of American Radicalism* (DeKalb, Ill., 1993), 123–48.

26. See James L. Huston, "The American Revolutionaries, the Political Economy of Aristocracy, and the American Concept of the Distribution of Wealth, 1765–1900," *American Historical Review* 98, no. 4 (Oct. 1993): 1079–105.

27. For all of their strengths, neither the republicanism nor the democratization schools of historiography offer a satisfying conceptual explanation for how material interests were managed and integrated into the federal framework or how political arrangements reflected and encouraged capital formation and particular species of business organization. This literature, though vast and impressive, is so grounded in broad ideological concerns that it cannot explain ground-level developments in American capitalism, and it rejects the idea that capital and practical anxieties about capital could be first-order drivers for the period's political actors or principal catalysts for its institutional development. A deep dive into this work would begin with Bernard Bailyn, *The Ideological Origins of the American Revolution* (Cambridge, Mass., 1967) and his student Gordon S. Wood, *The Creation of the American Republic, 1776–1787* (Chapel Hill, N.C., 1998) and Gordon S. Wood, *The Radicalism of the American Revolution* (New York, 1991); Pauline Maier, *From Resistance to Revolution: Colonial Radicals and the Development of American Opposition to Britain, 1765–1776* (New York, 1972); Lance Banning, *The Jeffersonian Persuasion: Evolution of a Party Ideology* (Ithaca, N.Y., 1978); Drew R. McCoy, *The Elusive Republic: Political Economy in Jeffersonian America* (Chapel Hill, N.C., 1980); Stanley Elkins and Eric McKitrick, *The Age of Federalism: The Early American Republic, 1788–1800* (New York, 1993). See also Bernard Bailyn, *The Origins of*

American Politics (New York, 1968) and Gordon S. Wood, "Rhetoric and Reality in the American Revolution," *William and Mary Quarterly*, 3rd ser., 32 (January 1966): 3–32. These works can be contrasted with Countryman, *A People in Revolution*; Young, *Democratic Republicans of New York*; James Oakes, *Slavery and Freedom: An Interpretation of the Old South* (New York, 1990). For a critique of this approach and its implications for capitalism, see Joyce Appleby, "The Vexed Story of Capitalism Told by American Historians," *Journal of the Early Republic* 21 (2002): 1–18, and Joyce Appleby, *Capitalism and a New Social Order: The Republican Vision of the 1790s* (New York, 1984). Cf. Gordon S. Wood, "The Enemy Is Us: Democratic Capitalism in the Early Republic," *Journal of the Early Republic* 16 (1996): 293–308. See also David Waldstreicher, "Appleby's Liberal America," Common-place, www.common-place.org.

28. Charles Sellers, *The Market Revolution: Jacksonian America, 1815–1846* (New York, 1991) is the classic work exploring the implications of a "market revolution." See also Richard Lyman Bushman, "Markets and Composite Farms in Early America," *William and Mary Quarterly*, 3rd ser., 55 (July 1998): 351–74; James A. Henretta, "Families and Farms: *Mentalité* in Pre-Industrial America," *William and Mary Quarterly*, 3rd ser., 35 (January 1978): 3–32; Michael Merrill, " 'Cash Is Good to Eat': Self-Sufficiency and Exchange in the Rural Economy of the United States," *Radical History Review* 4 (Winter 1977): 42–71; Robert E. Mutch, "Yeoman and Merchant in Pre-Industrial America: Eighteenth-Century Massachusetts as a Case Study," *Societas* 7 (Autumn 1977): 279–302. I am skeptical about the concept of a "Market Revolution" as put forward by this scholarship: see Brian Phillips Murphy, "The Market Revolution," in Sean Patrick Adams, ed., *A Companion to the Era of Andrew Jackson* (West Sussex, U.K., 2013), ch. 5. See also Winifred Barr Rothenberg, *From Market-Places to a Market Economy: The Transformation of Rural Massachusetts, 1750–1850* (Chicago, 1992), and Christopher Clark, *The Roots of Rural Capitalism: Western Massachusetts, 1780–1860* (Ithaca, N.Y., 1990).

29. Free banking and free incorporation policies were therefore continuations of "public" policies aiming to promote competition in the "private" sector. This literature is typified by Walt W. Rostow, *Stages of Economic Growth* (Cambridge, Mass., 1960), and Douglass C. North, *Economic Growth of the United States, 1790–1860* (Englewood Cliffs, N.J., 1960), as well as Stuart Bruchey, *The Roots of American Economic Growth 1607–1861: An Essay on Social Causation* (New York, 1965). See also Howard Bodenhorn, "Bank Chartering and Political Corruption in Antebellum New York," in Edward L. Glaeser and Claudia Goldin, eds., *Corruption and Reform: Lessons from America's Economic History* (Chicago, 2006).

30. On efforts to contain the influence of capital, see J. R. Pole, *The Pursuit of Equality in American History* (Berkeley, Calif., 1978); Steven Watts, *The Republic Reborn: War and the Making of Liberal America, 1790–1820* (Baltimore, Md., 1987); McCoy, *The Elusive Republic*, esp. 67–68; Banning, *The Jeffersonian Persuasion*, esp. 204–5; Gordon S. Wood, *The Creation of the American Republic* (Chapel Hill, N.C., 1969), esp. 72; J. G. A. Pocock, *The Machiavellian Moment: Florentine Political Thought and the Atlantic*

Republican Tradition (Princeton, N.J., 1975), 384–86. See also Dixon Ryan Fox, *The Decline of Aristocracy in the Politics of New York* (New York, 1919).

31. For the Pennsylvania case, see Bray Hammond's classic *Banks and Politics in America: From the Revolution to the Civil War* (Princeton, N.J., 1957). On Massachusetts, see Pauline Maier's article on corporations, "The Revolutionary Origins of the American Corporation," *William and Mary Quarterly*, 3rd ser., 50 (January 1993): 51–84.

32. See H. V. Bowen, *The Business of Empire: The East India Company and Imperial Britain, 1756–1833* (New York, 2008). See also Ann M. Carlos and Stephen Nicholas, "'Giants of an Earlier Capitalism': The Chartered Trading Companies as Modern Multinationals," *Business History Review* 62, no. 3 (Autumn, 1988): 398–419.

33. For more on this subject, see Stuart Banner's recently published book *American Property: A History of How, Why, and What We Own* (Cambridge, Mass., 2011).

34. Robert G. Kaiser, *So Damn Much Money: The Triumph of Lobbying and the Corrosion of American Government* (New York, 2009).

35. This book expands on insights offered by Cathy D. Matson and Peter S. Onuf, *A Union of Interests: Political and Economic Thought in Revolutionary America* (Lawrence, Kans., 1990). On the role of interests at the convention, see Gordon S. Wood , "Interests and Disinterestedness in the Making of the Constitution," in Richard Beeman, Stephen Botein, and Edward C. Carter III, eds., *Beyond Confederation* (Chapel Hill, N.C., 1987), 69–109. For an edited collection of the *Federalist Papers*, see Clinton Rossiter, ed., *The Federalist Papers* (New York, 2003).

36. Fox, *The Decline of Aristocracy*, ch. 1.

37. Barry Weingast, "The Economic Role of Political Institutions: Market-Preserving Federalism and Economic Development," *Journal of Law, Economics and Organization* 11 (1995): 1–31; Peter Temin, "Free Land and Federalism," *Journal of Interdisciplinary History* 21 (1991): 371–89.

38. See Ronald Formisano, "The Concept of Political Culture," *Journal of Interdisciplinary History* 31 (2001): 393–426, and Ronald Formisano, "State Development in the Early Republic: Substance and Structure," in Byron E. Shafer and Anthony J. Badger, eds., *Contesting Democracy: Substance and Structure in American Political History, 1775–2000* (Lawrence, Kans., 2001), 7–35.

39. Thomas M. Doerflinger, *A Vigorous Spirit of Enterprise: Merchants and Economic Development in Revolutionary Philadelphia* (Chapel Hill, N.C., 1986).

40. This book draws on intellectual, economic, legal, and political historians to craft narratives showing that "government" and "the economy" were inseparable entities—a distinct departure from older work in political economy that drew neat lines between public and private spheres of action. My approach to this material is inherently interdisciplinary and draws particular inspiration from three books, all improbably published by Johns Hopkins University Press in a series edited by Cathy Matson: Sharon Ann Murphy, *Investing in Life: Insurance in Antebellum America* (Baltimore, Md., 2010); Brian D. Schoen, *The Fragile Fabric of Union: Cotton, Federal Politics, and the Global Origins of the Civil War* (Baltimore, Md., 2009); and Sean Patrick Adams, *Old*

Dominion, Industrial Commonwealth: Coal, Politics, and Economy in Antebellum America (Baltimore, Md., 2004). See also Richard R. John, ed., *Ruling Passions: Political Economy in Nineteenth-Century America* (State College, Pa., 2006).

In *Building the Empire State*, I draw on two major thrusts of recent historiography: economic historians' examinations of the development and scale of commercial, savings, and investment banking in the early republic and nineteenth century and the work of "new institutionalist" political scientists and political and economic historians who argue that the cultural and literary turns in historiography underestimated and minimized the importance of institutions and the state in the early republic. These latter scholars advocate for us to "bring the state back in." For the former, see Howard Bodenhorn, *A History of Banking in Antebellum America: Financial Markets and Economic Development in an Era of Nation-Building* (Cambridge, U.K., 2000); Howard Bodenhorn, *State Banking in Early America: A New Economic History* (New York, 2002); Edwin J. Perkins, *American Public Finance and Financial Services, 1700–1815* (Columbus, Ohio, 1994); Richard Sylla, "Shaping the U.S. Financial System, 1690–1913: The Dominant Role of Public Finance," in Richard Sylla, Richard Tilly, and Gabriel Tortella, eds., *The State, the Financial System, and Economic Modernization* (Cambridge, U.K., 1999), 249–70; Peter L. Rousseau and Richard Sylla, "Emerging Financial Markets and Early U.S. Growth," *National Bureau of Economic Research Working Paper 7448* (December 1999); Robert E. Wright, *Origins of Commercial Banking in America, 1750–1800* (Lanham, Md., 2001); Robert E. Wright, *The Wealth of Nations Rediscovered: Integration and Expansion in American Financial Markets, 1780–1850* (New York, 2002); Robert E. Wright, *The First Wall Street: Chestnut Street, Philadelphia, and the Birth of American Finance* (Chicago, 2005). See also Robert E. Wright and David J. Cowen, *Financial Founding Fathers: The Men Who Made America Rich* (Chicago, 2006). For the latter, see John, "Governmental Institutions as Agents of Change."

This book also relies on political and economic studies exemplified by John L. Brooke, *The Heart of the Commonwealth: Society and Political Culture in Worcester County, Massachusetts, 1713–1861* (New York, 1989); William Cronon, *Nature's Metropolis: Chicago and the Great West* (New York, 1991); Price V. Fishback et al., eds., *Government and the American Economy: A New History* (Chicago, 2007); William H. Bergmann, "'A Commercial View of this Unfortunate War': Economic Roots of an American National State in the Ohio Valley, 1775–1795," *Early American Studies* 6 (2008): 137–64; Allan Kulikoff, "The Transition to Capitalism in Rural America," *William and Mary Quarterly*, 3rd ser., 46 (January 1989): 120–44; Edward Balleisen, *Navigating Failure: Bankruptcy and Commercial Society in Antebellum America* (Chapel Hill, N.C., 2001); Scott Sandage, *Born Losers: A History of Failure in America* (Cambridge, Mass., 2005); Jane Kamensky, *The Exchange Artist: A Tale of High-Flying Speculation and America's First Banking Collapse* (New York, 2008); Herbert Sloan, *Principle and Interest: Thomas Jefferson and the Problem of Debt* (New York, 1995).

41. See, for example, Christopher Hayes, *Twilight of the Elites: America After*

Meritocracy (New York, 2012), and George Packer, *The Unwinding: An Inner History of the New America* (New York, 2013).

Chapter 1

1. "The Committee appointed . . . General Washington," 24 November 1783, New York, Broadside, Evans 44426; James Grant Wilson, ed., *The Memorial History of the City of New-York*, vol. 2 (New York, 1892), 556 n.1. For more on pre-Revolutionary New York, see Richard M. Ketchum, *Divided Loyalties: How the American Revolution Came to New York* (New York, 2002). For a cultural history of the evacuation ceremonies' meaning, see Clifton Hood, "An Unusable Past: Urban Elites, New York City's Evacuation Day, and the Transformations of Memory Culture," *Journal of Social History* 37 (Summer 2004): 883–913.

2. Eric Homberger, *Historical Atlas of New York City* (New York, 1998), ch. 2.

3. Legislators in 1779 passed the Confiscation Act—shorthand for "an Act for the Forfeiture and Sale of the Estates of Persons who have adhered to the Enemies of this State, and for declaring the Sovereignty of the People of this State in respect to all property within the same." See New York *Laws* (1779, 3rd Sess.), ch. 29. See also Beatrice G. Reubens, "Pre-Emptive Rights in the Disposition of a Confiscated Estate, Philipsburgh Manor, New York," *William and Mary Quarterly*, 3rd ser., 22 (July 1965): 435–56; Catherine S. Crary, "Forfeited Loyalist Lands in the Western District of New York—Albany and Tryon Counties," *New York History* 35 (1954): 239–58; E. Wilder Spaulding, *New York in the Critical Period, 1783–1789* (1932; Ann Arbor, Mich., 1969), 77–78.

4. "'Brutus' to the Tories of New-York City," 15 August 1783, Broadside, New-York Historical Society. Hereafter abbreviated as NYHS. The Confiscation Act, passed during the legislature's second session in 1778, was initially vetoed by the state's Council of Revision. It was approved again and became law during the body's third session. See Edward Countryman, "Consolidating Power in Revolutionary America: The Case of New York, 1775–1783," *Journal of Interdisciplinary History* 6 (Spring 1976): 645–77, esp. 667 n. 49. The son of a blacksmith, Abraham Yates had become the Albany county sheriff in 1754 through the patronage of Robert Livingston Sr., the chancellor's father. But Yates rose to true prominence during the war, leading the Albany Committee of Correspondence, Safety and Security to draft the state's 1777 constitution, and thereafter serving in several state offices. See Stefan Bielinski, *Abraham Yates, Jr. and the New Political Order in Revolutionary New York* (Albany, N.Y., 1975).

5. Robert R. Livingston to Robert Morris, 20 December 1783, Reel 3, Robert R. Livingston Microfilm Papers, 37 reels (Stanford, N.C., 1980); RRL to Alexander Hamilton, 30 August 1783, Reel 3, RRLPM. Hereafter abbreviated as RRL, AH, and RRLPM.

6. RRL to Robert Morris, 20 December 1783, Reel 3, RRLPM.

7. AH to RRL, 13 August 1783, in Harold C. Syrett and Jacob E. Cooke, *The Papers of Alexander Hamilton*, 27 vols. (New York, 1961). Hereafter abbreviated as *PAH*.

8. John Jay to AH, 28 September 1783, *PAH*. See also John Jay to RRL, 12 September 1783, Reel 3, RRLPM. John Jay had succeeded Robert Livingston as Congress's minister of foreign affairs and helped negotiate the Treaty of Paris that ended the Revolution; he knew all too well that excessive abuses against Tories could do more than damage American credibility. Under the terms of the peace treaty, Tories who chose to remain in America were to be neither deprived of property nor stripped of political rights; Congress was called on to "earnestly recommend" that state legislatures undertake "a reconsideration and revision of all acts or laws" passed during wartime to confiscate Tory property so as to facilitate a "spirit of conciliation." See Articles V and VI of the Treaty of Paris (30 September 1783), www.yale.edu/lawweb/avalon/diplomacy/britain/paris.htm.

9. For more on New York during this period, see Anthony Gronowicz, "Political 'Radicalism' in New York City," in Paul A. Gilje and William Pencak, eds., *New York in the Age of the Constitution, 1775–1800* (Cranbury, N.J., 1992). For an overview of the period, see Spaulding, *New York in the Critical Period*, but note that Spaulding is unreliable on the issue of banking and credit; he confuses the land- and money-bank proposals throughout the book. See also Thomas C. Cochran, *New York in the Confederation: An Economic Study* (Philadelphia, 1932), and Jackson Turner Main, *The Sovereign States, 1775–1783* (New York, 1973). A more familiar study of the 1780s is Merrill Jensen, *The New Nation: A History of the United States During the Confederation, 1781–1789* (New York, 1950). See also John P. Kaminski, "New York: The Reluctant Pillar," in Stephen L. Schecter, ed., *The Reluctant Pillar: New York and the Adoption of the Federal Constitution* (Troy, N.Y., 1985), ch. 4. For more on the Bank of England, see H. V. Bowen, "The Bank of England During the Long Eighteenth Century, 1694–1820," in David Kynaston and Richard Roberts, eds., *The Bank of England: Money, Power, and Influence, 1694–1994* (New York, 1995), ch. 1; John Francis and I. Smith Homans, *History of the Bank of England, Its Times and Traditions, from 1694–1844* (New York, 1862); Tobias George Smollett and David Hume, *The History of England* (London, 1825), ch. 4.

10. See Richard Sylla, "Forgotten Men of Money: Private Bankers in Early U.S. History," *Journal of Economic History* 36 (1976): 173–88; Howard Bodenhorn, *State Banking in Early America: A New Economic History* (New York, 2003), ch. 2; Bray Hammond, *Banks and Politics in America from the Revolution to the Civil War* (Princeton, N.J., 1957), ch. 3; Lawrence Smith, *Money, Credit, and Public Policy* (Boston, 1959), 483; Charles Lee Prather, *Money and Banking* (New York, 1949), 200. Fritz Redlich, *The Molding of American Banking: Men and Ideas* (1951; repr., New York, 1968), 12. Robert E. Wright, *Hamilton Unbound: Finance and the Creation of the American Republic* (New York, 2002), 135; Joseph Stancliffe Davis, *Essays in the Earlier History of American Corporations* (Cambridge, Mass., 1917), 83.

11. The history of the Bank of New-York has been chronicled by several historians. A particularly hagiographic treatment was published to mark the bank's 175th anniversary: Edward Streeter, *Window on America: The Growth of a Nation as Seen by the Nation's First Bank* (New York, 1959). See also Fritz Redlich, *The Molding of American Banking: Men and Ideas*, 2 vols. (New York, 1951); Bray Hammond, *Banks and Politics in*

America from the Revolution to the Civil War (Princeton, N.J., 1957); Wright, *Hamilton Unbound*; Robert E. Wright and David J. Cowen, *Financial Founding Fathers: The Men Who Made America Rich* (Chicago, 2006).

12. RRL to Peter J. Van Berckel, 24 January 1784, Reel 3, RRLPM.

13. [Hamilton], "A Letter from Phocion to the Considerate Citizens of New-York, on the Politics of the Day," [January 1784], *PAH*.

14. AH to George Clinton, 14 May 1783, *PAH*.

15. Joseph Bucklin Bishop, *A Chronicle of One Hundred and Fifty Years: The Chamber of Commerce of the State of New York, 1768–1918* (New York, 1918). For the chamber's charter, see New York *Laws* (1784, 7th Sess.), ch. 30.

16. When Loyalist Tories appointed one of their own, Benjamin Moore, as Trinity Church's rector, Whigs responded by demanding that a patriot, Samuel Provoost, be made rector instead, demoting Moore to assistant. Robert Livingston thought the episode revealed the foolishness of some Tories. Their "imprudence," he told John Jay, "g[ave] a handle to warm Whigs to attack them." He feared that he and his allies' "extreme moderation," had only emboldened Tories by "g[iving] them confidence." "Not content with protection" from men like Livingston, Tory Loyalists had instead "sought for power, filling up the vacuum." Moore, the Loyalists' choice for rector, was, in the chancellor's word, a "reprehensible" man. But "in spite of the earnest request of the Whig members" of the church, the Tory vestrymen insisted on his appointment. Robert Livingston was one of the Whig parishioners who turned to the state legislature for aid. Lawmakers, the chancellor reported to John Jay, "void[ed] [Moore's] election" and "vest[ed] the temporalities of the church in nine trustees" until it could be reorganized. The episode painted in stark relief the political divisions in the city. At the one end were foolishly impolitic Loyalists. Somewhere in the middle were men like the chancellor and John Jay, "who wish . . . to suppress all violences [and] to soften the rigorous laws with respect to the Tories." And at the opposite end were "warm & hotheaded Whigs" who "are for the expulsion of all Tories from the state" and "wish to render the more moderate Whigs"—Livingston included himself—"in order to preserve [in] their own hands all the powers of Government." See RRL to John Jay, 29 November 1783, Reel 3, RRLPM.

17. From 1783 to 1789 during the Critical Period, the thirteen states created a total of twenty-six business corporations. Twelve were in Virginia and Massachusetts; North Carolina, South Carolina, Maryland, Pennsylvania, and Connecticut also chartered companies. New York chartered none. See Joseph Stancliffe Davis, *Essays in the Earlier History of American Corporations*, 2 vols. (Cambridge, Mass., 1917), 2:8, 22–23. The number of charters issued by states increased dramatically after 1789, with the highest concentration in New England.

18. Facing pressure to expand its operations and become more inclusive, the Bank of North America in Philadelphia decided to issue 1,000 new shares of stock, enabling a broader base of participation in an enlarged institution. This move would dilute the voting power of the bank's existing shareholders. Although they were promised financial

compensation for this loss, their enduring influence over the institution would become smaller than before, prompting them to begin organizing the new institution. John Chaloner to AH, 26 November 1783, and Gouverneur Morris to AH, 27 January 1784, both in *PAH*. See also Anna J. Schwartz, *Money in Historical Perspective* (Chicago, 1987), 4–6.

19. Competition among interests within comparative, dynamic, and partisan political circumstances is explored by Alan Tully, *Forming American Politics: Ideals, Interests, and Institutions in Colonial New York and Pennsylvania* (Baltimore, Md., 1994), ch. 10. A summary of recent, cross-disciplinary literature on the role of private interests in group formation can be found in Frank R. Baumgartner and Beth L. Leech, *Basic Interests: The Importance of Groups in Politics and Political Science* (Princeton, N.J., 1998), ch. 2. For more on the Federalist view of interests in the early republic's political economy, see Cathy D. Matson and Peter S. Onuf, *A Union of Interests: Political and Economic Thought in Revolutionary America* (Lawrence, Kans., 1990). My thinking on this subject has been particularly influenced by Joyce Appleby, *Capitalism and a New Social Order: The Republican Vision of the 1790s* (New York, 1984), and Joyce Appleby, "Commercial Farming and the 'Agrarian Myth' in the Early Republic," *Journal of American History* 68 (March 1982): 833–49. See also Isaac Kramnick, "Republican Revisionism Revisited," *American Historical Review* 87 (June 1982): 629–64.

20. Pauline Maier, "The Revolutionary Origins of the American Corporation," *William and Mary Quarterly*, 3rd ser., 50 (January 1993), 51–84; Davis, *Essays in the Earlier History of American Corporations*, 2: 6–9; Oscar Handlin and Mary F. Handlin, *Commonwealth: A Study of the Role of Government in the American Economy: Massachusetts, 1774–1861*, rev. ed. (Cambridge, Mass., 1969); Edwin Merrick Dodd, *American Business Corporations Until 1860, With Special Reference to Massachusetts* (Cambridge, Mass., 1954); Ronald Seavoy, *The Origins of the American Business Corporation, 1784–1855: Broadening the Concept of Public Service During Industrialization* (Westport, Conn., 1982); Hendrik Hartog, *Public Property and Private Power: The Corporation of the City of New York in American Law, 1730–1870* (Chapel Hill, N.C., 1993). See also Oscar Handlin and Mary F. Handlin, "Origins of the American Business Corporation," *Journal of Economic History* 5 (1945): 1–23.

21. RRL to Peter J. Van Berckel, 2 February 1784, Reel 3, RRLPM.

22. Although he had been born in New York, Stephen Sayre spent the most colorful of his forty-eight years living abroad; he returned to the city just before Evacuation Day, having lived in London prior to the Revolution. There he and an Irish-born partner named Bartholomew Coote Purdon had jointly owned and operated a bank on Oxford Street. In 1775 Sayre was arrested and imprisoned in the Tower of London after being implicated in a far-fetched plot to kidnap King George III during his ceremonial ride to Parliament on its opening day.

Freed in 1776 on a hefty £1,000 bail, Sayre returned to society only to have his partner abandon both him and their bank. Fleeing a personal debt, Purdon skipped off to Suez, leaving Sayre to clean up the mess and arrange for James Christie to auction off their joint assets. Sayre left London soon after and spent the rest of the Revolution traveling throughout Europe as an unofficial emissary for the American government and using his access to court the richest women he could find, including Catherine the Great. See John Richard Alden, *Stephen Sayre: American Revolutionary Adventurer* (Baton Rouge, La., 1983), 90–92. See also Sayre to George Washington, 15 October 1790 and 3 January 1795, in Theodore J. Crackel, ed., *The Papers of George Washington, Digital Edition* (Charlottesville, Va., 2008).

23. RRL to Peter J. Van Berckel, 24 January 1784, Reel 3, RRLPM.

24. Ibid.

25. Recent efforts to reconcile Tories and Whigs seemed to be failing, Livingston reported to John Jay the day after he penned his offer to the Dutch minister. The formerly Loyalist printer James Rivington had recently been beaten and "intimidated by the committee of mechanics so as to be induced to stop his press." Livingston blamed the "imprudence of the [T]ories" for creating a climate of aggression and "giv[ing] a handle to the warm Whigs to attack them." Meanwhile, he told Jay, "our extreme moderation—Livingston's way of referring to his and his associates' efforts to settle tempers—had temporarily backfired. It "gave [the Tories] confidence . . . they sought for power, filling up the vacuum," he wrote. The city was therefore left with "Tories who still hope for power" and "omit no occasion to show their attachment to Britain & their aversion to our government" on one side, and "warm & hotheaded Whigs" on the other, who are for the expulsion of all Tories" and "wish to render the more moderate Whigs suspected in order to preserve [in] their own hands all the powers of Government." See RRL to John Jay, 25 January. 1784, Reel 3, RRLPM.

26. RRL to John Jay, 25 January 1784, Reel 3, RRLPM. It is interesting to note that the paragraphs containing Livingston's invitation to join in land investments are crossed-through in the original manuscript version received and recorded by Jay. They are also redacted in Henry P. Johnston, A.M., ed., *The Correspondence and Public Papers of John Jay* (New York, 1890–93), vol. 3 (1782–93).

27. Peter J. Van Berckel to RRL, 27 January 1784, Reel 3, RRLPM.

28. Ibid., 2 February 1784, Reel 3, RRLPM.

29. New York *Packet*, 12 February 1784, 3, and 16 February 1784, 1; New York *Independent Gazette*, 12 February 1784, 3.

30. Bank directors would have to own at least four shares of stock.

31. For more on land banks, see Marshall D. Harris, *Origin of the Land Tenure System in the United States* (Ames, Iowa, 1953), ch. 10; Paul Wallace Gates, "The Role of the Land Speculator in Western Development," *Pennsylvania Magazine of History and Biography* 64 (1942): 314–33. A view of land speculation as an investment is William Chazanof, "Land Speculation in Eighteenth-Century New York," in Joseph R. Frese and Jacob Tudd, eds., *Business Enterprise in Early New York* (Tarrytown, N.Y., 1979), 55–76. See also Robert E. Wright, *Origins of Commercial Banking in America, 1750–1800* (Lanham, Md., 2001), 92.

32. See the advertisement for "European and India Goods" from John Turner Jr. & Co., New York *Packet*, 16 February 1784, supp. 1.

33. AH to John B. Church, 10 March 1784, *PAH*. Hamilton's intelligence about the land bank shapes the dominant narratives of the development of banking in New York, yet his information was far from complete.

34. Wadsworth, a Connecticut-born colonel, served as the Continental army's commissary-general until 1779, after which he took on the same role with Jean-Baptiste Donatien de Vimeur, Comte de Rochambeau's French troops. Church, a British merchant who fled debts and a duel to find a wife and fortune in the colonies, had lately returned to London with both. See John D. R. Platt, "Jeremiah Wadsworth: Federalist Entrepreneur" (Ph.D. diss., Columbia University, 1955).

35. Church owned 98 shares in the bank; Wadsworth held 104. Priced at $400 per share, their combined investment was nearly $82,000. Platt, "Jeremiah Wadsworth," 134–35. See also E. James Ferguson et al., eds., *The Papers of Robert Morris, 1781–1784*, 9 vols. (Pittsburgh, 1973–99), 8:342 n. 3.; Benson John Lossing, *The Life and Times of Philip Schuyler*, 2 vols. (New York, 1873), 2:207.

36. John Chaloner to Jeremiah Wadsworth and John B. Church, 4 January 1784, quoted in Platt, "Jeremiah Wadsworth," 137.

37. Church directed Hamilton to begin buying shares and "keep your Intentions a secret." See John B. Church to AH, 7 February 1784, *PAH*. Wadsworth instructed Hamilton to "strain at every nerve to buy in the new Shares," putting them in Hamilton's and Chaloner's names and using "my sisters and some other friends" to act as straw purchasers, all so that Robert Morris and Thomas Willing would not learn that they had caught on to their scheme. Jeremiah Wadsworth to Peter Colt, 6 February 1784, quoted in Platt, "Jeremiah Wadsworth," 138.

38. Wadsworth referred to the bank as an "engine" of regulation. Pennsylvania opponents of the Bank of North America referred to it as an "engine of power." See Platt, "Jeremiah Wadsworth," 58–59, and minutes of the Pennsylvania Assembly (Philadelphia, 1784), 253–54. Given the brevity of Hamilton's note to Church, it seems clear that this was not the first time he had suggested that the two merchants open their own bank; Church was already referring to it as "our Plan" by February. A 12 December 1783 letter to John B. Church is not extant but is referenced by Church in his 7 February 1784 letter to Hamilton. See John B. Church to AH, 7 February 1784, *PAH*. See also [John B. Church] to Jeremiah Wadsworth, 2 April 1783, Wadsworth Correspondence, Connecticut Historical Society (hereafter abbreviated as CtHi); Platt, "Jeremiah Wadsworth," 58–59. For the correspondence relating to the Bank of North America, see AH to John Chaloner, 11 December 1783; AH to John B. Church, 12 December 1783; John Chaloner to AH, 18 Dec ember 1783; John B. Church to AH, 7 February 1784, all in *PAH*.

39. Alden, *Stephen Sayre*, 137–38; AH to John B. Church, 10 March 1784, *PAH*.

40. AH to John B. Church, 10 March 1784, *PAH*.

41. New York *Packet*, 16 February 1784, 2.

42. For more on the insurance industry in the United States, see Sharon Ann Murphy, *Investing in Life: Insurance in Antebellum America* (Baltimore, Md., 2010);

Insurance Society of New York, *The Fire Insurance Contract: Its History and Interpretation* (New York, 1922); Martin F. Grace and Michael M. Barth, "The Regulation and Structure of Non-Life Insurance in the United States," Financial Sector Development Department Working Paper, Working Papers Series No. 1155, World Bank (July 1993).

43. Wadsworth was so confident in Hamilton's abilities that he instructed his Philadelphia agent John Chaloner to begin purchasing shares in a new second bank being opened in Philadelphia. Should he and John B. Church "pursue their Scheme of bank[in] g in New York," Wadsworth believed they would "Stand a Chance of mak[in]g better terms" and having stronger relationships with Philadelphia merchants if there were two banks in that city and "they [were] Interested in both." The profits they made on those shares would be reinvested in their New York bank once it opened. AH to John B. Church, 10 March 1784, *PAH*.

44. "A Merchant," New York *Packet*, 23 February 1784, 3.

45. New York *Packet*, 1 March 1784, 2.

46. "To the Worthy and Industrious Mechanicks of this State," [1783], New York, Broadside, Evans 44469. This was not the first time McDougall tried to unify merchants and mechanics. In 1774, as a member of the city's Chamber of Commerce, McDougall also represented the "Body of Mechanics" in elections to choose members of the state's delegates to the Continental Congress. See John Austin Stevens Jr., *Colonial Record of the New York Chamber of Commerce, 1768–1784* (New York, 1867), 90.

47. "To the Electors of this City at Large," 23 December 1783, New York, Broadside, Evans 44466. The phrase "Hewers of Wood, and Drawers of Water" refers to a state of slavery and is drawn from the Bible, namely, Joshua 9:23, which states, "Now therefore ye are cursed, and there shall none of you be freed from being bondmen, and hewers of wood and drawers of water for the house of my God."

48. AH to John B. Church, 10 March 1784, *PAH*.

49. Note dated 5 March 1784, New York *Independent Journal*, 6 March 1784, 2; repr. in New York *Packet*, 11 March 1784, 1. See also AH to John B. Church, 10 March 1784, *PAH*.

50. "Constitution of the Bank of New-York," [23 Feb.–15 March 1784], *PAH*. See esp. *PAH*, 3: 514 n. 1.

51. "To the Citizens of New-York No. 2," "A Citizen" [Robert R. Livingston], New York *Independent Journal*, 17 March 1784, 2, and RRL's "Bank Notes" memo, [1784], Reel 3, RRLPM.

52. My thinking on this matter was initially shaped by John J. McCusker and Russell R. Menard, *The Economy of British America, 1607–1789* (Chapel Hill, N.C., 1985), 332–37. "When private enterprise needed help, public promotive schemes were developed. When private enterprise seemed threatened, government intervened. And when private enterprise endangered the public good, government responded by regulating economic behavior," McCusker and Menard, 332. See also Louis Hartz, *Economic Policy and Democratic Thought: Pennsylvania, 1776–1860* (Cambridge, Mass., 1948), ch. 17.

53. New York Assembly *Journal*, 12 March 1784

54. Edmund Willis, "Social Origins of Political Leadership in New York City from the Revolution to 1815" (Ph.D. diss., University of California, Berkeley, 1967), 27.

55. For more on the merchants and mechanics' relations during the war, see Staughton Lynd, "The Mechanics in New York Politics, 1774–1788," *Labor History* 5, no. 3 (1964): 225–46.

56. Gouverneur Morris to Hamilton, 27 Jan. 1784, *PAH*; AH to Gouverneur Morris, 3 February 1784, *PAH*.

57. Thomas Tillotson to RRL, n.d. May 1784, Reel 3, RRLPM.

58. AH to Gouverneur Morris, 21 March 1784, *PAH*.

59. "Outline of a Charter for the Bank of New-York," [23 Feb.–15 March 1784], *PAH*.

60. "To the Citizens of New-York," "A Citizen" [Robert R. Livingston], New York *Independent Journal*, 13 March 1784, 2, and RRL's "Bank Thoughts" memo, [1784], Reel 3, RRLPM.

61. "To the Citizens of New-York No. 2," "A Citizen" [Robert R. Livingston], New York *Independent Journal*, 17 March 1784, 2, and RRL's "Bank Notes" memo, [1784], Reel 3, RRLPM.

62. "To the Citizens of New-York," "A Citizen" [Robert R. Livingston], New York *Independent Journal*, 13 March 1784, 2, and RRL's "Bank Thoughts" memo, [1784], Reel 3, RRLPM.

63. Thomas Tillotson to RRL, n.d. May 1784, Reel 3, RRLPM.

64. "The Following Queries Are Submitted to the *True Friends* to the Real Interest Happiness and Prosperity of This State," New York *Journal*, 18 March 1784, 2.

65. "A Real Whig," "Appeal to the Legislature" (part I), New York *Independent Gazette*, 11 March 1784, 3; part 2, New York *Independent Gazette*, 25 March 1784, 1.

66. "Intelligence Serious and Extraordinary, from a Correspondent," New York *Journal*, 18 March 1784, 2–3.

67. "A Mechanic," New York *Journal*, 25 March 1784, 2.

68. Richard Sylla, "Monetary Innovation in America," *Journal of Economic History* 42 (March 1982): 21–30. The potential for financial institutions to shape the regulation of their activities and convince their regulators of the mutuality of their interests, called cognitive regulatory capture, has been suggested to me by, among others, Willem H. Buiter, "Lessons from the North American Financial Crisis," paper delivered at "The Role of Money Markets" conference co-sponsored by Columbia Business School and the Federal Reserve Bank of New York, 29–30 May 2008, and Claire Priest, "Currency Policies and Legal Development in Colonial New England," *Yale Law Journal* 110 (2001): 1303–1405. On the role of institutions in economic development, see Peter Evans, "The Challenges of the 'Institutional Turn': New Interdisciplinary Opportunities in Development Theory," in Victor Nee and Richard Swedberg, eds., *The Economic Sociology of Capitalism* (Princeton, N.J., 2005), 90–116. See also Douglass C. North, *Institutions, Institutional Change and Economic Performance* (Cambridge, Mass., 1990), and Douglass C. North, "The New Institutional Economics," *Journal of Institutional and Theoretical Economics* 142 (1986): 230–37. For a view of institutions as sites of public choice and

deliberative politics oriented toward development, see Amartya Sen, "Rationality and Social Choice," *American Economic Review Papers and Proceedings* 85 (1995): 1–24; see also Amartya Sen, "The Possibility of Social Choice." Nobel Lecture, repr. in *American Economic Review Papers and Proceedings* 89 (1999): 349–78.

69. Staughton Craig Lynd, "The Revolution and the Common Man: Farm Tenants and Artisans in New York Politics, 1777–1788" (Ph.D. diss., Columbia University, 1962), 208–10; Alfred Young, *The Democratic Republicans of New York: The Origins, 1763–1797* (Chapel Hill, N.C., 1967), 78; Robert E. Wright, "Banking and Politics in New York, 1784–1829" (Ph.D. diss., SUNY Buffalo, 1996), 117–19.

70. Henry W. Domett, *A History of the Bank of New York, 1784–1884* (New York, 1884), ch. 3; New York Assembly *Journal* (1786), 94–95.

71. "A Subscriber to the Bank," New York *Journal*, 27 May 1784, 3.

72. William Seton to AH, 27 March 1784, *PAH.*

73. See the "Constitution of the Bank of New-York," [23 February–15 March 1784], *PAH.*

74. New York *Independent Journal*, 2 June 1784, 2.

75. New York *Packet*, 10 June 1784, 3.

76. During this period it is difficult to discern precisely how the bank's directors operated; because they were under no legal obligation to record the minutes of their meetings, they did not do so. Nor were they forced to submit to inspections from state officials or to other forms of executive branch regulation and oversight created by concerned or even curious legislators. Instead of operating within the definitions and constraints of a state-issued corporate charter, the bank's activities were shaped by the rules laid out in its 1784 constitution and by the judgments of its directors and managers. With its office open every day but Sundays, Christmas, New Year's Day, Good Friday, and the Fourth of July, from ten o'clock in the morning until one o'clock in the afternoon and then again from three to five o'clock, the bank promised to grant short-term credit—so-called *discounts*—each Thursday so long as bills were left with William Seton by Wednesday morning. See New York *Independent Journal*, 12 June 1784, 1. These and the bank's other rules, like the conversion tables for coins, were available for purchase at the bank and at other merchants' houses and at the Tontine and Merchants coffeehouses. See New York *Packet*, 1 July 1784, 4. From there, on any given day, one could book space for passengers and cargo on sloops sailing to Jamaica, sell saddle horses, or rent vacant space on the waterfront. For cash, one could buy cases of "Old St. Croix" rum, clocks, watches, silver, gold, hair brooms and brushes, paints and brass fittings used by cabinetmakers, China, candles, soap, linens, hats, and "Japaned ware." If someone lacked cash, in exchange for pearl or pot ash or flaxseed they could pick up shoe buckles, petticoats, window glass, stationery, loaf sugar, tea, rose butter, pepper, coffee, gin, brandy, molasses, chocolate, hay, lemons, oranges, copper tea kettles, mahogany logs, or Cheshire cheese. See "Murray, Sansom & Co., Hay Stevenson & Co., William Morewood," New York *Morning Post*, 28 May 1784, 1.

77. Wright, "Banking and Politics," 67; Allen S. Marber, "America's First Financiers,

Bankers, and Financial Executives: The New York Iron Merchants' Role in the First Banks and Insurance Companies," *Essays in Economic & Business History* 15 (1997): 85–94. Robert Wright contends that insider lending was less pervasive in New York than in New England, which was studied by Naomi Lamoreaux, *Insider Lending: Banks, Personal Connections, and Economic Development in Industrial New England* (New York, 1997).

Chapter 2

1. At the end of the eighteenth century, New York held roughly $74 million in public lands on which it disbursed about $367,600 annually in interest. Both figures were larger than for any other state. See Timothy Pitkin, *A Statistical View of the Commerce of the United States* (1817; repr., New York, 1967), 367–68; *An Account of the Receipts and Expenditures of the United States for the Year 1795* (Washington, D.C., 1796), 65. For more on the Phelps and Gorham tract, see Orsamus Turner, *History of the Pioneer Settlement of Phelps & Gorham's Purchase, and Morris' Reserve* (Rochester, N.Y., 1852).

2. For these and other Albany-area census figures, see www.nysm.nysed.gov/albany/census1790.html, retrieved on 12 January 2014.

3. For an overview of the geopolitics of law and dispossession, see Leonard J. Sadosky, *Revolutionary Negotiations: Indians, Empires, and Diplomats in the Founding of America* (Charlottesville, Va., 2009). For more on this subject as it specifically relates to upstate New York, see Laurence M. Hauptman, *Conspiracy of Interests: Iroquois Dispossession and the Rise of New York State* (Syracuse, N.Y., 2001); Laurence M. Hauptman and L. Gordon McLester III, eds., *The Oneida Indian Journey: From New York to Wisconsin, 1784–1860* (Madison, Wis., 1999).

4. Alfred B. Street, *The Council of Revision of the State of New York* (Albany, N.Y., 1859), 301–2.

5. See *Laws of the State of New York*, 16th Sess., ch. 8. See also Alfred Young, *The Democratic Republicans of New York* (Chapel Hill, N.C., 1967), 538–41.

6. As examples of this literature, see Henry W. Domett, *A History of the Bank of New York, 1784–1884* (New York, 1884); Cadwallader D. Colden, *Memoir, Prepared at the Request of a Committee of the Common Council of the City of New York, and Presented to the Mayor of the City, at the Celebration of the Completion of the New York Canals* (Albany, N.Y., 1825); Charles King, *A Memoir of the Construction, Cost, and Capacity of the Croton Aqueduct* (New York, 1843); Gustavus Meyers, *The History of Public Franchises in New York City: Boroughs of Manhattan and the Bronx* (New York, 1900).

7. See Cadwallader Colden, "A Memorial Concerning the Fur Trade of the Province of New York," reprinted in David Hosack, *Memoir of DeWitt Clinton* (New York, 1829), 232–45. See also Orsamus Turner, *Pioneer History of the Holland Purchase of Western New York* (Buffalo, N.Y., 1849); Cadwallader Colden, *The History of the Five Indian Nations* (New York, 1784). My thanks also to Mary-Jo Kline and her deft facility with maps.

8. Christopher Colles, *Proposal for the Speedy Settlement of the Waste and Unappropriated Lands on the Western Frontiers of the State of New York* (New York, 1785). The

scale of this proposal is minimized in Robert Troup, *A Vindication of the Claim of El-kanah Watson, Esq. to the Merit of Projecting the Lake Canal Policy, as Created by the Canal Act of March, 1792: And Also, a Vindication of the Claim of the Late General Schuyler, to the Merit of Drawing that Act, and Procuring Its Passage Through the Legislature* (Geneva, N.Y., 1821), 6–7.

9. Troup, *Vindication*, 6–7; Colles, *Proposal*, 10.

10. Troup, *Vindication*, 6–7. This is supported by my review of the New York Assembly and Senate *Journals* between 1784 and 1791.

11. Carter Goodrich, *Government Promotion of American Canals and Railroads, 1800–1890* (Westport, Conn., 1974), 19.

12. Robert E. Wright, *The First Wall Street: Chestnut Street, Philadelphia, and the Birth of American Finance* (Chicago, 2005). For more on Hamilton's role in this development, see Max M. Edling, *A Revolution in Favor of Government: Origins of the U.S. Constitution and the Making of the American State* (New York, 2003), 159. For Hamilton's bank plans, see "First Report on the Public Credit," in Harold C. Syrett et al., eds., *Papers of Alexander Hamilton*, 27 vols. (New York, 1961–79), 6:78–83. See also Jacob E. Cooke, "The Compromise of 1790," *William and Mary Quarterly*, 3rd ser., 27 (1970): 523–45; Kenneth R. Bowling, "Politics in the First Congress, 1789–1791" (Ph.D. diss., University of Wisconsin, 1968), 200–227; (Hamilton) Federalist No. 30, available in Jacob E. Cooke, ed., *The Federalist* (Middletown, Conn., 1961).

13. Winslow C. Watson, ed., *Men and Times of the Revolution; or, Memoirs of Elkanah Watson, Including Journals of Travels in Europe and America, from 1777 to 1842, with His Correspondence with Public Men and Reminiscences and Incidents of the Revolution* (New York, 1856), 327.

14. Ibid., 245–46. See also Douglas R. Littlefield, "The Potomac Company: A Misadventure in Financing an Early American Internal Improvement Project," *Business History Review* 58 (Winter 1984): 562–85.

15. Ibid., 311.

16. In Smith's thinking, turnpikes were so immediately useful that users did not object to paying a toll so long as the toll was not so high that it consumed profits. Likewise, the turnpike's operators hesitated to levy a toll high enough to discourage its use. Therefore, the profit motives of the travelers on the channel and the operators of the channel reached an equilibrium that was expressed in a toll. E. G. West, "Adam Smith's Public Economics: A Re-Evaluation," *Canadian Journal of Economics* 10, no. 1 (February 1977): 1–18. See also Martha E. Gross, "Aligning Public-Private Partnership Contracts with Public Objectives for Transportation Infrastructure" (Ph.D. diss., Virginia Polytechnic Institute, 2010).

17. See Robert Troup, *A Letter to the Honorable Brockholst Livingston, Esq. One of the Justices of the Supreme Court of the United States, on the Lake Canal Policy of the State of New-York, with a Supplement, and Additional Documents* (Albany, 1822), 14, 22. Watson published the articles in the New York *Journal and Patriotic Register* editions of 28 January 1792 and 17 March 1792.

18. Watson, ed., *Men and Times of the Revolution*, 312. For more on New York's interest in developing western rural farmland in order to expand its available marketplace, see Paul Kantor with Stephen David, *The Dependent City: The Changing Political Economy of Urban America* (Glenview, Ill., 1988), 48–55.

19. The idea that there was something uniquely American about these financing ideas was later echoed explicitly in an 1818 text on canal promotion printed at DeWitt Clinton's behest, [Charles G. Haines], *Considerations on the Great Western Canal, from the Hudson to Lake Erie: with a View of its Expence, Advantages, and Progress* (New York, 1818), 14–5, 17–20. This text was printed by the New-York Corresponding Association for the Promotion of Internal Improvements, whose goal was to "[open] an extensive correspondence, with gentlemen of the first distinction, throughout the Union" concerning internal improvements. The committee's president was DeWitt Clinton and one of the vice presidents was Cadwallader D. Colden. It was composed of several office-holders and merchants, including William Bayard, James Tallmadge Jr., and John Pintard. Charles G. Haines, who penned the volume, was the secretary of the association and to DeWitt Clinton.

20. Watson, *Men and Times of the Revolution*, 360.

21. For further details, see Noble E. Whitford, *History of the Canal System of the State of New York: Together with Brief Histories of the Canals of the United States and Canada* (Albany, 1906), 1:33–46. It should be noted that Whitford's account is biased toward demonstrating that publicly financing the Erie Canal, because of the scale and cost of the project, was preferable to entrusting it to corporations or private-capital associations.

22. See Caroline Elizabeth MacGill, *History of Transportation in the United States Before 1860* (Washington, D.C., 1917), 177. The landowner I refer to is Jeremiah Van Rensselaer, the canal promoter is Thomas Eddy, and the onetime Bank of New-York director is Robert Bowne.

23. Philip Schuyler to Thomas Eddy, August 1803, quoted in Nathan Miller, *The Enterprise of a Free People: Aspects of Economic Development in New York State During the Canal Period, 1792–1838* (Ithaca, N.Y., 1962), 24.

24. *New York Journal and Patriotic Register*, 24 July 1793. See also Miller, *Enterprise of a Free People*, 23–24.

25. Watson, *Men and Times of the Revolution*, 328.

26. Hosack, *Memoir of DeWitt Clinton*, 423; Wendell E. Tripp, "Robert Troup: A Quest for Security in a Turbulent New Nation 1775–1832" (Ph.D. diss., Columbia University, 1973), 151–53.

27. Miller, *Enterprise of a Free People*, 27; Hauptman, *Conspiracy of Interests*, 68–70; Barbara Ann Chernow, "Robert Morris: Land Speculator, 1790–1801" (Ph.D. diss., Columbia University, 1974).

28. Nathan Miller, "Private Enterprise in Inland Navigation: The Mohawk Route Prior to the Erie Canal," *New York History* 31 (1950): 399–401.

29. See [Goldsbrow Banyar, Philip Schuyler, and Elkanah Watson], *The Report of a*

Committee Appointed to Explore the Western Waters in the State of New-York: for the Purpose of Prosecuting the Inland Lock Navigation (Albany, 1792).

30. The state eventually lent the Western Company so much support that New York's state government became the company's largest shareholder.

31. *Second Report of the Western Inland Lock Navigation Company* (Albany, N.Y., 1798); Elkanah Watson, *History of the Rise, Progress, and Existing Condition of the Western Canals* (Albany, N.Y., 1820), 93; Noble E. Whitford, *History of the Canal System of the State of New York: Together with Brief Histories of the Canals of the United States and Canada* (Albany, 1906), 38–45.

32. Tacitus [DeWitt Clinton], *The Canal Policy of the State of New York, Delineated in a Letter to Robert Troup, Esq.* (Albany, 1821), 16–17.

33. Platt quoted in "Letter from Jonas Platt, Esq. to David Hosack, M.D.," 3 May 1828, printed in n. 10, appendix, of Hosack, *Memoir of DeWitt Clinton*. See also Tacitus, *Canal Policy*, viii.

34. Albert Gallatin, *Report of the Secretary of the Treasury; on the Subject of Public Roads and Canals made in pursuance of a Resolution of the Senate, of March 2, 1807* (Washington, D.C., 1808), 5–6.

35. Ibid., 18–19.

36. Lance E. Davis and Douglass C. North, *Institutional Change and American Economic Growth* (Cambridge, 1971), chs. 1–4; the authors write, "[I]t is the possibility of profits that cannot be captured within the existing arrangemental structure that leads to the formation of new (or the mutation of old) institutional arrangements." See also Willard Hurst, *Law and Social Process in United States History* (Ann Arbor, Mich., 1960); Lawrence M. Friedman, *History of American Law* (New York, 1973), 10–14.

Chapter 3

1. In this chapter, Democratic-Republicans, Democrats, and Republicans will be referred to as "Republicans" when suitable. Varietals of Federalists will be called "Federalists."

2. Edward Livingston to Thomas Jefferson, 11 April 1800, in Julian Boyd et al., eds., *The Papers of Thomas Jefferson*, 31 vols. to date (Princeton, 1950–). Hereafter abbreviated as TJ and *PTJ*.

3. Howard Bodenhorn, *State Banking in Early America: A New Economic History* (New York, 2003), 3–19.

4. TJ to Judge Spencer Roane, 6 September 1819, *PTJ*.

5. Bray Hammond, in his seminal history of American banking, writes of the Bank of New-York and Bank of the United States, "both were Federalist." See Bray Hammond, *Banks and Politics in America: From the Revolution to the Civil War* (Princeton, N.J., 1957), 149; Beatrice G. Reubens, "Burr, Hamilton and the Manhattan Company: Part II: Launching a Bank," *Political Science Quarterly* 73 (March 1958): 578–607. See also Matthew L. Davis, *Memoirs of Aaron Burr*, 2 vols. (New York, 1836), 1:413; Alfred F. Young,

The Democratic-Republicans of New York: The Origins, 1763–1797 (Chapel Hill, N.C., 1967), 229–30; Henry Wysham Lanier, *A Century of Banking in New York, 1822–1922* (New York, 1922), 16; Bodenhorn, *State Banking in Early America*, 133; Henry W. Domett, *A History of the Bank of New York* (New York, 1884), 42.

6. For recent insight on the controversial nature and character of Aaron Burr, see Joanne B. Freeman, *Affairs of Honor: National Politics in the New Republic* (New Haven, Conn., 2001), 192–95, 205–13; Nancy Isenberg, "The 'Little Emperor': Aaron Burr, Dandyism, and the Sexual Politics of Treason," in Jeffrey L. Pasley, Andrew W. Robertson, and David Waldstreicher, eds., *Beyond the Founders: New Approaches to the Political History of the Early American Republic* (Chapel Hill, N.C., 2004), 129–58; Nancy Isenberg, *Fallen Founder: The Life of Aaron Burr* (New York, 2007). For more on the charter battle surrounding the Manhattan Company, see Beatrice G. Reubens, "Burr, Hamilton and the Manhattan Company: Part I: Gaining the Charter," *Political Science Quarterly* 72 (December 1957): 100–125; Gregory S. Hunter, *The Manhattan Company: Managing a Multi-Unit Corporation in New York, 1799–1842* (New York, 1989).

7. Howard Bodenhorn suggests that legislators, aware of opposition to new banks, approved of charters with hidden banking clauses and later claimed to have been duped to give themselves political cover; "[S]uch mistakes were repeated too often to have resulted from legislative oversight, laxity, or incompetence." See Bodenhorn, *State Banking in Early America*, 134. Robert Wright offers an alternative narrative to the common Burr-as-trickster story by proposing two explanations of the documented events. The first is that the legislators, rather than being "duped," were too pressed for time to read the amended charter in its final form. The second is that Hamilton in fact supported the Manhattan Company's entry into banking—for reasons of ideology and political economy—and opposed it publicly solely to politically injure Aaron Burr. See Robert E. Wright, "Artisans, Banks, Credit, and the Election of 1800," *Pennsylvania Magazine of History and Biography* 122 (July 1998): 21–39. The first explanation may be possible, in theory, because the company charter did indeed sail through the legislature in a matter of days, guided by Burr himself. Yet the swift timing of the bill, then, would indeed have been a component of Burr's overall effort; the clause was vague enough to escape the scrutiny of readers, and the bill moved quickly enough to escape the eyes of lax legislators. Wright's contention of a form of legislative incompetence, however, contradicts Pauline Maier's claim that legislatures took a keen interest in drafting corporate charters. See Pauline Maier, "The Revolutionary Origins of the American Corporation," *William and Mary Quarterly*, 3rd ser., 50 (January 1993): 51–84. It also does not change a simple fact: the New York legislature, like the New York City Common Council, was engaged in creating a water company, not a bank. Likewise, there is no evidence to support the claim that Hamilton thought it appropriate for the Manhattan Company to open a discount office; his support of banks in general was contingent on the needs of local economies and the speculative risks posed by both stock subscriptions and the discounting of bank notes.

8. Milton Lomask, *Aaron Burr: The Years from Princeton to Vice President, 1756–1805* (New York, 1979), 221–30.

9. Hamilton quoted in a speech of 24 June 1788 at the New York ratification convention. See *Debates and Proceedings of the Constitutional Convention of the State of New York* (Poughkeepsie, N.Y., 1788), 71.

10. Max M. Edling, *A Revolution in Favor of Government: Origins of the U.S. Constitution and the Making of the American State* (New York, 2003), 228.

11. Peter S. Onuf, *The Origins of the Federal Republic: Jurisdictional Controversies in the United States, 1775–1787* (Philadelphia, 1983); Pauline Maier, *Ratification: The People Debate the Constitution, 1787–1788* (New York, 2010); David C. Hendrickson, *Peace Pact: The Lost World of the American Founding* (Lawrence, Kans., 2006).

12. Douglas Bradburn, *The Citizenship Revolution: Politics and the Creation of the American Union, 1774–1804* (Charlottesville, Va., 2009), ch. 3; David Waldstreicher, *In the Midst of Perpetual Fetes: The Making of American Nationalism, 1776–1820* (Chapel Hill, N.C., 1997), 85–92.

13. For a brief account of Hamilton's plan and congressional opposition, see Stanley Elkins and Eric McKitrick, *The Age of Federalism: The Early American Republic, 1788–1800* (New York, 1995), 226–36. For Hamilton's bank plan, see AH, "Second Report on the Public Credit," 13 December 1790, *PAH*.

14. James Kent to Theodorus Bailey, 27 February 1791, in William Kent, ed., *Memoirs and Letters of James Kent* (Boston, 1898), 41–42.

15. James Watson to James Wadsworth, 16 January 1791, Wadsworth Papers, Connecticut Historical Society. Hereafter abbreviated as CtHi.

16. Steven Kirk Bane, "'A Group of Foreign Liars': Republican Propagandists and the Campaign Against the Federalists, 1789–1801" (Ph.D. diss., Texas Christian University, 1993), ch. 7.

17. Rufus King to Nicholas Low, 18 December 1791, Nicholas Low Papers Supplement, New-York Historical Society. Hereafter abbreviated as NYHS.

18. Ibid., 25 December 1790, Nicholas Low Papers Supplement, NYHS. This was indicative of the "divisive particularism" feared by Hamiltonians and Federalists who saw state banks as impermanent devices created by states to undermine the effectiveness and efficiency of the national bank. See Stuart Bruchey, "Alexander Hamilton and the State Banks, 1789 to 1795," *William and Mary Quarterly*, 3rd ser., 27 (July 1970): 347–49.

19. Alexander Hamilton to Nicholas Low, 21 December 1791, in Harold C. Syrett and Jacob E. Cooke, *The Papers of Alexander Hamilton*, 27 vols. (New York, 1961). Hereafter abbreviated as AH and *PAH*.

20. See Bodenhorn, *State Banking in Early America*, 128–33; Bruchey, "Alexander Hamilton and the State Banks," 349.

21. Freeman, *Affairs of Honor*, xv.

22. Rufus King to Nicholas Low, 21 March 1792, Nicholas Low Papers Supplement, NYHS.

23. Hammond, *Banks and Politics*, 69–70, 149.

24. For more on the Panic of 1792, see Scott Reynolds Nelson, *A Nation of Deadbeats: An Uncommon History of America's Financial Disasters* (New York, 2013), ch. 1.

25. Richard Sylla, Robert E. Wright, and David J. Cowen, "Alexander Hamilton, Central Banker: Crisis Management During the U.S. Financial Panic of 1792," *Business History Review* 83 (2009): 61–86.

26. AH to William Seton, 18 January 1791, Box 1, Record Group 1, Chase Manhattan Bank Archives.

27. According to Joyce Appleby, institutional "novelties" were suspect during this period. Hamilton, as a Revolutionary hero and financial expert, was in a powerful position to determine what reception was given to a new financial institution in the city. Without his approval, to many any new bank would be unwelcome. See Joyce Appleby, "Thomas Jefferson and the Psychology of Democracy," in James P. Horn, Jan Lewis, and Peter S. Onuf, eds., *The Revolution of 1800: Democracy, Race, and the New Republic* (Charlottesville, Va., 2002), 159.

28. AH to William Seton, 6 February 1791, *PAH*.

29. Ibid., 18 Jan. 1792, 24 January 1792, *PAH*.

30. Young, *Democratic-Republicans*, 227.

31. This is from a review of the journals of the New York Assembly and the New York Senate, 1792–99. No serious debate was entertained over the chartering of a third bank for the city by either house, and I have found no evidence that an application was received by the legislature during this period.

32. Naomi R. Lamoreaux, *Insider Lending: Banks, Personal Connections and Economic Development in Industrial New England* (New York, 1996), 2–5.

33. Rufus King to Nicholas Low, 11 March 1792, Rufus King Papers, NYHS.

34. Ibid., 29 April 1792, Rufus King Papers, NYHS. King wrote, "I don't yet hear that Brockholst [Livingston] has gone [illegible] . . . nor have I any reason to change my opinion that he will come out with Property. I presume you will do what is proper respecting his note, and the Bank shares—it is my Judgment that he should make us a compensation for canceling the contract."

35. Joanne Freeman observes that "[the] political elite remained profoundly uncomfortable with . . . political methods" during the 1790s. See Joanne B. Freeman, "Corruption and Compromise in the Election of 1800: The Process of Politics on the National Stage," in Horn et al., *The Revolution of 1800*, 89.

36. Of course it would be unwise for a prominent person to advertise a denial of credit, for whatever reason. From Philadelphia, Rufus King wrote to Nicholas Low of news that William Duer, signer of the Articles of Confederation and patriarch of one of New York's most prominent families, had fallen on hard times. "Poor Duer! [Philadelphia] is in an uproar with a report that he has failed in making his payments at the NYork Bank." Rufus King to Nicholas Low, 21 March 1792, Rufus King Papers, NYHS. King appreciated that financial failures could damage a reputation and outlast financial considerations. As he wrote of Brockholst Livingston, "[W]e are confounded with the conduct of Brockholst. His sentiments however, I hope are too extravagant, for the extravagance of the Times." Rufus King to Nicholas Low, 21 March 1792, Rufus King Papers, NYHS.

37. There is some dissent from this view. One writer, for example, described the Bank of New-York as "violently Federalist" and making decisions "always with a view to contributing to Federalist success. The directors loaned money to their personal and party friends with gross partiality and for questionable purposes. If a merchant dared help the opposite party or offended the directors he was taught to repend his independence by rejection of his paper when he most needed cash." Gustavus Myers, *The History of Tammany Hall* (1917; repr., New York, 1971), 13–14. This account seems to stem from the 1799 experience, however, as such complaints cannot be found in either print or letters earlier in the 1790s.

38. Freeman, "Corruption and Compromise," 89.

39. Sidney I. Pomerantz, *New York: An American City, 1783–1803* (New York, 1938), 131. See also Peter Jay to John Jay, 3 May 1799, Jay Papers, Columbia University; Edmund Philip Willis, "Social Origins of Political Leadership in New York City from the Revolution to 1815" (Ph.D. diss., University of California, Berkeley, 1967), 55.

40. Merchant and former general John Lamb, a creditor to Burr, indicated that the Bank of New York "had always exercised an important influence upon the elections, its power upon the approaching struggle [in 1792], was not weakened by the stability which it had acquired by its charter." See Isaac Q. Leake, *Memoir of the Life and Times of General John Lamb . . .* (1850; repr., New York, 1971), 338–39.

41. Young, *Democratic-Republicans*, 218–19; Domett, *A History of the Bank of New York*, 132–35; James O. Wettereau, "New Light on the First Bank of the United States," *Pennsylvania Magazine of History and Biography* 61 (July 1937): 263–85.

42. Jabez D. Hammond, *The History of Political Parties in the State of New York, from the Ratification of the Constitution to December, 1840,* 2 vols. (Buffalo, 1842), 1:325.

43. Ibid., 1:324.

44. The city, with only about 50,000 persons in 1795, did not extend beyond the area that became Canal Street. The northernmost wards, the Sixth and Fifth, were just south of this boundary, and the southernmost and wealthiest neighborhoods of the First, Second, and Third wards were located near Battery Park, Wall Street, and City Hall. Hence the location of the Tontine Coffee House, the center of the city's commercial life, and Trinity Church, both on Wall Street, made them central focal points of the city's economic and social landscape. For an overview, see Edwin G. Burrows and Mike Wallace, *Gotham: A History of New York City to 1898* (New York, 1999), 475 (map). For wealth distribution calculations, see Willis, "Social Origins," 58 (map), 60 (table II-5).

45. Willis, "Social Origins," 60.

46. Ibid., 49–54, 72–73. Currency conversion done with aid of http://www.measuringworth.com/.

47. New York *Commercial Advertiser*, 24 January 1799.

48. Jeffrey L. Pasley, "*The Tyranny of Printers*": *Newspaper Politics in the Early American Republic* (Charlottesville, Va., 2001), ch. 1.

49. New York *Commercial Advertiser*, 21 January 1799. In a 22 January 1799 New York *Commercial Advertiser* article, "Howard-Merchant" writes that he was told by a

Federalist merchant to sign a petition to "the stupid Legislature" protesting Burr's bankruptcy bill. He demurred, writing, "[B]eing in the habit of confiding in our constitutional authorities, and attending to my own business, I did not walk up stairs" at the Tontine Coffee-House. While Federalists portrayed merchants as a monolithic group, such were the divisions within their ranks. See also New York *Commercial Advertiser*, 19 January 1799, "Sixth Ward" asking "what are we to understand by 'the Democrats being on the [right] side for once, all of them except ten having voted against [the Bankruptcy bill]' . . . are we to infer from this that all the prisoners confined for debt . . . differ from [the aristocracy] on political subjects, and therefore [should be] revenged?"

50. Hammond, *The History of Political Parties in the State of New York*, 1:199.

51. James Smith, M.D., 10 September 1798, Broadside, Evans 44469, NYHS. For more detail on the water-supply needs of the city, see Nelson M. Blake, *Water for the Cities: A History of the Urban Water Supply Problem in the United States* (Syracuse, N.Y., 1956), 5–8, 44–45.

52. The council was the board of directors for the corporation of the city of New York. Aligning itself with the state legislature to alleviate concerns that it was usurping state sovereignty or an inappropriate relic of monarchy, the corporation attempted to become republican. For an explanation of this strategy, see Hendrik Hartog, *Public Property and Private Power: The Corporation of the City of New York in American Law, 1730–1870* (Chapel Hill, N.C., 1989).

53. New York (N.Y.) Common Council and Joseph Browne, *Proceedings of the Corporation of New York to Supply the City with Pure and Wholesome Water with a Memoir of Joseph Browne, M.D. on the Same Subject* (New York, 1799).

54. Maier, "Revolutionary Origins of the American Corporation."

55. The committee was composed of Hamilton and Federalists John Murray, president of the Chamber of Commerce, and Gulian Verplanck, president of the Bank of New-York. The Republicans were Burr; Peter Wendover, president of the Mechanic Society; and John Broome, a Republican merchant. *Minutes of the Common Council*, 2:514–15.

56. New York (N.Y.) Common Council and Arthur Everett Preston, ed., *Minutes of the Common Council of the City of New York, 1784–1831*, 19 vols. (New York, 1917), 2:520.

57. Several historians have explored the labyrinthine details of the Manhattan Company charter's passage. See Reubens, "Burr, Hamilton and the Manhattan Company: Part I," and Hunter, *The Manhattan Company*.

58. See New York (State), *An Act of Incorporation of the Manhattan Company* (New York, 1799). For comparisons with other charters for water companies, see Blake, *Water for the Cities*, passim.

59. In December 1796, Burr asked William Eustis for a copy of the charter of the Union Bank, Boston. On 1 February 1797, he wrote to Thomas Morris that he had formulated a plan for a bank but was hesitant to submit it for review even to friends. See Aaron Burr to William Eustis, 16 December 1796, and Aaron Burr to Thomas Morris, 1

February 1797, in Mary-Jo Kline et al., eds., *Political Correspondence and Public Papers of Aaron Burr*, 2 vols. (Princeton, N.J., 1983), 1:286–88.

60. *Act of Incorporation*, 11.

61. Davis, *Memoirs of Aaron Burr*, 1:414.

62. Pervill Squire and Keith E. Hamm, *One Hundred and One Chambers: Congress, State Legislatures, and the Future of Legislative Studies* (Columbus, Ohio, 2005), chart at 141.

63. The Federalist directors were John B. Church, Hamilton's brother-in-law and, for a time, the second-largest stockholder in the Bank of North America. Hamilton acted as his attorney and agent in New York, even while secretary of the Treasury; John Watts, a former state assembly speaker, city recorder, and director of the Branch Bank of the United States; John B. Coles, a flour merchant with wide business ties and a recent member of the Common Council. The Republican members were no less impressive. Six of the nine were founders of the Tontine Coffee-House, the nexus of the city's commerce. They were Aaron Burr; Daniel Ludlow, a former Tory and the wealthiest merchant in the city; William Edgar; William Laight, a director of the New York branch of the Bank of the United States; Paschal N. Smith; Samuel Osgood, the nation's first postmaster-general and DeWitt Clinton's stepfather-in-law; John Broome, a Clintonian with extensive New York political ties; Brockholst Livingston, an attorney and cousin of Chancellor Robert R. Livingston; John Stevens, an engineering and transportation entrepreneur and a relation of Robert R. Livingston. Reubens, "Burr, Hamilton and the Manhattan Company: Part II: Launching a Bank," 100.

64. Robert R. Livingston to James Madison, 6 November 1795, James Madison Papers, Library of Congress. Hereafter abbreviated as RRL.

65. Young, "The Democratic Republicans," 577–78. Young writes, "Republican factionalism, so scorned by historians, actually was a symptom of a competition for power healthy to a new party." Factionalism, however, was scorned by some Republicans for the divisions it caused within the party, and Young's admission works to weaken his claim that the party had a coherent credo and leadership structure by 1797. Clearly, Burr recognized that more than "love" was lost among the three factions, as evidenced by the composition of the Manhattan Company's board of directors.

66. DeWitt Clinton bought 1,000 shares; Burr's associate and fellow assemblyman John Swartwout and Chancellor Robert R. Livingston each purchased 2,000 shares, making them the largest shareholders. See Stock Dividend Book, Manhattan Company, Chase Manhattan Bank Archives.

67. Hammond, *The History of Political Parties*, 1:125. The member, Thomas Storm, pled ignorance after being accused of aiding Burr's Republican cause. See "The American," New York *Commercial Advertiser*, 1 May 1799.

68. Nicholas Low to Rufus King, 17 April 1799, Rufus King Papers, NYHS.

69. Stock Dividend Book, Manhattan Company, Chase Manhattan Bank Archives.

70. Davis, *Memoirs of Aaron Burr*, 1:415–16.

71. Robert Troup to Rufus King, 19 April 1799, Rufus King Papers, NYHS. Troup

subscribed for Manhattan Company shares on 22 April 1799. Federalist shareholders included city recorder Richard Harrison, who was also an ex officio director of the Manhattan Company. He bought a thousand shares for himself and pushed the city to exercise its buying option. See Minutes of the Common Council, 2:535. Included among shareholders were James Roosevelt; A. L. Bleecker; Charles Cammann, a director of the Bank of New-York; and Isaac Governeur, a director of the New York branch of the Bank of the United States. Federalists Richard Varick, the mayor of New York, and state lieutenant governor Stephen Van Rensselaer, who was Hamilton's brother-in-law, also became stockholders.

72. Alfred B. Street, *The Council of Revision of the State of New York* (Albany, 1859), 423. See also Robert Troup to Rufus King, 5 June 1799, Rufus King Papers, NYHS.

73. Robert Troup to Rufus King, 19 April 1799, Rufus King Papers, NYHS.

74. John Stevens to RRL, 12 April 1799, Livingston Papers, NYHS. The company did not require its subscribers to fully pay for their shares up front, thus the company only had $400,000 by the summer of 1799 and did not reach $1 million until the close of its first year of business. Spending $200,000 on supplying water from the Collect—though imperfect—was preferable to the far more costly project of diverting water from the Bronx River, a project that the company did not have the capital to complete at this time. The company initiated a well near the Collect in May 1799 and constructed a reservoir on Chambers Street in 1800, near the present-day Manhattan-side anchor of the Brooklyn Bridge, that held approximately 130,000 gallons of water, considerably less than the one million gallons they had hoped to store. See Blake, *Water for the Cities*, 46–47, 56–58.

75. New York *Daily Advertiser*, 4 April 1799.

76. Peter Jay to John Jay, 3 May 1799, Jay Papers, Columbia University.

77. "C," New York *Commercial Advertiser*, 26 April 1799.

78. Fisher Ames to Rufus King, 12 June 1799, vol. 41, Rufus King Papers, NYHS.

79. New York *Commercial Advertiser*, 1 May 1799. Emphasis in original.

80. "The Anti-Revolutionist" 2 and 4, New York *Commercial Advertiser*, 27 and 31 April 1799.

81. "The Anti-Revolutionist 4," New York *Commercial Advertiser* , 31 April 1799. One of Burr's earliest biographers suggested that the ambition of the project made legislators generous in granting Burr wide latitude in his proposal, particularly because state funds were not being used for the enterprise; see Davis, *Memoirs of Aaron Burr*, 1: 416. Bray Hammond, arguing from the opposite side, suggests that legislators were too attentive to charters to have made such a mistake; Burr, therefore, had tricked them. See Bray Hammond, "Long and Short Term Credit in Early American Banking," *Quarterly Journal of Economics* 49 (November 1934): 79–103, esp. 85.

82. "A Merchant," New York *Commercial Advertiser*, 8 June 1799.

83. New York *Commercial Advertiser*, 26 April 1799.

84. Robert Troup to Rufus King, 5 June 1799, Rufus King Papers, NYHS. Sidney Pomerantz writes that "responsibility for the passage of the Manhattan Company

charter must be placed squarely on the Federalists" and contends that the controversy raised by Federalists in the election of 1799 was "artful political maneuvering that had made Burr the arch-conspirator" in the Manhattan Company's chartering. It was, he wrote, "so skillfully executed that historians to this day have uncritically accepted the accusations heaped upon him in the bitterness of an election campaign." See Pomerantz, *New York*, 187–91. Hartog sees a far greater sin in the legislature's actions: "Federalist legislators were either duped, bribed, or convinced to vote for a project that its sponsors intended to use for ends entirely distinct from the purposes stated in the charter: a direct and manifest violation of standard republican principles and an important event in the evolution of the business corporation form." This latter view dismisses the political character of banks prior to the founding of the Manhattan Company and the flag raised by Judge Lansing on the Council of Revision but ignored by fellow Federalists. See Hartog, *Public Property and Private Power*, 149.

85. New York *Journal and Patriotic Register*, 1 May 1799. For more on discounts and accommodation loans, see Robert E. Wright, *Origins of Commercial Banking in America, 1750–1800* (Lanham, Md., 2001), 129–33.

86. Reubens writes that "appealing to the deeply rooted anti-bank, anti-corporation views of Republican voters, the Federalist arguments [in the campaign of 1799] made them uneasy about Burr's Republicanism, as they occasionally had been in the past." Although the latter appears to be valid—Burr first held office as a Federalist in the 1780s—essentially no evidence has been uncovered during my research to suggest that Republican voters were any less enthusiastic about corporations or banking than Federalists. Rather, the Republicans' role in the creation of the Manhattan Company and its transformation into a bank seems to be prima facie evidence of the acceptability of chartered financial institutions among Republican leaders in the city. See Reubens, "Burr, Hamilton and the Manhattan Company: Part II," passim.

87. The decision was made on 8 May 1799. New York *Journal and Patriotic Register*, 22 May 1799.

88. Laight wrote that he believed it was "improper to hold an office of similar import in any other institution whose object is pointed to the same end and whose mode of producing the same effect may possibly contravene each other." See Minutes of the Board of Directors, 16 May 1799, Chase Manhattan Bank Archives. James Wettereau has written that in 1793, Thomas Fitzsimons, a director for the Bank of North America, was elected to the board of the Bank of the United States, but he declined the honor. Wettereau interpreted this as evidence that interlocking directorships between banks, like interlocking stock ownerships, were frowned upon earlier in the decade. Laight's move, therefore, was not without precedent. See James O. Wettereau, "The Branches of the First Bank of the United States," *Journal of Economic History* 2 (December 1942): 66–100 at 75.

89. Bank of Manhattan records. See also Joseph A. Scoville, *The Old Merchants of New York City*, 2 vols. (New York, 1863), 2:190–94.

90. "A Merchant," New York *Commercial Advertiser*, 8 June 1799.

91. "Socrates," New York *Commercial Advertiser*, 22 May 1799.

92. "The American," New York *Commercial Advertiser*, 13 May 1799. For the pro-corporation article, see New York *Commercial Advertiser*, 11 May 1799.

93. "Socrates," New York *Commercial Advertiser*, 22 May 1799. The "State of Manhattan" reference may have come from the suggestion that the Manhattan Company start an "East India company" with its surplus capital. Such an idea may have conjured recollections of the British East India Company, which was labeled and feared in the Old Regime as a "nation" independent of Parliament by virtue of its royal charter. See Minutes of the Board of Directors, 29 April 1799.

94. "Julius," New York *Commercial Advertiser*, 25 May 1799; Nicholas Low to King, 14 June 1799, Rufus King Papers, NYHS.

95. Nicholas Low to Rufus King, 15 April 1799, Rufus King Papers, NYHS.

96. Robert Troup to Rufus King, 19 April 1799, Rufus King Papers, NYHS. See also New York *Commercial Advertiser*, 10 February 1800.

97. Among the prominent Federalists who took a pass on Manhattan Company shares was Nicholas Gouverneur, president of the Bank of New-York and an original petitioner. The full list of the original subscribers and petitioners can be found in the Minutes of the Board of Directors, 15 and 22 April 1799. This has been compared with the names appearing in the list of stockholders registered in July 1800. See First Stock Dividend Book, Manhattan Company. Beatrice Reubens and Gregory Hunter have both examined this material well and I have relied on their work as a guide. Reubens undertook the formidable task of determining the partisan associations of many of the shareholders in her examination of the origins of the Manhattan Company. Her evidence leads her to conclude, "Undoubtedly, in numbers and wealth, the Federalists who rejected the Manhattan Company greatly exceeded the Federalists who did buy stock." This is of course true, but the limited availability of stock must also be considered as a contributing factor in addition to the self-selection of shareholders, as should the discretion Burr had in determining who was eligible to be an original subscriber or petitioner, a shareholder class distinct from the public. See Reubens, "Burr, Hamilton and the Manhattan Company: Part II," 108–10.

98. New York Assembly *Journal*, 23rd Sess., 238.

99. Ibid., 240.

100. Domett, *A History of the Bank of New York*, 57. The Bank of New-York, unlike the Manhattan Company, was required to retire several directors each year, and it had a capitalization of only $1 million. This is garnered from a side-by-side comparison of the two companies' charters. See New York *Laws*, 1791, ch. 37, for the Bank of New-York, and 1799, ch. 84, for the Manhattan Company charters. Although Federalists predicted that the Manhattan Company would enter all forms of business and attempt to undermine existing partnerships and merchants, this did not occur, although the company did hold significant amounts of real estate in Manhattan and trade in both government and business stocks. An 1815 report concluded that the Manhattan Company behaved more responsibly and cautiously than many of its peers. See "A Citizen" [C.

Sigourney], *An Appeal to the Public in the Conduct of Banks in the City of New York* (New York, 1815), 6.

101. New York *Laws*, 1801, ch. 104.

102. Nicholas Fish to Arthur Noble, 13 February 1800, Box 1, RG 1, Chase Manhattan Bank Archives.

103. New York *Commercial Advertiser*, 15 May 1799.

104. Joseph Browne to Aaron Burr, 7 July 1799, *The Papers of Aaron Burr, 1756–1836*, microfilm ed., 27 reels (Glen Rock, N.J., 1978).

105. Minutes of the Board of Directors, 19 September 1799.

106. (Cheetham), *An Impartial Enquiry*, 9–11.

107. John Stevens to RRL, 28 August 1799, Livingston Papers, NYHS.

108. Minutes of the Board of Directors, 23 December 1799.

109. "Julius," New York *Commercial Advertiser*, 25 May 1799. The author criticized Coles for "len[ding] support to such an institution."

110. Robert Troup to Rufus King, 12 December 1799, Rufus King Papers, NYHS.

111. New York *Weekly Museum*, 4 January 1800.

112. Ledger entries for 30 March 1800 and 30 June 1800, Manhattan Company, RG 1, Chase Manhattan Archives. Thanks also to Robert Wright for his assistance; see Robert Wright, "Banking and Politics in New York, 1784–1829" (Ph.D. diss., SUNY Buffalo, 1996), 239–64.

113. *American Citizen*, 29 April 1800.

114. Ibid., 25 April 1800.

115. Willis, "Social Origins," 72 (Table II-11).

116. "Portius," New York *Commercial Advertiser*, 4 May 1800. The author also reflects, "[O]f two persons equally industrious and skillful, if I give the preference to the man who thinks as I do and lends his support to that course of public measures which in my estimation will promote the happiness of the community, I assuredly violate no law of justice and do nothing which can offend the most rigid moralist."

117. Freeman, "Corruption and Compromise," 99.

118. "Philander," *American Citizen*, 5 May 1800.

119. *American Citizen*, 5 May 1800.

120. (Cheetham), *An Impartial Enquiry*, 9.

121. DeWitt Clinton to Henry Remsen, 16 March 1808, quoted in Reubens, "Burr, Hamilton and the Manhattan Company: Part I," 122.

122. Thomas Jefferson to James Monroe, 4 March 1800, quoted in Davis, *Memoirs of Aaron Burr*, 2:54–55.

123. AH to J. A. Bayard, 16 January 1801, *PAH*.

124. "Mentor," *American Citizen*, 8 May 1801.

125. *American Citizen*, 21 January 1801.

126. As a specific example, see New York *Commercial Advertiser*, 19 March 1799. See also E. Wilder Spaulding, *New York in the Critical Period, 1783–1789* (New York, 1932), 27–29. For a discussion of the ways in which debt was feminized, see Bruce H. Mann,

Republic of Debtors: Bankruptcy in the Age of American Independence (Cambridge, Mass., 2002), 120–21, 162–64. For historians, the Republican identity of the Bank of the Manhattan Company complicates the assertion that the Jeffersonians of 1800 rose to power on voters' suspicions of banks, capital, and credit. For a summary of Jefferson's objections to the Bank of the United States, see Herbert Sloan, *Principle and Interest: Thomas Jefferson and the Problem of Debt* (Charlottesville, Va., 1995), 171–73, 179–80, 192. Concern about the speculative aspects of banking were also voiced by Robert R. Livingston in a letter to Thomas Jefferson; see RRL to TJ, 20 February 1791 in TJP, 19:296. See also Elkins and McKitrick, *The Age of Federalism*, 242–44.

127. For a discussion of the Republicans' vision of a classless society, see Joyce Appleby, *Capitalism and a New Social Order: The Republican Vision of the 1790s* (New York, 1984), 74; Doron Ben-Atar and Barbara B. Oberg, "The Paradoxical Legacy of the Federalists," in Doron Ben-Atar and Barbara Oberg, eds., *Federalists Reconsidered* (Charlottesville, Va., 1998), 12. Within that volume, see also Rosemarie Zagarri, "Gender and the First Party System," 131–32. For anecdotal evidence of Federalists' demand for deference from artisans and mechanics, see Howard B. Rock, *Artisans of the New Republic: The Tradesmen of New York City in the Age of Jefferson* (New York, 1979), 5–7.

128. The work of Richard John and the "new institutionalism" associated with scholarship of twentieth-century state formation stress the degree to which institutions are changed through interactions with each other. The matrix of political institutions within which Burr and other political actors operated was altered by the founding of the Manhattan Company, deliberately but also with unforeseen consequences. By considering the corporation as an extension of the state and a part of political culture, I hope to illuminate the role of institutions in the formation of political parties and as agents of change within the state itself. For an introduction to this approach, see Richard R. John, "Governmental Institutions as Agents of Change: Rethinking American Political Development in the Early Republic, 1787–1835," *Studies in American Political Development* 11 (Fall 1997): 347–80. See also Richard R. John, "Ruling Passions: Political Economy in Nineteenth-Century America," *Journal of Policy History* 18, no. 1 (2006): 1–20. See also Karen Orren and Stephen Skowronek, "Beyond the Iconography of Order: Notes for a 'New Institutionalism,'" in Lawrence C. Dodd and Calvin C. Jillson, eds., *The Dynamics of American Politics: Approaches and Interpretations* (Boulder, Colo., 1994), 311–30.

129. For an overview of the role directors played in banks in the early republic, see Lamoreaux, *Insider Lending*, passim. The role of private benefit as a catalyst for collective action and group formation is a limited one, of course, subject to contingent identities and events. Among a limited set of Federalists and Republicans, therefore, the Manhattan Company's partisan project eliminated the need for voters to mute their partisan leanings for fear of compromising their financial viability. Republicans could identify one another through subsidiary credit networks that centered on Republican Manhattan Company directors, while Federalists could openly purge Republicans from their networks and reify their existing relationships. A summary of recent, cross-disciplinary literature on the role of private interests in group formation can be found in

Frank R. Baumgartner and Beth L. Leech, *Basic Interests: The Importance of Groups in Politics and in Political Science* (Princeton, N.J., 1998), ch. 2. For a view of post-Revolutionary New York politics based on competition among interest groups, albeit classes rather than institutions, see Edward Countryman, *A People in Revolution: The American Revolution and Political Society in New York, 1760–1790* (Baltimore, Md., 1981), 294–96.

130. In light of the more controversial aspects of the Manhattan Company and the eventual assumption of its water-utility responsibilities by the city decades later, the civic nature of the Manhattan Company has been particularly neglected by historians. Yet at the time of the election of 1800, the company was engaged in constructing the city's first water system, having departed from an unworkably ambitious agenda to divert water from the Bronx (East) River, in favor of an achievable and a sustainable plan to use wells and a reservoir. See Blake, *Water for the Cities*, passim.

131. For the importance of civic ceremony and the public sphere in partisan politics, see Waldstreicher, *In the Midst of Perpetual Fetes*, 216–45.

132. (James Cheetham), *An Impartial Enquiry into Certain Parts of the Conduct of Governor Lewis . . . Particularly in Relation to the Merchants' Bank* (New York, 1806), 9.

Chapter 4

1. Robert R. Livingston Receipt Book (1808–13), LeBoeuf Collection, New-York Historical Society. Hereafter abbreviated as NYHS.

2. See John Mair, *Book-Keeping Modernized, or Merchant-Accounts by Double Entry, According to the Italian Form* (1736; Edinburgh, 1800), Book 1, "The nature and use of the Waste-book explained," 5. My thanks to John McCusker for explaining the importance and hierarchy of various types and forms of account books, and to Ted Crackel of the George Washington Papers for inviting me to participate in a conference on the Financial Papers of George Washington at Mount Vernon in October 2009, where I was first introduced to this subject.

3. Bound volume (BV) Fulton & Livingston, Account Book (1809–14), NYHS.

4. 9 Wheat. 1 (1824). See Albert Abel, "The Commerce Clause in the Constitutional Convention and in Contemporary Comment," *Minnesota Law Review* 25 (1940–41): 432–94, esp. 432. See also W. Howard Mann, "The Marshall Court: Nationalization of Private Rights and Personal Liberty from the Authority of the Commerce Clause," *Indiana Law Journal* 38 (1962–63): 193–214.

5. The notoriety and import of *Gibbons v. Ogden* invited subsequent historical examinations into the political context in which the Livingston-Fulton monopoly existed, but the outcome of *Gibbons* colors much of this historiography. Although Maurice Baxter displays sensitivity to the role partisan identities played in managing the monopoly, his focus in the *Gibbons* decision is on the federal implications of monopoly and lead him to conclude: "[T]he history of the Livingston-Fulton monopoly . . . is also one of popular complaints, continuing attacks by competitors, various compromises and final

legal defeat." Maurice Baxter, *The Steamboat Monopoly: Gibbons v. Ogden, 1824* (New York, 1972), 19. Similarly, Wallace Mendelson's brief examination of the legislative history of the monopoly asserts that it was plainly unpopular both in the public and among the members of the legislature; "the New York legislature was obviously in sympathy with the desire to abolish it but the doctrine of vested interests prohibited direct legislative relief." Mendelson concludes that the Marshall Court's mandate in *Fletcher v. Peck* compelled the legislature to view the monopoly grant as a contract that had to be upheld despite the legislature's desire to repeal the grant and open the steamboat industry to competition. Wallace Mendelson, "New Light on *Fletcher v. Peck* and *Gibbons v. Ogden*," *Yale Law Review* 58 (1949): 567–67; see also *Fletcher v. Peck*, 1810 U.S. LEXIS 322.

6. See New York *Laws*, 1787, ch. 57, ch. 55 (1798), ch. 94 (1803), ch. 223 (1808), ch. 200 (1811). See also New Jersey *Laws*, 1811, 223–25, and Connecticut *Laws*, 1822, ch. 28.

7. See T. J. Stiles, *The First Tycoon: The Epic Life of Cornelius Vanderbilt* (New York, 2009).

8. George Rogers Taylor, *The Transportation Revolution, 1815–1860* (White Plains, N.Y., 1951).

9. Sidney I. Pomerantz, *New York: An American City, 1783–1808* (New York, 1938), 147–225.

10. Pomerantz, *New York*, 416.

11. As John Larson's examination of internal improvements in New York revealed, "[L]ocal [public] resources seldom could support expensive, experimental works . . . taxpayers resisted public expenditures." Private investors were not a guaranteed source of financial support to entrepreneurs, as they often "found greater immediate return in commerce, agriculture and manufacturing." John Lauritz Larson, *Internal Improvement: National Public Works and the Promise of Popular Government in the Early United States* (Chapel Hill, N.C., 2000), 71. A useful, if dated, review of scholarship on internal improvements can be found in Carter Goodrich, "Internal Improvements Reconsidered," *Journal of Economic History* 30 (June 1970): 289–311.

12. L. Ray Gunn, *The Decline of Authority: Public Economy Policy and Political Development in New York, 1800–1860* (Ithaca, N.Y., 1988), 100.

13. This view dissents from Gunn, *The Decline of Authority*, 80. See also Theodore H. Lowi, "Business, Public Policy, Case Studies, and Political Theories," *World Politics* 16 (July 1964): 677–715.

14. Gunn, *The Decline of Authority*, 99–100. See also Nathan Miller, *The Enterprise of a Free People: Aspects of Economic Development of New York During the Canal Period, 1792–1838* (Ithaca, N.Y., 1962).

15. Gunn, *The Decline of Authority*, 100. Harry Scheiber provides two useful categories for distinguishing between forms of state support. The first is "public largess": financial grants, bounties, prizes, loans, and stock purchases. The second is grants of privileges; rights; and immunities to individuals, groups, and communities. See Harry Scheiber, "Federalism and the American Economic Order," *Law and Society Review* 10 (Fall 1975): 57–100, 88. Khan's examination of patent litigation revealed that "the early

focus on securing the rights and benefits of patentees, rather than on the social-welfare consequences of monopoly grants, enhanced private return on patent protection." See B. Zorina Khan, "Property Rights and Patent Litigation in Early Nineteenth-Century America," *Journal of Economic History* 55 (March 1995): 58–97.

16. Legislators, who had a "fascination with the construction of constitutions," recognized that charters could "enlist or encourage private efforts to improve or develop their states and. . . spare taxpayers the cost of such projects" while being modified to embrace the ideals of republicanism. Exploring the question of why states chartered corporations in great numbers after the Revolution, given Old Regime anxieties concerning the aristocratic origins of corporations and the alternatives available to state legislatures, Maier concludes that although the anti-charter doctrine deployed against corporations in the 1780s and 1790s created a ready source of opposition, it was based on antiquated models of corporations. See Pauline Maier, "The Revolutionary Origins of the American Corporation," *William and Mary Quarterly*, 3rd ser., 50 (January 1993): 51–84.

17. Larson, *Internal Improvement*, 82.

18. Joyce Appleby, *Capitalism and a New Social Order: The Republican Vision of the 1790s* (New York, 1984), 22. Appleby notes that "increasingly private arrangements were counted upon to supply the public's material needs . . . money becomes capital through the changed intentions of those with money, that is, with the decision to invest rather than spend or hoard wealth" (22–23). Capital aggregation, a consequence of mercantile commerce, was feared because it could lead to idleness and excessive opulence, thereby threatening liberty. See Lance Banning, *The Sacred Fire of Liberty: James Madison and the Founding of the Federal Republic* (Ithaca, N.Y., 1995), 63. For a contemporary explanation, see Adam Smith, *An Inquiry into the Nature and Causes of the Wealth of Nations*, 2 vols. (London, 1778), Book 4. Smith's principal interest in Book 4 is in the enrichment of a nation through trade rather than through agricultural productivity. As Peter Onuf writes, the concept of "virtue" emerged from "a distinctly agrarian bias; the true patriots were freeholding farmers and planters . . . by contrast, the loyalties of merchants followed their ever changing interests: they had no country." Peter S. Onuf, *Jefferson's Empire: The Language of American Nationhood* (Charlottesville, Va., 2000), 77.

19. This predates the state-binding Contract Clause decision, based on Art. I, Sec. 10, Cl. 1, of the U.S. Constitution, rendered by the Marshall Court in its 1810 decision *Fletcher v. Peck*. See 1810 U.S. LEXIS 322.

20. Robert R. Livingston to Thomas Tillotson, 12 November 1802, Robert R. Livingston Papers Microfilm, 37 reels (Stanford, N.C., 1980). Hereafter abbreviated as RRL and RRLPM.

21. An account of this event can be found in Robert H. Thurston, *Robert Fulton: His Life and Its Results* (New York, 1891), 113. Thurston mistakenly identifies the date as 9 August. A contemporary account indicates that the actual date was 21 Thermidor on the French calendar, or 8 August. An even more detailed version is from "Recueil Polytechnique des Ponts et Chaussées" (Paris, 1808), quoted in full in Alice Crary Sutcliffe,

Robert Fulton and the "Clermont": The Authoritative Story of Robert Fulton's Early Experiments, Persistent Efforts, and Historic Achievements (New York, 1909), ch. 3.

22. RRL to Thomas Tillotson, 29 May 1803, Robert R. Livingston Papers, NYHS.

23. Cynthia Owen Philip, *Robert Fulton: A Biography* (New York, 1985), ch. 8.

24. Cadwallader D. Colden, *The Life of Robert Fulton* (New York, 1817), 167.

25. N.B.: The Hudson River was then called the North River. For the original grant to Livingston, see New York *Laws*, 1798, ch. 55.

26. Robert Fulton to Cadwallader Colden, 2 April 1813, quoted in Archibald D. Turnbull, *John Stevens: An American Record* (New York, 1928), 235.

27. John Stevens to Cadwallader Colden, [n.d.] April 1813, quoted in Turnbull, *John Stevens*, 235.

28. Quoted in Turnbull, *John Stevens*, 231.

29. See [James Madison] No. 39, *Federalist Papers*.

30. See Joyce Chaplin's discussion of Eli Whitney's cotton gin in Chaplin, *An Anxious Pursuit: Agricultural Innovation and Modernity in the Lower South, 1730–1815* (Chapel Hill, N.C., 1993).

31. Robert Fulton, Edward Livingston, and Aaron Ogden, *Memorial & Petition of Robert Fulton and Edward Livingston in Behalf of Themselves and the Heirs of the Late Robert R. Livingston* (Albany, N.Y., 1814), 5. The boat was originally called *The Steamboat* before being renamed the *Clermont*, which was the name of the Livingston estate in the Hudson Valley.

32. Howard H. Morse, *Historic Old Rhinebeck: Echoes of Two Centuries* (Rhinebeck, N.Y., 1908), 327

33. RRL to unknown recipient, 18 July 1807, Robert R. Livingston Papers, NYHS.

34. See New York *Laws*, 1808, ch. 223.

35. John Stevens to RRL, [n.d.] 1808, quoted in Turnbull, *John Stevens*, 245.

36. Ibid.

37. RRL to John Stevens, fragment of unsigned draft, [n.d.] Jan. 1808, Robert R. Livingston Papers, NYHS.

38. RRL to John Stevens, [n.d.] January 1808, quoted in Turnbull, *John Stevens*, 238.

39. RRL to John Stevens, 13 January 1808, Robert R. Livingston Papers, NYHS.

40. Turnbull, *John Stevens*, 262.

41. Ibid., 255.

42. Throughout the first two decades of the 1800s, New York claimed territory reaching to the low-tide watermark of its neighboring states. This was particularly galling to New Jersey leaders who believed they shared the Hudson River equally with New York. Yet the city of New York leased land in the harbor up to the edge of New Jersey's shoreline and John Stevens's home. See New Jersey Legislative Council *Journal*, March 1807.

43. "Now by this writing the said Robert R Livingston and Robert Fulton do agree for themselves, their heirs, executors and administrators and assigns to *give and grant* to the said John Stevens his heirs executors administrators and assigns the full entire and

exclusive right to use all their said patent rights for constructing steamboats on the Delaware, Chesapeake, Tantee, Saranac and Connecticut Rivers and from Road Island to Providence. Yet if from any unforeseen event there should at the experatur of seven-years from the date of this writing being one or more of the beforementioned waters on which there shall not be at least one steamboat constructed by and under the authority of the said John Stevens this and in such case the said patent rights to navigate steamboats on such waters as shall then not have a steamboat shall devolve to the said Robert R Livingston and Robert Fulton and the said John Stevens shall have the use for said water on which he shall construct or cause to be constructed a steamboat within the seven-years mentioned all and every improvement which the said Fulton and Livingston may make in navigating steamboats And the said John Stevens engages for himself his heirs administrators and assigns to relinquish to the said Robert R Livingston and Robert Fulton all claim to navigate steamboats on the waters of the State of New-York including Lake Champlain and the run to any point between New York and New Brunswick in New Jersey . . . And should the said John Stevens discover invent or adapt any thing in the construction of the steamboats which the said Livingston and Fulton may deem an improvement they shall be at liberty to use any such discovery or invention in their boats for the waters beforementioned except in the case of establishing steam ferry boats to run between New York and Jersey. But should the said Livingston and Fulton use any improvement of the said John Stevens on any of the water of the United States then they already specified they shall make him a reasonable compensation." Robert Fulton, "Memorandum of an agreement," 1 December 1809, Box 1A, Fulton Papers, NYHS.

44. Stock Subscription Sheet (Philadelphia, 19 November 1810), LeBoeuf Collection, NYHS.

45. Jabez D. Hammond, *The History of Political Parties in the State of New York, from the Ratification of the Constitution to December, 1840*, 2 vols. (Buffalo, 1842), passim. Only one was nominally a Federalist: Peter Jay Munro, the nephew of deceased New York governor John Jay.

46. Brian Phillips Murphy, "'A very convenient instrument': The Manhattan Company, Aaron Burr, and the Election of 1800," *William and Mary Quarterly*, 3rd ser., 65 (April 2008): 233–66.

47. Robert Fulton to John Stevens, 24 January 1811, quoted in Turnbull, *John Stevens*, 304.

48. Thus, Livingston and Fulton's enthusiasm for the Erie Canal was more than New York boosterism; not only could they regulate commercial steamboat traffic on the canal—their power could reach throughout the Great Lakes.

49. RRL to Robert L. Livingston, 2 September 1807, Robert R. Livingston Papers, NYHS.

50. There is no record of the North River Steam Boat Company applying for a state charter of incorporation until 1815.

51. Robert Fulton to RRL, 12 July 1808, Robert R. Livingston Papers, NYHS.

52. See Baxter, *The Steamboat Monopoly*, 21; George Dangerfield, *Chancellor Robert R. Livingston of New York, 1746–1813* (New York, 1960), 418; Colden, *Life of Robert Fulton*, 144.

53. The Albanians could have used the steamboat design of John Fitch's expired federal patent. They opted to replicate Fulton's design instead. Colden, *Life of Robert Fulton*, 146.

54. Robert Fulton to John Stevens, 24 January 1811, quoted in Turnbull, *John Stevens*, 304. Livingston and Fulton had good reason not to rely on the latter's federal patent to protect their steamboat rights. In 1809 Fulton met with President James Madison and reported to Livingston,

> The conversation turned on our exclusive right to navigate with steam boats on the North River and the waters of the State of New York. Mr. Madison is decidedly of our opinion—that the legislature of a State has a right to preclude any patentee from the exercise of his invention in their particular State, and to favor whom they please and for as long as they please. I think we should give it out, and strictly adhere to it, that we will not permit any vessel moved by steam to navigate the waters of the State of New York on any consideration whatsoever.

For eight years, James Madison, in his capacity as secretary of state, had been one of the three federal cabinet officials charged with assessing patent applications (the others were the secretary of war and the attorney general). That he believed a state monopoly law could be the superior legal authority to a federal patent confirmed Livingston's legal strategy of insulating his and Fulton's enterprise through that law. See Robert Fulton to RRL, 12 July 1809, Robert R. Livingston Papers, NYHS.

55. Andrew Bartholomew to RRL, 17 August 1811, Robert R. Livingston Papers, NYHS.

56. Dangerfield, *Chancellor Robert R. Livingston*, 416.

57. RRL to John Stevens, [n.d.] 1811, Robert R. Livingston Papers, NYHS. Also cited in Turnbull, *John Stevens*, 305.

58. New York Assembly *Journal*, 34th Sess., 27 March and 8 April 1811.

59. Ibid., 8 and 9 April 1811.

60. The public right Lansing cited is called *jus publicum*, which bars the state from conveying a private right to collectively held public assets. It is possible, too, that Lansing had other motivations in opposing the monopoly. In 1823 he filed suit against John R. Livingston to challenge the legality of the monopoly after seeking and being denied a license. For more on this case, see Morton J. Horowitz, *The Transformation of American Law, 1780–1860* (Cambridge, Mass., 1977), 123. The case citation is *Livingston v. Van Ingen et al.*, 9 Johnson's Re 507.

61. RRL to James Mease, 24 March 1812, Robert R. Livingston Papers, NYHS.

62. *Examination of the Chancellor's Opinion in the Case of Robert R. Livingston . . .* (Albany, N.Y., 1812), 40–54, Broadside, Evans S26269.

63. For more on Kent's role, see Thomas Campbell Jr., "Chancellor Kent, Chief Justice Marshall and the Steamboat Cases," *Syracuse Law Review* 25 (1974): 497–534.

64. RRL to John Yates, 25 June 1812, LeBoeuf Collection, NYHS. John Yates was a relation to Justice Joseph Yates.

65. 9 Johnson 507 (1812).

66. RRL to John Stevens, [n.d.] 1811, Robert R. Livingston Papers, NYHS.

67. RRL to Edward Livingston, 19 March 1812, Robert R. Livingston Papers, NYHS.

68. Robert Fulton to Edward Livingston and Robert L. Livingston, 1 September 1813, Robert R. Livingston Papers, NYHS.

69. RRL to Messrs. Parker, Lansing, Winnie, and Townsend, et al., 5 September 1812, Robert R. Livingston Papers, NYHS. It is unclear if Livingston received a response to the letter.

70. Robert Fulton to RRL, 24 September 1812, RRLPM.

71. An examination of the passenger list from one of the Livingston-Fulton boat's voyages confirms that partisan identities did not dampen the enthusiasm of patrons or their willingness to use the boats. See Sutcliffe, *Robert Fulton*, 278–82.

72. RRL, "My Essay on Steamboats . . . ," [1811], RRLPM.

73. Ogden's petition to the New York legislature can be found in *Proceedings of the New Jersey Historical Society*, vol. 9 (Newark, N.J., 1864), 121–23. See also Baxter, *The Steamboat Monopoly*, 35.

74. Henry R. Stiles, *A History of the City of Brooklyn, Including the Old Town and Village of Brooklyn, the Town of Bushwick, and the Village and City of Williamsburgh*, vol. 3 (Brooklyn, N.Y, 1870), 536–39.

75. James Grant Wilson and John Fiske, eds., *Appleton's Cyclopedia of American Biography*, vol. 2 (New York, 1888), 245.

76. William Duer, *A Review of the Letter, Addressed by William Alexander Duer, Esq., to Cadwallader Colden, Esq.* (New York, 1818), 56.

77. Aaron Ogden, *Petition* ([n.d.] 1814) quoted in Kirkpatrick Sale, *The Fire of His Genius: Robert Fulton and the American Dream* (New York, 2001), 166.

78. See New York *Laws*, 1814, ch. 52.

79. Cadwallader D. Colden, *A Vindication by Cadwallader D. Colden, of the Steamboat Right Granted by the State of New-York: In the Form of an Answer to the Letter of Mr. Duer, Addressed to Mr. Colden* (New York, 1819), 62–63.

80. Ibid., 65.

81. Nicholas Roosevelt to Aaron Ogden, 15 December 1814, Robert Fulton Papers, NYHS. For more on Roosevelt's "Mississippi expedition," see Sutcliffe, *Robert Fulton*, 284.

82. This fact led many historians, including Wallace Mendelson and Maurice Baxter, to conclude that Colden and his partner Emmet saw the contractual nature of the monopoly grant as their strongest line of defense. It is more likely, however, that Colden and Emmet made the argument out of necessity. Because they did not have access to Fulton or to his patents and drawings, Colden and Emmet could not argue for the

originality of the Livingston-Fulton steamboats as intellectual property. Instead, the lawyers argued for the legitimacy of the state monopoly grant, focusing on its contractual facets in addition to its public benefits and the achievements of Livingston and Fulton. See Colden, *Vindication*, 80–90.

83. Colden, *Life of Robert Fulton*, 249–50.

84. New York Assembly *Journal* 37th Sess., 246–49.

85. (Friend of John Fitch) [William Duer], *An Examination of Cadwallader D. Colden's Book, Entitled A LIFE OF ROBERT FULTON* (New York, 1817), 8.

86. Colden, *Life of Robert Fulton*, 7.

87. Excerpt from Fulton's petition to the Legislature, in Colden, *Vindication*, 68.

88. (Friend of John Fitch), *An Examination*, 36.

89. Colden, *Life of Robert Fulton*, 247–49.

90. William Duer, *A Letter, Addressed to Cadwallader D. Colden* (Albany, N.Y., 1817), 65–66.

91. New York Senate *Journal*, 37th Sess., 19 March 1814.

92. Robert Fulton to unknown recipient, 20 March 1814, Box 1, Fulton Papers, NYHS.

93. Duer, *A Letter, Addressed to Cadwallader D. Colden*, 80. Emphasis in original.

94. See John R. Livingston, *Petition of John R. Livingston and Robert J. Livingston to the Legislature of New Jersey . . .* (New York, 1814), quoted in John D. Ward, *An Account of the Steamboat Controversy Between the Citizens of New York and New Jersey from 1811 to 1824* (Newark, N.J., 1863), 11–15, and quoted at 12–13. Aaron Ogden submitted a rebuttal petition to the New Jersey legislature, according to its journals, but no text is quoted and no extant copy can be found. Emphasis in original.

95. See New Jersey General Assembly *Proceedings*, 3 February 1815 (Trenton, N.J., 1815).

96. Sale, *The Fire of His Genius*, 172.

97. Colden, *Life of Robert Fulton*, 167.

98. See Duer, *A Letter, Addressed to Cadwallader D. Colden*.

99. Ibid., 16.

100. Ibid., 21. Emphasis in original.

101. See Robert Fulton to James Madison, 23 March 1814 and 5 November 1814, Madison Papers, Manuscript Division, Library of Congress.

102. Colden, *Life of Robert Fulton*, 255.

103. Duer, *A Review of the Letter*, 66.

104. Ibid., 18.

105. Baxter, *The Steamboat Monopoly*, 38.

106. Larson, *Internal Improvement*, 76.

107. New York Assembly *Journal*, 45th Sess., 1822.

108. Even within these corporations, however, the political implications of financial associations could lead to disruptive disagreements. In 1820 a legal dispute erupted among shareholders of the North River Steam Boat Company over whether the

company would bank with the Manhattan Company or the Bank of New-York, each of which had differing partisan histories and ties to factions within the state. See *E. Livingston v. D. Lynch, June et al.* (1820), 4 Johnson 574. See also *Roorbach and Bartholomew v. Dale et al.* and *North River Steam Boat Company* (1822), 6 Johnson 468; *Lansing and Thayer v. North River Steam Boat Company* (1823), 7 Johnson 163.

109. Cf. Gunn, *The Decline of Authority*, 81.

110. Robert G. Albion, *The Rise of the New York Port* (New York, 1939), 151–52.

111. See *State v. Thomas Gibbons* (1818), 4 N.J.L. 45, and *Ogden v. Gibbons* (1819), 5 N.J.L. 612. Even after their Supreme Court showdown, litigation continued between the two; see *Thomas Gibbons v. Aaron Ogden* (1826), 8 N.J.L. 288.

112. Many of the injunction cases arose in New York City and originated with Tompkins's ill-conceived partnership with Thomas Gibbons. See *Ogden v. Gibbons* (1819), 4 Johnson 150, 162. See also *Ogden v. Gibbons* (1819), 4 Johnson 173; *Livingston v. Ogden and Gibbons* (1819), 4 Johnson 47; *J. R. Livingston v. Gibbons and Ogden* (1819), 4 Johnson 93; *J. R. Livingston v. D. D. Tompkins* (1820), 4 Johnson 416; *J. R. Livingston v. Gibbons* (1820), 4 Johnson 517; *J. R. Livingston v Gibbons, impleaded with Ogden* (1821), 5 Johnson 240; *North River Steamboat Company v. John R. Livingston* (1825), 3 Cow. 713; *Gibbons v. Ogden* (1820), 17 Johnson 488; *Thomas Gibbons v. John R. Livingston* (1822), 6 N.J.L. 236; *Thomas Gibbons v. Aaron Ogden* (1822), 6 N.J.L. 285.

113. In 1793 Congress adopted a federal coasting license law that established a registry for U.S. vessels engaged in coastal interstate trade. Furthermore, in 1812 Congress adopted a law allowing resident aliens in the United States to enroll and license steamboats to operate in American rivers and bays. Unlike the 1793 enrollment act for U.S. citizens, this law did not mandate an oath on the part of the boat's owner. See *Act* 18 February 1793; c. 8, §2, 1 Stat. 305, and *Act* 12 March 1812; c. 40, §1, 2 Stat. 694.

114. 22 U.S. 1, 185; 22 U.S. 1, 6.

115. For a more thorough examination of the case, see T. J. Stiles, *The First Tycoon*, ch. 2.

116. The idea that economic growth can be accompanied by increasingly liberal ideologies of political economy, social mobility, and institutional democratization is posed in Benjamin Friedman, *The Moral Consequences of Economic Growth* (New York, 2005). Compare this with the causal emphasis Douglass North places on property rights as the catalyst for economic growth in democratic society, and with Amartya Sen's focus on the benefits and capabilities individuals derive from growth. See Douglass North, *Institutions, Institutional Change and Economic Performance* (Cambridge, 1990) and Amartya Sen, *Development as Freedom* (Oxford, 1999).

117. Fulton contended that his originality lay in the "ratio" he applied to the scale of his steamboat.

118. (Friend of John Fitch), *An Examination*, 34–35.

119. The view of the federal courts as the ultimate enemy to the monopoly seems to have first been advanced in a legal brief written by Aaron Burr on 10 September 1812. In it, he writes, "[W]hatever may be the opinion of Lawyers however logical & just it is to

be lamented that they are in this case useless & idle, suing that . . . the highest Court of Law of the State, hath declared this act to be *valid* and *reasonable* and for the *public good* and that the Legislature is 'Sovereign.' . . . This is manifestly an abridgement of the general right of the Citizens of the United States and an interference with the powers of the General Government and ought to be so declared *whenever the question can be brought judicially before the Supreme Court of the United States.*" Burr outlines much of what became Daniel Webster's argument in *Gibbons v. Ogden*, citing the federal coasting license law as the statute to use to make the monopoly vulnerable in a federal judicial venue. See Aaron Burr, Legal brief, New York, 10 September 1812, Connecticut Historical Society.

120. Ibid., 36.

121. The following year, Bayard introduced legislation allowing resident foreigners to operate and license steamboats with the national government; the law was later cited by the Marshall Court as evidence of the authority of Congress to regulate steamboats. 12th Congress, Senate, "A Bill for the Relief of Robert Fulton and His Associates" (Washington, D.C., 1811); *Memorial of Isaiah Townsend and Others of the City of Albany . . .* (Washington, D.C., 1811), 4; *Memorial of Aaron Ogden of Elizabethtown, N.J.* (Washington, D.C,, 1811); Senate *Journal*, 31 December 1811; *Act* 12 March 1812; c. 40, §1, 2 Stat. 694.

122. "Facts and Considerations . . . Why Is Steam-Boat Navigation Interesting to Connecticut?" (Hartford, Conn., 1819), 7. Emphasis in original. The term "obnoxious" could be equated to "servility" or a "predicament of those who live at the mercy of other people"—the opposite of the virtuous and independent yeoman farmer idealized in republican ideology. See Quentin Skinner, *Liberty Before Liberalism* (Cambridge, 1998), 94–95.

123. DeWitt Clinton, *A Discourse Delivered Before the American Academy of the Arts* (New York, 1816), quoted at 27, 29, 30.

124. [Robert R. Livingston], *An Examination of the Chancellor's Opinion in the Case of Robert R. Livingston and Robert Fulton vs. James Van Ingen, Lansing, and Others* (Albany, N.Y., 1812), 18, 22. Emphasis in original.

125. "Facts and Considerations . . . Why Is Steam-Boat Navigation Interesting to Connecticut?" 7.

126. Duer, *A Letter, Addressed to Cadwallader D. Colden*, 9. Emphasis in original.

127. Ibid., 82.

128. *Amendments Proposed by Select Committee of the House . . . "an Act for the Benefit of the Widow and Children of Robert Fulton"* (Washington, D.C., 1816); Ferdinando Fairfax, *Memorial of Ferdinando Fairfax Against the Extension of the Patents Granted to Robert Fulton . . .* (Washington, D.C., 1816), 2–4.

129. William Alexander Duer, *A Reply to Mr. Colden's Vindication of the Steam-Boat Monopoly* (Albany, N.Y., 1819), 108.

130. Ibid., 181–82.

131. Ibid., 142

132. Ibid., 172.

133. Ibid., 118.

134. Ibid., 14–15.

135. See Drew R. McCoy, *The Elusive Republic: Political Economy in Jeffersonian America* (Chapel Hill, N.C., 1980), ch. 9, esp. 231.

136. An Act Respecting Navigable Communications Between the Great Western and Northern Lakes and the Atlantic Ocean, 15 April 1817, ch. 262, p. 301, §5.

Chapter 5

1. Cadwallader D. Colden, *Memoir, Prepared at the Request of a Committee of the Common Council of the City of New York, and Presented to the Mayor of the City, at the Celebration of the Completion of the New York Canals* (Albany, 1825), appendix.

2. Enos Throop to Martin Van Buren, 15 March 1817, Ser. 2, Reel 5, Martin Van Buren Papers, Library of Congress. Hereafter abbreviated as LC.

3. See Colden, *Memoir*, appendix.

4. Ibid.

5. Heritage Auction Galleries September 2009 U.S. Coin Auction Catalogue, Sale No. 1129.

6. Colden, *Memoir*, appendix.

7. "From the N.Y. Evening Post of Nov. 2," *Cooperstown Watch-Tower*, 14 November 1825, 2.

8. The canal was called both the "Grand Canal" and the "Erie Canal" by contemporaries; it encompasses both the Hudson-Erie route and a separate canal linking the Hudson to Lake Champlain. This chapter does not consider subsequent expansions of the canal through branch canals. For the sake of clarity, only the term "Erie Canal" will be used because this chapter is more concerned with the institutions of the canal than with the physical structure itself; the canal projects' funding and operations were consolidated among the New York canal commissioners and the governing board of the Canal Fund. See John Lauritz Larson, *Internal Improvement: National Public Works and the Promise of Popular Government in the Early United States* (Chapel Hill, N.C., 2001); Carol Sheriff, *The Artificial River: The Erie Canal and the Paradox of Progress, 1817–1862* (New York, 1996); John Joseph Wallis and Barry R. Weingast, "Equilibrium Impotence: Why the States and Not the American National Government Financed Economic Development in the Antebellum Era" (June 2005), NBER Working Paper No. W11397; Stanley L. Engerman and Kenneth L. Sokoloff, "Digging the Dirt at Public Expense: Governance in the Building of the Erie Canal and Other Public Works" (December 2004), NBER Working Paper No. W10965.

9. Thomas Jefferson, Sixth Annual Message (2 December 1806), http://millercenter.org/president/speeches/detail/3495.

10. Albert Gallatin, *Report of the Secretary of the Treasury; on the Subject of Public Roads and Canals made in pursuance of a Resolution of the Senate, of March 2, 1807* (Washington, D.C., 1808), 113.

11. "Letter from Joshua Forman" in David Hosack, *Memoir of DeWitt Clinton: With an Appendix, Containing Numerous Documents, Illustrative of the Principal Events of His Life* (New York, 1829), 343–44.

12. Noble E. Whitford, *History of the Canal System of the State of New York: Together with Brief Histories of the Canals of the United States and Canada* (Albany, 1906), ch. 24.

13. Simeon De Witt to Joseph Ellicott, 13 June 1808, repr. in Frank Severance, ed., *The Holland Land Co., and Canal Construction in Western New York* (Buffalo, N.Y., 1910), 3–4; New York *Laws* (1801) ch. 195.

14. Many of the bankers had personally negotiated with John Adams in 1782 to become lenders to the Continental Congress during the Revolution, and subsequently extended nearly a dozen loans to the U.S. government.

15. Patrick R. Weissend, "The Life and Times of Joseph Ellicott," Holland Land Office Museum (Batavia, N.Y., 2002); Ellicott Evans, "Joseph Ellicott," in *Publications of the Buffalo Historical Society*, vol. 2 (Buffalo, N.Y., 1880), 341–43.

16. Weissend, "The Life and Times of Joseph Ellicott," 8.

17. Joseph Ellicott to Simeon De Witt, 30 July 1808, repr. in Frank Severance, ed., *The Holland Land Co.*, 4–15.

18. Simeon De Witt to Joseph Ellicott, 24 August 1808, and Joseph Ellicott to David E. Evans, 20 October 1808, in Severance, *The Holland Land Co.*, 16–17.

19. Simeon De Witt to William Darby, 25 February 1822, in *Canal Laws*, I, 38–42.

20. See New York (State) Canal Commissioners, *Laws of the State of New York in Relation to the Erie and Champlain Canals: Together with the Annual Reports of the Canal Commissioners and Other Documents*, 2 vols. (Albany, 1825), 1:13–38.

21. Richard L. Hall and Alan V. Deardorff, "Lobbying as Legislative Subsidy," *American Political Science Review* 100 (2006): 69–84.

22. DeAlva Stanwood Alexander, *A Political History of the State of New York*, 3 vols. (New York, 1906–1909), 1:156.

23. Nathan Miller, *The Enterprise of a Free People: Aspects of Economic Development in New York State During the Canal Period, 1792–1838* (Ithaca, N.Y., 1962), 28–29; New York *Laws* 1808 ch. 222; Joel Munsell, *Annals of Albany*, vol. 4 (Albany, 1853), 309, 313.

24. Hosack, *Memoir of DeWitt Clinton*, 382; Samuel L. Knapp, *The Life of Thomas Eddy; Comprising an Extensive Correspondence with Many of the Most Distinguished Philosophers and Philanthropists of This and Other Countries* (New York, 1834), 153.

25. Hosack, *Memoir of DeWitt Clinton*, 382.

26. For the legislative history of the survey and commission, see New York (State) Canal Commissioners, *Laws of the State of New York*, 1:8–10, 46–47. For the 1811 report, see ibid., 1:48–69.

27. For biographers of both DeWitt Clinton and the Erie Canal, the 1810 summer sojourn of the commissioners through the taverns, boardinghouses, and backcountry of western New York marks the birth of the Erie Canal. Five of the seven commissioners traveled together by boat, sharing jokes, cigars, and rooms where they tolerated vermin, bats, and drunks. Peter Porter often slept outside in his own tent, and early in its survey

the group rewarded Thomas Eddy with the title "commodore," as he was the youngest and the only one who did not hold an office or a military rank. In a typical diary entry, DeWitt Clinton wrote of a house run by a "violent Federalist" named Maggie, where his sleep was assaulted by "an army of bed bugs, aided by a body of light infantry in the shape of fleas and a regiment of mosquito cavalry" and where one of their party was so impressed at the ability of Ann, "the girl of the house," to down three glasses of whiskey "successively" that he rewarded her with a dollar. William W. Campbell, *Life and Writings of DeWitt Clinton* (New York, 1849), 70. Van Rensselaer and Morris, meanwhile, rode separately in their own stately carriages. Chosen as the commission's president, the fifty-eight-year-old Morris was traveling with his new bride, thirty-six-year-old Anne "Nancy" Randolph, sister of Thomas Jefferson's son-in-law Thomas Mann Randolph Jr. Morris made the trip his honeymoon and brought along a second carriage packed with food, servants, an English portrait painter, and a French chef. A particularly amusing account can be found in Richard Brookhiser, *Gentleman Revolutionary: Gouverneur Morris, the Rake Who Wrote the Constitution* (New York, 2003), 188.

28. New York (State) Canal Commissioners, *Laws of the State of New York*, 1:68.

29. Ibid., 1:68–69.

30. See "An Act to Provide for the Improvement of the Internal Navigation of the State," 8 April 1811, in New York (State) Canal Commissioners, *Laws of the State of New York*, 1:70.

31. "Message to the Senate and House of Representatives," 23 December 1811, in New York (State) Canal Commissioners, *Laws of the State of New York*, 1:95.

32. New York (State) Canal Commissioners, *Laws of the State of New York*, 1:93.

33. Ibid.

34. Ibid., 1:92.

35. [New York (State) Canal Commissioners], *Report of the Commissioners* (Albany, 1812).

36. New York (State) Canal Commissioners, *Laws of the State of New York*, 1:81.

37. Ibid., 1:84.

38. Ibid., 1:85.

39. Ibid.

40. Ibid.

41. Ibid., 1:81.

42. Ibid., 1:83.

43. Ibid., 1:85, 101. For the full report, see "Report of the Commissioners Appointed to Attend at the Seat of the General Government," 4 March 1812, in New York (State) Canal Commissioners, *Laws of the State of New York*, 1:71-101.

44. When Federalists backed DeWitt Clinton for president in 1812, challenging incumbent President James Madison, Root was one of the leading Republicans who stood against awarding New York's twenty-nine electoral votes to the dissident candidate.

45. Albany *Argus*, 1 February 1814, 1.

46. New York (State) Canal Commissioners, *Laws of the State of New York*, 1:104-5.

47. Ibid., 1:115.

48. The year 1814 had been a uniquely ripe moment to make an attack on the commission; legislators were already distracted by the war then being fought on and around Lake Erie. On the domestic political front, two major issues consumed what oxygen was left in Albany: controversial bank charter applications and the effort of Governor Aaron Ogden of New Jersey to overthrow the monopoly grant held by canal commissioners Robert Fulton and the late Robert R. Livingston. With gold and silver specie payments suspended in New York and twenty-two applications for bank charters before the legislature, along with a bill to allow any association to freely open a bank, the state was poised to add more than $15 million to the state's existing $20 million in bank capital; *Niles' Weekly Register* labeled the charter frenzy a "mania" that was "truly alarming." In the words of the Albany correspondent for the *New York Spectator*, the capital was crawling with "agents, lobby members, & c." with stakes and interests in the legislature's work. When just one of these bank bills was narrowly rejected with the aid of the lieutenant governor's tie-breaking vote, the state senate's crowded gallery broke into applause. Both banking and the steamboat monopoly divided pro- and anti-canal legislators, showing that canal politics and policies were, for the moment, too immature to displace more long-standing interest-driven issues. *Niles' Weekly Register*, vol. 5 (1813–14): 276; "From Our Correspondent—Albany," New York *Spectator*, 13 April 1814, 2.

49. Paul Busti to Joseph Ellicott, 30 December 1813, in Severance, *The Holland Land Co.*, 36–37.

50. Freeman Hunt, *Lives of American Merchants*, vol. 1 (New York, 1858), 329–43.

51. Platt filled a vacancy created when James Kent ascended to become the state's new chancellor.

52. Swartwout wanted to keep fighting, but Clinton walked away from the encounter; his quarrel had never been with Swartwout, he said, but with Burr. Swartwout got revenge when his brother Robert wounded Richard Riker, Clinton's "second," in a duel one year later, giving Riker a limp he would endure for the rest of his life. See [Joseph Alfred Scoville], *The Old Merchants of New York City* (New York, 1863), 250; John Bigelow, "DeWitt Clinton as a Politician," *Harper's New Monthly Magazine* (New York) 50 (1875): 565.

53. Charles Haines, "Swartwout's Meadows," *The Plough Boy* (Albany, 1820), 82–83.

54. New York (State) Canal Commissioners, *Laws of the State of New* York, 1:106–7. After Bayard's selection, John Pintard was chosen to be the meeting's secretary. Pintard, a merchant and Republican, had been city inspector under DeWitt Clinton's mayoralty; he, Clinton, and Swartwout had been officers in the city's Tammany Society during its earliest days. And like Eddy, Pintard had recently been occupied by founding the New-York Historical Society. Although he and Bayard belonged to opposing political parties, they were both longtime Clinton pals and each would eventually lead the city's Chamber of Commerce.

55. Minutes, DeWitt Clinton Papers, New-York Historical Society (hereafter

abbreviated as NYHS); Knapp, *Life of Eddy*, 306. Eddy mistakenly recalled that the completed memorial was adopted at the meeting; compare with Samuel Ruggles, *Writings and Speeches of Samuel B. Ruggles* (New York, 1860), 8. Judge Platt said that the "memorial alone was sufficient to entitle [Clinton] to the character of an accomplished writer, an enlightened statesman, and a zealous patriot." Platt to Hosack in Hosack, *Memoir of DeWitt Clinton*, 102–4.

56. [DeWitt Clinton], *Memorial of the Citizens of New-York*, in New York (State) Canal Commissioners, *Laws of the State of New York*, 1:129.

57. Sterling Goodenow, *A Brief Topographical and Statistical Manual of the State of New-York* (New York, 1822), 34.

58. New York (State) Canal Commissioners, *Laws of the State of New York*, 1:119–22. See also Gideon Granger, *Speech of . . . Jan. 8, 1817 on the Subject of a Canal from Lake Erie to Hudson's River* (New York, 1817).

59. Joseph Ellicott to DeWitt Clinton, 20 January 1816, DeWitt Clinton Papers, Rare Books and Manuscripts Collection, Columbia University Library. Hereafter abbreviated DWC and DWCP.

60. Uri Tracy to DWC, 22 January 1816, DWCP.

61. Thomas Eddy to DWC, 28 February 1816, DWCP.

62. There were 139 investors in the loan. The smallest holding was $164 and the largest $50,000, with thirty subscriptions under $1,000, thirty between $1,000 and $2,000, twenty-four between $3,000 and $5,000, fourteen between $5,000 and $10,000, and sixteen more than $10,000. Two investors subscribed for $50,000 each. See "List of Holders of New-York State Stock, Resident in the Southern District of This State and Out of This State, on 31 Mar 1816, Showing the Amounts Held by Each with the Interest Due and Payable on the First Monday of April 16," Misc. Canal Papers, New York State Library. Hereafter abbreviated as NYSL. See New York Assembly *Journal*, 40th Sess., 520, for details on geographical distribution. See Miller, *Enterprise of a Free People*, 83, for more on occupational information cross-checks with New York directories of the day.

63. DWC to unknown recipient, [February 1816], DWCP. Nathan Miller thinks the loan is a signal moment in the canal's history, yet it does not figure in the correspondence of canal commissioners.

64. Robert Troup to DWC, 26 January 1816, DWCP.

65. DWC to unknown recipient, 21 February 1816, DWCP.

66. New York (State) Canal Commissioners, *Laws of the State of New York*, 1:323–30.

67. Henry Varnum Poor, *Sketch of the Rise and Progress of the Internal Improvements and of the Internal Commerce of the United States* (New York, 1881), xii–xiii.

68. John R. Harding, *One Hundred Years of Trinity Church, Utica, N.Y.* (Utica, N.Y., 1898), 108–9. At one point John Pintard, a longtime Clinton ally who had been secretary at the 1816 New York City canal meeting, thought he too might find a home in the canal operation, confiding to his daughter Eliza that he half-expected Clinton to offer him a position overseeing the finances of the canal's construction. He would accept the job, he

told her, not merely for the salary but because it would surely offer opportunities to enrich his "posterity" by purchasing land in "favourable locations." The appointment, however, was not offered. See John Pintard to Eliza Noel Pintard Davidson, 28 January 1817, in *Letters from John Pintard to His Daughter Eliza Noel Pintard Davidson*, 4 vols. (New York, 1940), 1:54–55.

69. Whitford, *History of the Canal System*, 789–90.

70. DWC to John Pintard, 18 August 1816, Folder 4, DWC Papers, New York Public Library. Hereafter abbreviated as NYPL.

71. New York (State) Canal Commissioners, *Laws of the State of New York*, 1:268, 312; Paul Busti to DWC, 22 Feb. 1817, in ibid., 1:309–11; DWC to John L. Sullivan, Esq., 3 March 1817, DWCP; John L. Sullivan to DWC, 7 March 1817, in *Laws of the State of New York*, 1:320–22.

72. Philetus Swift to DWC, 5 March 1817, in ibid., 1:312–13; Augustus Porter to Myron Holley, 5 Jan. 1817, in ibid., 1:313–15; Matthew Brown Jr. and Francis Brown to One of the Commissioners, 1 January 1817, in ibid., 1:315–16; Wilhelm Mynderse to Myron Holley, 17 February 1817, in ibid., 1:317–19; George S. Conover, ed., *History of Ontario County, New York* (Syracuse, N.Y., 1893), 278.

73. New York (State) Canal Commissioners, *Laws of the State of New York*, 1:271–72.

74. See "DeWitt Clinton to the Members of Congress from the State of New-York," 22 January 1817 in ibid., 1:311–12.

The Bonus Bill was vetoed by James Madison on his last day in office. Madison supported neither the reasoning nor the structure of the bill and would not tolerate a capacious reading of congressional power to justify physical improvements to interstate commerce. In the message attached to his veto, the soon-to-be-former president renewed his call for a constitutional amendment that would explicitly empower Congress to appropriate funds for roads and canals. In the absence of such an authorization, Madison believed that factions threatened to corrupt the lawmaking process, assaulting his ideal conception of a balanced Constitution. See Larson, *Internal Improvement*, 68. See veto message at www.constitution.org/jm/18170303_veto.htm. For the debates, see *Annals of Congress*, House of Representatives, 14th Congress, 2nd Sess., passim.

Many historians have analyzed this in the light of Madison's earlier statements about the constitutionality of federally funded improvements, as well as Clinton's sarcastic reference in 1812 to Madison's constitutional "scruples." The opinion he then offered to the canal commissioners and his subsequent veto of the Bonus Bill in 1817 represented his long-held belief that powers not enumerated in the Constitution were unavailable to the federal government. Madison was not, however, an opponent of improvements altogether. In August and September 1787, he supported Benjamin Franklin's recommendation that the Constitutional Convention grant Congress the power to authorize canals, suggesting on 14 September 1787 that the power of incorporation be added as well. At the time, Gouverneur Morris made arguments that such powers were implicitly granted to Congress. Lance Banning suggests that Madison's 1787 position is best understood in the light of his fear, expressed in Federalist Paper No. 41, that a lack of clarity in the Constitution would lead to "necessary usurpations of power." Madison and Franklin's motions failed at the Convention.

Although the canal commissioners were correct in apprehending that their canal proposals were bundled with the congressional politics of bank rechartering, Madison's position had been consistent. He supported internal improvements in principle, but his opposition to federal funding absent a constitutional amendment echoed his arguments with Gouverneur Morris twenty-five years earlier. See Lance Banning, *The Sacred Fire of Liberty: James Madison and the Founding of the Federal Republic* (Ithaca, N.Y., 1995), 161–62; [James Madison] No. 41, Federalist Papers; Max Farrand et al., eds., *The Records of the Federal Convention of 1787*, 4 vols. (New Haven, Conn., 1937), 2:615–16. Clinton believed that the veto had created a "total interruption of the interposition of the national government in favor of" such projects. "Some will oppose because they believe the power is already vested in Congress," he told New York Federalist Senator Rufus King, "and others will object because they think that it ought not to be deposited in that body." As for Madison, Clinton thought his veto was inconsistent with past actions. "After swallowing the National Bank and the Cumberland Road & c.," Clinton wrote, "[I]t was not to be supposed that Mr. Madison would strain at Canals. But so it is . . ." DWC to Rufus King, 13 December 1817, in Charles R. King, ed., *The Life and Correspondence of Rufus King*, vol. 6 (New York, 1900), 83–84.

75. Robert Troup, *Letter to the honorable Brockholst Livingston, Esq. One of the justices of the Supreme Court of the United States, on the Lake Canal Policy of the State of New-York* (Albany, 1822); Services of George Tibbits in Hosack, *Memoir of DeWitt Clinton*, appendix.

76. DWC to William D. Ford, 10 March 1817, in New York (State) Canal Commissioners, *Laws of the State of New York*, 1:323–28.

77. Jacob Rutsen Van Rensselaer to DWC, 11 March 1817, DWCP.

78. For additional material on Jacob R. Van Rensselaer, see John L. Brooke, *Columbia Rising: Civil Life on the Upper Hudson from the Revolution to the Age of Jackson* (Chapel Hill, N.C., 2010), ch. 7.

79. Ellicott to Busti, 13 May 1816; Ellicott to Busti, 12 February 1817; Ellicott to Busti, 21 June 1817, in Severance, *Holland*, 126–28.

80. New York (State) Canal Commissioners, *Laws of the State of New York*, 1:287.

81. "A List of the Names of Holders of the New York State 6% Stock of a Million Loan and of 5% and 6% Cl. Loans for the Years 1818–1821, for the Quarter Ending 31 December 1821," Misc. Canal Papers, NYSL. See also Miller, *Enterprise of a Free People*, A3 for a more comprehensive quantitative analysis of this and subsequent canal loans. The total figure of available bank capital is drawn from state comptroller William Marcy's estimate in New York Assembly *Journal*, 49th Sess., 418–19.

82. Thomas Eddy and William Bayard were both bank directors, yet neither invested in the canal fund personally until the loans began attracting more wealthy investors in the early 1820s. For more on the Bank for Savings, see Miller, *Enterprise of a Free People*, 88–89.

83. *Niles' Weekly Register* of 17 March and 2 June 1821, quoted in Miller, *Enterprise of a Free People*, 98.

84. Lawmakers also set aside the first $33,500 of each year's auction duties for a hospital, an orphanage, an "economical school," and "the support of foreign poor." New York (State) Canal Commissioners, *Laws of the State of New York*, 1:362.

85. In both houses, the New York City delegations were unified in opposing the bill. See George E. Baker, ed., *Works of William Seward*, 3 vols. (New York, 1853), 2:106. Troup, *Letter to the Honorable Brockholst Livingston, Esq.*, appendix B. For a comparison, see Lee William Formwalt, *Benjamin Henry Latrobe and the Development of Internal Improvements in the New Republic, 1796–1820* (New York, 1982); Joseph Hobson Harrison Jr., "The Internal Improvement Issue in the Politics of the Union, 1783–1825" (Ph.D. diss., University of Virginia, 1954). The most comprehensive study of the Chesapeake and Delaware Canal is Ralph D. Gray, *The Natural Waterway: A History of the Chesapeake and Delaware Canal, 1769–1985* (Urbana, Ill., 1989). See also Hisayo K. Ushida, "Search for Federal Aid: The Petitioning Activities of the Chesapeake and Delaware Canal Company," *Japanese Journal of American Studies* 14 (2003): 87–103.

86. For more on the Council of Revision, see Daniel J. Hulsebosch, *Constituting Empire: New York and the Transformation of Constitutionalism in the Atlantic World, 1664–1830* (Chapel Hill, N.C., 2005), 176–80.

87. Hosack, *Memoir of DeWitt Clinton*, 387–88.

88. For more on Kent, see Hulsebosch, *Constituting Empire*, 277–95.

89. Hosack, *Memoir of DeWitt Clinton*, 387–88.

90. Elkanah Watson, *History of the Rise, Progress, and Existing Condition of the Western Canals* (Albany, 1820); New York Corresponding Association for the Promotion of Internal Improvements, *Public Documents, Relating to the New-York Canals: Which Are to Connect the Western and Northern Lakes, with the Atlantic Ocean* (New York, 1821); Troup, *Letter to the Honorable Brockholst Livingston* (Albany, 1822).

91. A. C. Flagg, "Internal Improvements in the State of New York: A Sketch of the Rise, Progress, and Present Condition of Internal Improvements in the State of New York," *Hunt's Merchants' Magazine and Commercial Review* 24 (June 1851): 34. See Ronald E. Shaw, *Erie Water West: A History of the Erie Canal, 1792–1854* (Lexington, Ky., 1966), part 4 passim. See also Petitions and Appeals to the Canal Board, 1828–1926, Comptroller's Office Records, Ser. A1140, NYSL.

92. For an overview of this literature, see Cathy D. Matson, "Capitalizing Hope: Economic Thought and the Early National Economy," *Journal of the Early Republic* 16, no. 2, Special Issue on Capitalism in the Early Republic (Summer 1996): 273–91. On the potential for local boosterism to be linked to a vision of national unity, see John Seelye, "'Rational Exultation': The Erie Canal Celebration," *American Antiquarian Society Proceedings* 94 (1984): 261–67; John Seelye, *Beautiful Machine: Rivers and the Republican Plan, 1755–1825* (New York, 1991), 293–302, 319–53. See also Sheriff, *The Artificial River*, 47–51; C. Knick Harley, "Oligopoly Agreement and the Timing of American Railroad Construction," *Journal of Economic History* 42, no. 4 (December 1982): 797–823. On

institutional dynamism, see Guy S. Callender, "The Early Transportation and Banking Enterprises of the States in Relation to the Growth of Corporations," *Quarterly Journal of Economics* 17 (1903): 111–62. For more on the "American" political economy, see Robert H. Wiebe, *The Opening of American Society: From the Adoption of the Constitution to the Eve of Disunion* (New York, 1984), 200–203; Harry Scheiber, "The Transportation Revolution and American Law," in [Indiana Historical Society], *Transportation and the Early Nation: Papers Presented at the Indiana American Revolution Bicentennial Symposium Allen County-Fort Wayne Historical Society Museum, Fort Wayne, Indiana, April 24–26, 1981* (Indianapolis, Ind., 1982), 12; James Willard Hurst, *Law and the Conditions of Freedom in the Nineteenth-Century United States* (Madison, Wis., 1956), 43–50.

Conclusion

1. Joseph S. DeSalvo, *Perspectives on Regional Transportation Planning* (Lexington, Mass., 1973), 203. For more on how the canal's contemporaries viewed the project's benefits, see James L. Barton, *Commerce of the Lakes, and Erie Canal; Its Nationality and Character* (Buffalo, N.Y., 1851).

2. Governor DeWitt Clinton Annual Message, 1828, in Charles Z. Lincoln, ed., *Messages from the Governors . . .* (New York, 1909), 3:200.

3. Ballard C. Campbell, *The Growth of American Government: Governance from the Cleveland Era to the Present* (Bloomington, Ind., 1995); Colleen A. Dunlavy, *Politics and Industrialization: Early Railroads in the United States and Prussia* (Princeton, N.J., 1994); William J. Novak, *The People's Welfare: Law and Regulation in Nineteenth-Century America* (Chapel Hill, N.C., 1996); Barbara Young Welke, *Recasting American Liberty: Gender, Race, Law, and the Railroad Revolution, 1865–1920* (New York, 2001); Victoria Saker Woeste, *The Farmer's Benevolent Trust: Law and Agricultural Cooperation in Industrial America, 1865–1945* (Chapel Hill, N.C., 1998); Robin L. Einhorn, "Slavery and the Politics of Taxation in the Early United States," *Studies in American Political Development* 14 (Fall 2000): 156–83; Robin L. Einhorn, *American Taxation, American Slavery* (Chicago, 2006).

4. Michael F. Holt, "Change and Continuity in the Party Period: The Substance and Structure of American Politics, 1835–1885," in Byron E. Shafer and Anthony J. Badger, eds., *Contesting Democracy: Substance and Structure in American Political History, 1775–2000* (Lawrence, Kans., 2001), 106. Compare with Richard L. McCormick, *The Party Period and Public Policy: American Politics from the Age of Jackson to the Progressive Era* (New York, 1986); Joel H. Silbey, *The American Political Nation, 1838–1893* (Stanford, Calif., 1991).

5. Howard Bodenhorn, *State Banking in Early America: A New Economic History* (New York, 2003), 155–83. For more on the discretionary use of canal proceeds, see Carol Sheriff, *The Artificial River: The Erie Canal and the Paradox of Progress, 1817–1862* (New York, 1996).

6. The canal sped up the liquidation of the Holland Land Company's extensive

holdings by opening parts of the state to farming, transforming land ownership in those areas from idle speculations into actively productive investments, thereby intensifying Iroquois removal in upstate New York. For more on the linkage between private interests and state power vis-à-vis the displacement of New York tribes, see Laurence M. Hauptman, *Conspiracy of Interests: Iroquois Dispossession and the Rise of New York State* (Syracuse, N.Y., 1999); Henry S. Manley, "Buying Buffalo from the Indians," *New York History* 28 (1947): 313–29; Thomas S. Abler, "Factional Dispute and Party Conflict in the Political System of the Seneca Nation (1845–1895): An Ethnohistorical Analysis" (Ph.D. diss., University of Toronto, 1969). For more on New York's economic development, see Robert G. Albion, *The Rise of New York Port, 1815–1860* (New York, 1939); Clifton Hood, "Robert G. Albion's *The Rise of New York Port, 1815–1860*," *Reviews in American History* 27, no. 2 (June 1999): 171–79; Robert E. Wright, *The First Wall Street: Chestnut Street, Philadelphia, and the Birth of American Finance* (Chicago, 2010), 85–102. See also Sven Beckert, *The Monied Metropolis: New York City and the Consolidation of the American Bourgeoisie, 1850–1896* (New York, 2003). For more on the implications of public-infrastructure spending on local economies, see Robert J. Barro, "Government Spending in a Simple Model of Endogenous Growth," *Journal of Political Economy* 98, no. 5, pt. 2 (October 1990): S103–25. My thinking about financial agglomeration has been influenced by the economic-geography work of Paul Krugman. See Paul Krugman, "Increasing Returns and Economic Geography," *Journal of Political Economy* 99, no. 3 (June 1991): 483–99.

7. Mathew Carey, *Brief View of the System of Internal Improvement of the State of Pennsylvania* (Philadelphia, 1831), chs. 4–5, 20.

8. Julius Rubin, *Canal or Railroad? Imitation and Innovation in the Response to the Erie Canal in Philadelphia, Baltimore, and Boston* (Philadelphia, 1961).

9. See Nathaniel H. Carter and William L. Stone et al., *Reports of the Proceedings and Debates of the Convention of 1821* (Albany, N.Y., 1821). For more on the 1821 New York Constitution, see Daniel J. Hulsebosch, *Constituting Empire: New York and the Transformation of Constitutionalism in the Atlantic World, 1664–1830* (Chapel Hill, N.C., 2006), 271–73. For more on chartering, see L. Ray Gunn, *The Decline of Authority: Public Economic Policy and Political Development in New York State, 1800–1860* (Ithaca, N.Y., 1988), 70–71.

10. Charles Z. Lincoln, *The Constitutional History of New York: From the Beginning of the Colonial Period to the Year 1905, Showing the Origin, Development, and Judicial Construction of the Constitution*, 5 vols. (Rochester, N.Y., 1906), 2:165. For more on the Panic of 1837, see Jessica M. Lepler, *The Many Panics of 1837: People, Politics, and the Creation of a Transatlantic Financial Crisis* (New York, 2013).

11. For more on the emergence of laissez-faire policies nationally, see John Lauritz Larson, *Internal Improvement: National Public Works and the Promise of Popular Government in the Early United States* (Chapel Hill, N.C., 2001), esp. Introduction and Epilogue.

12. Gunn, *Decline of Authority*, 241. Other historians who deal with 1846 include

Charles W. McCurdy, *The Anti-Rent Era in New York Law and Politics, 1839–1865* (Chapel Hill, N.C., 2001); John J. Dinian, *The American State Constitutional Tradition* (Lawrence, Kans., 2006); Peter J. Galie, *Ordered Liberty: A Constitutional History of New York* (New York, 1996); Patricia McGee, "Issues of Factions: New York State Politics from the Panic of 1837 to the Election of 1848" (Ph.D. diss., St. John's University, 1970); Marvin Meyers, *The Jacksonian Persuasion: Politics and Belief* (Stanford, Calif., 1960), ch. 11. Gunn is therefore far from the only historian to look at the document, but his interpretation of its meaning for New York's political economy holds much sway among his peers in the literature. See also Arthur A. Ekirch Jr., "Democracy and Laissez Faire: The New York State Constitution of 1846," *Journal of Libertarian Studies* 1 (Winter 1977): 319–23. One example of a growth model that relies on rationalization is Walt Rostow's take-off theory as argued in W. W. Rostow, *The Stages of Economic Growth: A Non-Communist Manifesto* (New York, 1960). For more on general incorporation, see William F. Shughart II and Robert D. Tollison, "Corporate Chartering: An Exploration in the Economics of Legal Change," *Economic Inquiry* 23 (1985): 585–99. Note that New York in 1811 passed a general incorporation statute to aid domestic manufacturing and industry in advance of the War of 1812. The act covered the textile, metals, and glass industries, and it was renewed in 1821. The maximum capitalization authorized for corporations created under this act was $100,000. Some companies created under special acts were below this figure, suggesting that the cap did not necessarily create a deficiency across all industries. Yet companies created by special legislation, which had capitalizations in excess of $100,000 were principally in the metal industry. Their charters were limited to twenty years. And a clause inserted into the statute nullified limited liability, making shareholders fully responsible for future debts. The New York legislature in 1822 also passed a Limited Partnership Act to extend protections to unincorporated associations; this did not extend to stock associations, however. Upon forming a company that issued stocks for the purpose of capital formation, liability limitations ceased and the partners faced full risk exposure for the debts of their enterprise. See W. C. Kessler, "A Statistical Study of the New York General Incorporation Act of 1811," *Journal of Political Economy* 48 (December 1940): 877–82. Kessler believes that the 1811 statute's importance is overlooked, in contrast to Shaw Livermore, "Unlimited Liability in Early American Corporations," *Journal of Political Economy* 43 (October 1935): 674–87. For more on the history of the limited partnerships, see William Draper Lewis, "The Uniform Limited Partnership Act," *University of Pennsylvania Law Review and American Law Register* 65 (June 1917): 715–31.

13. Erasmus Peshine Smith, *A Manual of Political Economy* (New York, 1853), 258–59.

14. William G. Bishop and William H. Atree, eds., *Report of the Debates and Proceedings of the Convention for the Revision of the Constitution of the State of New York, 1846* (Albany, N.Y., 1846), 980.

15. Smith, *A Manual of Political Economy*, 259.

16. Ibid., 259–60.

17. Ibid., 259–61, 269.

18. A. B. Johnson, "The Legislative History of Corporations in the State of New York," *Merchants' Magazine and Commercial Review* 23 (December 1850): 611.

19. Howard Bodenhorn, "Bank Chartering and Political Corruption in Antebellum New York," in Edward L. Glaeser and Claudia Goldin, eds., *Corruption and Reform: Lessons from America's Economic History* (Chicago, 2006); Bray Hammond, "Free Banks and Corporations: The New York Free Banking Act of 1838," *Journal of Political Economy* 44 (April 1936): 184–209. See also Bray Hammond, *Banks and Politics in America: From the Revolution to the Civil War* (Princeton, N.J., 1957), 572–84; Fritz Redlich, *The Molding of American Banking: Men and Ideas,* 2 vols. (New York, 1951), 187–90; James Roger Sharp, *The Jacksonians Versus the Banks: Politics in the States After the Panic of 1837* (New York, 1970), 316; Gunn, *The Decline of Authority,* 108–12.

20. Samuel Ruggles to Charles Ruggles, 5 December 1834, Charles Ruggles Papers, Letters from Samuel B. Ruggles, 1834–55 Folder, NYPL; see also Daniel G. B. Thompson, *Ruggles of New York: A Life of Samuel B. Ruggles* (New York, 1946).

21. Samuel Ruggles to Charles Ruggles, 27 December 1834, Charles Ruggles Papers, Letters from Samuel B. Ruggles, 1834–1855 Folder, NYPL. Emphasis in original.

22. For more on the intersection of railroads and the post office during the J. Q. Adams and Jackson administrations, see Richard R. John, *Spreading the News: The American Postal System from Franklin to Morse* (Cambridge, Mass., 1995), ch. 6.

23. Samuel Ruggles to Charles Ruggles, 27 December 1834, Charles Ruggles Papers, Letters from Samuel B. Ruggles, 1834–1855 Folder, NYPL. Emphasis in original.

24. Although Ruggles's letter echoed a report he had prepared for the legislature earlier in the year, it was far more concerned with linking an improvement agenda to the Erie Railroad and the future of the Whig Party. Cf. New York Assembly, Committee on Ways and Means, *Report upon the Finances and Internal Improvements of the State of New York, 1838* (New York, 1838).

25. Samuel Ruggles to William H. Seward, 17 December 1838, Charles Ruggles Papers, Box 2, Folder 10, William H. Seward Letters, NYPL. Emphasis in original. In this way, it is possible to see how the Democratic Party emerged to become an antidevelopment party, an issue explored in Richard R. John, "Affairs of Office: The Executive Departments, the Election of 1828, and the Making of the Democratic Party," in Meg Jacobs, William Novak, and Julian Zelizer, eds., *The Democratic Experiment: New Directions in American Political History* (Princeton, N.J., 2003), 50–84.

26. See J. B. Scoles to Samuel Ruggles, 17 February 1839, Charles Ruggles Papers, Letters from Samuel B. Ruggles, 1834–1855 Folder, NYPL. See also Harry Hubert Pierce, *Railroads of New York: A Study in Government Aid* (Cambridge, Mass., 1953), 14. For broader political context and the role of internal improvements in partisan battles of the 1840s, see Michael F. Holt, *The Rise and Fall of the American Whig Party: Jacksonian Politics and the Onset of the Civil War* (New York, 1999), 80–82. See also Herbert D. A. Donovan, *The Barnburners: A Study of Internal Movements in the Political History of New York State and the Resulting Changes in Political Affiliation, 1830–1852* (New York, 1925), 22–24.

27. The equation of a railroad with a canal or road was just as much a fiction as the corporation's legal personhood. The railroad was a different enterprise than either. Although its security to the state may have been its right-of-way, this was not its only asset. It was neither a road nor a fixed asset right-of-way like a canal or a bridge. Rather, a railroad's holdings were widely allocated and mobile. It possessed a route and owned iron rails made from a commodity and fashioned through a manufacturing process that gave them additional value. And, significantly, a functioning railroad owned at least one very expensive and technically advanced piece of equipment: a steam locomotive powered by coal or timber, built by a contractor using a catalog of domestic and imported parts of varying sophistication. A railroad was therefore a far more complex and specialized business than the already specialized businesses on which it depended. Railroads maintained a wide network of relationships with agricultural, mining, iron, copper, brass, and glassworks. They employed unskilled laborers; highly trained engineers and surveyors; and a bevy of bookkeepers, clerks, and accountants in their offices, as well as professional attorneys. These material and personnel needs made railroads dependent on channels of commerce to carry the goods and services they required and dependent on market and pricing information to carry on their work. They were users of the same conduits and markets they promised to extend. See Naomi R. Lamoreaux and Kenneth L. Sokoloff, "Intermediaries in the U.S. Market for Technology, 1870–1920," in Lance E. Davis and Stanley L. Engerman, eds., *Finance, Intermediaries and Economic Development* (New York, 2003), 209–46. For more on the managerial challenges presented by the railroad's complexities, see Alfred D. Chandler Jr., *The Visible Hand: The Managerial Revolution in American Business* (Cambridge, Mass., 1977), ch. 3, esp. 87.

Also, unlike the steamboats of the Fulton-Livingston era, these steam locomotives enjoyed an important legal protection. Since 1836, the federal Patent Office operated under rules requiring technical examinations of applications. This made a patent more difficult to obtain, thus it also made a patent more valuable and legally defensible in court. Steam locomotives did not require monopoly protection from the state because they and their owners were already protected by the national government. The nineteenth-century patent system has attracted a great deal of attention. See Hugo Meier, "Technology and Democracy, 1800–1860," *Mississippi Valley Historical Review* 43 (March 1957): 618–40; Brooke Hindle, *Emulation and Invention* (New York, 1983), 16–23, 42–43; Morgan Sherwood, "The Origins and Development of the American Patent System," *American Scientist* 71 (1983): 500–506; Kenneth L. Sokoloff and B. Zorina Khan, "The Democratization of Invention During Early Industrialization: Evidence from the United States," *Journal of Economic History* 50 (June 1990): 363–78; Carolyn C. Cooper, *Shaping Invention: Thomas Blanchard's Machinery and Patent Management in Nineteenth-Century America* (New York, 1991); Steven Lubar, "The Transformation of Antebellum Patent Law," *Technology and Culture* 32 (October 1991): 932–59; I. Bernard Cohen, *Science and the Founding Fathers: Science in the Political Thought of Thomas Jefferson, Benjamin Franklin, John Adams, and James Madison* (New York, 1995), 237–43; B. Zorina Khan, "Property Rights and Patent Litigation in Early Nineteenth-Century

America," *Journal of Economic History* 55 (March 1995): 58–97; and B. Zorina Khan, *The Democratization of Invention: Patents and Copyrights in American Economic Development, 1790–1920* (New York, 2005). My thanks to Jeffrey Matsuura, whose paper "Thomas Jefferson and the Evolution of a Populist Vision of Intellectual Property Rights and Democratic Values" shaped my understanding of this subject. It was presented on 3 November 2006 at a Smithsonian Institution–International Center for Jefferson Studies cosponsored conference titled "Inventing America: The Interplay of Technology and Democracy in Shaping American Identity."

28. For an interesting discussion of this subject, see Michael Kammen, "A Different 'Fable of the Bees': The Problem of Public and Private Sectors in Colonial America," in John Parker and Carol Urness, eds., *The American Revolution: A Heritage of Change* (Minneapolis, 1975).

29. New York (State), *Report of the Joint Committee of Canals*, 18 March 1817, 4–6, 7.

INDEX

ACKNOWLEDGMENTS

If I have learned anything in writing, rewriting, and revising this book for publication, it is that a project like this is the product of years of collaborations.

My thanks, first and foremost, go to Peter S. Onuf. Peter's wisdom, honesty, support, and friendship helped me cross this finish line.

In 2004 I met Richard John at a conference where he offered a comment on a paper I had written (many revisions later it is Chapter 3); since then, Richard has generously read my work and offered thoughtful advice. When I needed to place this book, Richard took time out of a holiday weekend to convince me to include it in this series. I cannot thank him enough for his support.

At the University of Virginia, I held a fellowship supported by the Jefferson Scholars Foundation. I thank Jimmy Wright, Julie Innes Caruccio, Doug Trout, and Sara Neher for their friendship, along with the rest of the staff at the foundation and the donors who made this work possible.

I also held a fellowship at the International Center for Jefferson Studies at Monticello, and I thank Andrew O'Shaughnessy and the staff, especially Anna Berkes, Eric Johnson, Jack Robertson, and Mary Scott-Fleming, with whom I shared tea every afternoon, for their friendship and support.

At the McNeil Center for Early American Studies at the University of Pennsylvania, I met colleagues who have since become some of my best friends. Dan Richter is one of the warmest and most brilliant people in our profession, and I feel incredibly lucky to have had the chance to be associated with the center and my class of fellows: Jo Cohen, Ken Cohen, Simon Finger, Matt Garrett, Robb Haberman, Adam Jortner, Julie Kim, and Patrick Spero were wonderful colleagues, and my life is much better for having met Christina Snyder and Zara Anishanslin.

During my time in Charlottesville I had many fun and engaging experiences with Christa Dierksheide, Leonard Sadosky, Rob Parkinson, Johann Neem, Matt Speiser, Josh Botts, Seth Center, Marty Rojas, Caitlin Thompson, and Lee Dunham. At the University of Virginia, Brian Balogh, Gary Galla-gher, Chuck McCurdy, Sophie Rosenfeld, and Maya Jasanoff were the best supporters one could ask for. Other historians who either read portions of this book or offered encouragement to me at crucial moments include An-drew Shankman, John Brooke, Robert Wright, Pauline Maier, Joanne Free-man, Stephen Mihm, Amanda Moniz, Max Edling, Douglas Bradburn, Jessica Lepler, and Cathy Matson.

I also thank the library and special collections staffs at the New-York His-torical Society, the New York Public Library, the New York State Archive, the Library of Congress, the Chase Manhattan Bank Archives, and the Bank of New York, as well as the interlibrary loan officers at the Alderman Library at UVA and Newman Library at Baruch College.

I thank my colleagues in the Baruch College history department—Carol Berkin, Charlotte Brooks, Julie DesJardins, Bert Hansen, Thomas Heinrich, Clarence Taylor, Jed Abrahamian, TJ Desch-Obi, Vince DiGirolamo, Johanna Fernandez, Veena Oldenburg, Cynthia Whittaker, Tansen Sen, the late Al-fonso Quiroz, and my chair, Kathy Pence—as well as my dean, Jeff Peck, our associate provost, Dennis Slavin, and our department assistant, Ana Calero. I am incredibly lucky to have found a warm and welcoming department full of productive scholars.

Research for this book was supported by the Gilder-Lehrman Institute for American History, the Bankard Fund for Political Economy at the Uni-versity of Virginia, and the PSC-CUNY research fund.

I also want to thank everyone at the University of Pennsylvania Press who has assisted with this book, including Erica Ginsburg and my editor Robert Lockhart. Thanks also to John Larson and Sharon Murphy for their com-ments on the book manuscript.

I am very lucky to have enjoyed the friendship, guidance, and advice of so many former colleagues from my days as a journalist (which never truly ended). Michael Sivy, Peter Keating, Beverly Goodman, Adrienne Carter, Duff McDonald, Ellen Stark, and Suzanne Woolley helped make the *Money* magazine newsroom one of the most interesting places I've ever been, where omnivorous curiosity was the norm. Peter then convinced me to hop over to *George* magazine, where I met the indefatigable Sasha Issenberg. I then spent several summers at the *BusinessWeek* proofreading and copy desks with Larry Dark and Alethea Black.

Wally Edge (who I later learned was David Wildstein) put faith in me when he handed me an all-access pass to the inner sanctum of New Jersey politics at PoliticsNJ.com. Chris Eilert, Paul Sarlo, Dick Codey, Bill Baroni, Julie Roginsky, Ken Kurson, Peter Eagler, Bill Martini, Frank Vespa-Papaleo, and Cory Booker each had a part in making a book like this possible, and I owe a tremendous debt to Steve Kornacki for showing me breathtaking generosity during the most difficult time of my life.

Thanks also to David J., Aimee Mann, the Johns, and Jonathan Schwartz for pulling me along, and to Maxfield for making it all possible. At Haverford College, thanks particularly to Roger Lane and Lisa Jane Graham, as well as Wilson Carey McWilliams, who frequently visited from Rutgers.

Finally, I owe everything to my family. Sarah, Seamus, Catriona, and Juno are the world to me. My parents, James and Joan Murphy, sacrificed more than I will ever know and instilled in me a love of history. They put me through college, supported me in every endeavor, and have always been there for me. I never imagined I would have to finish this book without my father, who fell ill just weeks after our daughter was born in the fall of 2013. He was a gentle and great man, and this is for him.